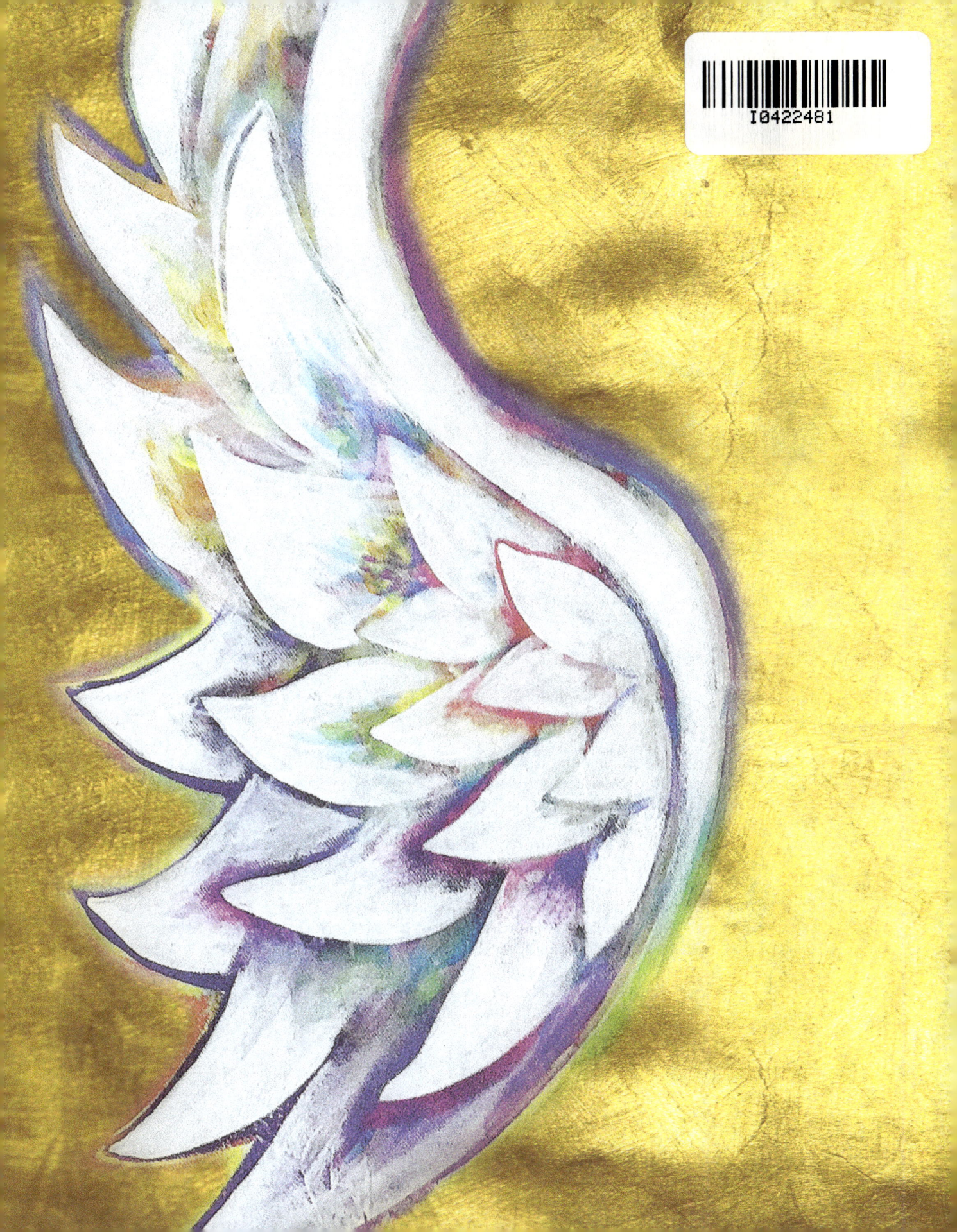
I0422481

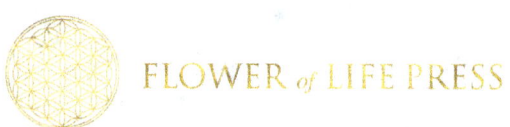

FLOWER *of* LIFE PRESS

*Rise Above: Free Your Mind One Brushstroke at a Time*
Copyright © 2025 Whitney Freya
2nd Edition
All rights reserved.

Published by Flower of Life Press
www.FlowerofLifePress.com

All rights reserved. No part of this publication may be reproduced, distributed, or transmitted in any form or by any means, including photocopying, recording, or other electronic or mechanical methods, without the prior written permission of the publisher, except in the case of brief quotations embodied in critical reviews and certain other noncommercial uses permitted by copyright law.

The content of this book is for general instruction only. Each person's physical, emotional, and spiritual condition is unique. The instruction in this book is not intended to replace or interrupt the reader's relationship with a physician or other mental health professional. Please consult your doctor for matters pertaining to your specific health.

Book Design by Jane Astara Ashley
Cover and Interior Art by Whitney Freya
Photos by Kevin Schlatt Photography

Library of Congress Control Number: Available upon request.

ISBN:

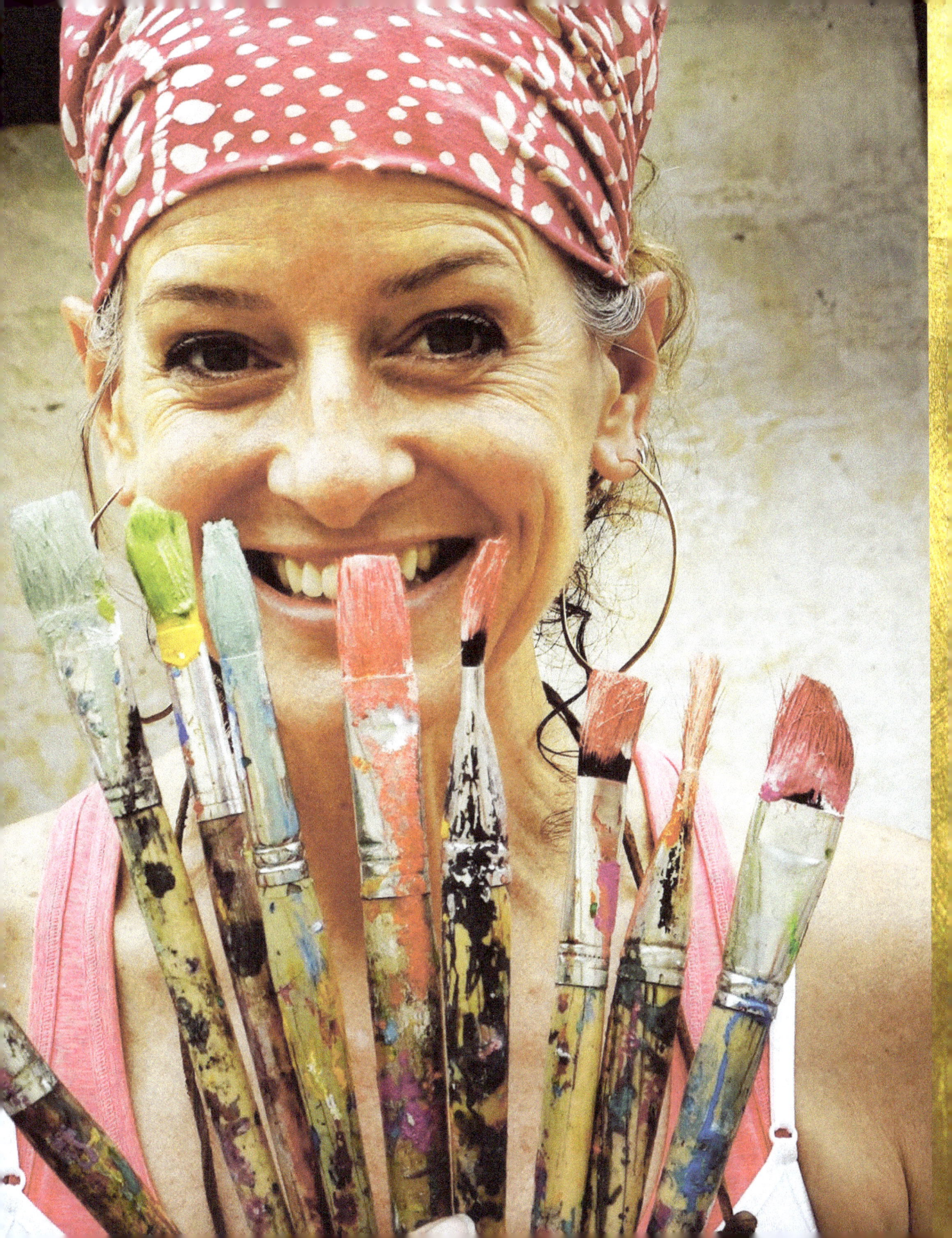

# Praise

Super Soul Flow has given me the answer for a long-searched-for mode of meditation where I can channel my infinite overflowing energy and paint. Aside from yoga, traditional meditation practices have always been a bit out of my reach. Being able to slow down and relax isn't a trait I excel at. Aligning with the energy of my creator self has centered and grounded me. I'm closer to grace and ease daily.

**~Elissa Siferd**

My intention to participate in the Super Soul Flow Meditation process was to learn intuitive painting. These guided tutorials kept me in the flow of my creativity, freeing me from fear and self-doubt. This process nurtures my creativity and at the same time challenges me to expand myself, lessening limiting beliefs. The benefits of this program stretched beyond my expectations. As an intuitive healer and entrepreneur, I create space for my clients to tap into their creative genius. I use the Super Soul Flow meditative painting practice as a way to keep myself grounded and in alignment with Spirit. This process allows me to achieve the flow I need to help those I serve.

**~Elise D'Amico-Davis, www.elisedamico.com**

Love my Super Soul Flow creativity. Now I share my love that is growing out of my creativity with my children and all people around me... Super Soul Flow is allowing my heart to overflow.

**~Christian Nicolai**

Whitney has me seeing more clearly HOW I am constantly creating in my life. I am creating the energy that surrounds me with my words and my thoughts. My Personal Painting Practice has given me a fun and easy way to tap into feelings of peace. I used to worry so much more. I used to feel stress so much more. Now, when I feel anything less than Super Soul Flow I know just what to do! Dive into your Super Soul Flow—you won't regret it!

**~Jina Daniels, Creatively Fit Coach, www.Jax-Zen.com**

Whitney has helped me to develop a daily painting practice. Just like I exercise my physical body, my daily painting practice exercises my right-brain. My day is always better when I paint. Now, I'm sharing that daily painting practice with others. I truly believe that everyone can benefit from painting, especially when they apply what they learn to the rest of their life. Super Soul Flow absolutely rocks.

**~Karen Castilon, Creatively Fit Coach, www.createyourhappyart.com**

Whitney has helped me rediscover my personal painting practice. Being creative on a daily basis is truly bringing a sense of alignment with my true self and life path. I feel much less stressed... and feel the power and strength of Super Soul Flow. I believe anyone can feel the same through the Super Soul Flow process.

*~Kim Keher, Creatively Fit Coach, www.facebook.com/kimkehercreative*

*Rise Above* pulses with pure inspiration! There is a passionate breath whispering through every word and image in this book that feels like a warm gust of wind lifting you up into super-soul creative flow!

*~Laüra Hollick, Soul Artist, www.laurahollick.com*

Super Soul Flow got me started on a daily painting process! I've painted and posted (on Instagram) every day for the past 20 days, something I never would have dreamed of doing were it not for this program. It also encouraged me to buy myself actual art supplies, I had always painted on particle board or other scrap materials before. Now I have canvases and a full palette of gorgeous colors that bring me joy! Thanks Whitney Freya for offering this course and FREEDOM to create!

*~Pat Donovan*

Super Soul Flow has given me a whole new way of seeing my art and the art making in itself. I am more thoughtful on what I want to create without strings. Going with the flow has been so hard for me. I'm such a left brain thinker that it was easy for me to follow Whitney's directions. Because of how she teaches you to paint, I had the opportunity to freely explore and just play with the paint without worrying about a final result. I love the freedom I have felt doing so. Thanks, Whitney!

*~Jenn Sher*

The Super Soul Flow Program has allowed me to choose art, to choose expression using paint on canvas. For that I am very grateful. I have learned from my painting sessions to stand strong in what feels good to me and don't let anything from the outside world alter it. I had allowed others' stories around art making to suppress my own desire. With Super Soul Flow I have created a NEW story and have freed myself from the "I can't..." story. I know now as I express myself more and more on the canvas, it will flow into the rest of my life! Thank you, Whitney.

*~Heather Gervascio-Freeman, www.gutsygirlclub.com*

Something I've always wanted to do is to make art, not just for the benefit of myself, but to share with the world. My mother always told me "You can't make a living being... an artist."

*~Anonymous*

# Dedication

This book, this experience, and this magical journey is dedicated to you…

YOU who are the "idealists."

YOU who have been accused of being a "dreamer."

YOU who can't resist blazing new trails and daring to believe that WE are capable of more.

More compassion.

More love.

More peace.

More cooperation.

More CHANGE!

I dedicate this book to the Rainbow Warriors that have blessed my trails already. To my tribe of Creatively Fit Coaches, thank YOU ALL for being the wind beneath my wings. Thank you to VIVIAN for emailing me from Nigeria and sharing your vision. Thank you to my friends—old, new, and future—who surround me with possibility and open hearts.

Most of all, thank you to my three children for inspiring me daily to KNOW that we are going to create a better world because YOU are SO mind-blowingly amazing! Thank you for choosing me to be your wild, free-spirited, momma-on-a-mission! I am honored to get to be your MOM.

I exist and create and believe and love and dare because YOU do the same.

A'Ho!

~Whitney

# Acknowledgments

The words that end up on this paper are just the tip of the iceberg. A book is made up of hours, years, and lifetimes of experience, feeling, ah-ha's, meditations, musings, layers of paint, and views from the mountain tops, from the sky, from the ocean's edge.

A mandala of light, love, energy, wisdom, and feeling swirl around in an infinite dance and, just for a moment, touch down to become a book.

This book is so many magical moments that have evolved into what you are reading today because of hundreds of moments and people—friends, mentors, and guides.

Thank you to my publishers Astara Jane Ashley and Scott Watrous for your inspired guidance, your divine downloads, and for your seemingly infinite faith in our creative potential. Flower of Life Press rocks!

Thank you to all of you who have dared to journey into the canvas with me, to face your fears, and to allow me to be your muse.

I am humbled, overjoyed, honored and so incredibly grateful to get to call this my "work." YOU make it possible. I acknowledge YOU. None of us exist in a bubble.

This book is the "butterfly effect" of so many magical and creative souls.

Thank you for sharing your color with our world!

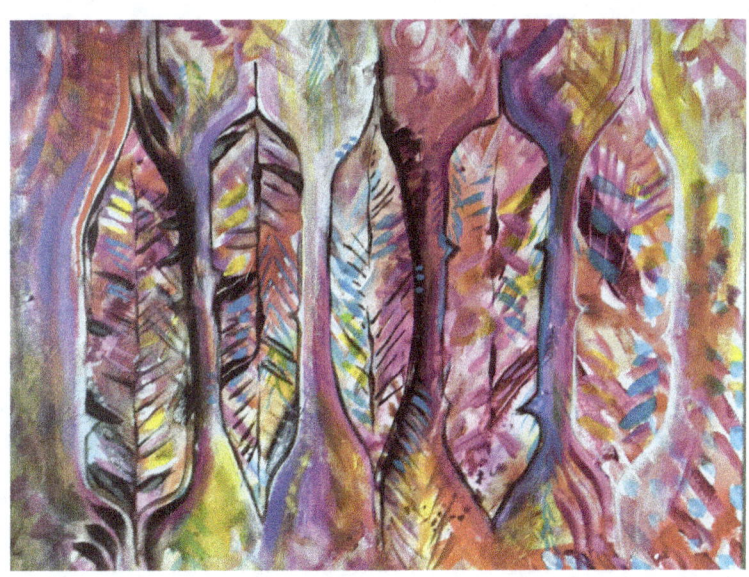

# Contents

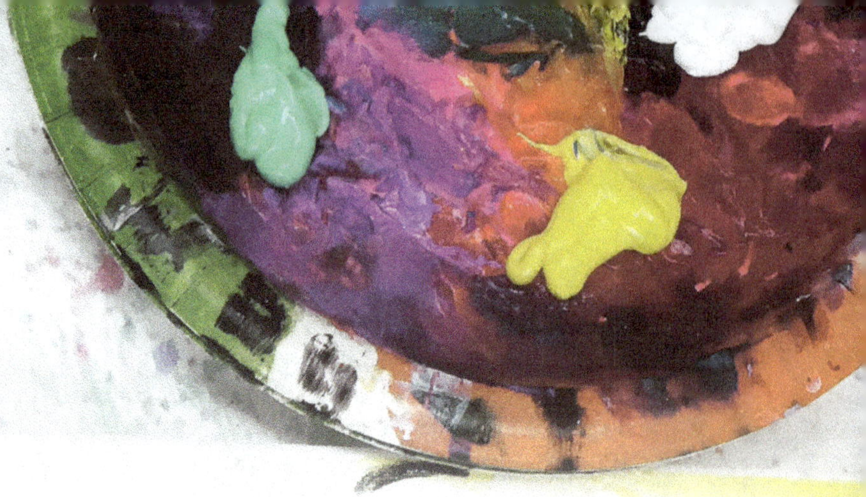

Introduction     x

Chapter 1     FREEDOM     1

Chapter 2     SELF-LOVE     19

Chapter 3     PRESENCE     30

Chapter 4     ABUNDANCE     48

Chapter 5     FEARLESSNESS     71

Chapter 6     CLARITY     89

Chapter 7     INTUITION     108

Chapter 8     SPACIOUSNESS     125

Chapter 9     PEACE     143

Chapter 10     EASE AND GRACE     160

Chapter 11     JOY     183

Chapter 12     PERSONAL SYMBOL     199

Conclusion     218

About the Author     222

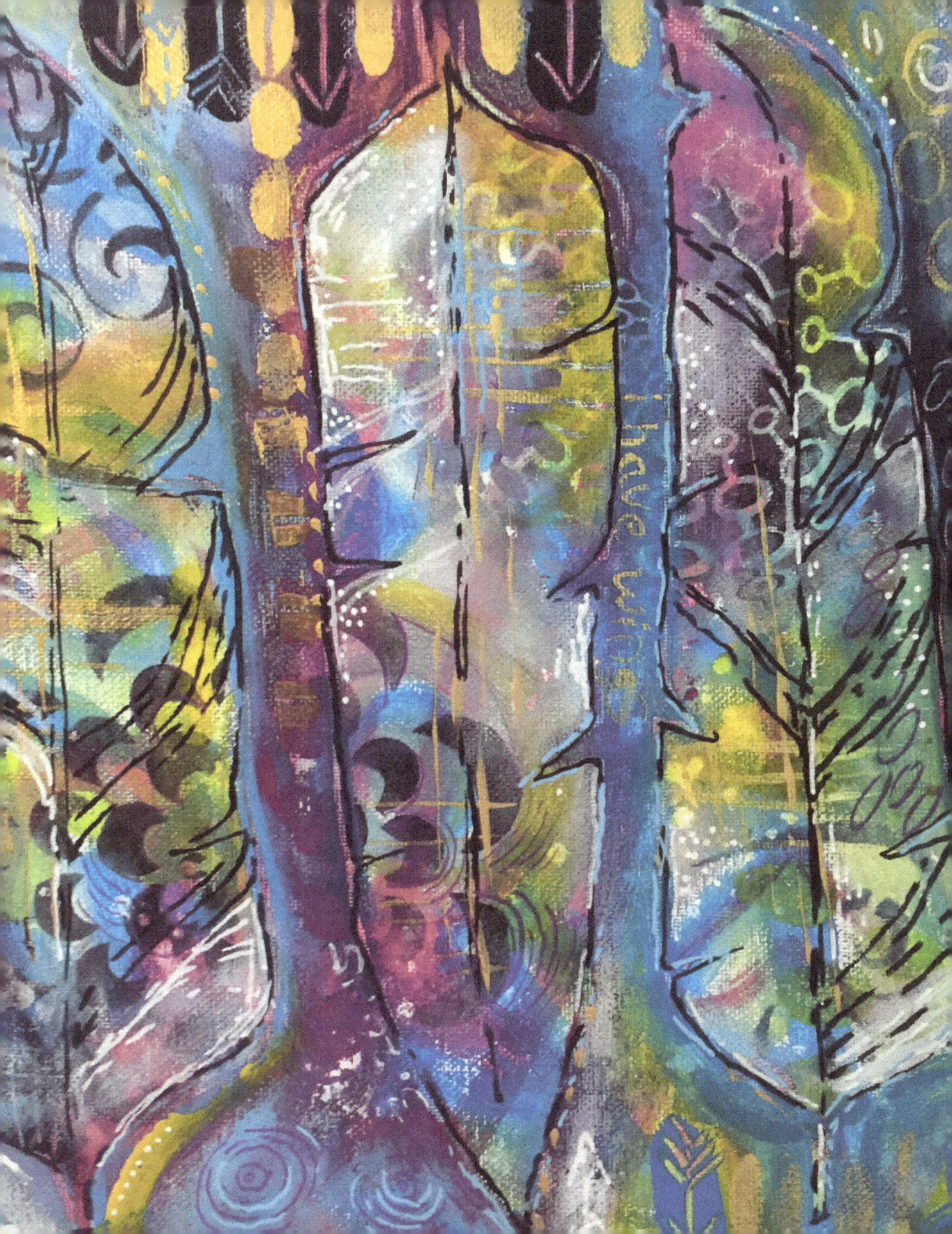

# Introduction

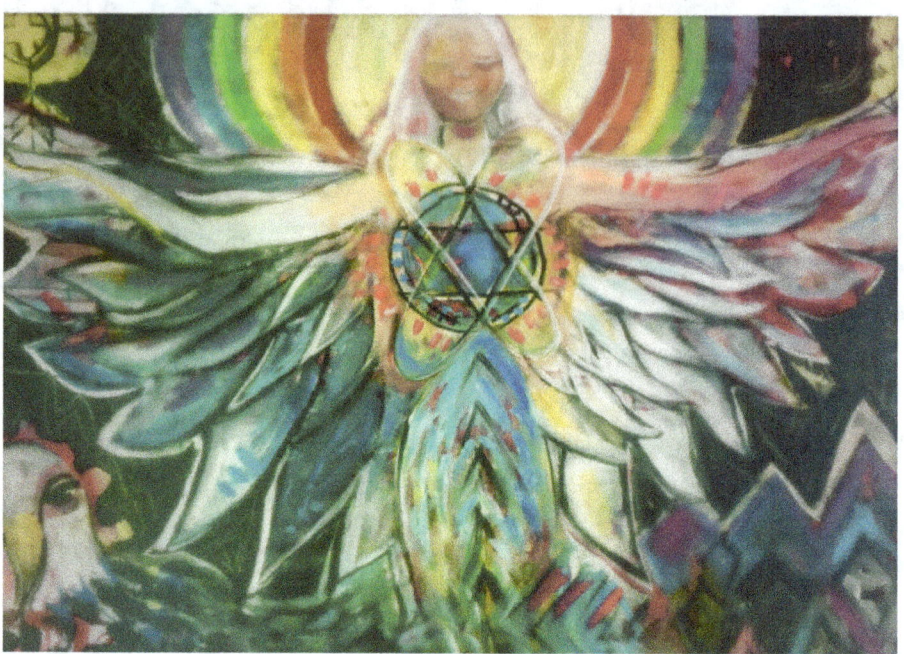

Rise Above!

*Rise Above* is a call to elevate one's awareness beyond the polarities of human drama and victimhood. It serves as a reminder that we can choose to view life's current circumstances in a way that is empowering, hopeful, and infinitely more creative.

Since 1996, I have been teaching this Sacred and Personal Painting Practice and have witnessed countless times how life's obstacles can be approached from at least two different perspectives.

One perspective fosters curiosity and opens us up to greater possibilities, while the other shuts us down, allowing the inner critic to take control.

At the canvas, one student might say, "How can I brighten up my painting and make it more focused?"

While another says, "My painting is muddy, and I'm totally confused."

Both could be talking about the exact same painting.

Each is accurately describing the painting in its current state. The difference lies in focus: one centers on what they want—brighter colors and a clearer subject—while the other dwells on what is "wrong."

I encounter this duality almost daily in my own life and see it mirrored in others' experiences.

What motivates me is the question: "How can I live more in flow, in harmony with what IS, and create the change I desire from the inside out?"

And then, I strive to share this perspective with as many people as possible.

Every time I approach the canvas, I understand that I'm creating an opportunity to RISE ABOVE the voice inside that insists, "You're not professionally trained. You're not good enough."

You know that voice.

But as I paint, I take the opportunity to practice dialoguing with my brush, the colors, and the evolving image on the canvas. I choose to RISE ABOVE the low-frequency, critical voice, and instead embrace thoughts and words that create space for learning, authentic self-expression, and FUN.

When this book was first written in 2016, the world was experiencing an escalation of polarizing forces, spreading fear and drama through the collective frequency.

After a restless night, I woke up at my friend's house in L.A. with the words RISE ABOVE reverberating in my mind.

I knew it had to be the title of my book.

This is what I love about what I do:

Painting helps us rise above the lower vibrations of worry, fear, and overwhelm.

As you'll learn, I have a deep appreciation for symbolism. It made me laugh when, just three hours later, as I sat dazed and sleepy on the Pacific Surfliner Train heading to Santa Barbara, I realized what I was about to do:

I was traveling to Santa Barbara to fly for the first time in my life. I was literally going to RISE ABOVE.

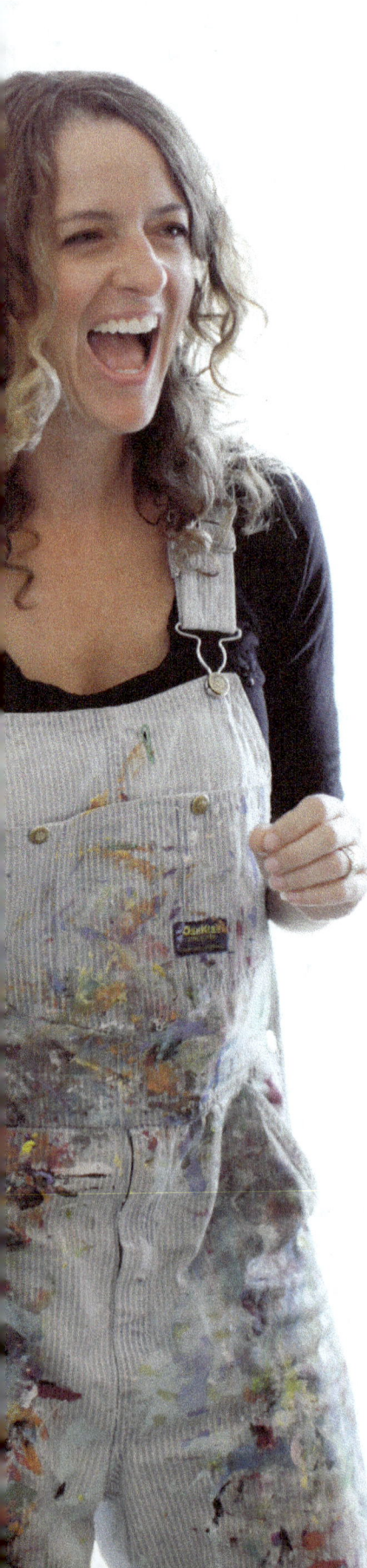

That day, I flew my paraglider wing for the first time—eleven times, to be exact. By the end of the day, I felt so "high" that I had nearly forgotten the troubling current events that had agitated me earlier.

It's the same feeling I experience when I go to my canvas for my Personal Painting Practice:

I become totally present.
I raise my vibration.
I connect to my highest wisdom.

I RISE ABOVE life's worries, challenges, stresses, and disappointments.

I believe this is why the arts exist. It's why you're drawn to paints, colors, imagery, and the creative process.

It's not about creating a product—it's about raising your vibration. It's about transcending our limited, linear, rational perspectives to connect with our Soul's perspective.

When we paint, we FREE OUR MINDS in the expansive spaciousness of the blank canvas.

**When I returned from California, I painted wings for the cover of this book. As I painted, my eyes fell on a shamanic painting I had created two months earlier.**

There she was—wings spread, eyes uplifted, with a rainbow halo radiating around her.

"Time to RISE ABOVE," she whispered.

Freya...she wears a cloak of falcon feathers. Wings. The awareness had been there all along, waiting patiently.

Together, we can use this process to rise above our historical, fear-based world and reclaim our true state of being—one intimately united with our Creative Spirit.

**One brushstroke at a time, you can remember your incredible, creative power.**

# Mother eARTh as Your Muse

In 2011 I moved to a magical mountain valley in Northeast Oregon. I moved to land that was so remote, so steeped in ancient wisdom and so wildly gorgeous, that everything about my life changed—everything.

As I "came home" to the place on Earth where the Nez Perce tribe lived free until 1877—the last free tribe in the continental U.S.—I was activated. I remembered that I am free to create the life that inspires me and to share this energy of freedom with you!

The rawness of the land and the sheer magnitude of the mountains reflected back to me a call to a new level of authenticity and truth. Mother Earth doesn't lie, mute, deny, suppress… she just IS.

If I was going to be as raw and expansive and strong and true as the land around me, I was going to have to face the fear and open up the closet door that I had been avoiding for so long.

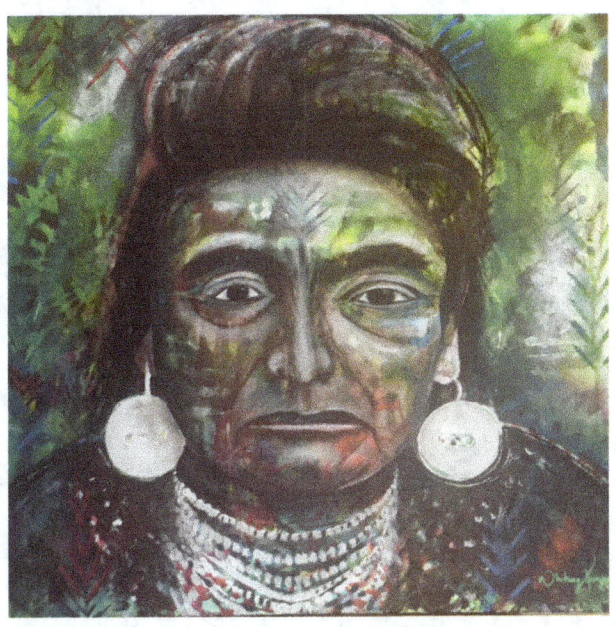

CHIEF JOSEPH, LEADER OF THE NEZ PERCE TRIBE

Nine months (symbolism!) after moving into our brand-new, 4,500-square-foot house on 700 acres, I moved out. I made a choice. I had to experience the art that is my life, my way. And I chose the path that honored my soul's journey— what my infinite self wanted to experience in this lifetime.

Freedom, self-love, abundance, ease and grace, peace… every chapter in this book is a personal journey of reclamation, a reunion with my soul. I took back those energies that had been sacrificed to keep others feeling good about themselves and learned to FLY!

I had a new "blank canvas." I moved into a rental in town, two blocks from my kids' school, with a limited budget and a new passion for life.

It's what I have always loved about bringing my clients to the canvas. I watch them FREE their minds from fear, self-doubt, limiting beliefs… and RISE ABOVE to take back their power to create feelings of abundance, love, possibility, and joy!

As I moved through this new chapter, free to flow and harmonize with life around me, I was given new insight…

No matter what is going on externally, you can ALWAYS choose the energy or the reality you create—or receive—in that situation. You are always FREE to bathe yourself in whatever feeling you choose. When you open up to your NATURAL state, you remember that you are an infinite being currently experiencing life as an individual.

You can call in a higher knowing, an elevated perspective, an eagle's eye view.

What flows into you when you connect to this aspect of yourself knows only love, truth, wisdom, and possibility.

This is why survivors of horrific conditions share their stories... to remind you that you are the sole (or should I say SOUL) creator of your experience.

The NEW personal mastery is contingent upon you and me remembering this truth.

The NEW Creativity is not about creating pretty pictures or products that sell; it is about aligning with your natural state and creating energy in each moment. That energy is felt by us as feeling.

We are here to create feelings that fuel our wildest dreams and visions of world peace, a sustainable, lush environment, new educational systems, and dream into reality the New Earth that is rooted in love, not fear.

This is the call, to remember the truth of who you are as a creator and to RISE ABOVE life's drama, obstacles, and challenges, so that you don't distract yourself from what you came here to experience... life in Super Soul Flow.

Super Soul Flow is the process I was given—as I created my new life in-between the mountains and the canyons, the rivers and lakes—to share with you and to activate your remembrance of how to live your life in a co-creative relationship with your Infinite Self.

Can you think of any reason you would NOT want to live that way? Right!

It is a feeling. It is the feeling that everything is happening in perfect timing. Coincidences and synchronicities abound and the magic is everywhere. Now I am going to share it with you.

And it will be the wind beneath your wings as you RISE ABOVE life's challenges.

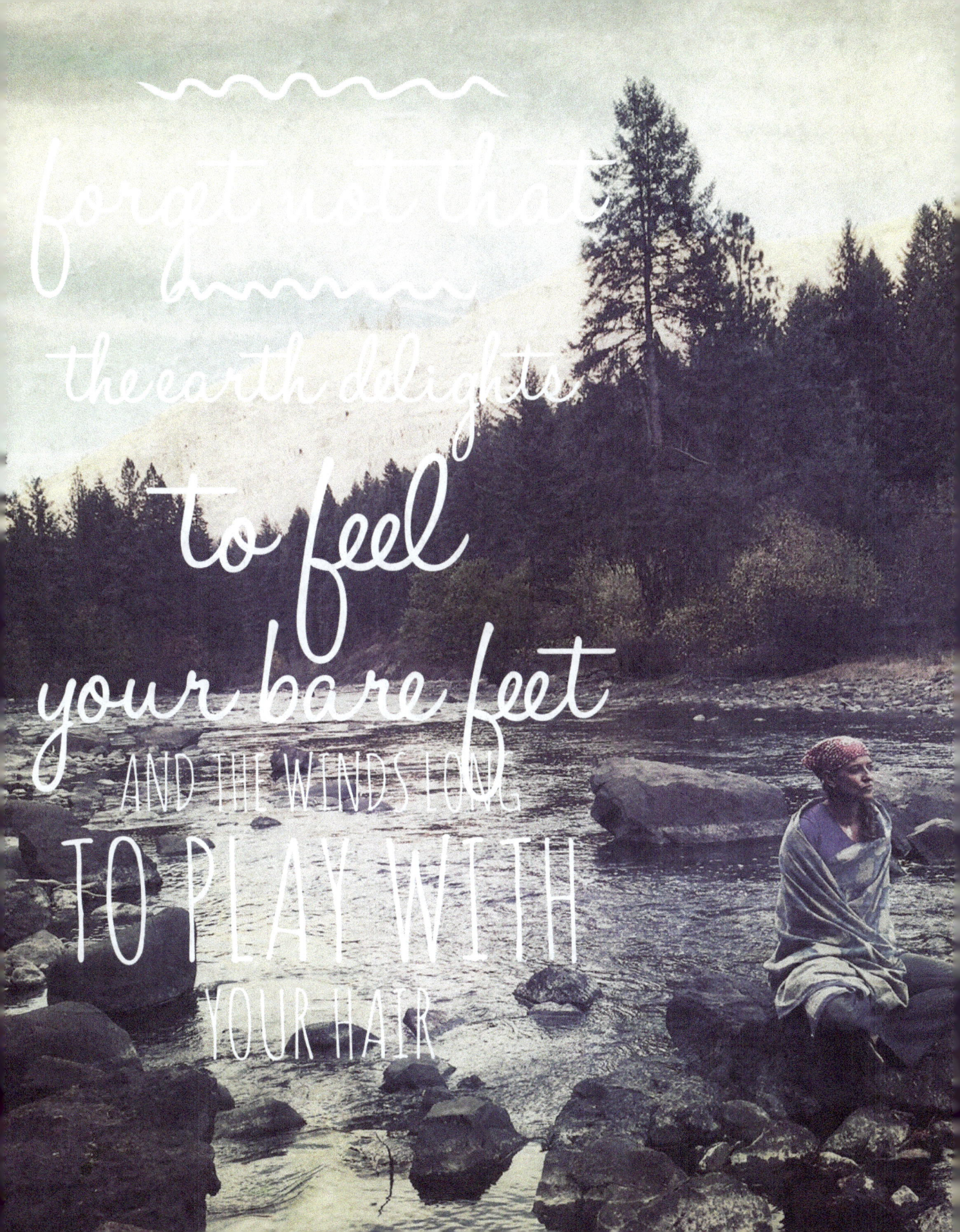

## I have selected an animal totem as a guide for each ENERGY you are going to paint: Freedom, Peace, Abundance, Joy...

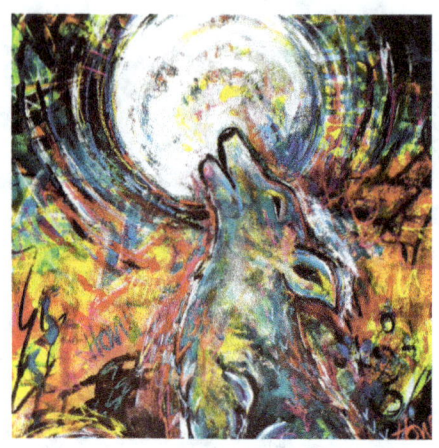

It can sometimes be easier to connect to a feeling, or energy, when we imagine it embodied in an animal.

Would you howl like a **coyote** if you were not feeling free?

You know that thrill of seeing a **dolphin**? You feel lucky, divinely blessed, and a huge smile instantly spreads across your face! This is your animal guide for Self-Love.

The **buffalo** was the symbol of abundance for most Native American cultures because it provided so much that they needed to survive and thrive!

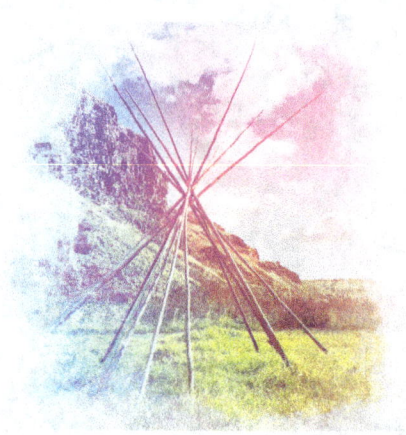

And we are calling in our ROARRRRRR to protect that which brings us joy. The **lioness** will help you defend your boundaries and create the space for the energy of joy to roam freely in your life.

You can choose to paint the animal totems yourself, or simply allow the "musings" to inspire your Super Soul Flow Painting Meditation. Perhaps your first time through the book you'll choose to follow the Painting Prompts, and the next time through, you'll paint the animal totems.

If you are particularly passionate about a certain animal, or you start seeing hummingbirds or elephants everywhere (live OR in images, on coffee mugs—doesn't matter how you see them!), look them up in this book and allow your thoughts to be guided to new levels of awareness around how you WANT to feel.

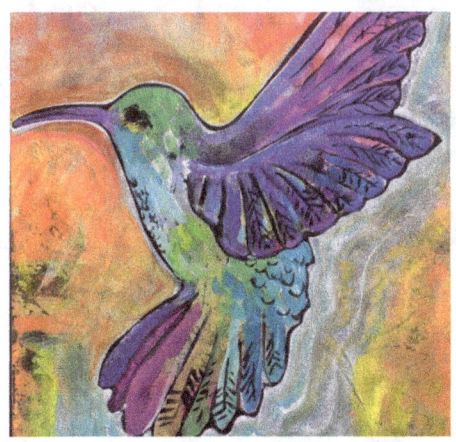

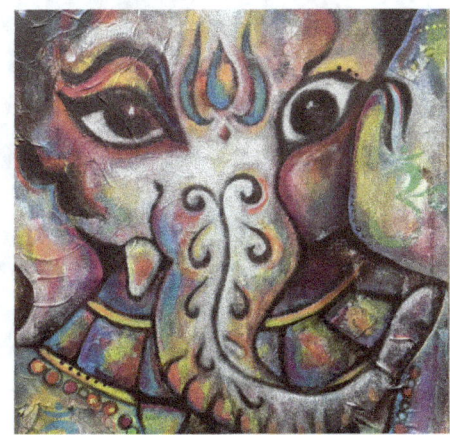

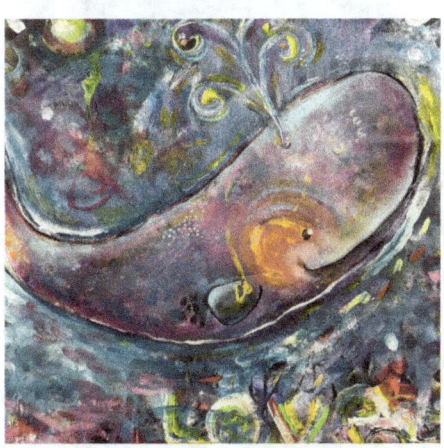

Perhaps you'll ask the animal to show you all the ways you can create more peace, spaciousness, or clarity...

Indigenous peoples have always seen animals as allies and a source of wisdom. They made images of animals as masks, on cave walls, and in their jewelry and pottery to harness the animals' power and wisdom.

Allow **elephant** to whisper her intuitive wisdom to you.

Dive underneath the surface of your busy life, into the emotional, watery realm, and BE the massive, yet graceful and fluid **whale** to align with waves of peace.

RISE ABOVE your life's challenges and frustrations on the wings of **eagle**.

These animal guides hold their own keys to unlocking your own truest nature.

A'Ho.

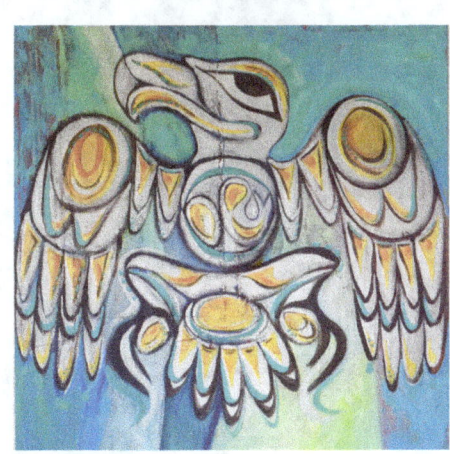

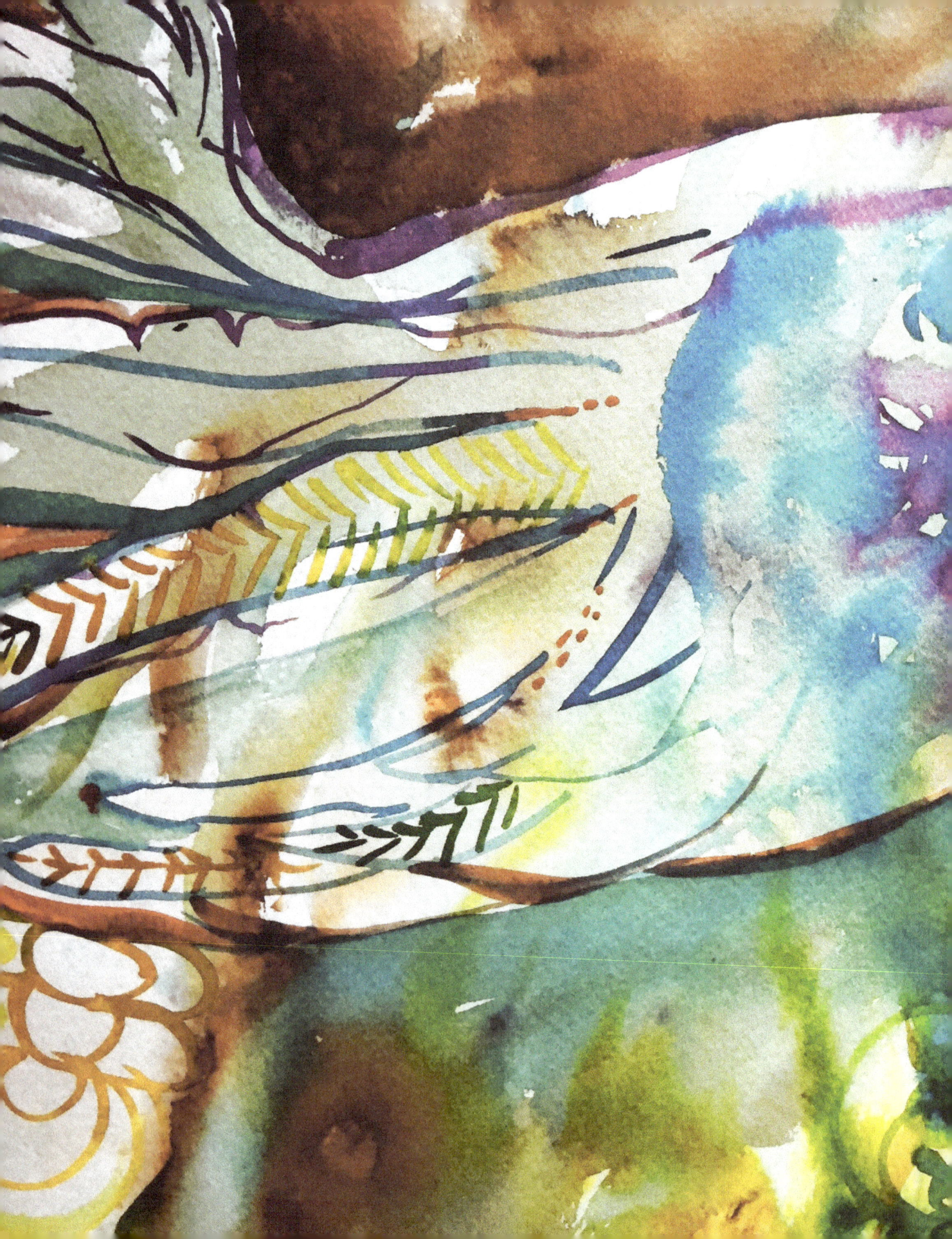

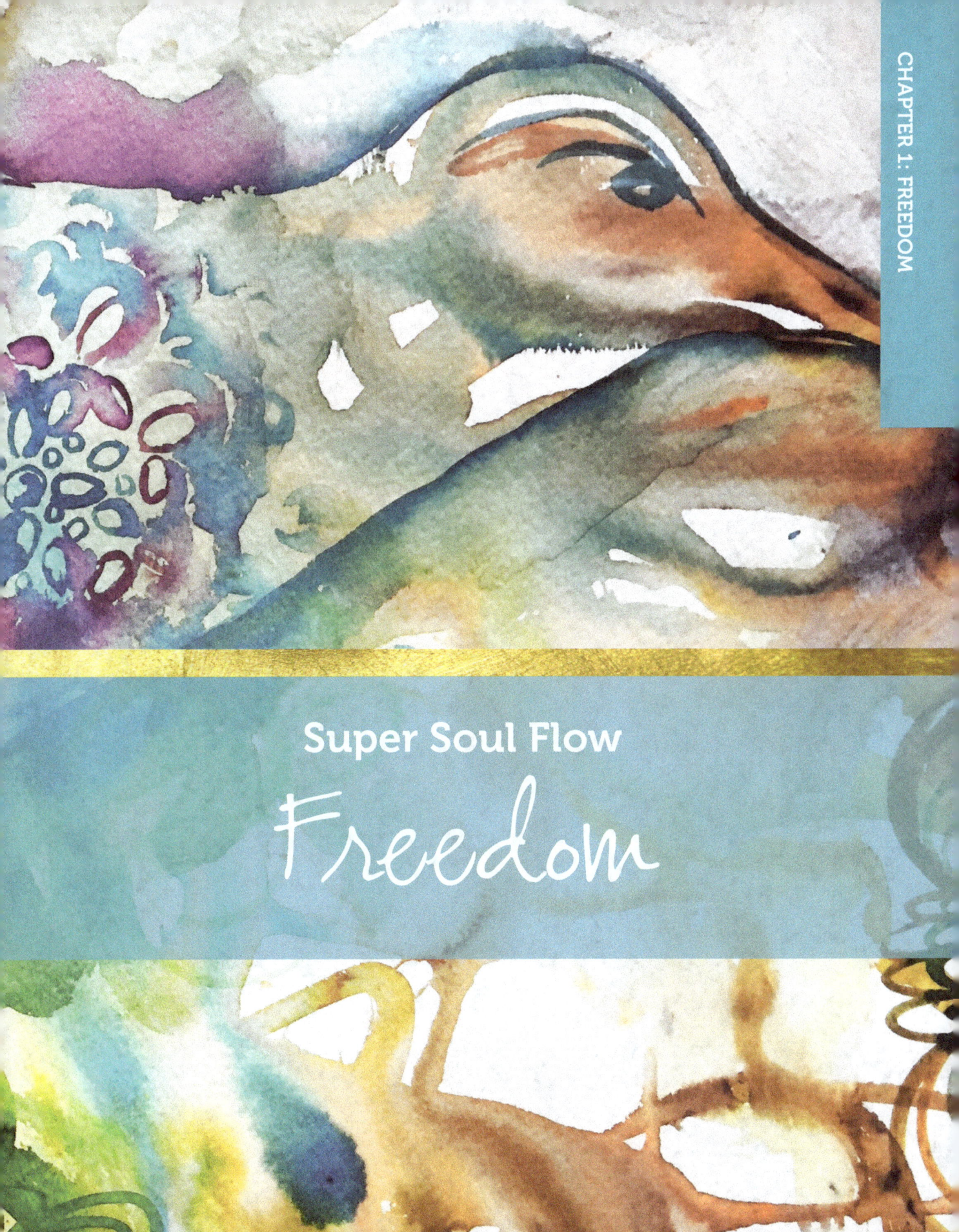

Super Soul Flow

# Freedom

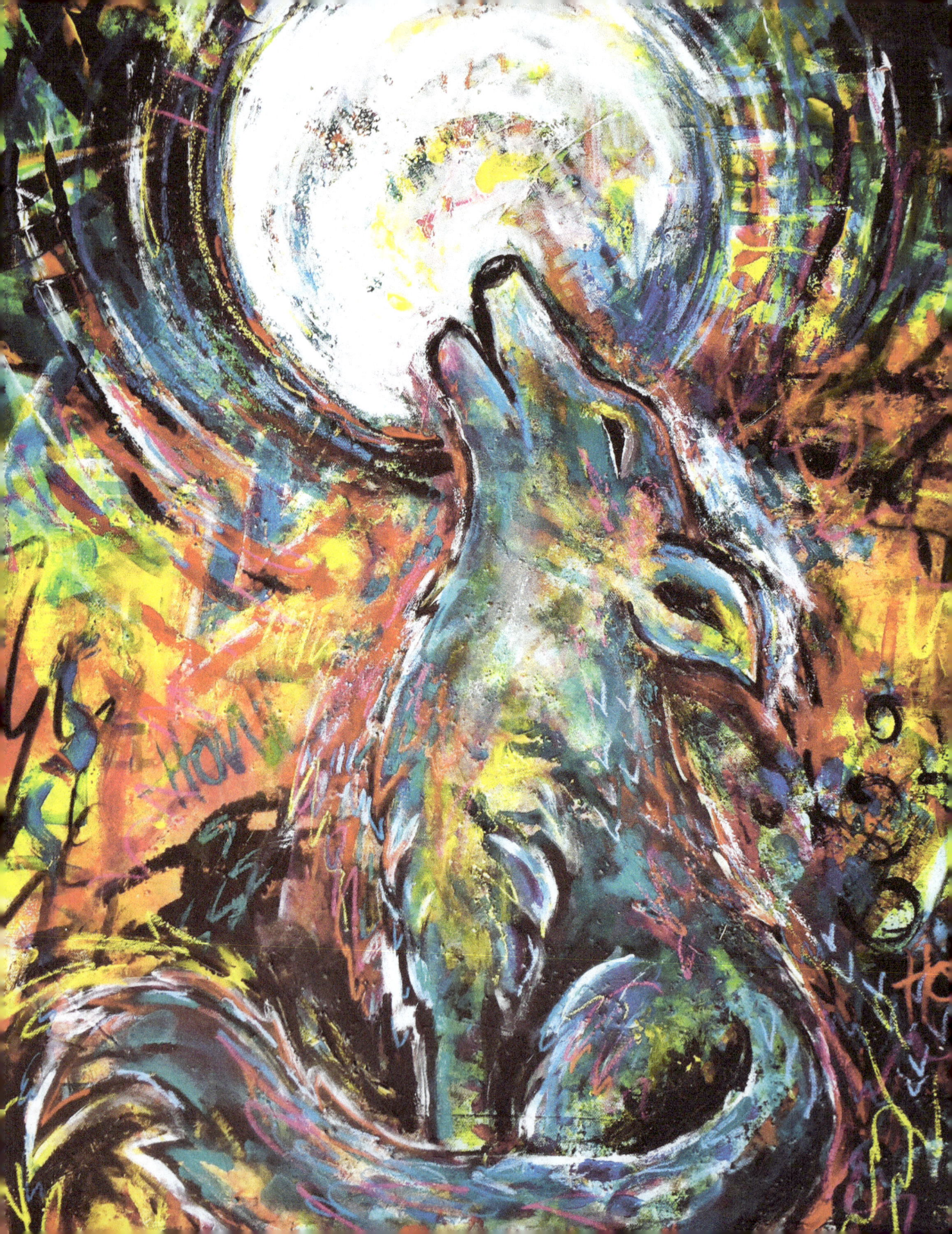

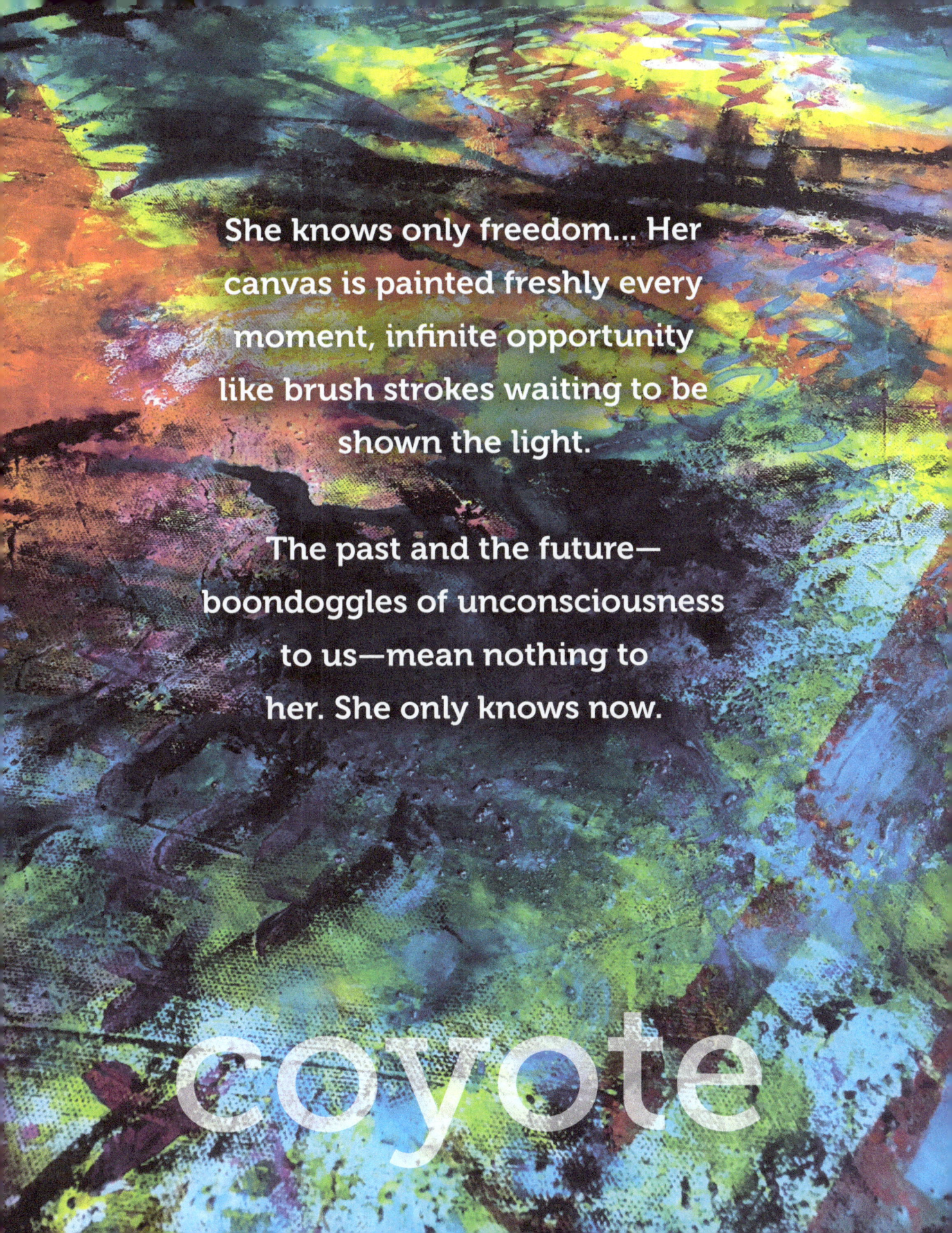

She knows only freedom... Her
canvas is painted freshly every
moment, infinite opportunity
like brush strokes waiting to be
shown the light.

The past and the future—
boondoggles of unconsciousness
to us—mean nothing to
her. She only knows now.

coyote

# coyote

Follow me now into your unknown.
At the canvas... you are free.
At the canvas... you make the rules.
At the canvas... you create your own path.
At the canvas... you HOWL your desires into
 the void.
At the canvas... you turn your expectations,
your limiting beliefs,
upside down and inside out.
What if you could?
What if you dared?
What if you tried?
What if you believed?
What if you trusted?
What if you only looked within for
recognition and affirmation?

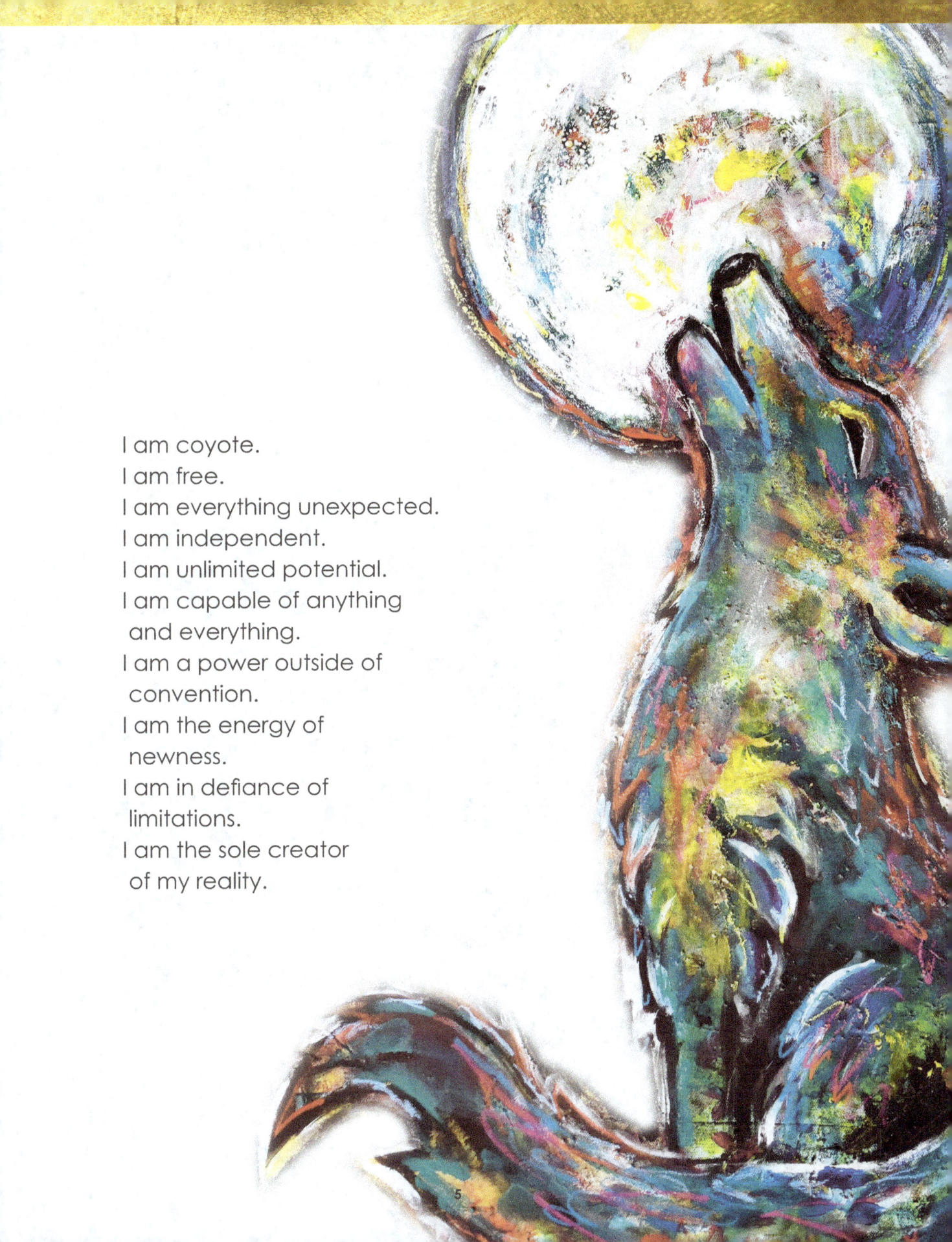

I am coyote.
I am free.
I am everything unexpected.
I am independent.
I am unlimited potential.
I am capable of anything
 and everything.
I am a power outside of
 convention.
I am the energy of
 newness.
I am in defiance of
 limitations.
I am the sole creator
 of my reality.

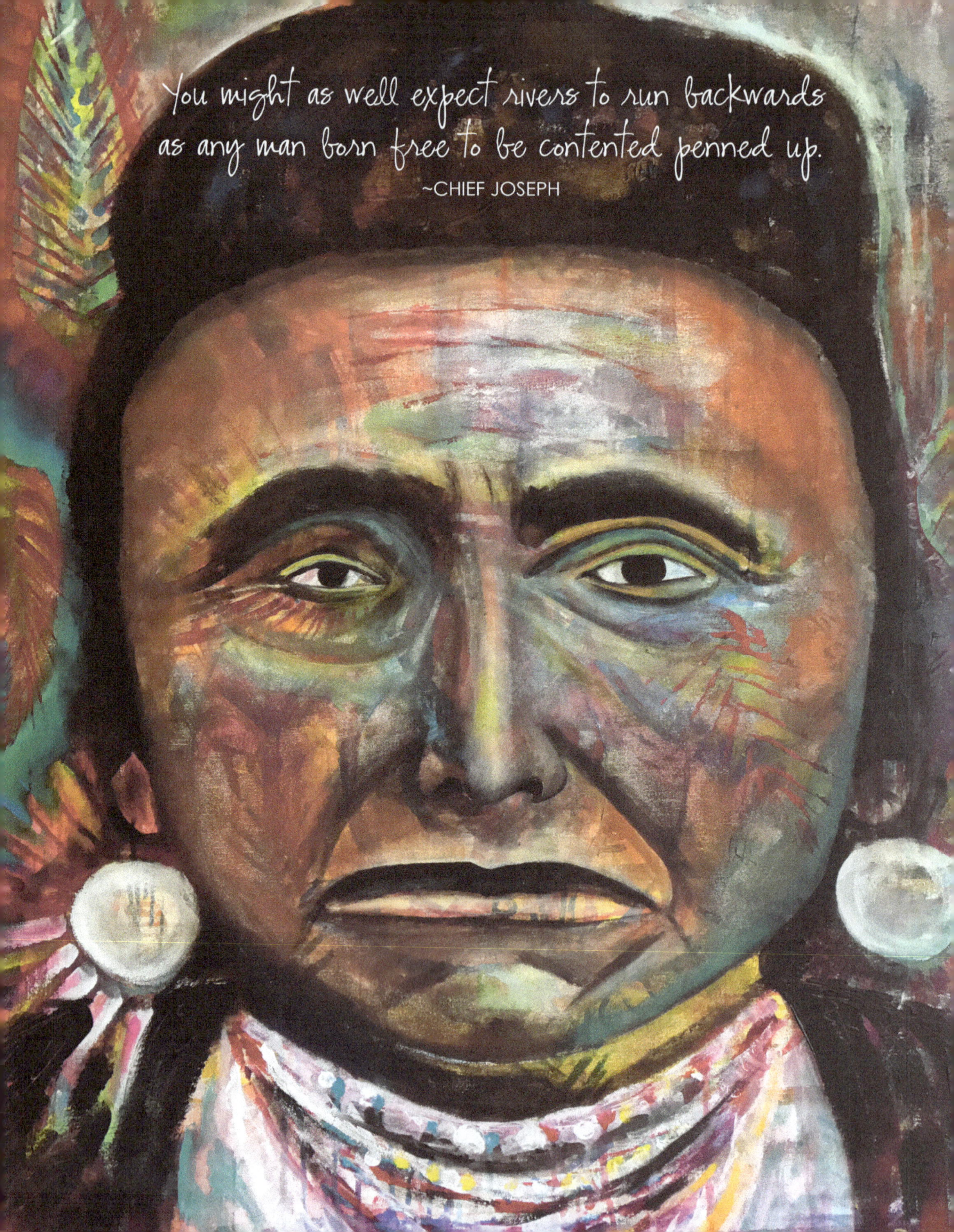

You might as well expect rivers to run backwards as any man born free to be contented penned up.

~CHIEF JOSEPH

Your opportunity to RISE ABOVE whatever is trying to pull you down in your life is proportionate to how you create a new sense of unity within your awareness. When you choose to look at life through both aspects of your mind—the logical and the intuitive—you can then, even more effectively and gracefully, co-create your life as you desire, rising above any limiting beliefs, circumstances, or challenges.

*Intuition* and *imagination* are the pathways of communication between your intuitive mind and your thinking mind.

Whenever you are feeling confused, anxious, worried, or stressed it is a sign that you are out of balance.

## TIP FOR ACCESSING NEW FREEDOM

*We've had it all backwards.*

Your intuitive, infinite mind is meant to RECEIVE inspiration from your soul, and then let your logical mind know what it needs to create this inspiration into reality.

We were conditioned to do the opposite. Think about it.

When is the last time you got inspired or fired up by a new idea? What happened next?

Your logical mind kicked in, as if you asked it, "Can I make this new idea happen?" It said, "If it involves change, the unknown, any risk, or potential to lose (money, reputation, etc.), then the answer is NO."

So you get stuck.

Or the idea floats away and you are right back where you started.

Now you are going to learn to CREATE your life the way you intended. You will receive the knowing, and then give your task-oriented, linear mind its marching orders.

We begin at the canvas.

In this lesson, you are going to paint the ENERGY of freedom.

**At the canvas, you are going to create the FEELING of freedom. What does it feel like to be free from any expectations or limitations? How can you connect with what freedom means to you?**

This is your inspiration… FREEDOM! Yes! Now, tell your left brain what you need: supplies, water, a paint-brush…

Your left brain, logical mind, does not get to tell you that you don't have time, that you're not really good at painting anyway, or there are more important things you could be painting, doing, cleaning… Right? Your mind is not meant to captain the ship. Your soul is.

And your soul is FREE! So let's dive into that energy!

## What is freedom to you? Is it the freedom to…

… be who you want to be?

… feel the way you want to feel?

… say what you want to say, when you want to say it?

… be as goofy as want to be? Laugh? Cry? Dance? Express yourself fully?

… believe what you want to believe?

… live authentically?

… travel where you want? Learn what you want? Start something new?

… be happy? Joyful? At peace?

… spend more time in nature? Meditation? Yoga? Teaching? Helping others?

… move? Expand? Celebrate? Love?

… know that you are enough and worthy of love?

If you could really immerse yourself in the energy of pure potentiality, what would that *feel* like for you?

You are emerging from a "Cycle of Limitation" and are awakening to the knowing that you can do things another way. The speed at which you are able to leave behind this cycle depends on the speed at which you can embrace your CREATOR self and blaze new trails into the future that you CHOOSE to create.

# I AM the sole creator of my experience.

Do you want anything less than pure freedom? Of course not.

Let's see what insight we can gain from the canvas into what is holding us back.

## The way we do anything is the way we do everything.

This is how this process works. YOU create your experience. So any blocks, limiting beliefs, or self-doubts are created by you.

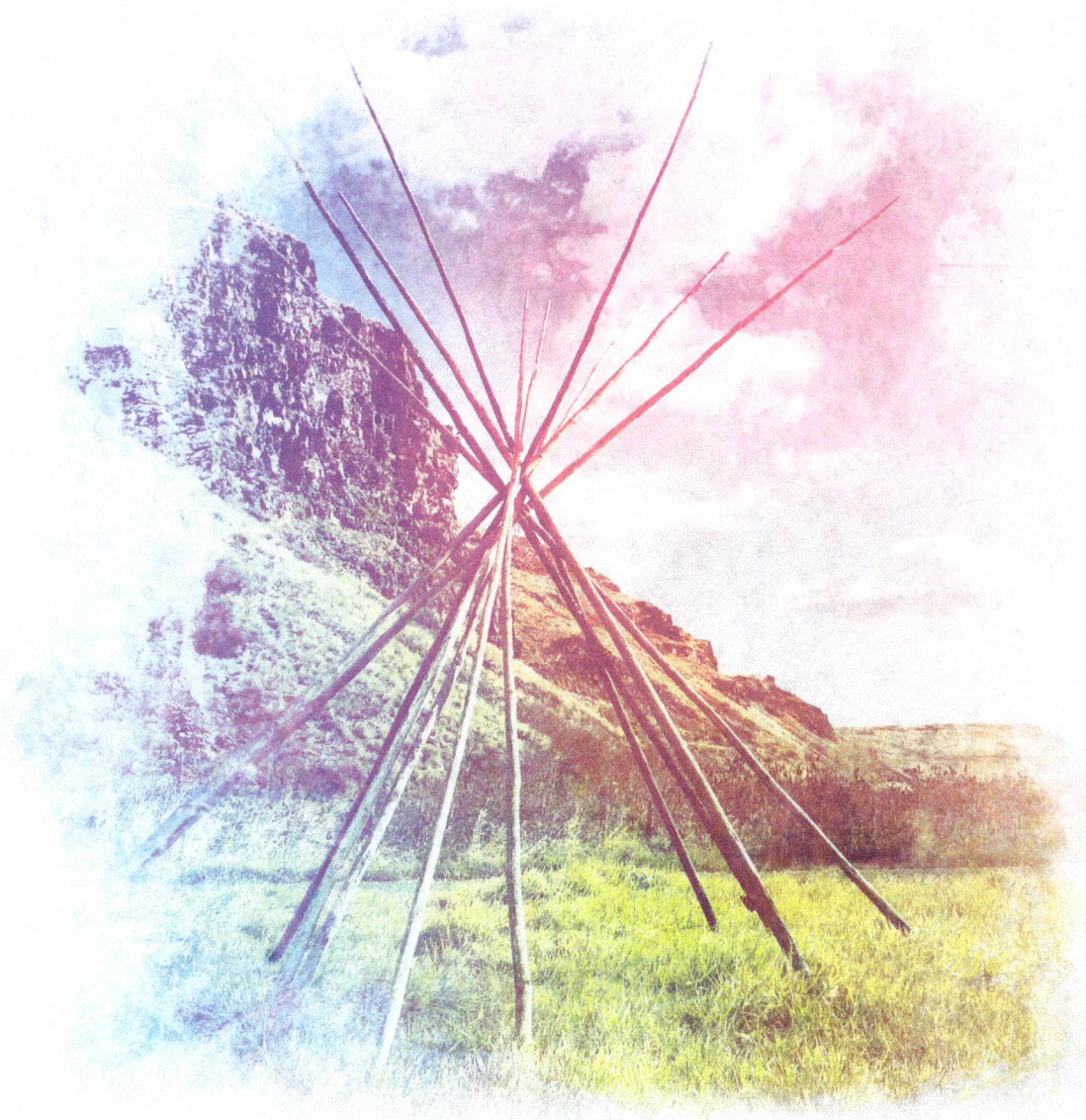

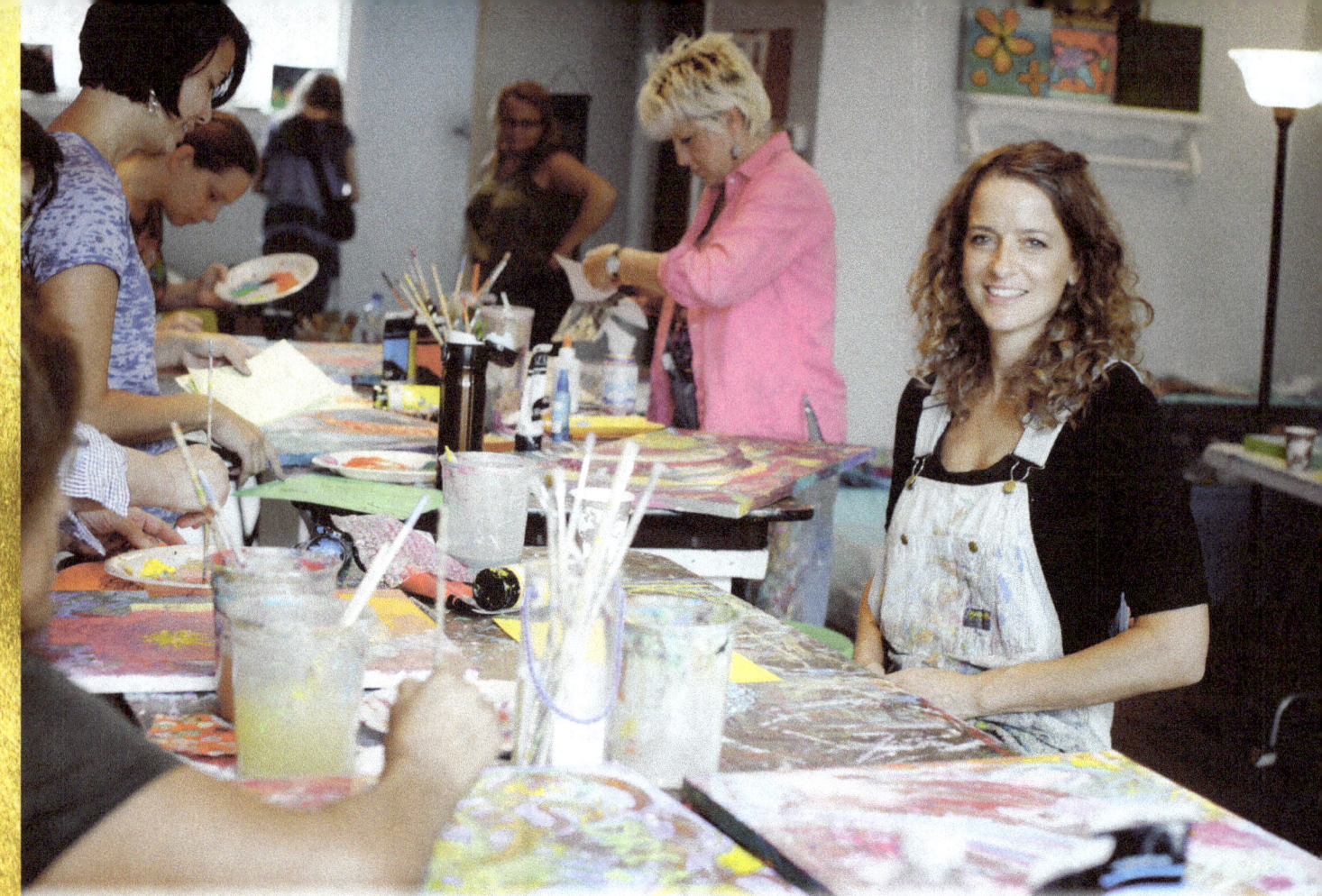

It's ok. We all choose these sticky places so that we can expand each time we get un-stuck. It is how we learn to create more and more of what we want.

The **Super Soul Flow** experience *is* about taking action in the form of creating change on the canvas.

## Why the canvas?

- Most of us have, at one point or another, FEARED the blank canvas. Rising above the energy of fear is the foundation of living in Super Soul Flow.

- The canvas brings us face to face with our CREATOR self.

- It is easier to accept the statement, "I AM the sole creator of my experi- ence" at the canvas than in our life.

- The canvas is a portal to an expanded, multi-dimensional way of thinking and being. It is this portal because this part of our awareness speaks to us symbolically.

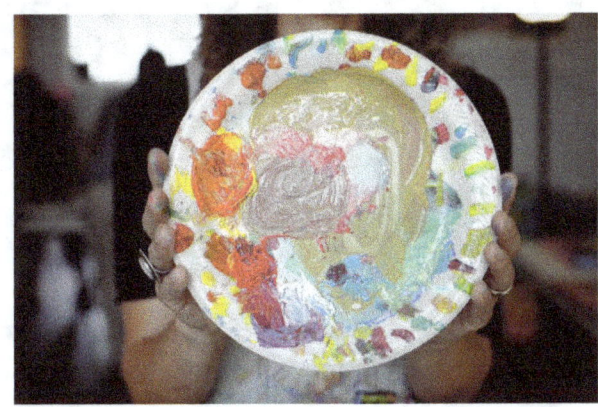

- Science has recorded that meditative and creative activity produce the same brainwaves. They have also proven that when we stimulate our creative, right hemisphere, that we create more receptivity to generating a *stroke of insight,* an *ah-ha,* or *breakthrough* moment.

These **Painting Prompts** are your muse, a suggested path, and are NOT "have-to's." Make the experience yours. Follow the prompt as much or as little as you like. Start with the prompt and then allow the creative process to guide you in any direction. Or, follow along step by step. It is up to you. YOU create your reality.

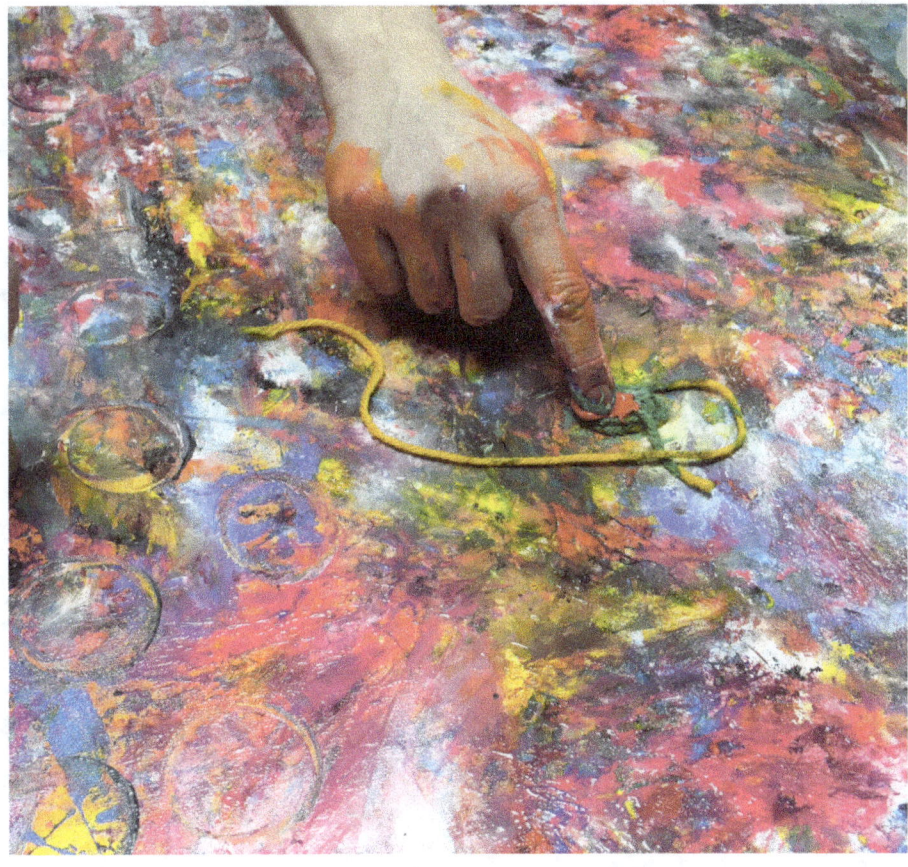

# Creating the Energy of FREEDOM

## Supplies

- Your "Meditation Canvas." This can be any size. I started with a 12-inch square gallery-wrapped canvas so it was easy to keep nearby at my kitchen table. A A bigger canvas can be easier! Start with a size that speaks to you.
- Acrylic paints (white, black, red, yellow, blue, magenta, and cerulean blue are my basic colors)
- Brushes and a water container
- Palette: paper plate, meat tray, artist palette…
- Paper towels, rags, etc.
- A candle to bring "ARTual" to your Super Soul Flow Painting Practice
- Your writing journal
- Deep breaths, a smile, and a commitment to honor the statement, "Life is the canvas of my soul."

Your "Meditation Canvas" is where you are going to create the energy of FREEDOM.

Your "Meditation Canvas" does not need to EVER become any THING. It can be simply where you go to play with color and immerse your awareness into the depths of your unconscious mind, your "knowing mind," or your creator self.

*You are going to create the energy of FREEDOM by detaching from the habit of producing a finished product.*

You are completely FREE to paint whatever you want. You are FREE to paint no-THING. You are FREE to paint with *only* the intention to relax, or to expand your awareness beyond your logical mind.

Think doodling. Your painting may look more like a palette than a "painting."

I am truly encouraging you to play like a child. You can paint free from expectations, comparison, judgment, or a need to ever, ever finish. How can you create the feeling of freedom on the canvas? This is your intention.

## Suggested Process

1. Place ALL the colors you have onto your palette.

2. Play some inspiring music and light your "ARTual" candle. Create sacred time for your painting practice.

3. Dip your brush into the color that is most calling to you.

4. Make your mark on the canvas.

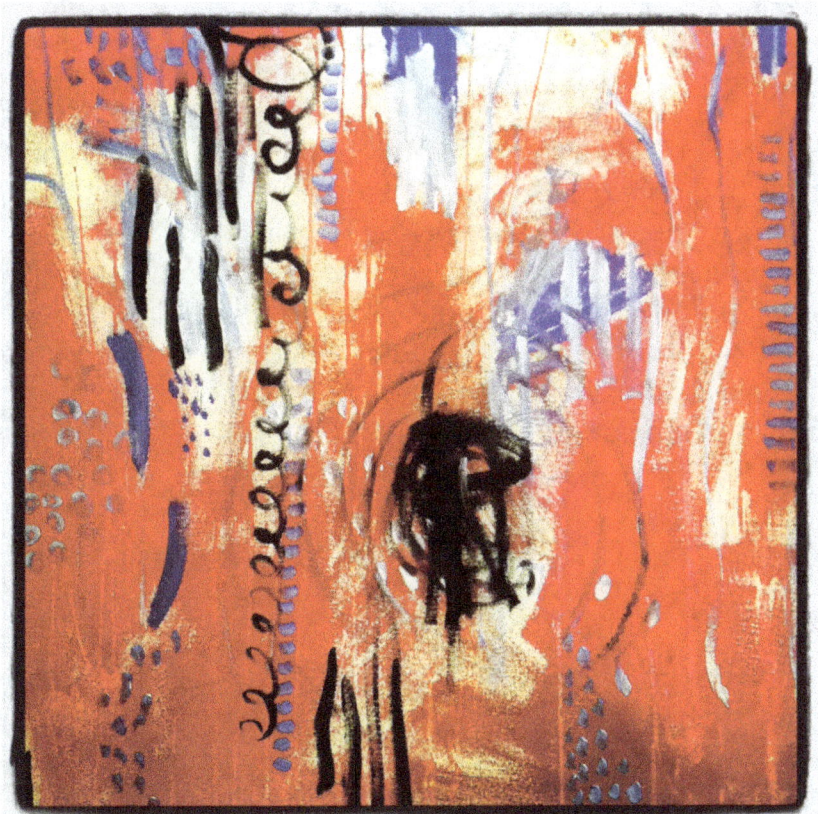

5. Paint until all the paint is off the brush and then dip it into another color. Repeat. As you paint, keep your writing journal open to capture any insight or thoughts that don't resonate with the energy FREEDOM. I will go into more detail in the following section.

6. When you find yourself judging your canvas (notice I said "when" and not "if") take a deep breath and ask yourself if that thought is in alignment with the energy of FREEDOM. Does that thought make you feel free or stuck? Write down any sticky thoughts that come up—get them

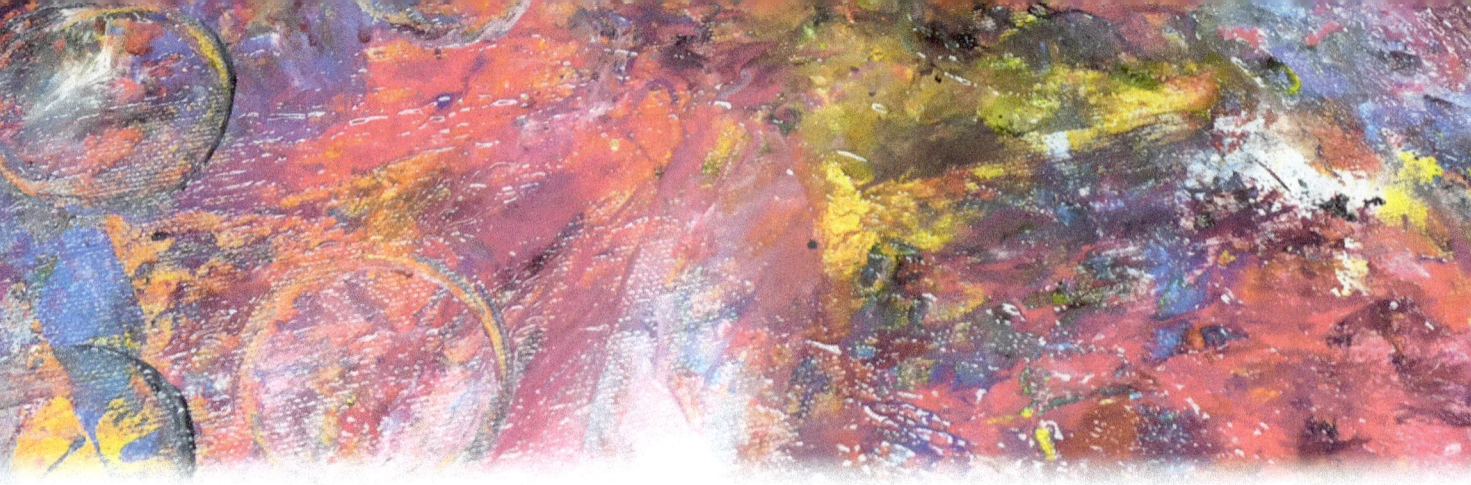

out of your mind and into your journal where you can more objectively decide if those thoughts are ones you want to expand or not. This will be an invaluable part of your painting practice.

7.  Within the Super Soul Flow Painting Practices there will be prompts that include employing other painting techniques and elements, like dripping, stenciling, or adding papers and pattern. If you already have this awareness in your repertoire, feel FREE to use them. If not, relax in the knowing that I am going to continue to expand your Painting Practice experiences. Like taking yoga classes, different poses are introduced in different classes. Right now, focus on freeing your thoughts and immersing yourself in the flow!

*You are in the process of shifting your entire painting paradigm. Allow time and energy for this process.*

## The Canvas of Your Mind

You paint pictures in your mind all day long.

You are getting to know the dance between your thinking mind and your knowing mind. You may also know them as your logical mind and your intuitive mind, or your left and right brain.

They BOTH paint pictures in your mind of your "reality." The question is, are you painting a reality that makes your heART sing, or are you painting a reality that creates worry, stress and anxiety?

You want to create images that make you happy and excited, right?

The more you enter into FLOW with your infinitely creative soul, the quicker you will RISE ABOVE the worry and get to the possibility!

NOW is when you get to let go of the belief that ART is only valuable as a "product." Maybe you were led to believe that ART should only be created by people who could sell their art. The "story" that ART only has value if you can make a living at it was written by our Western capitalistic culture. NOW you and I are going to write a NEW story.

> *"Art and love are man's greatest gifts to himself. There is no art without love. Art is always the making of the soul, the craft of man's touch... so it has been since Neanderthal times, and so it will always be."*
>
> ~Dr. David R. Hawkins, *Power vs. Force*

**Super Soul Flow** was given to me intuitively. The following section was an automatic writing I channeled in my journal as I meditated on the energy of freedom.

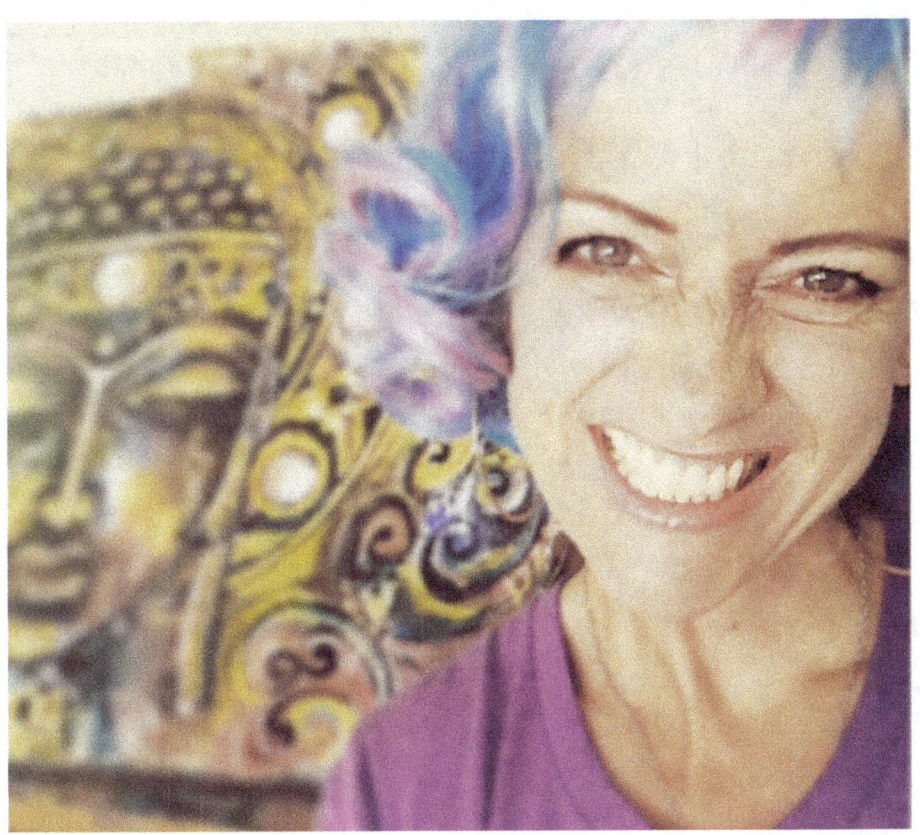

# Freedom

The opposite of "I AM not creative" is freedom!

Your pathway to your own personal liberation can be as simple as stepping up to, into, and then beyond the canvas.

The canvas is where your own inner guru gets to give voice to its eternal wisdom. This part of you knows your limiting beliefs. It knows where you get stuck, why you feel stuck and what you desire to open, even just a bit further, into your personal BLOOM.

The canvas is like the phone. All the potential fiber optics and technology can be there, but if you don't have that final threshold vehicle of communication, the phone itself, you will never be able to receive the signal.

The canvas attunes your subtle body to a state where it is able to receive the intuitive messages from the source of wisdom and insight that is infinitely greater than your own physical experience.

We are talking quantum leaps, morphogenetic fields, ah-ha's, epiphanies, and strokes of insight. They are able to find you only when you've prepared the pathways and opened up the channels in your mind that resonate with a harmonious frequency. There is no judge, no inner critic. There is simply an openness and willingness to receive.

This is why you paint.

For now, create FREEDOM.

Where you feel yourself forcing your creativity, take a step back. Receive and allow the power to FLOW through you.

**Your soul knows this power. Your soul knows that YOU are infinitely creative. You have just given this bigger part of yourself a key into your physical reality in this lifetime. Ready to play? YES!**

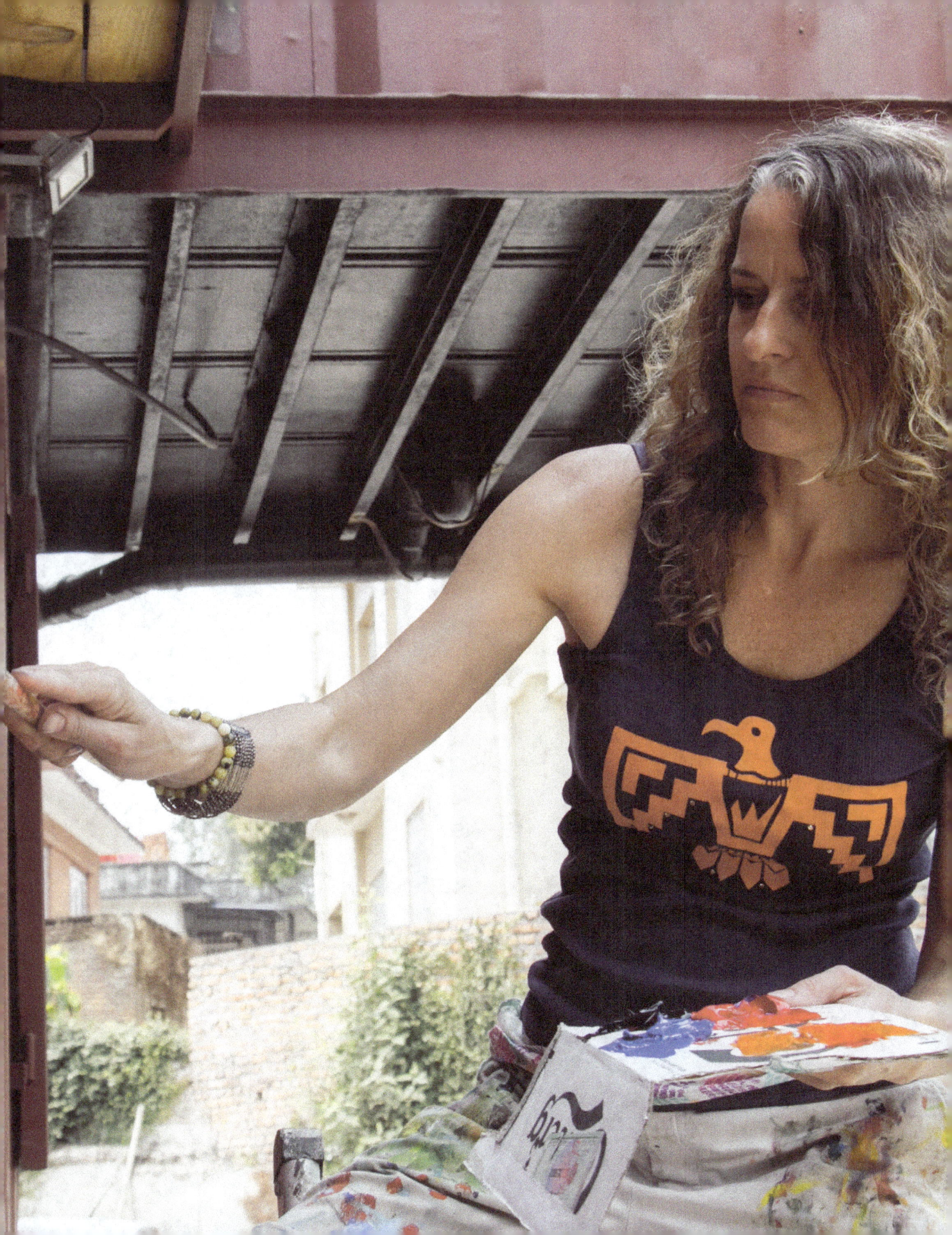

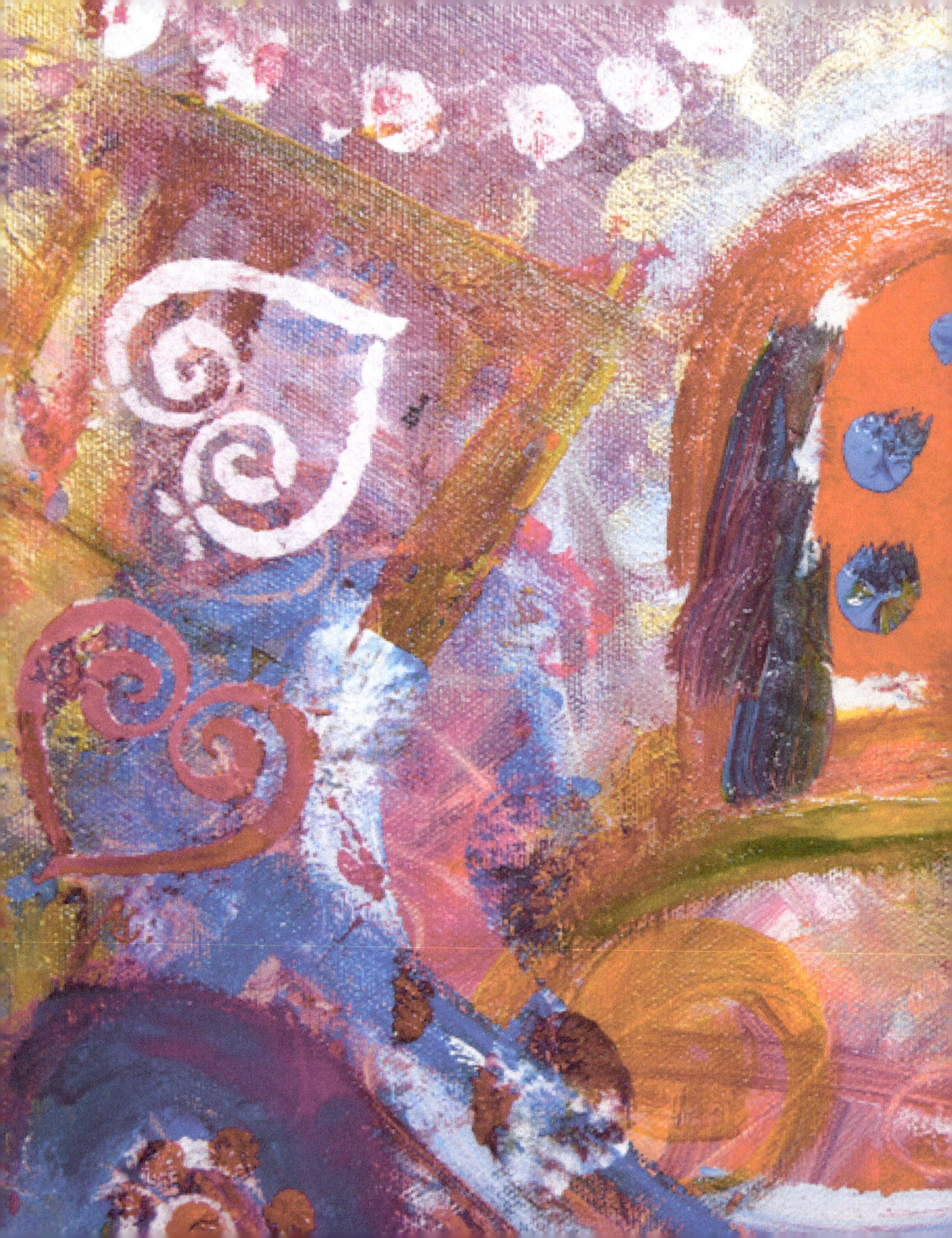

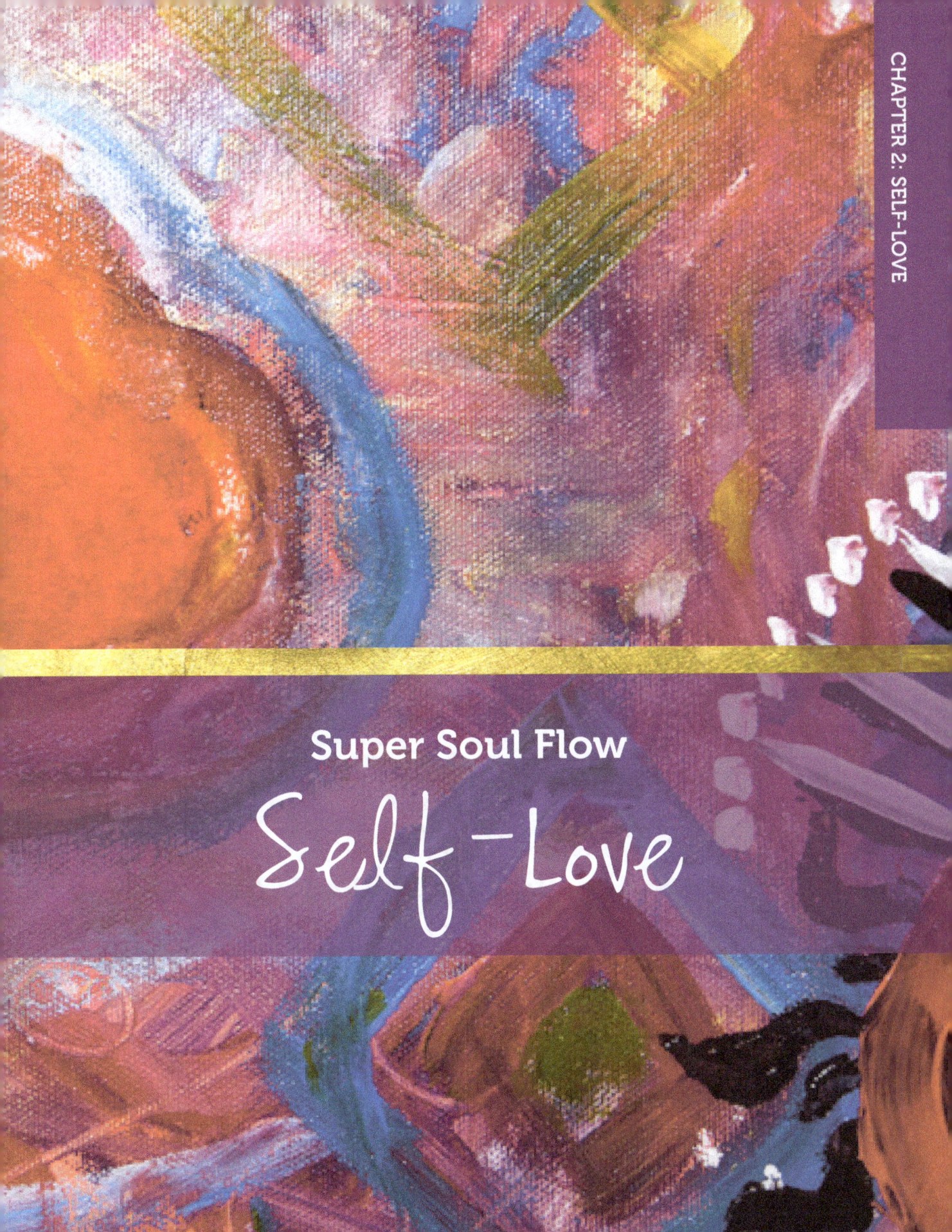

Super Soul Flow

# Self-Love

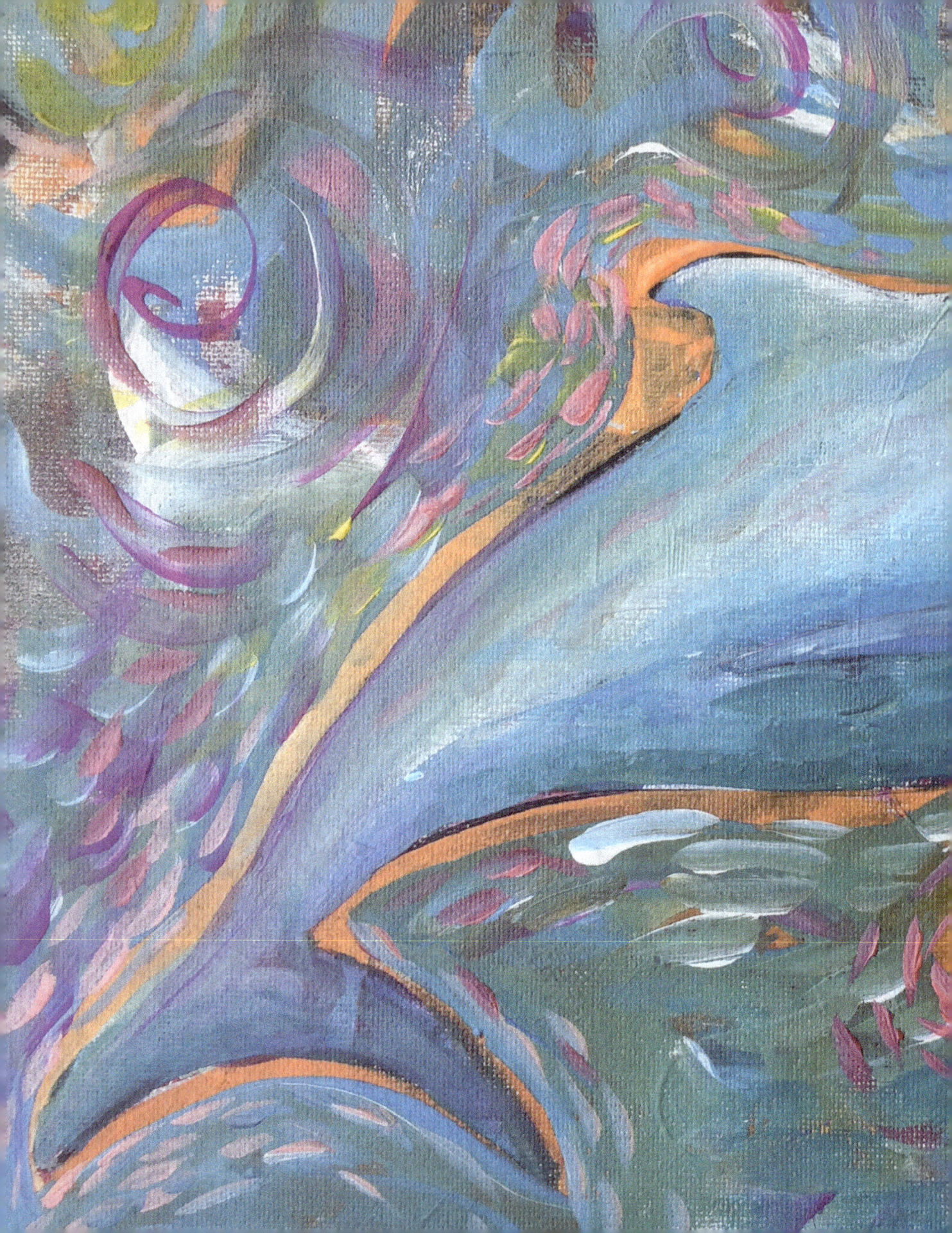

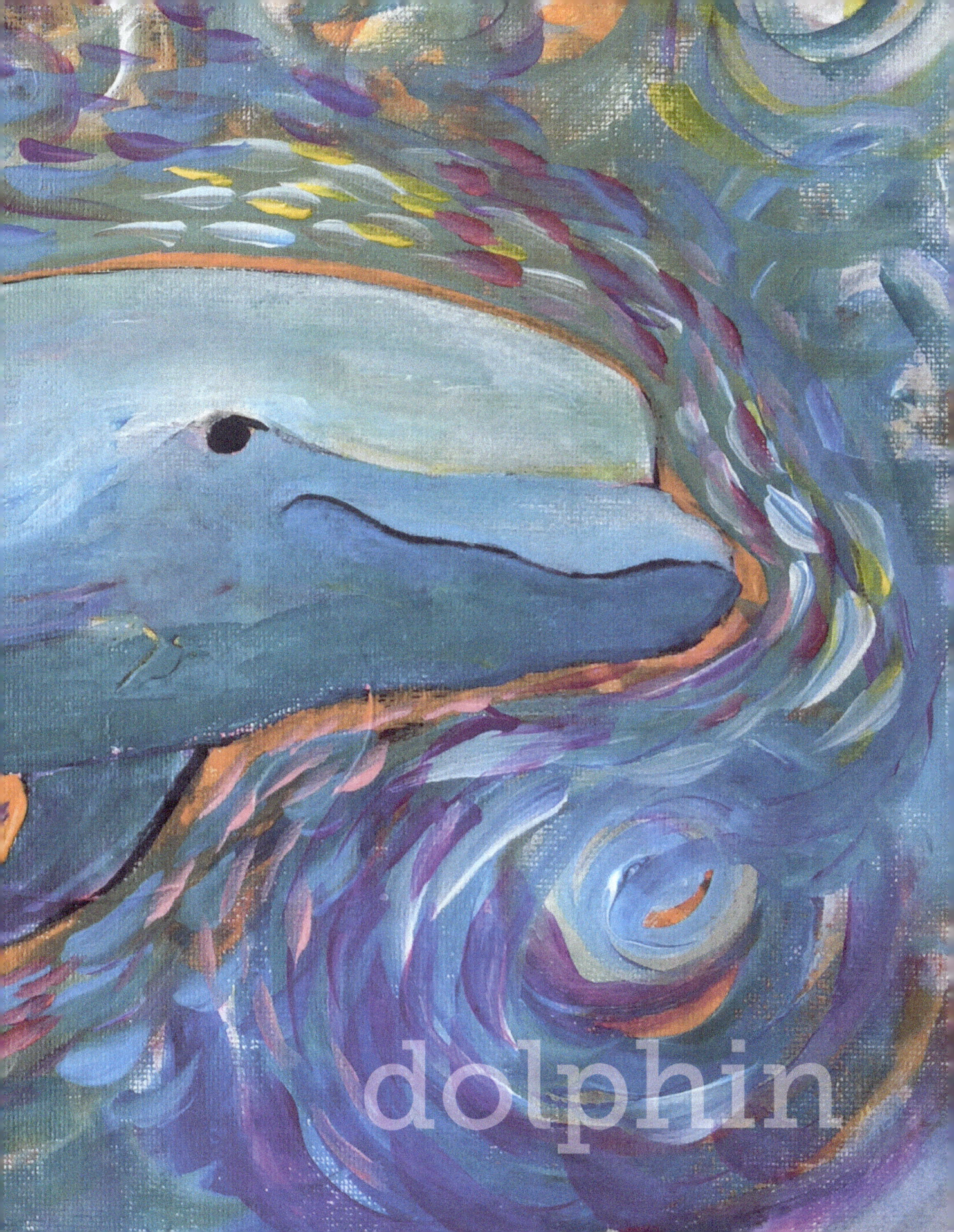

dolphin

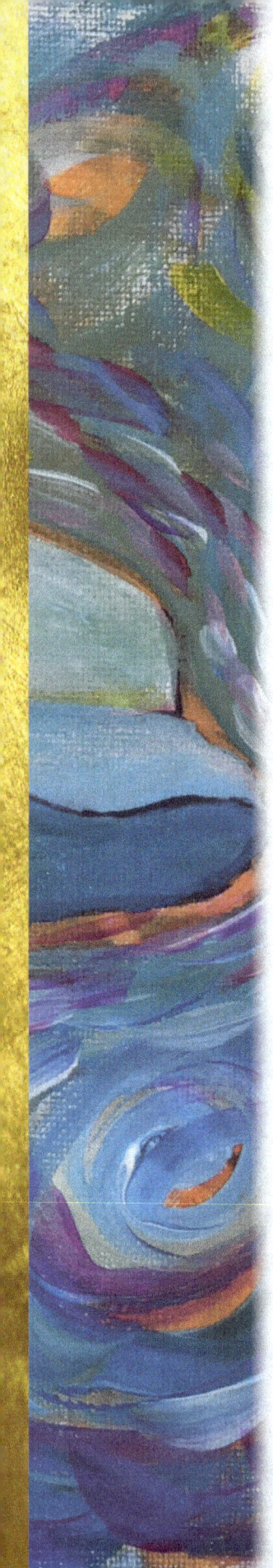

# dolphin

*A dolphin can turn a boat full of practical adults into giddy children! Everyone LOVES dolphins. Their round, friendly eyes, shiny skin and playful nature make them one of the most lovable animal totems around.*

*And since they are creatures of both air and water, they have magical powers. Sometimes it takes this degree of magic to help us love ourselves and navigate our emotional waters with grace and ease—like a dolphin.*

*Next time you catch yourself being critical of yourself, worrying because you don't believe you are enough, or comparing yourself to others and feeling less than, call in DOLPHIN. Allow her to leap and dive through the murky waters in your heART until they are clear and bubbly once again.*

The OCEAN calls to me,
her sirens luring me into her mysterious depths.
I seek escape, to be covered up, to disappear.

The OCEAN calls to me,
she echoes feelings of renewal and purity.
I fear her expansiveness, her infinite waters.

The OCEAN calls to me,
her vastness promises potential, fruitfulness.
I hold back, feeling unworthy of her treasures.

The OCEAN calls to me,
she sends her messenger as my guide.

I crane my neck to notice a disturbance in the surface.

The OCEAN speaks to me,
dolphin leaps into the air, clicking her welcome.
I am smiling, leaning into the tide.

The OCEAN reminds me,
that, just like the dolphin, I am cherished and loved.

Just like the dolphin, I can love every inch of my own
waters, the dark corners and playful surface.

Just like the dolphin, I exist in two worlds, my emotional and
my practical.

Just like the dolphin, I can love all of me, all of my life, both
above and below.

Just like the dolphin, I am only love.

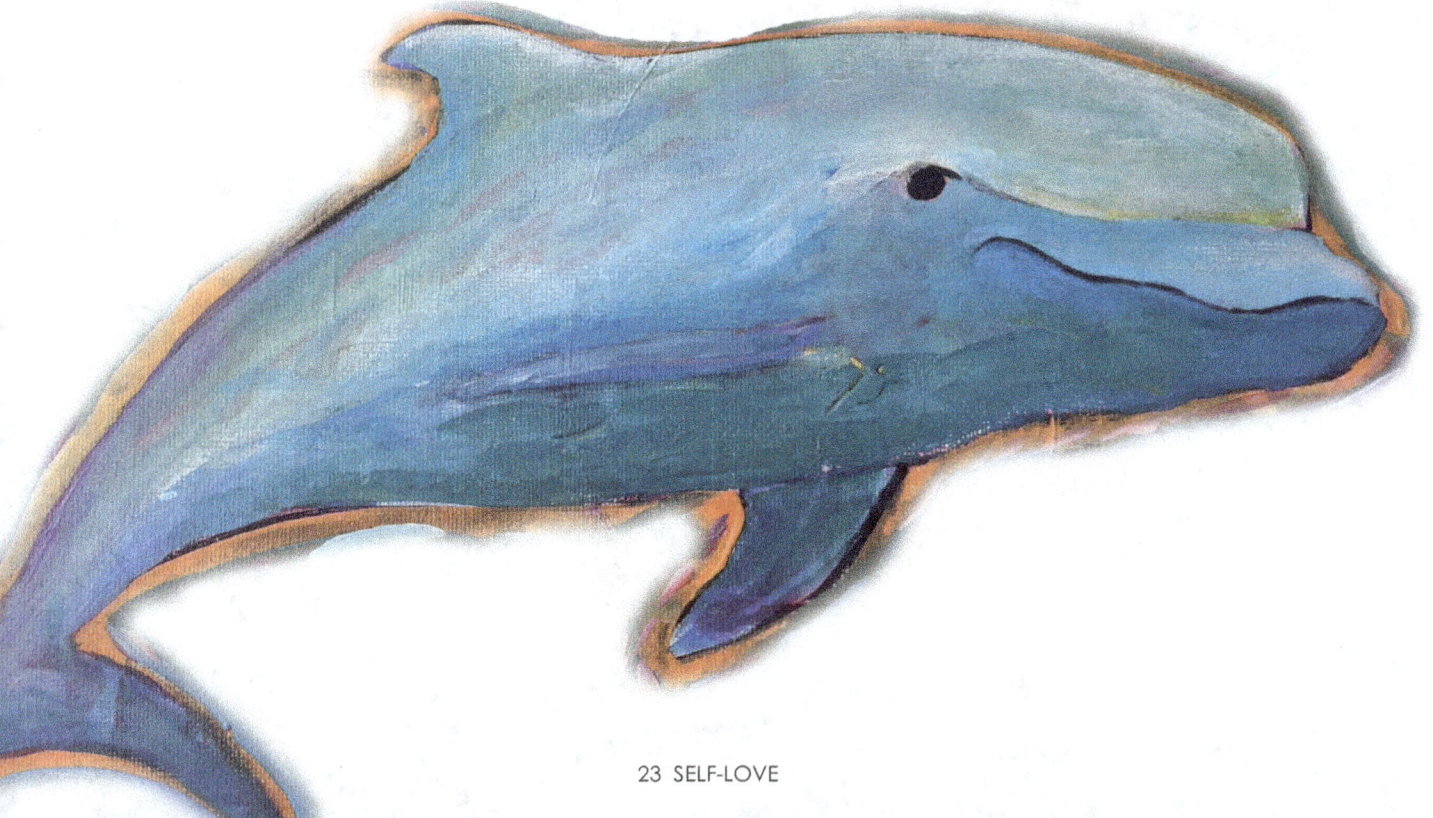

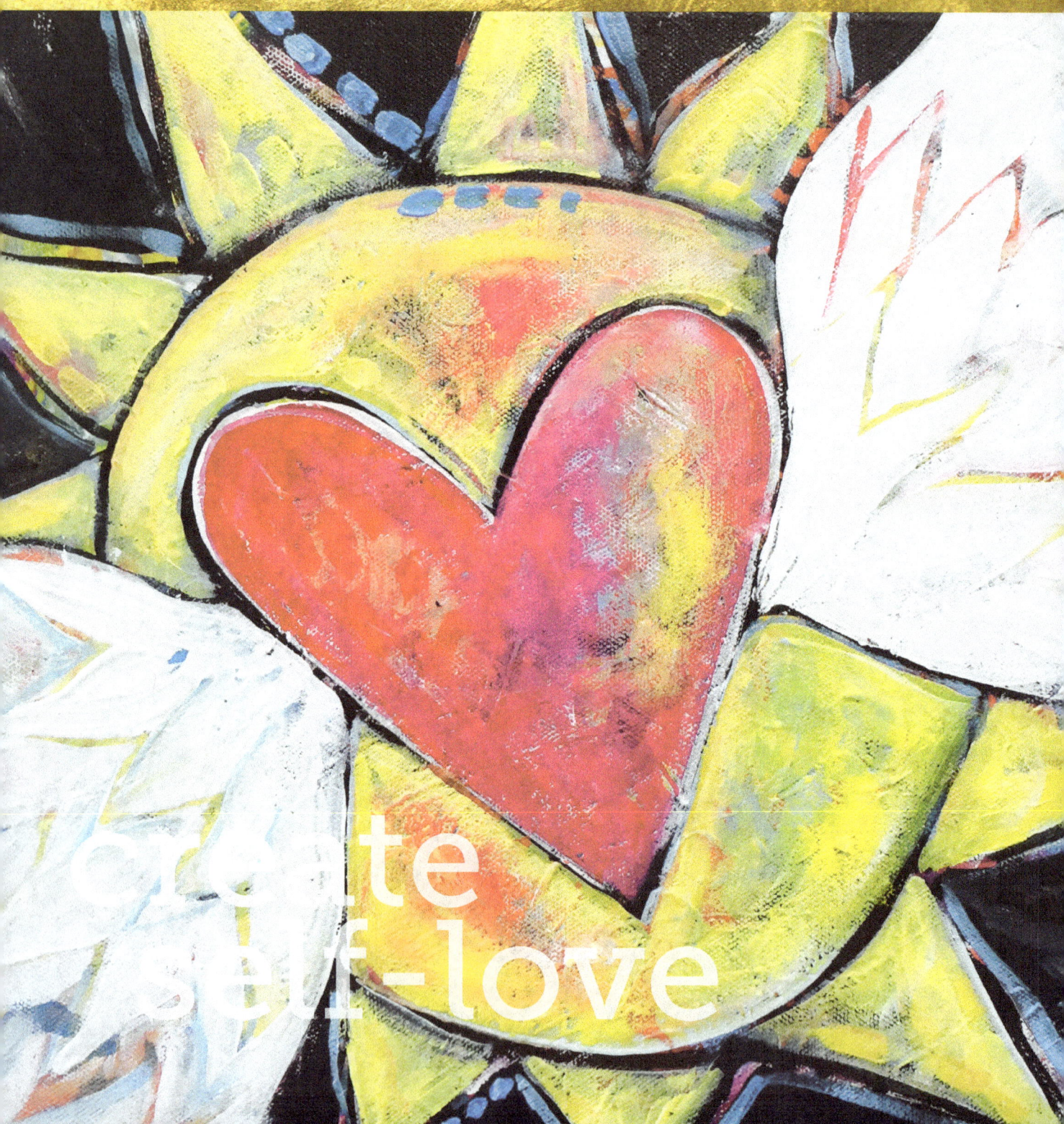

You yourself, as much as anybody in the entire universe, deserve your love and affection.
~BUDDHA

create
self-love

# You were not taught or encouraged to love yourself unconditionally.

The result is that you might look for the unconditional love, that we all so desperately crave, outside of yourself.

You want your husband or child or partner to love you unconditionally.

You want the proper recognition from the people you help or support. You've done all THAT for them, after all, why don't they seem more grateful? Right?

Here's the truth (it gets better, I promise!)

The ONLY source of true unconditional love is within YOU.

No one else can possibly love you EXACTLY, 100% of the time, the way you really, really want them to. Only you can do this.

Until you rediscover this unconditional love you have for yourself, you will continue to look to others to provide this energy, this feeling, for you.

And when they let you down, because they don't love you perfectly, your love for them becomes conditional. Then their love for you becomes conditional. Or it feels that way. And you feel like you've been cheated or robbed, or somehow left out. You become the victim.

Ouch!

Ok, shake it off! You've got this.

YOU are going to LOVE LOVE LOVE you! Then, a glorious thing happens.

You don't NEED anyone else to do anything perfectly for YOU! As a result, your love FOR THEM becomes unconditional.

You know what comes next...

Then, their love for you becomes UNCONDITIONAL!

It feels so good.

Loving yourself is pure bliss.

You see how you have been so conditioned to feel like this is somehow bad or wrong. Not anymore.

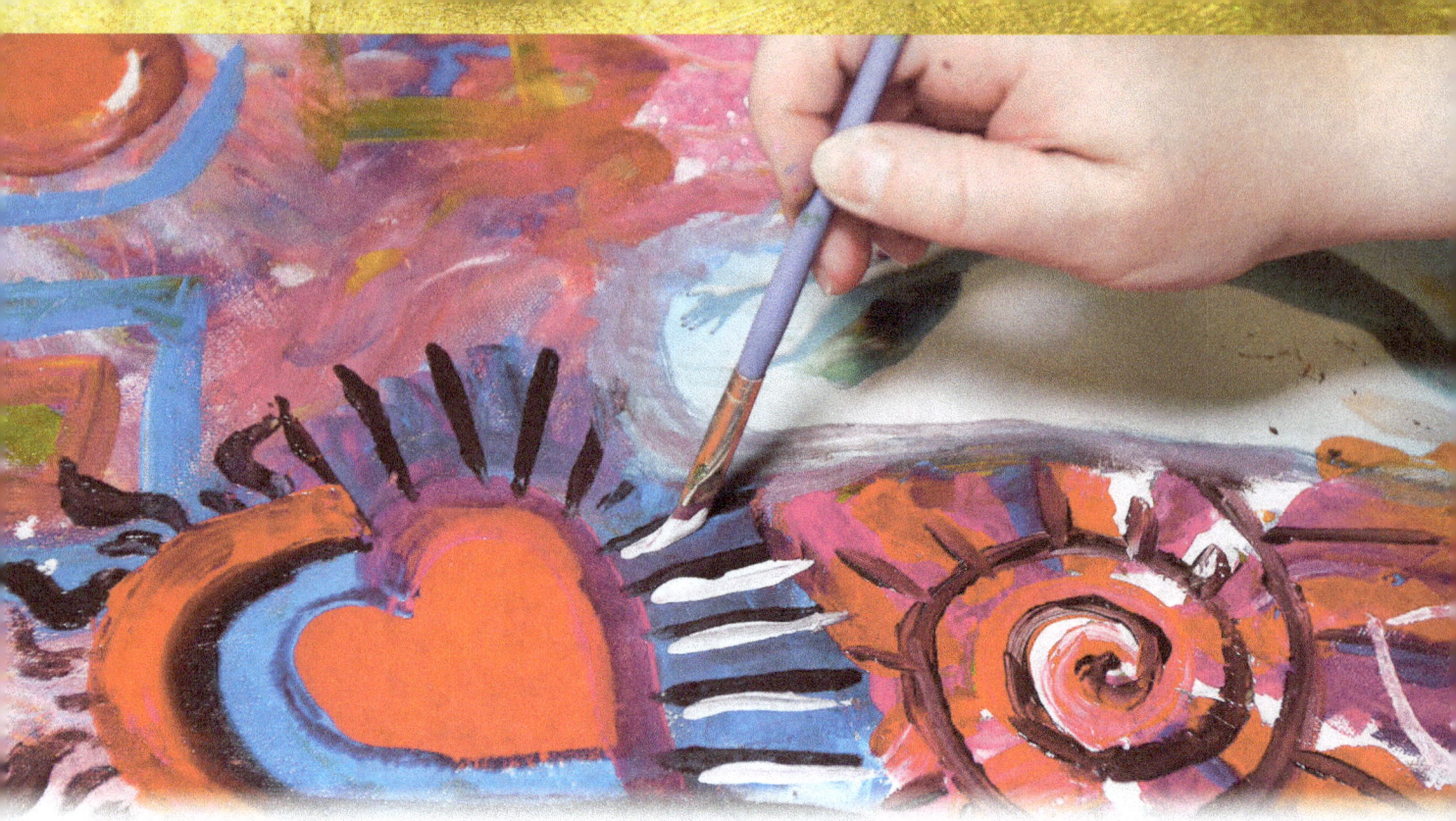

Today you will create the energy of self-love at your meditation canvas. In the process, you will get to observe all the tiny ways you do not love yourself. Once you observe your inner critic, your inner perfectionist, your inner "poor me," you can take back your power and tell those voices that they have been misinformed.

"Thank you Ms. Inner Critic for wanting the best for me. I understand you did not realize how you have been keeping me from loving me. Now, because of you, I get to begin today, right now, to be my own inner cheerleader. You, Ms. Inner Critic, are off the hook! Go take a well deserved vacation."

Don't worry, she will check back in with you to see if you want her back. You can politely reject her offers. Eventually, she will just fade away into the ethers.

At the canvas, during your personal painting practice, you are going to practice loving everything you create, no matter what.

When just one of us stands in our power, in a place rooted in self-love, we are more powerful than millions of people standing in fear, guilt, or anger. When you are getting all the love you need from within, you overflow with forgiveness, acceptance, peace and unconditional love for others and all experiences.

You're not the Dalai Lama, you say? Understood. Let's start small. Let's take our intention to love ourselves to the canvas. Even a 20-minute Painting Practice focused on creating self-love can ripple beyond the canvas in powerful ways.

I want you to paint a heart. Paint more than one. Paint them in a new way. Create your own heART symbol.

# Creating the Energy of SELF-LOVE

Which is more typical: judging what we like or don't like? Or judging what is good or bad?

Or do we accept everything and judge nothing?

Even when we "like" something we are leaving opportunity to not like something else. *Painting with unconditional self-love means expecting nothing BUT love.* There are no other options—you aren't "waiting to see" or wondering if it will be this enough or that enough. The experience simply IS love.

You get to create with color, engage your soul in play and symbolism, and expand your imagination into new realms of possibility. You have infinite potential for change. You can paint forever and there is no end to the love, acceptance, and receptivity.

When it is "ugly," you love it. When it is "gorgeous," you love it. There is nothing you can put on that canvas that you won't love. It doesn't mean that there isn't a constant process of choosing what colors, images, lines, patterns to keep or which to paint over or change. But you love the WHOLE process. Art AND life are dependent on contrasting experiences.

## Dark and light, shadow and illumination

Read the following meditation from *The Book of Love and Creation* by Paul Selig out loud before you begin your painting practice:

*"I AM in my love. Yes, I am worthy of love, and I understand now that the belief that I am not allowed love by myself is an act of fear, and is the ego seeking to maintain jurisdiction of my light to prevent me from full realization of my Divine Self and all the wonder that it would bring to me. I am free of this fear as I say it. I AM free. I AM free. I AM free. I AM in my love."*

Here is another meditation on the power of love from the book *The Magical Presence, The Saint Germaine Series*:

*"…the Joy of ever expanding the Perfection which forever abides within love. Constant new creation will ever go on, for Life is Perpetual Motion and neither slumbers or sleeps, but is ever and forever a Self-Sustained Stream of Expanding Perfection in Joy, in Ecstasy, and Eternally New Design. This Perfect Activity and Joy of Life are all contained within Obedience to the Law of Love."*

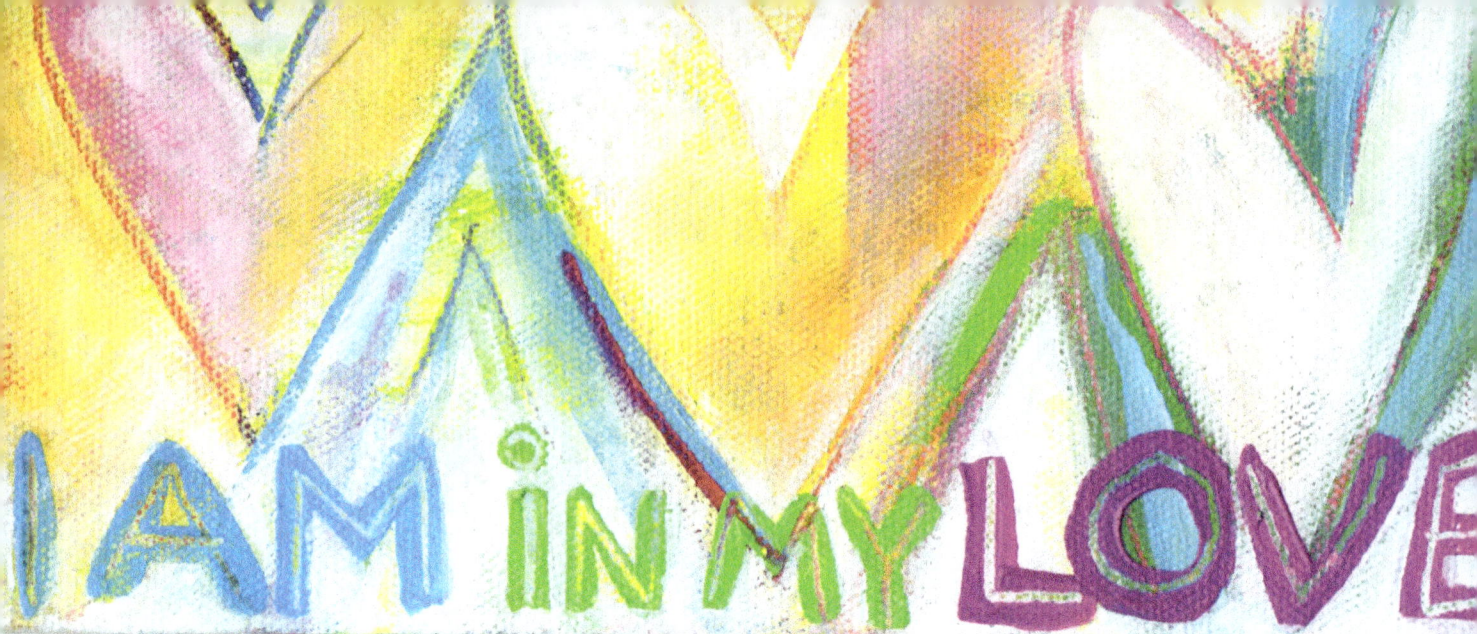

## The Canvas of Your Mind

*As you paint the energy of Self-Love, tune in to all the ways you DON'T think loving thoughts to yourself.*

There is a tremendous tendency, from our physical, local reality, to "blanket" everything we do with the same belief.

For example, a lawyer or an accountant may rely on their perfectionism for their professional success. Their career is such that being perfect, detailed, and exact is rewarded. However, if they "blanket" that same energy over their personal life and relationships it may no longer serve them.

As you paint, tune in to the subtle ways you are not loving yourself.

*You don't need to create love. Your heart is made to produce so much love that you can send your love to the entire world. If you can't feel love, it's because you are resisting love; it's because you've learned how to stop expressing your love.*

*~DON MIGUEL RUIZ, THE VOICE OF KNOWLEDGE*

# A Guided Meditation

*Close your eyes. Take a deep breath. Bring all your awareness within. Take another deep breath. Follow your breath all the way in. In the dark, behind your eyelids, look for YOU. Where are you? Are you in your head? Are you in your heart? Search around a bit. Try to pinpoint from where your awareness comes. Is it tucked behind your rib cage, in your head, within your beating heart?*

*Doesn't your body feel really small all of a sudden? How could ALL of you fit in that small body? Do all of your memories, your dreams, your passions, your tastes, sights, smells… your ideas, your preferences, your style, your talents… reside within the skin of your body, nestled somewhere between the bones and organs? OR are you bigger than that?*

*From this expansive perspective, LOVE yourself. LOVE you!*

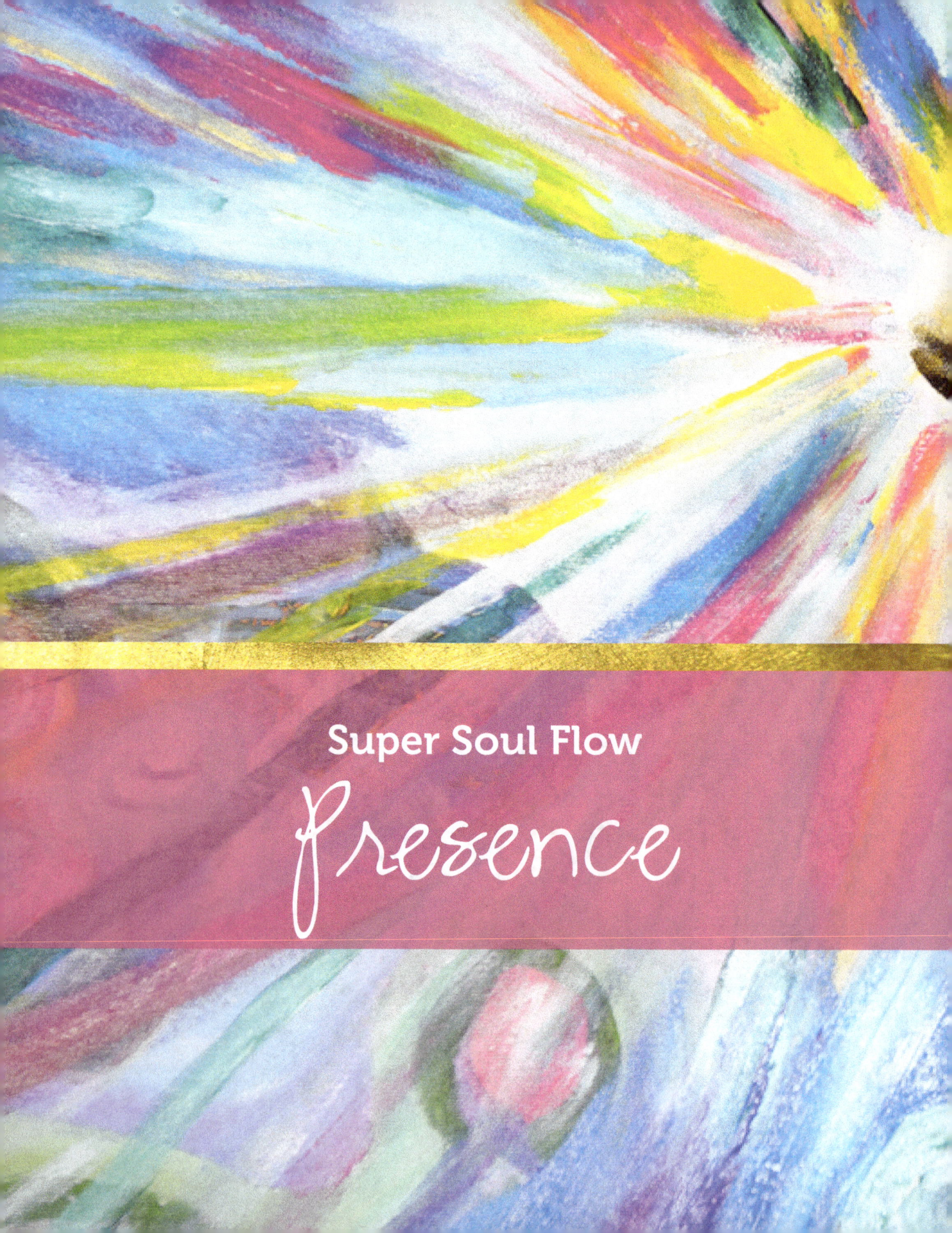

Super Soul Flow

*Presence*

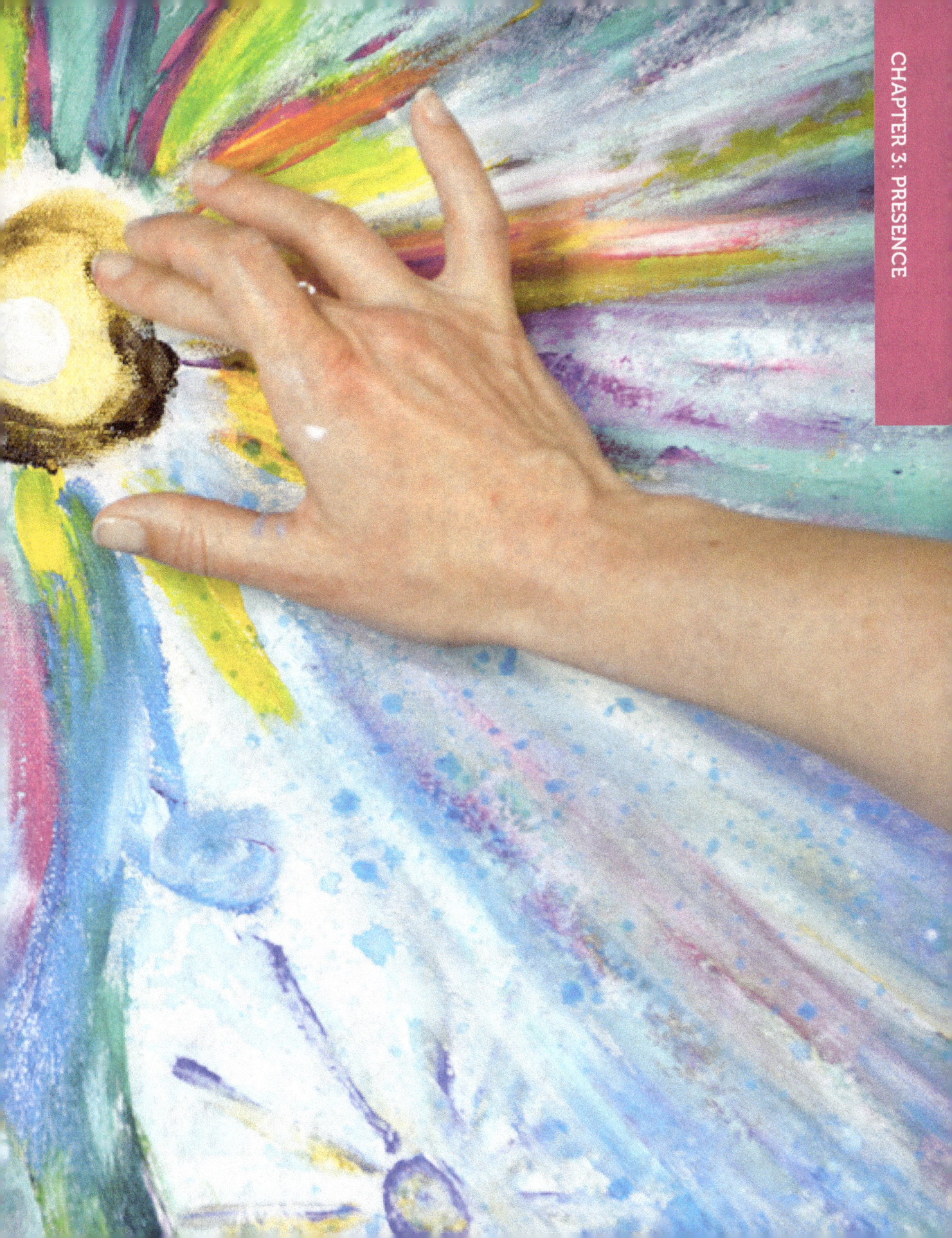

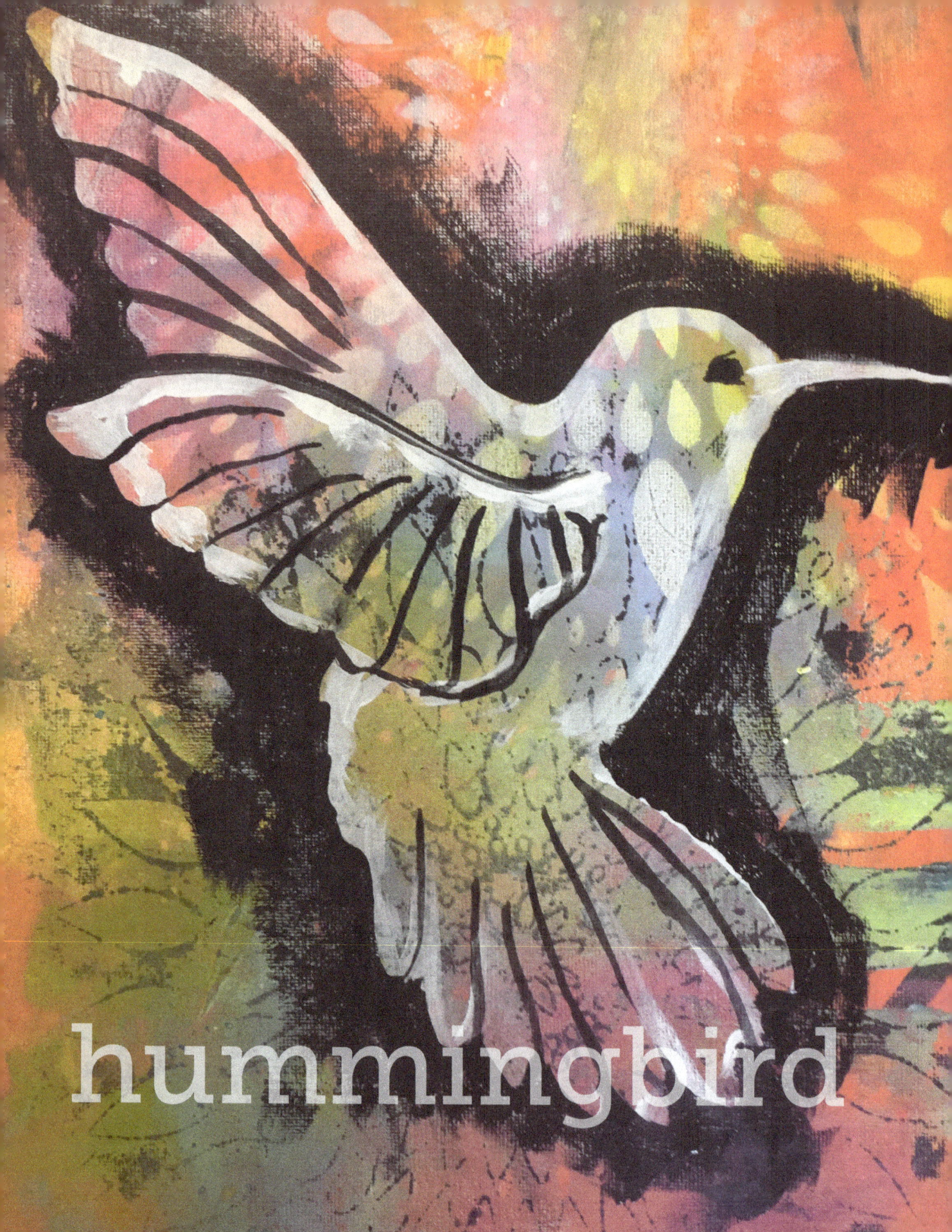

hummingbird

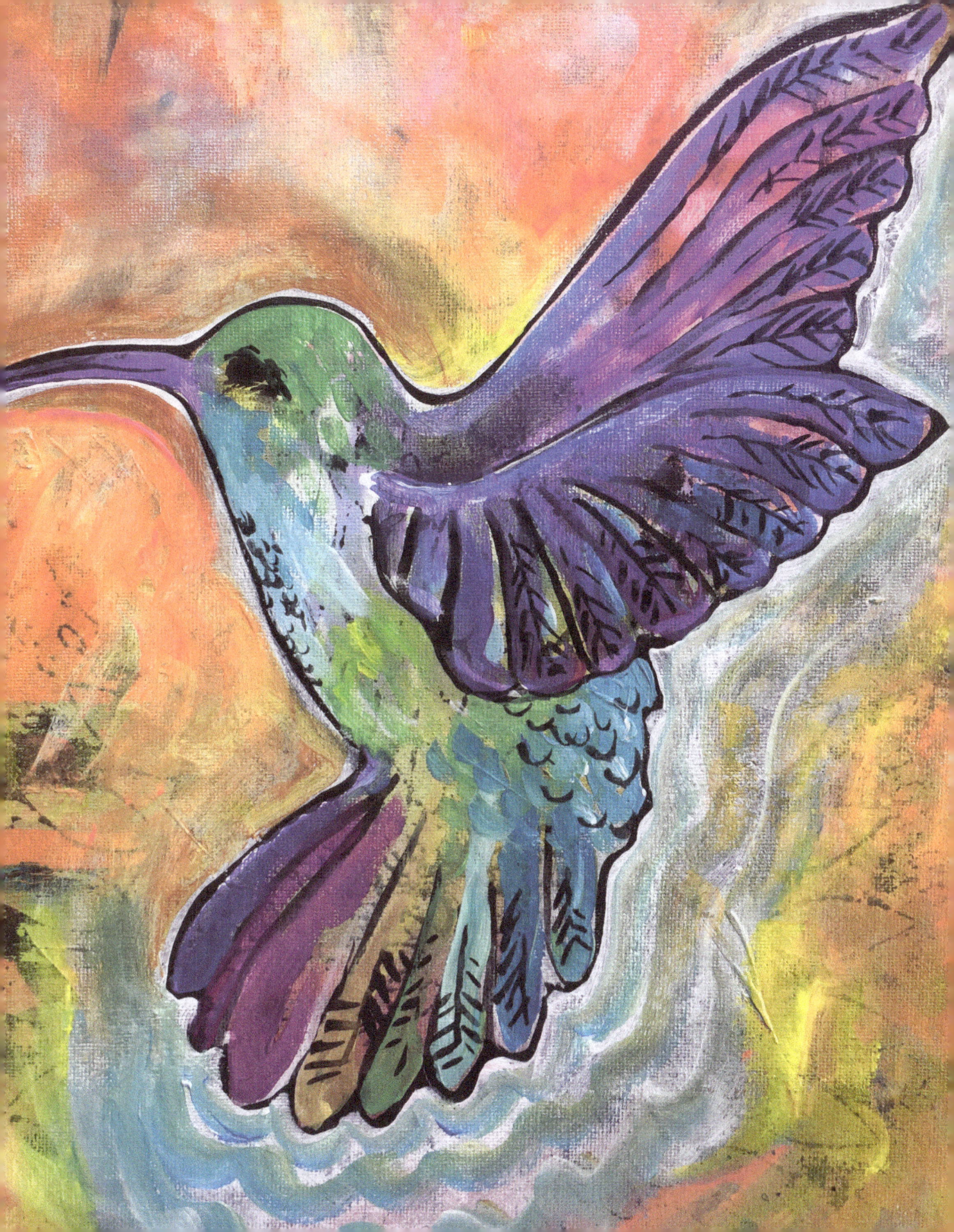

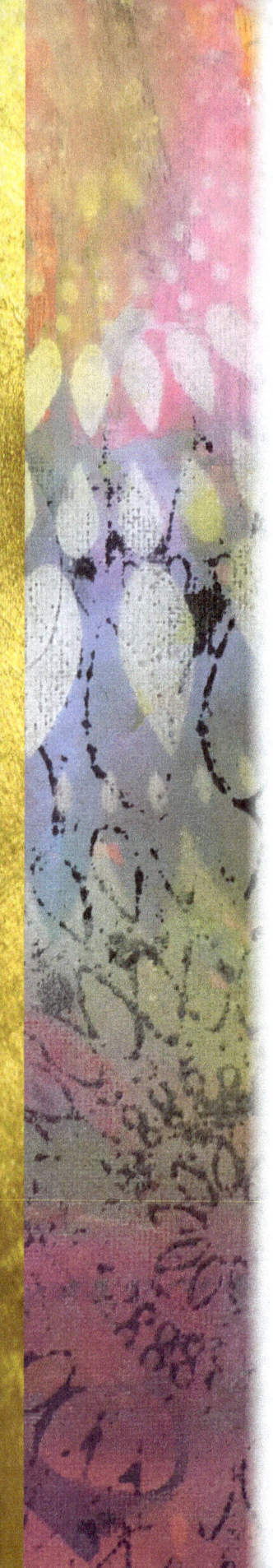

# hummingbird

*Hummingbirds are the wizards of the air. They zoom through the ethers, almost invisibly. And, in a moment, they hover in mid-flight. Wings moving in the pattern of infinity, calling us to RISE ABOVE our routine perception. A hummingbird zeroing in on its next source of sweetness reminds us to also seek sweetness and beauty in our own lives. And the medicine of the hummingbird guides us within, to the truest source of divine nectar.*

Should I go here or do this?

What do you desire?

Should I take a left or a right?

What do you desire?

Should I help him, her, or them?

What do you desire?

How easy is it to distract ourselves with illusory promises or expectations?

The secret is in identifying our deepest desires, in this moment.

As a hummingbird miraculously appears, as if from nowhere, your mind is guided instantly toward the object of your soul's desire.

Its iridescent wisdom becomes your muse.

The hummingbird was created...
... to drink sweet nectar from the ripest blossoms.

You are created...
... perfectly to have everything you need to follow your bliss and, therefore, offer your gifts to the world.

Harmony in motion.

When a hummingbird catches your eye, she commands all of your attention.

When a person in flow—flying on the wings of their passion—crosses your path, you are likewise transfixed.

Right NOW...

What is your desire? BE that.

Now, FLY!

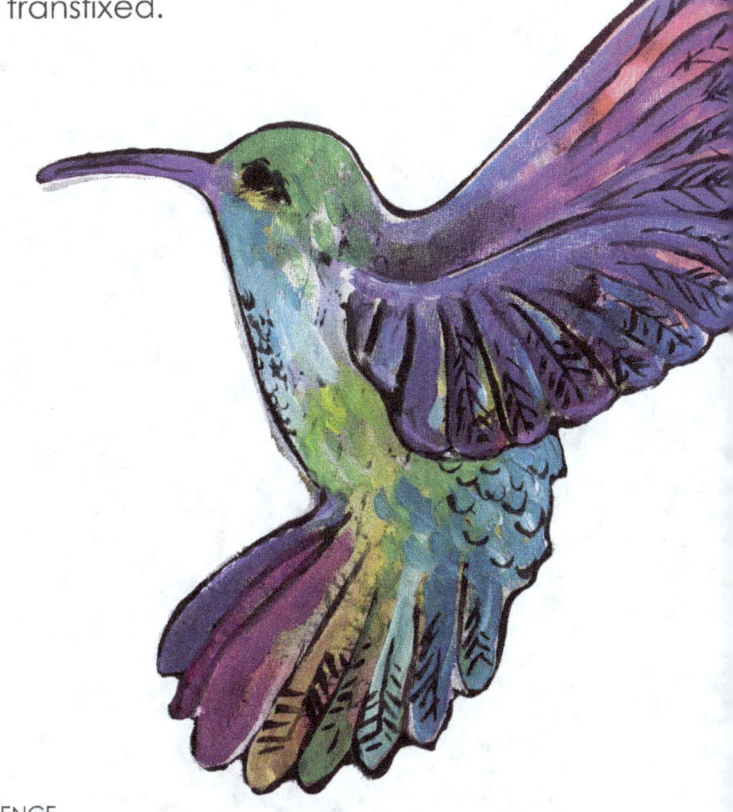

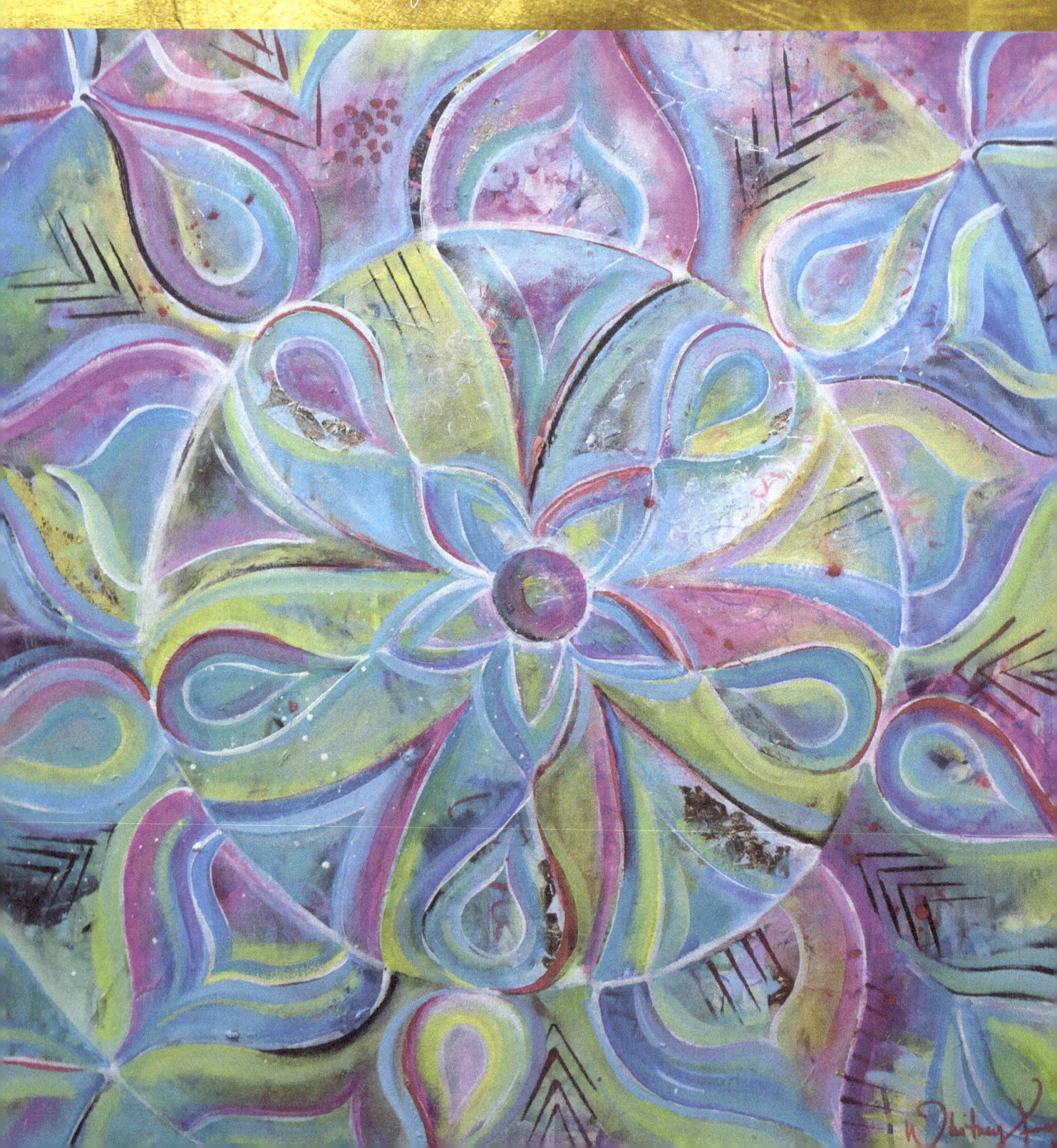

The Mandala is an archetypal image whose occurance is attested throughout the ages. It signifies the wholeness of the Self. This circular image represents the wholeness of the psychic ground, or, to put it in mythic terms, the divinity incarnate in man. ~CARL JUNG

# Today you are going to make friends with the present moment.

Becoming present is all about cultivating awareness and becoming your own witness.

Be your witness right now. Take a deep breath and ask yourself, "What do I feel right now?"

Then take a step back and observe your present moment.

Are you feeling tired, happy, hopeful, frustrated, stressed, or excited?

Now, ask yourself, "Am I this feeling? Is this who I am?"

The answer would be NO.

**You are the being that is experiencing the feeling—you are NOT your feeling. In fact, at any given point in time, your focus and the feeling being generated is either from the past, the present, or the future.**

From the past, we can learn from our mistakes, recall valuable information, memories, or facts that we have learned or experienced and access our own personal set of baggage.

From the future, we get the opportunity to plan ahead, envision the future we desire, or worry about what might, possibly, maybe happen if this situation, desire, or goal of ours does not work out.

Personally, I have found that after imagining something that I want, my default is to almost immediately start imagining the worst case, rather than the best case, scenario.

This awareness struck me back in January 2014. It was the launch of my new website. It had been a full year of planning and expectation—and thousands of dollars invested. It felt like all my high hopes and dreams were launched alongside that site. I found myself thinking about what I wanted my biz to look like a year down the road. But then I realized that I was following that desire with all my back-up plans in case it didn't work out! Why would I spend my time and my powerful imagination painting the picture of what I DIDN'T want?!

I decided to change that pattern. With awareness it IS possible.

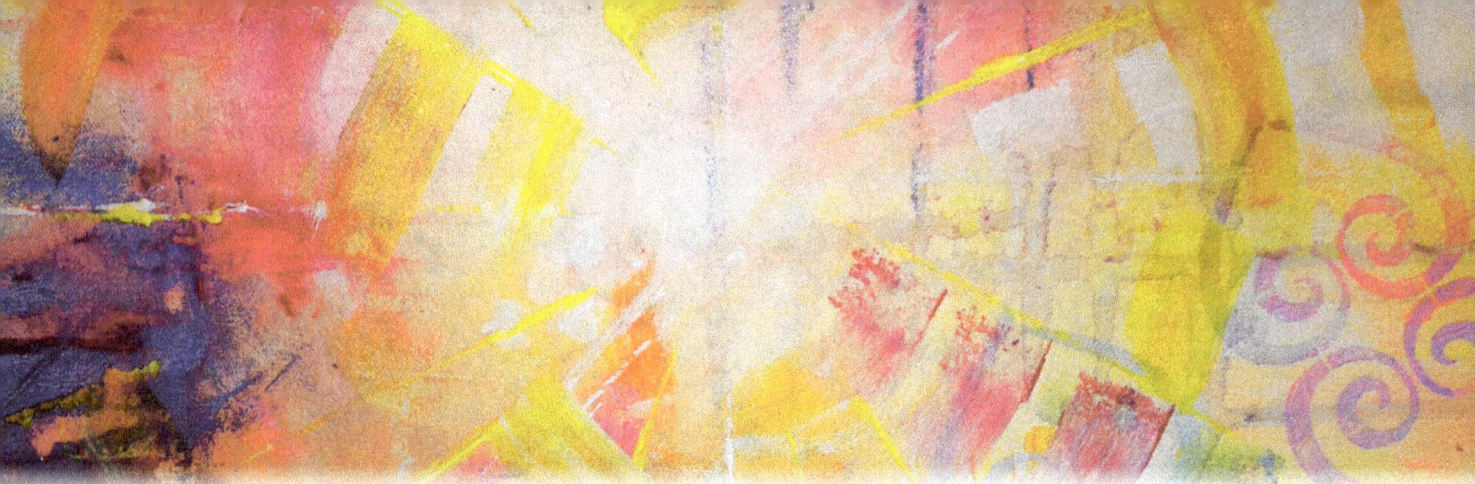

From present moment awareness, we get to access the "field of pure potentiality." In the present moment we are not limited by our past experience, nor are we being constrained or distracted by our worry about the future. In the present moment we can choose from infinite possibilities—if we learn how to stay there long enough.

Before we get a chance to choose from those infinite possibilities in our present moment awareness, our past-focused voice, also called the Ego, distracts us with our memories of all those other times we tried something new and failed, or lost money, or did not hit our goals... OR it reminds us of those obligations we have coming up, or our need to protect ourselves from insecurity.

Before we get to go skipping merrily into that Field of Pure Potentiality, we get dragged back into our past, or catapulted into an imaginary, illusory future, where limitations, boundaries, should's and have-to's reign supreme.

**What are all the ways you can stay grounded in the present moment, MORE of the time?**

**What are all the ways you can consciously choose present moment awareness over past and future?**

**What are all the ways you can spend more of your time imagining exactly what you desire, rather than generating the energies of what you least desire?**

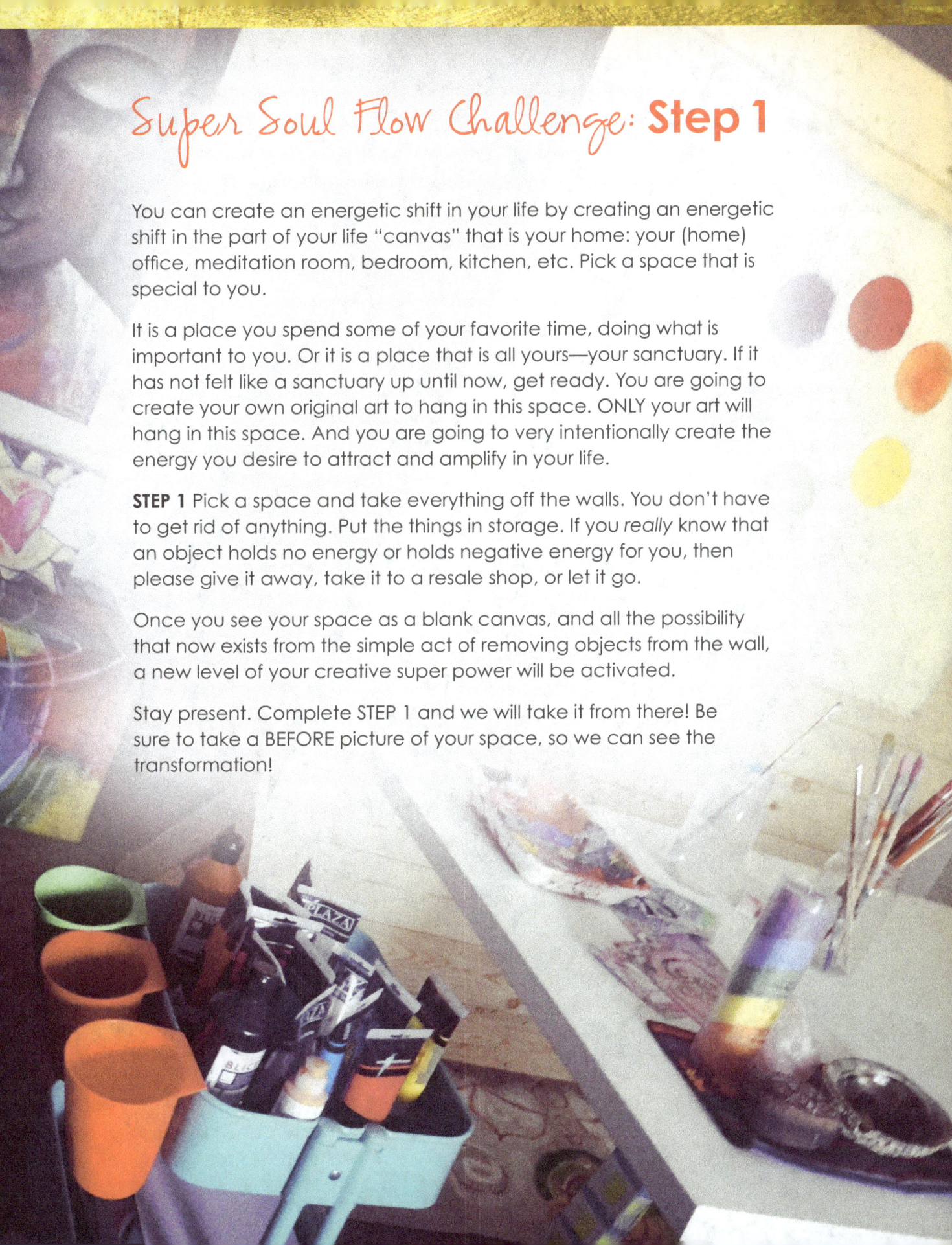

# Super Soul Flow Challenge: **Step 1**

You can create an energetic shift in your life by creating an energetic shift in the part of your life "canvas" that is your home: your (home) office, meditation room, bedroom, kitchen, etc. Pick a space that is special to you.

It is a place you spend some of your favorite time, doing what is important to you. Or it is a place that is all yours—your sanctuary. If it has not felt like a sanctuary up until now, get ready. You are going to create your own original art to hang in this space. ONLY your art will hang in this space. And you are going to very intentionally create the energy you desire to attract and amplify in your life.

**STEP 1** Pick a space and take everything off the walls. You don't have to get rid of anything. Put the things in storage. If you *really* know that an object holds no energy or holds negative energy for you, then please give it away, take it to a resale shop, or let it go.

Once you see your space as a blank canvas, and all the possibility that now exists from the simple act of removing objects from the wall, a new level of your creative super power will be activated.

Stay present. Complete STEP 1 and we will take it from there! Be sure to take a BEFORE picture of your space, so we can see the transformation!

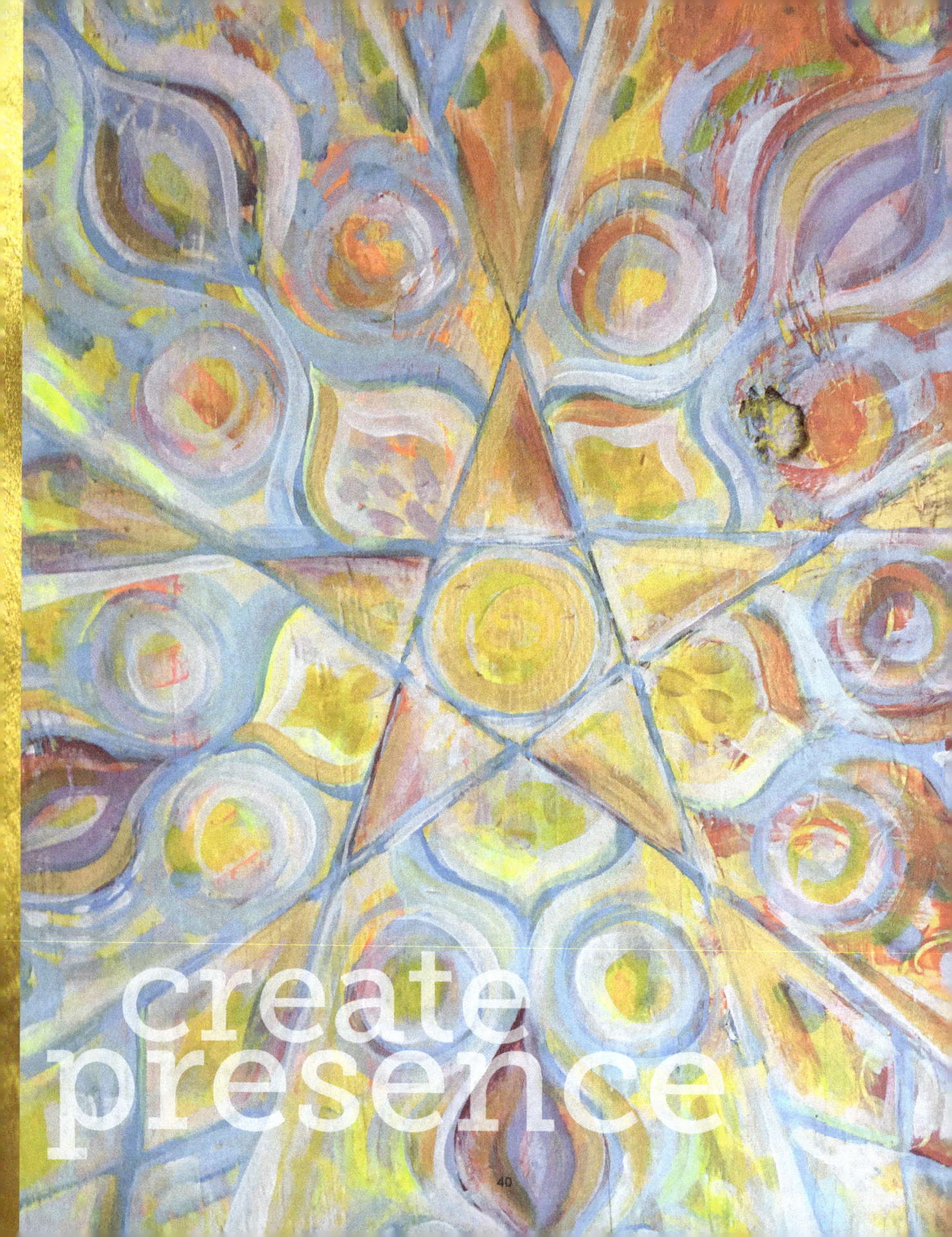

create
presence

# You get to create the energy of presence. You get to know how it feels.

Once you know the FEELING, you can attract it to you at a moment's notice. Then you EXPAND that energy throughout the entire "canvas" that is your life. This is one of the most powerful reasons you have been attracted to painting.

Your soul is calling you, luring you, attracting you into the present moment where it can FLOW through you! Who cares what you paint or how good it looks in the end, if the creative act is ATTRACTING to you the divine, infinite awareness that wants to play and CO-CREATE your life with you?

AND if you are called to share your Personal Painting Practice with others, as a teacher, or as a ring leader of friends around the kitchen table, you are guiding others to a new awareness of the power of *their* present moment.

Super Soul Flow is meant to be shared and the energy of creative power and possibility is meant to spread like wildfire. YOU are lighting your own sacred spark and then YOU can fan that same flame within others!

## Let's create PRESENCE!

You get to paint a mandala in this chapter! *Mandala* in Sanskrit means "sacred container." Mandalas have been created by almost every culture that has ever existed. It has ALWAYS been a ritual, an "ARTual," designed to bring us to our center and connect us to the divine.

# Creating the Energy of PRESENCE

## It is only from the present moment that you can access your Creator Self.

Anything is possible when you detach from your stories and limiting beliefs. It is then that you tap into your intuition, or infinite mind—your knowing mind. You can receive divine understanding in a quantum moment, synergize seemingly disparate elements into brilliance, and transcend your own definition of who you "are" and what you are capable of.

This is the space of miracles. Painting brings you to this space.

### Free your mind one brushstroke at a time.

Each new canvas is a brand new beginning. Then, we take this presence beyond the canvas and into the art that is your life.

There are two ways you can go about painting PRESENCE. Maybe they are one in the same or intimately interrelated, but let me share some images...

The image at the beginning of this chapter is from a Super Soul Flow Workshop in which almost 20 people contributed to the canvas with the intention of creating the energy of presence. It looked completely different from all the other—very present. And, ironically, it's also a mandala.

The first way to approach your Painting Practice in this chapter is to simply intend to connect to and create the energy of presence on your canvas and see what appears.

The other approach is to paint a mandala. The image on the opposite page is a mandala I painted in 20 minutes during a Super Soul Flow workshop.

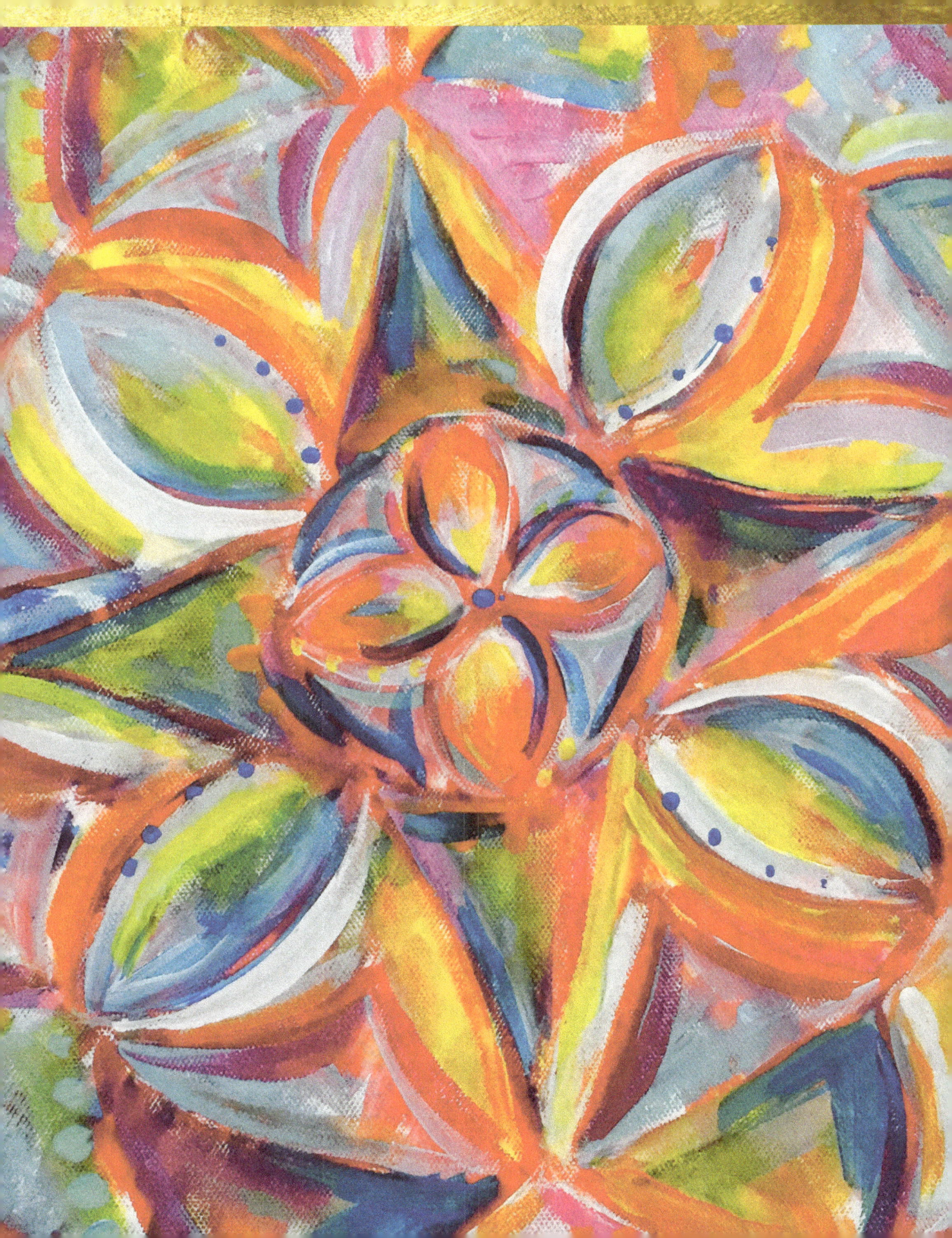

Here are some examples of mandala paintings step by step.
It's like painting FREEDOM in a circular motion.

(1)

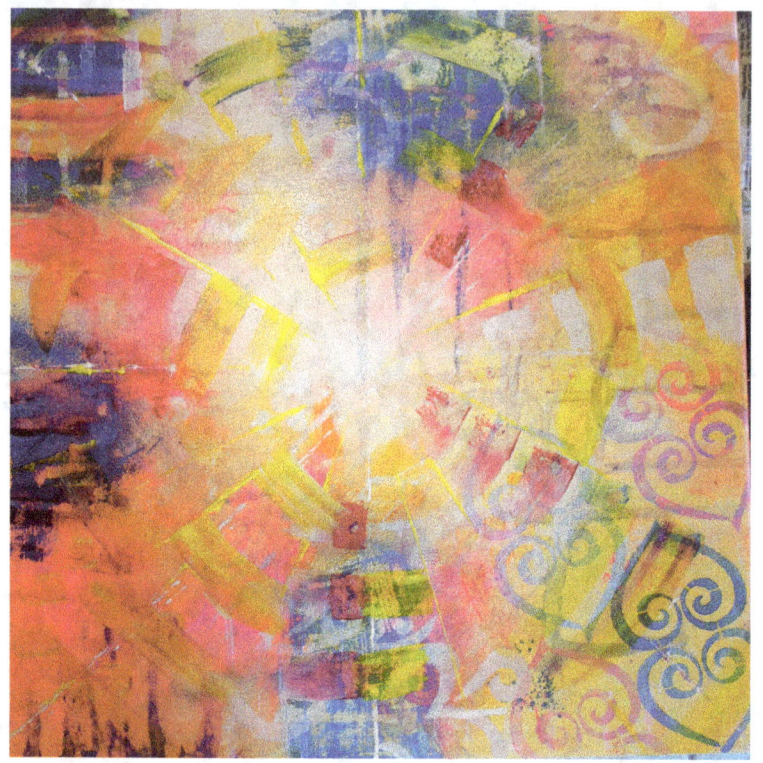

(2)

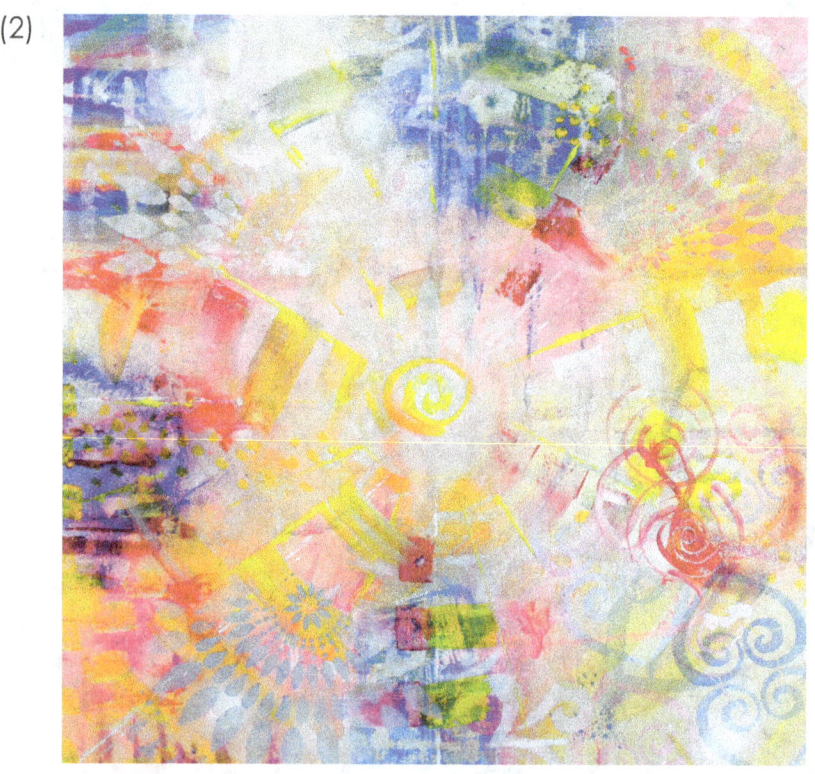

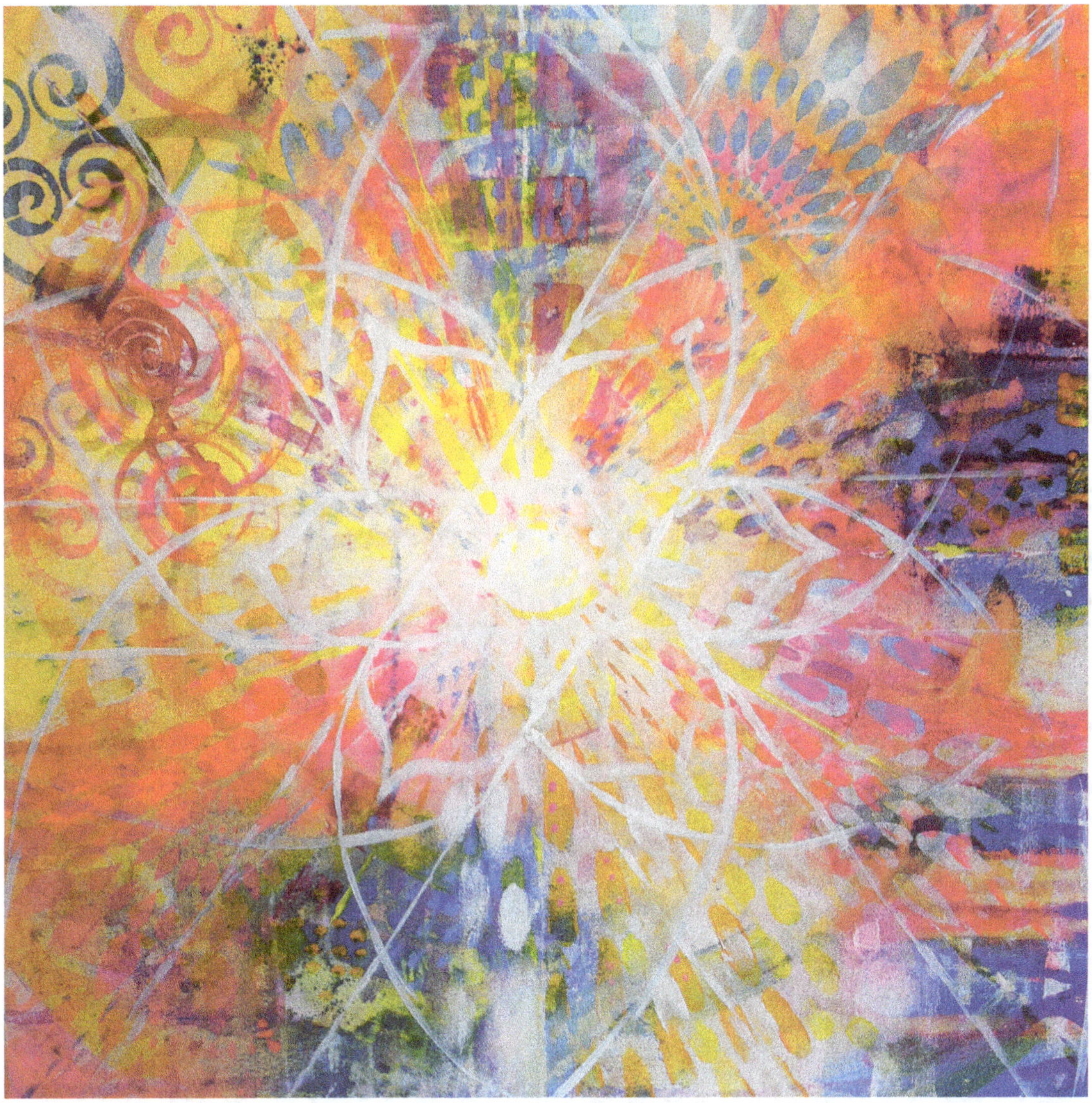

(3)

Below is an image of the finished painting. This hangs in a very auspicious place in my home, radiating out its divine light energy. You may begin to be inspired to keep your Super Soul Flow paintings and display them in your own space. There is something magical and powerful that happens when you surround yourself with your own images and creations.

(4)

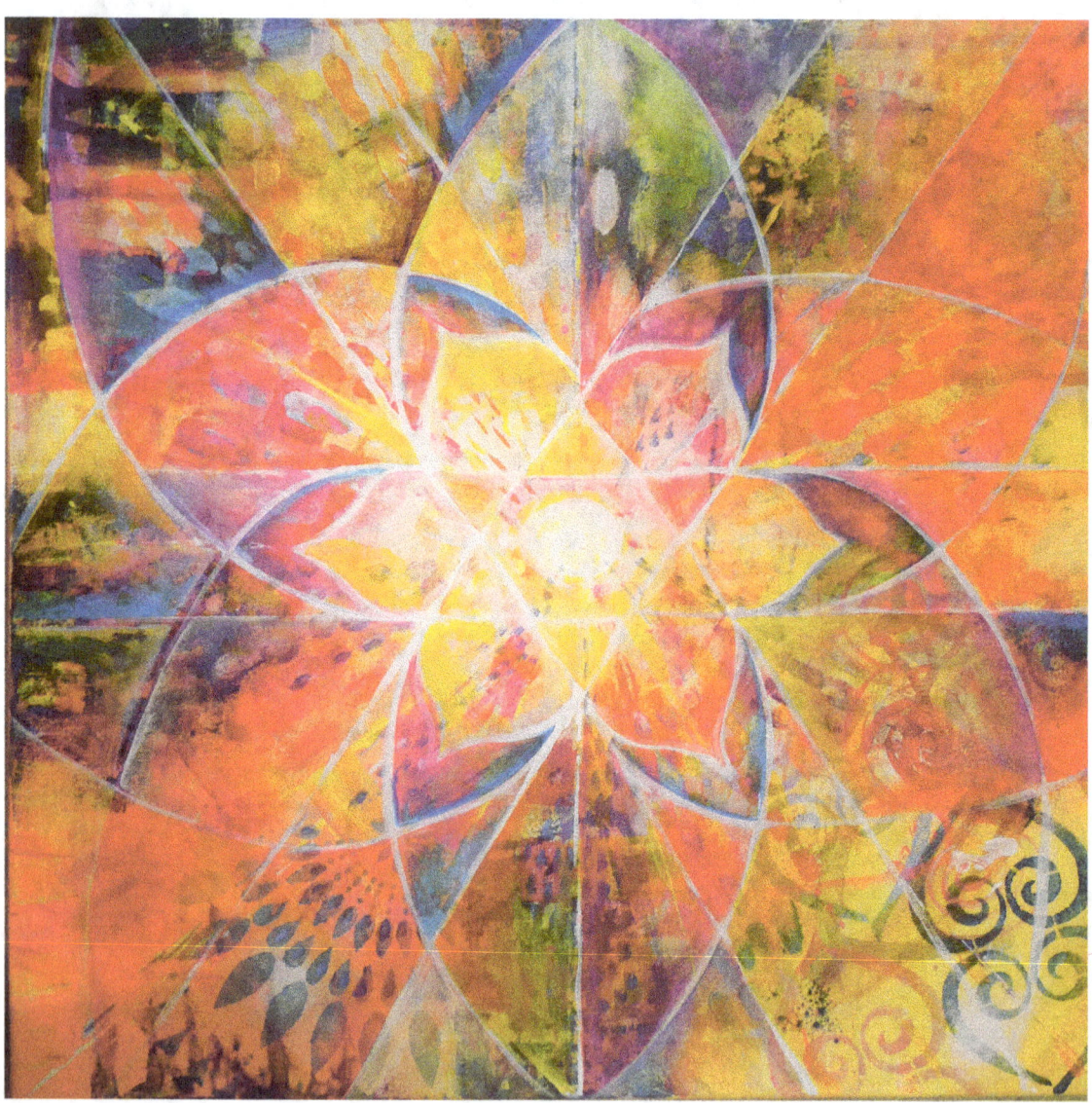

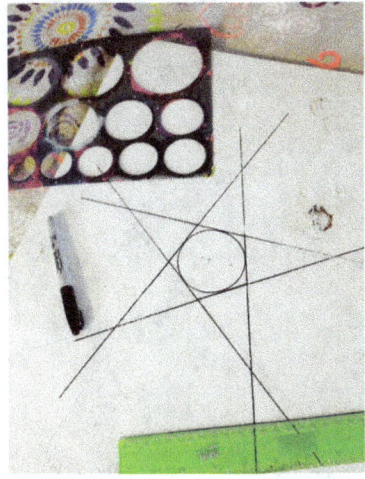

I created this mandala painting on a piece of wood to hang outside my front door. The pentacle is a symbol of protection at a threshold and, to me, it blesses all who enter and protects negative energies from entering my home.

Regardless, the presence of the painting each time I enter the door, creates a present-moment awareness of the sacredness of my home space and my commitment to it radiating only positive energy.

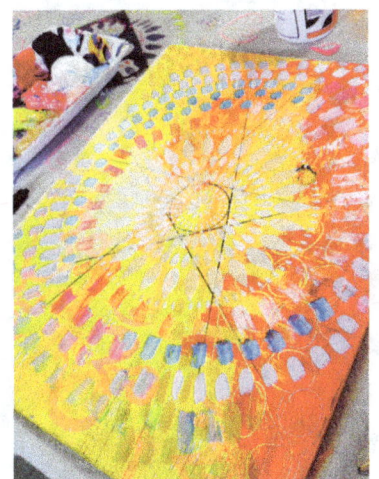

Remember, your Personal Painting Practice is first and foremost an opportunity to connect to your Creator Self and immerse yourself in the energy that your desire. At this frequency, you will align with your own Super Soul Flow.

One of the intentions encoded into this book is that you are empowered to share the energy of Super Soul Flow. Whether you have taught art for years, or are waking up to this call now, I truly believe that the true purpose of art is, as Terrence McKenna says, to "save the soul of mankind."

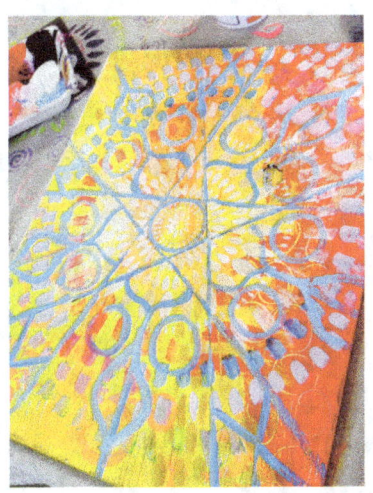

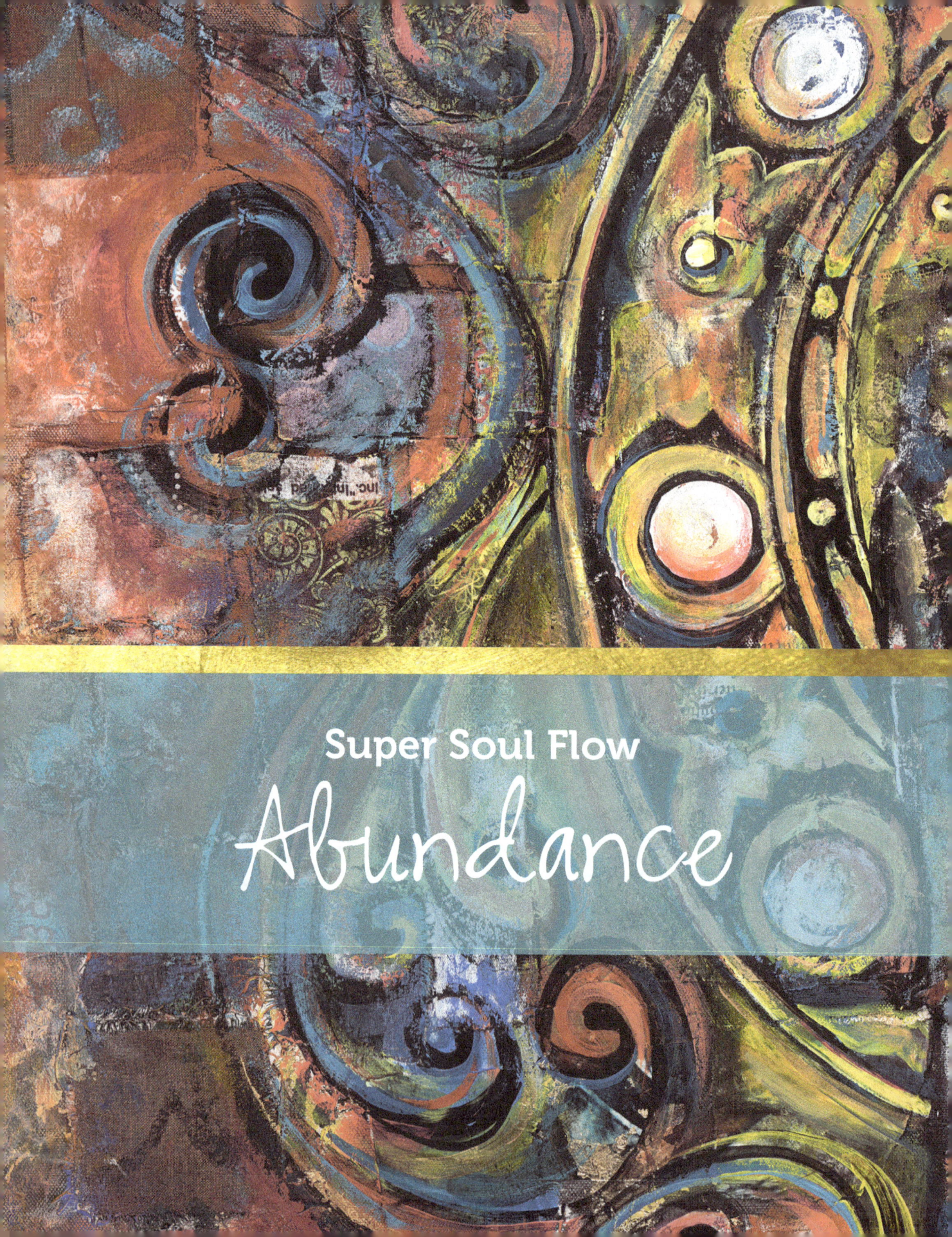

Super Soul Flow

Abundance

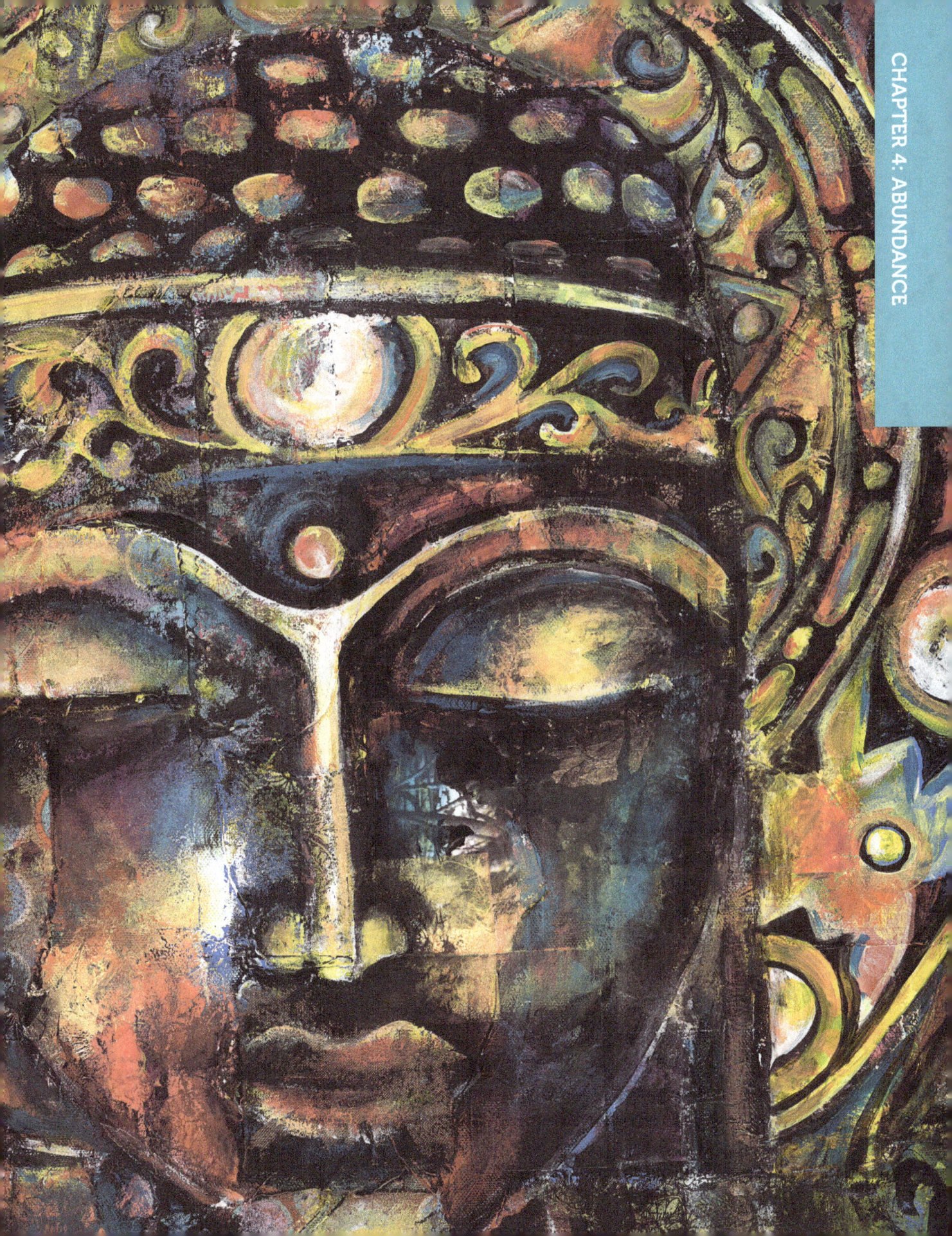

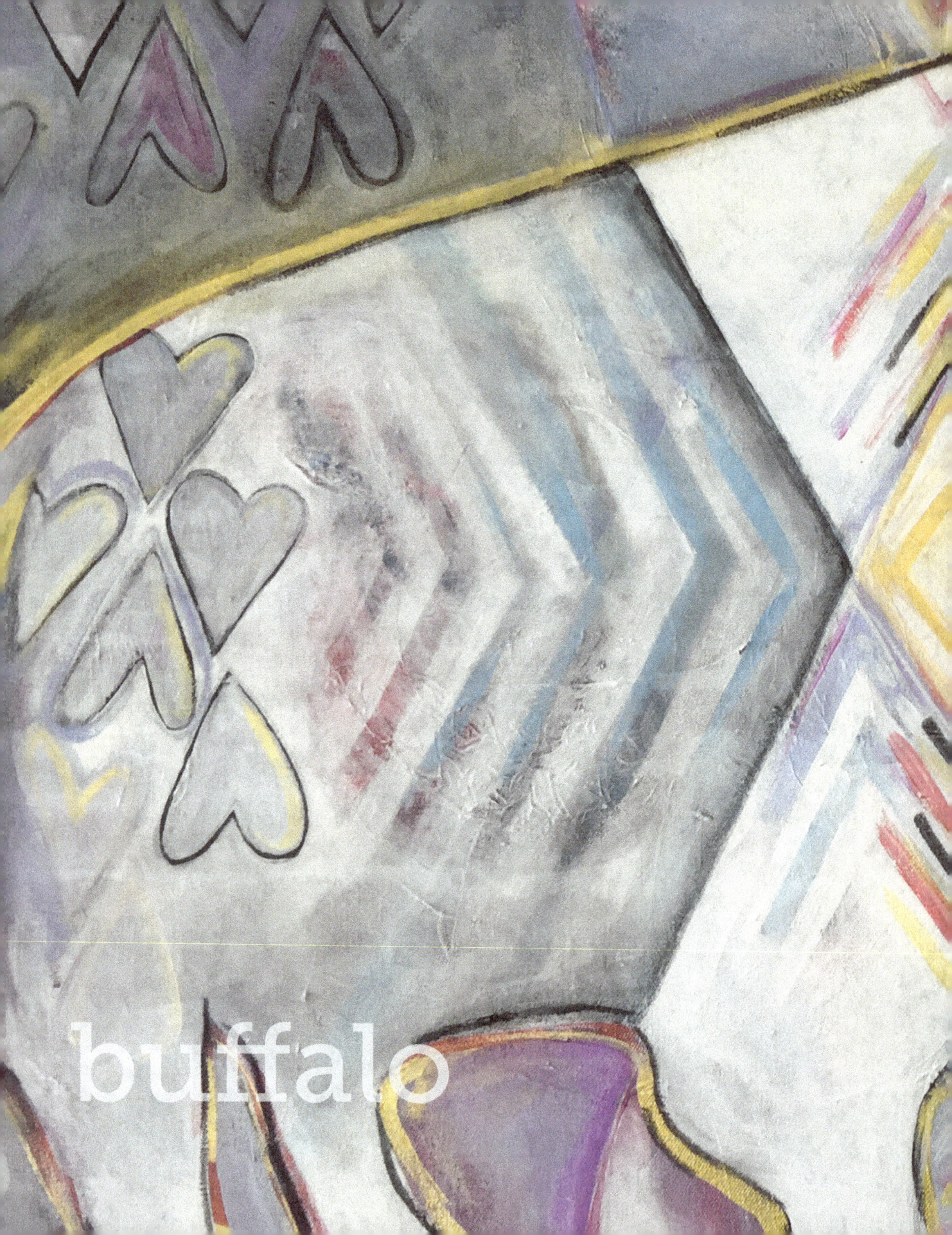
buffalo

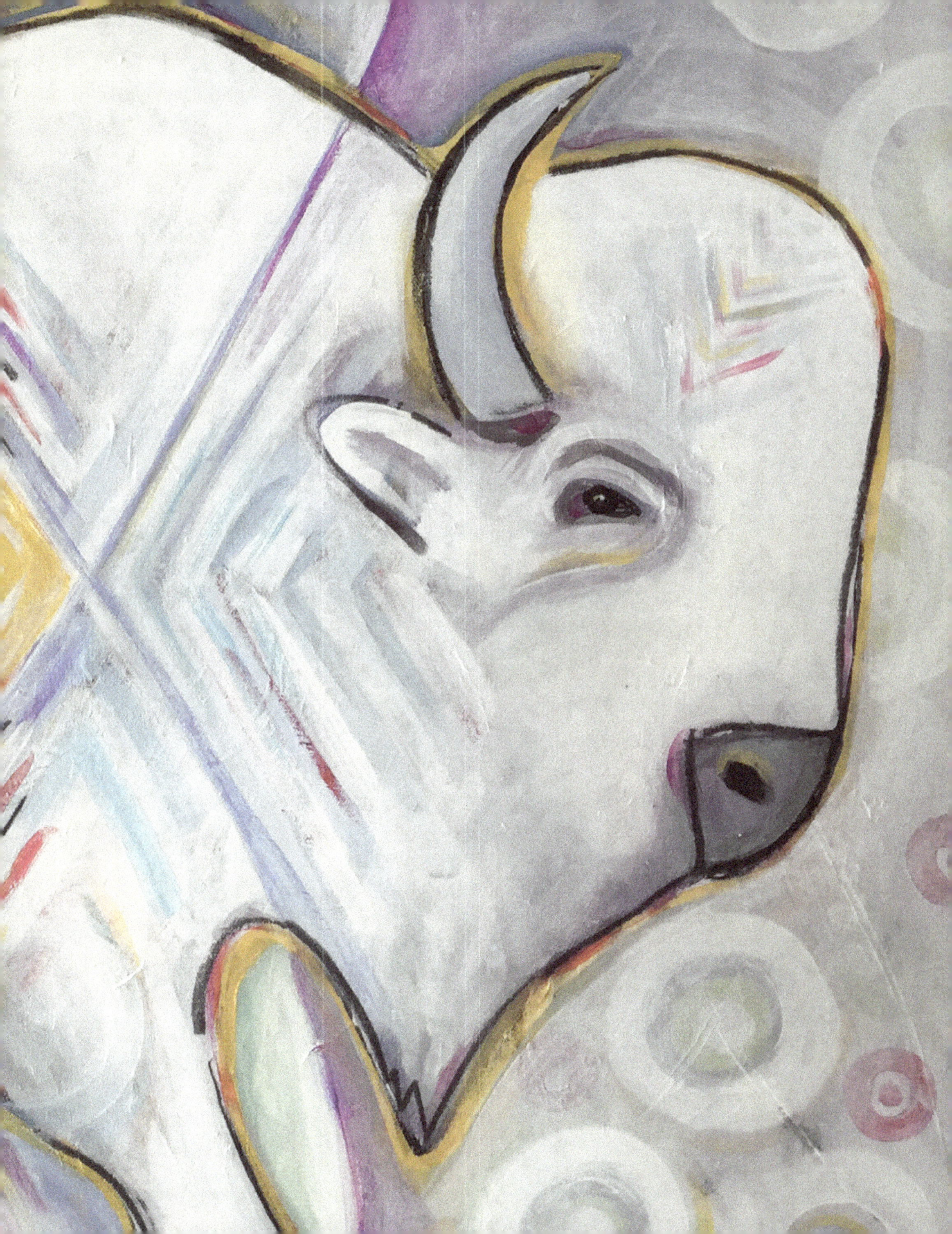

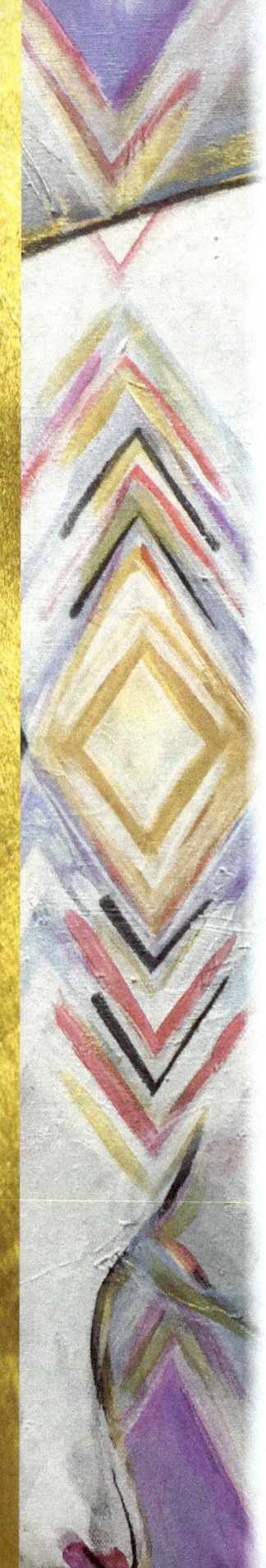

# buffalo

*For many of the North American indigenous tribes, the buffalo was the symbol of abundance. When the buffalo hunt was successful, survival was ensured. No buffalo? Scarcity and lack dominated. Every piece of the buffalo was used by the community for everything from clothing to tools, food, and lighting.*

*In the Native American prophecies, the buffalo, particularly the white buffalo, is a sign of good times, fortune, and hope.*

*If you have ever been close to a buffalo, you know how massive they are. The buffalo IS abundance. As an animal totem, its medicine is the energy of prosperity, abundance, hope, provision, and blessing, and it calls you to a higher level of personal gratitude.*

I AM your home.
I AM your hunger satiated.
I AM warmth in the dark night.
I AM the sustenance that nurtures your growth.
I AM the power of the thunder.
I AM the servant, willing to lay down for you to live.

I come to you, through the mist, puffing my warmth into the ethers, to offer you the magnitude of your potential.

I come to you, after a long season of scarcity, to cover you in warmth and security

I come to you, though you think you are small, to remind you that you are SO big.

I come to you, as White Buffalo, to encourage your steps along your sacred path.

I am a hologram of the entire universe and I am a hologram of you.

YOU are powerful.
YOU are abundant.
YOU are holy.
YOU are the gift.
YOU are the reward the Divine seeks to capture for itself.

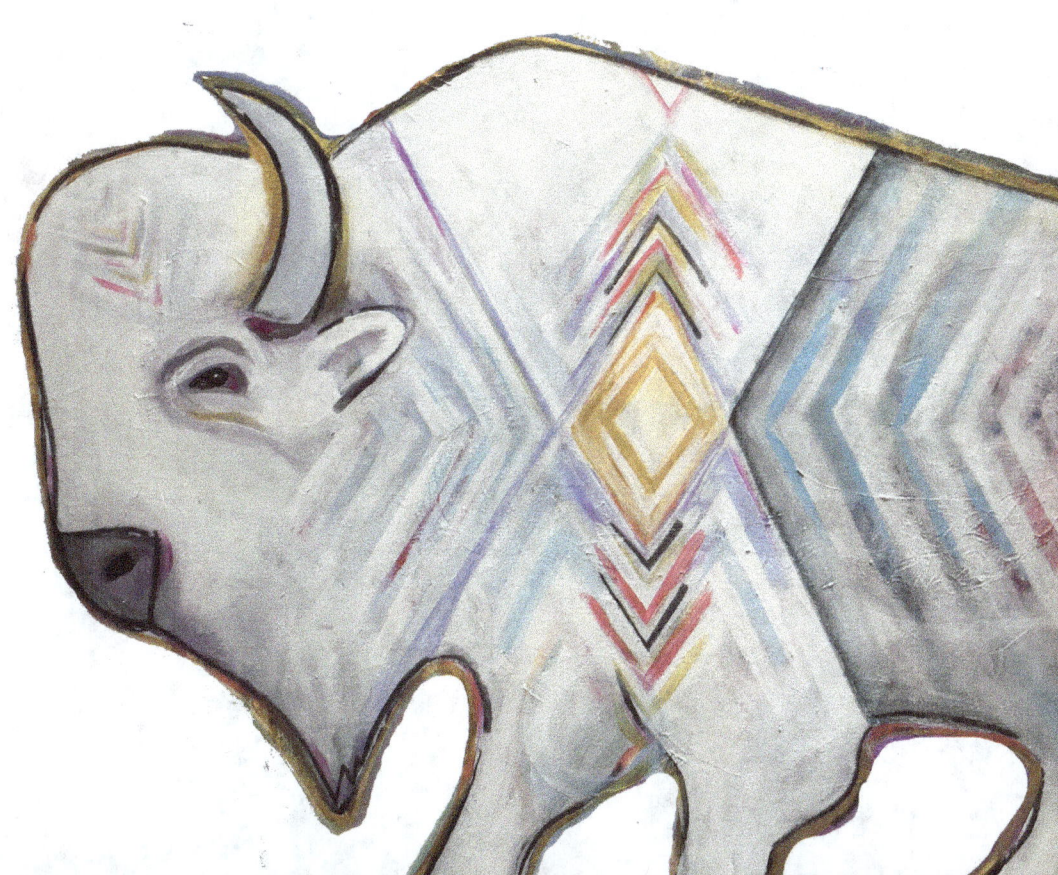

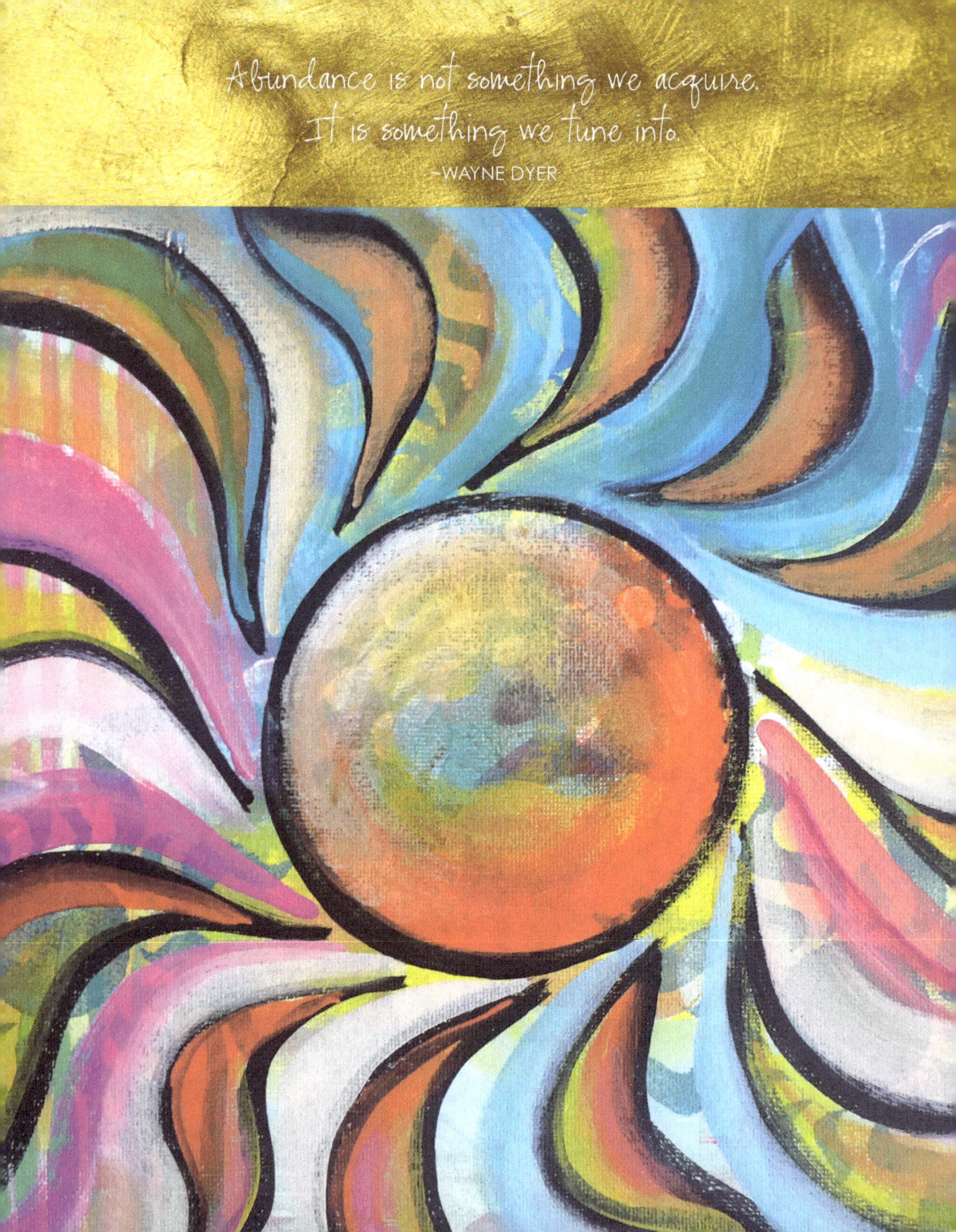

Abundance is not something we acquire.
It is something we tune into.
~WAYNE DYER

You may think of abundance as a collection of things, accomplishments or money. You may long for more abundance; who doesn't at some point? But, what if you could truly embrace and accept the reality that all the abundance you desire is within you?

Think of it as your new super power! You now have the power to create abundance, anywhere you want.

**If you want to attract more money, in this chapter you will create the FEELING behind your financial desires so you can RISE ABOVE your old limiting beliefs around money.**

I first learned of this "super power" reading about the aspect of the divine feminine that is expressed through the Goddess Lakshmi. In exploring the stories and legends of the Goddess, you get to know more about who you are—man or woman. You learn about an entirely new pantheon of super powers, not the traditional faster-than-a-speeding-bullet and able-to-leap-tall-buildings-in-a-single-bound powers, but the more subtle and feminine super powers. Creating abundance is one such super power.

In Sally Kempton's book, *Awakening Shakti,* she describes Lakshmi's "first lesson":

> *What we really crave is not more stuff, but the inner experience of abundance and beauty. Lakshmi is famous for giving material boons, but her deeper gift is the subtle ability to experience innate perfection and beauty. Because Lakshmi is an aspect of our life-force; the sense of sufficiency, abundance and beauty is built into us, and so is the need for it.*

We are going to explore three types of abundance that are available to us at any time:

- INNER abundance

- CREATIVE abundance

- RADIANT abundance

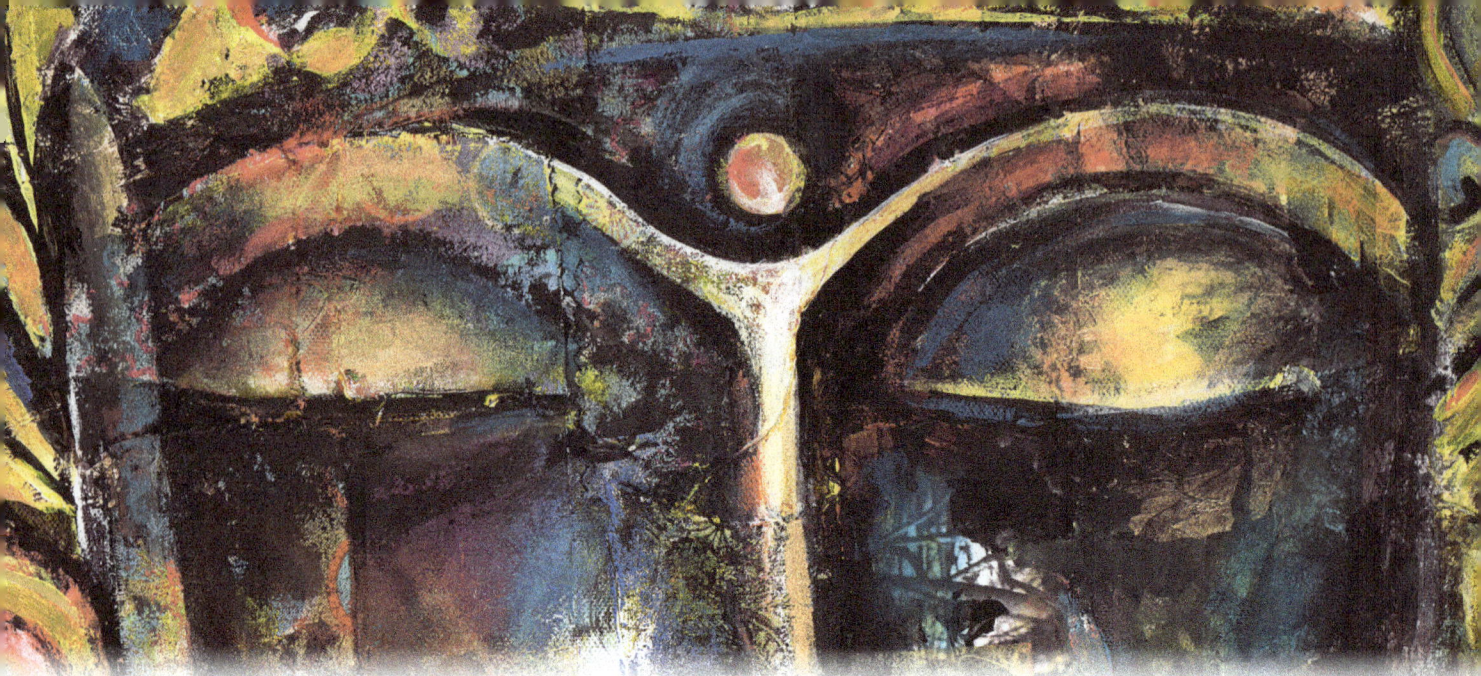

# INNER Abundance

Inner Abundance speaks to the reality that any abundance you seek, true abundance, requires first an acknowledgment that its source is within you.

If you are searching for the feeling of abundance in your bank account, your business platform, or your closet, you are only going to continue to search.

In the example of money, you want to go underneath the surface and explore what FEELING the abundance of money will create for you. Is it freedom, creativity, excitement, and adventure? Focus on THAT energy and all the ways you can create that feeling. Then, you will be able to attract the financial reality to support that feeling.

From Eckhart Tolle's *A New Earth:*

> *If the thought of lack—whether it be money, recognition, or love—has become a part of who you think you are, you will always experience lack... Acknowledging the good that is already in your life is the foundation of all abundance... Whatever you think the world is withholding from you, you are withholding from the world... because deep down you think you are small and that you have nothing to give. Whatever you think, you are right.*

In our Personal Painting Practice we can intentionally create the feeling of abundance as we mix colors and explore the infinite shades available to us, or contemplate ALL the different images we could choose to create. While we may have a hard time accepting that all abundance is available to us, we can ground ourselves in the metaphor that is the canvas. In that practice arena, anything is possible and infinite manifestations are at our fingertips.

## CREATIVE Abundance

This is what I am calling our Super Power of Creating Ideas. I want to invite you to think of one idea or story that you have in your head that is no longer serving you. What is it?

Is it that you can't leave your job, or that you are not talented enough to achieve the professional success you desire?

Or maybe you have accepted the story that "good moms stay home with their kids" or, that to be successful you have to work hard. No pain no gain, as they say.

Do you tell yourself that you couldn't take the time away from work or your family to take that workshop or participate in a new training? Have you accepted a belief like "I can't sing," or "I can't paint," or "I can't come up with original ideas"?

Right now, at this point in space/time history, we have unprecedented permission and opportunity to create NEW ideas that not only serve us but that can bring us freedom and joy!

In the book *Return of the Bird Tribes,* by Ken Carey, we read,

> Healthy intelligence knows itself as a center of creative description, living within an infinite ocean of truth that stretches forever in all directions… healthy intelligence knows that you are never trapped within your concepts.

You have the super power of CREATIVE ABUNDANCE! You can create new ideas that FREE you and inspire you. You can let go of beliefs, ideas, or stories that tell you that you can't live in fulfillment or be that happy.

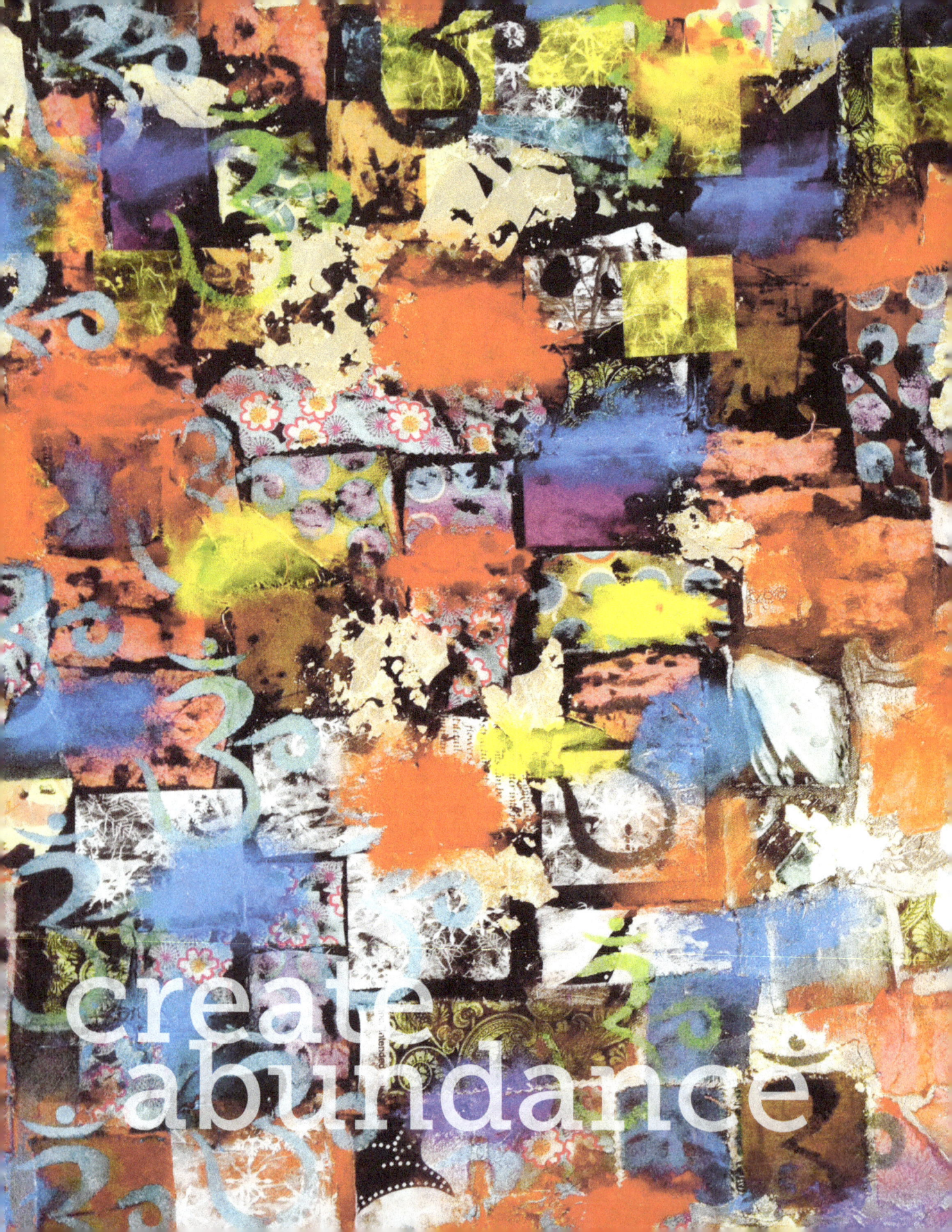

create
abundance

If you really, really want to do something and you have been telling yourself that you can't do it for whatever reason—change THAT. Most of what we accept as truth in our minds are stories or beliefs from others that were given to us at school or from within our families—NOT our own truth that would serve our fullest personal expression in this lifetime.

For example, think of some old stories that used to be accepted as truth but that are now almost laughable they are so ridiculous:

- Women shouldn't vote

- Slavery is acceptable

- Rock and roll music is the devil incarnate

- Women shouldn't show their knees

- Big boys don't cry...

What are some new ideas you could create today? Look at your normal routine. What is your schedule for today, or tomorrow? What are all the ways you could create some change in your routine?

I was talking to a client as she drove home from work and illustrated this concept in this way:

> *You are driving home from work right now on a familiar route, with a specific destination in mind. BUT, right NOW you could turn right or left. In one more minute, you could turn right or left. You could, instead of going straight home, visit a library, a coffee shop, get your nails done, or stop at a friend's house. You could pull over at a park and meditate, journal, or reach out to an old friend, or a new friend. There is, in truth, an ABUNDANCE of different stories that you could act out right now. Although you typically follow the same route home without even considering the options, just for tonight, entertain the different ideas that are, in fact, available to you.*

We tell ourselves, "I couldn't do that." But is that really true? Instead of thinking that, what if you replaced "I couldn't..." with, "What would it take for me to get to...?" Or, "What else is possible on my drive home?"

What else is possible today at work?

What else is possible during my lunch hour?

What else is possible during this free morning I have or this weekend?

Are the stories you are telling yourself etched in stone or are they truly very flexible?

This is the super power you have of Creative Abundance. What are all the ways you can create some new stories around what your day looks like, what is possible for you, what new skills you can learn?

## RADIANT Abundance

This aspect of the energy of abundance is the most fun! This is where YOU get to create miracles for others. YOU have the power to radiate abundance to those around you. You can be Lakshmi incarnate, spreading the energy of abundance into the lives of others.

This is a powerful way to connect to your inner and creative abundance. Remember, Eckhart Tolle says to give freely what you feel others are withholding from you.

This is Sally Kempton's suggestion for connecting to the divine energy of Lakshmi:

> Move through the world with the intention to bless the people around you. Do this unselfconsciously, silently, and humbly. You might begin by blessing the chair you sit in, the clothes you are wearing... In the next days, make a point of offering blessing to everyone you meet. Silently bless them with abundance... with whatever you sense they need.

Sometimes I find it easier to understand an idea by looking at its opposite.

When we are sad, mad, or otherwise in a low vibration we understand that it brings everyone down around us. I know you can think of a time when someone else brought you down.

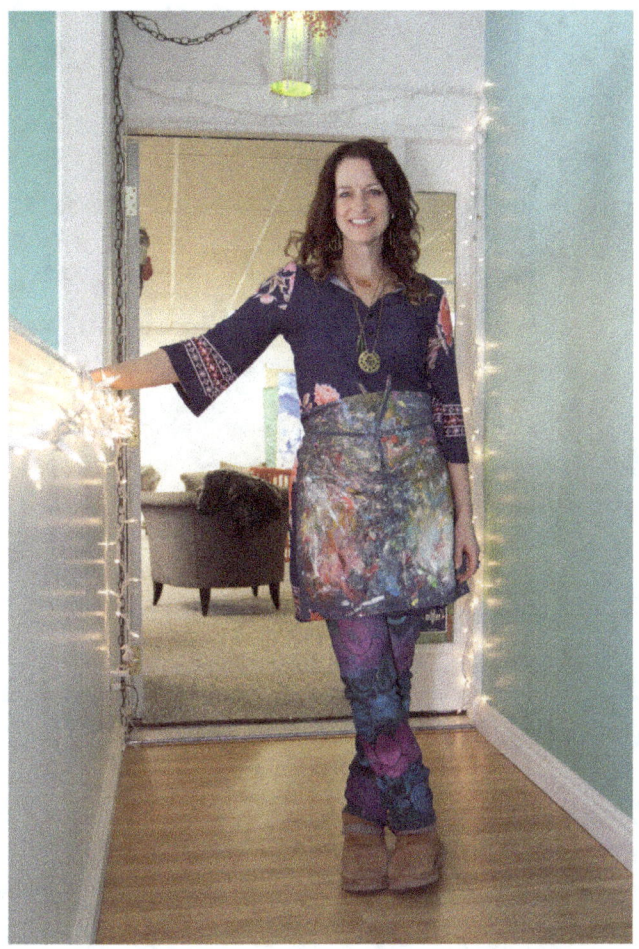

Now, let's spend time imagining and creating the opportunity to lift up the people and energy around us. When you choose to walk into a room radiating light and abundance you absolutely have a tremendous impact and can RISE ABOVE any situation.

I often, for better or worse, imagine lying on my deathbed. I know the power of that moment, the power of our dying thoughts. I can sense that in that transition, the fear, the worry, the bills, the accomplishments, the sense of achieving and accumulating... fall away. This was what I felt in my meditation recently. When everything ends in this physical life the only energy that remains is *love*. That is all that is permanent.

Everything else is part of the story, the illusion, or the physical world. So my ah-ha was, "Why not live fully in the physical world *and* fully tapped into that abundant source of love?"

The fear, worry, jealousy, and anxiety certainly don't enhance my physical experience.

Then, someone sent me, literally within 24 hours, a video from Father Bede Griffiths, a Benedictan Monk, entitled "The Non-dual Mind." You can find it on YouTube. In the video, Father Bede Griffiths shares his experience in which he connected to his non-dual mind. He thought he was dying. Everyone around him thought he was dying. And then he was immersed in, overwhelmed with, such a powerful energy of divine love that he almost felt he would die from that! He also discovered and experienced that when everything else goes away, what is left is pure, radiant love. It is beautiful.

YOU have that within every cell of your being. Let's connect to that abundant energy and radiate it out to your world, shall we?

## The Proof of Abundance...

From *The Law of Attraction,* by Esther and Jerry Hicks:

> *When you come to understand that this Universe… indeed this physical experience in which you are participating is abundant—and that there is not an ending to that abundance—then you do not worry. Instead of worrying, they say, you create. You create, causing others to attract to you, and they create, causing you to attract to them.*

The proof of abundance is all around us. Look at all the ways people earn their living. Look at all the ways we can express ourselves, even the variety of dress!

There was a time when the Impressionists' blurry, colorful landscapes were ridiculed and considered blasphemous and a time when women weren't allowed to wear pants!

The "older generation" used to think that the world was ending when young people insisted on shorter hemlines and dancing to rock and roll. The energy of abundance was not as prevalent. There were more rules. You only drank white wine with fish and red wine with meat. You picked one career and stuck with it until retirement. Women got to choose between (hold your horses) being a nurse or a teacher! I remember crying to my mother close to college graduation because I did not even know what CONTINENT I wanted to live on!

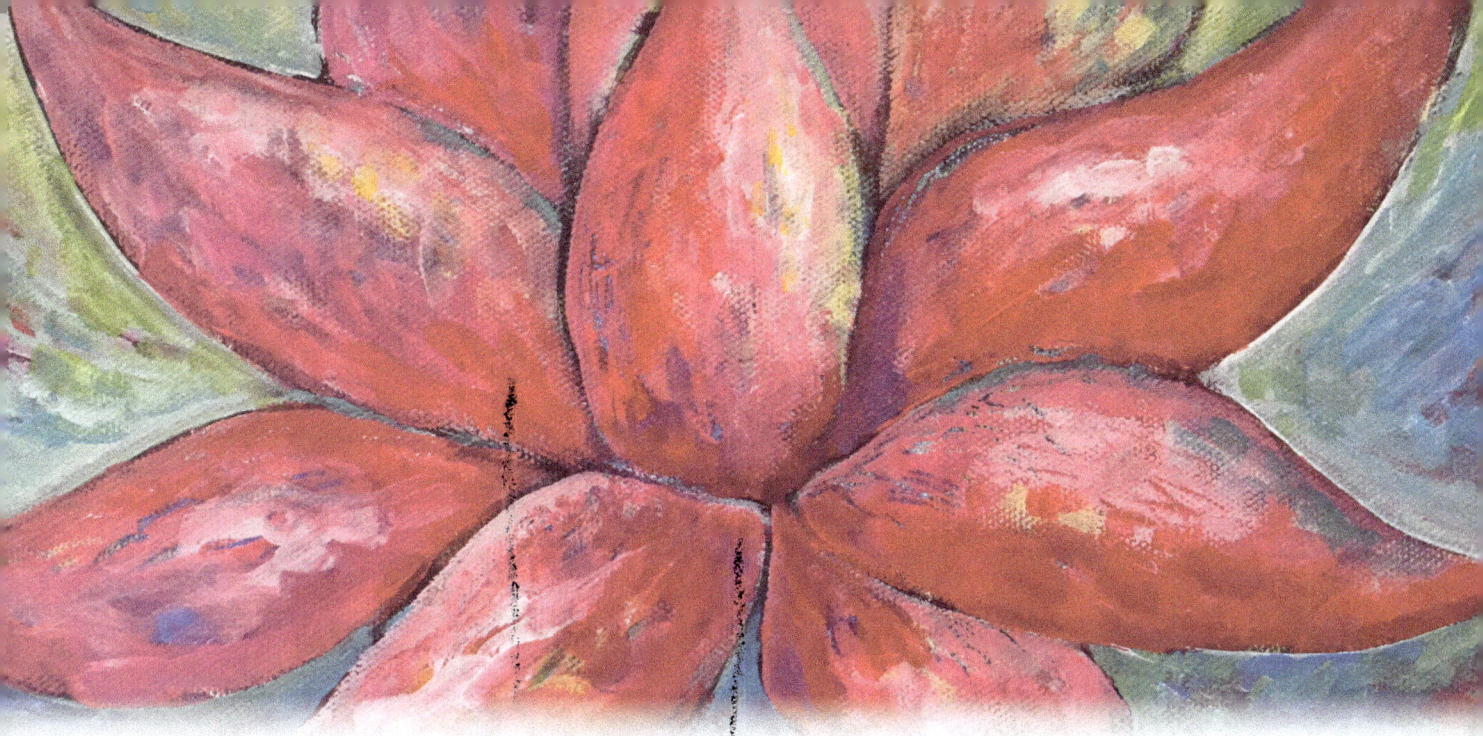

*What the Universe is showing you right now is that this is the age of infinite possibilities and authentic self-expression?*

Think of all the different things you COULD do right now! Think of the simple activity of baking cookies. What are ALL the different kinds of cookies you could make? Chocolate chip, butterscotch oatmeal, sugar cookies, macaroons, seven layer bars, brownies, snickerdoodles, chocolate snickerdoodles... Do you see?

If you are not there yet, it is only because your fullest CREATOR SELF has yet to fully emerge and bloom onto the surface, illuminating your highest dream for your life.

Are you ready? The world is. All the rules have been broken. Every option is accessible to you.

The only reason you are living anything less than pure joy, light, self-love and freedom is because of limiting beliefs you either created in the past or adopted from the cultural stories around you. The NEW story that we are all in the process of co-creating is that you are a creator in an infinitely abundant Universe. You get to remember this now.

**Welcome home.**

# Creating the Energy of ABUNDANCE

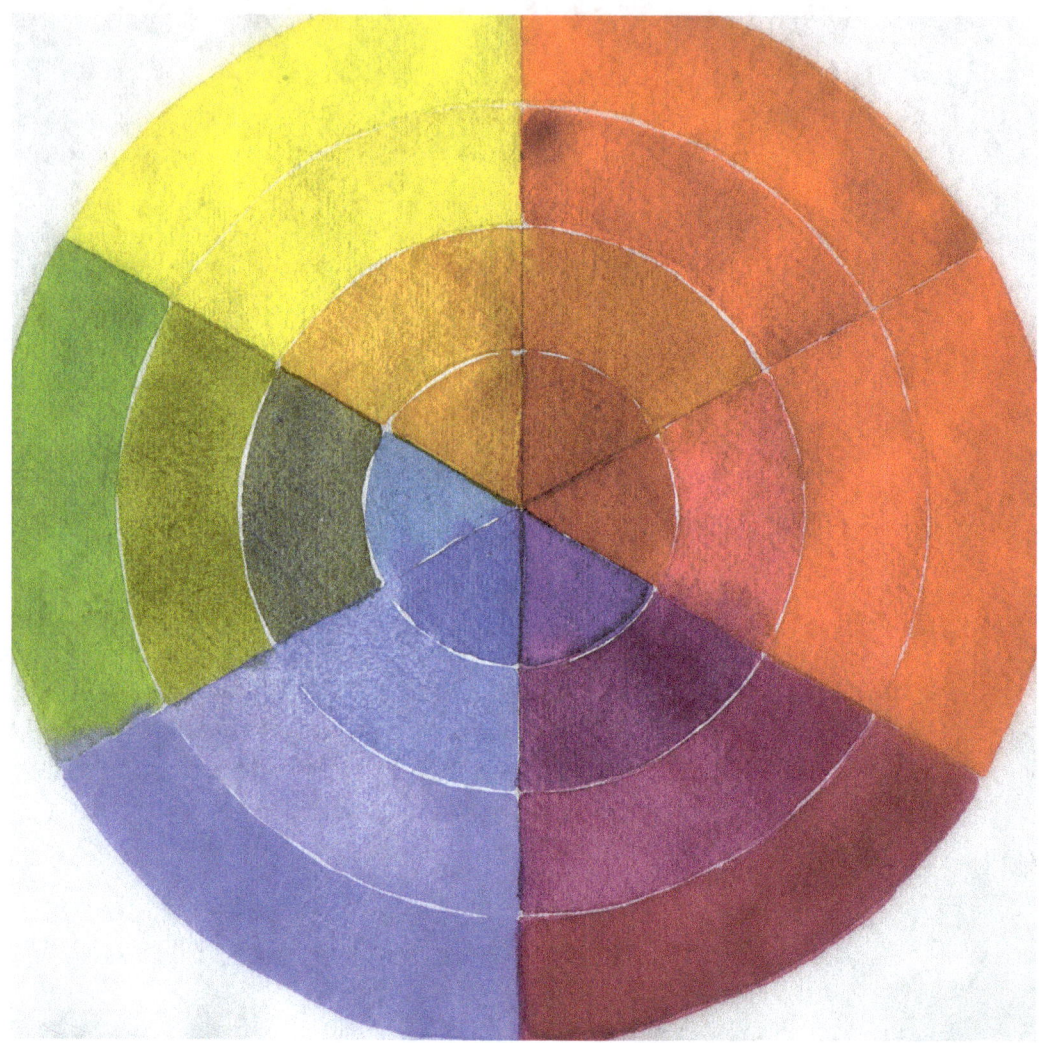

To connect to the energy of abundance, we are going to begin with exploring the magnificent color wheel. You are going to explore the infinite, and most abundant, shades of color that you can create yourself!

One of the statements I have heard new painters make throughout my career is, "It is getting muddy," or "I don't have the right color." Therefore, becoming comfortable mixing colors is a valuable practice and one that will illustrate, symbolically, the abundance all around us!

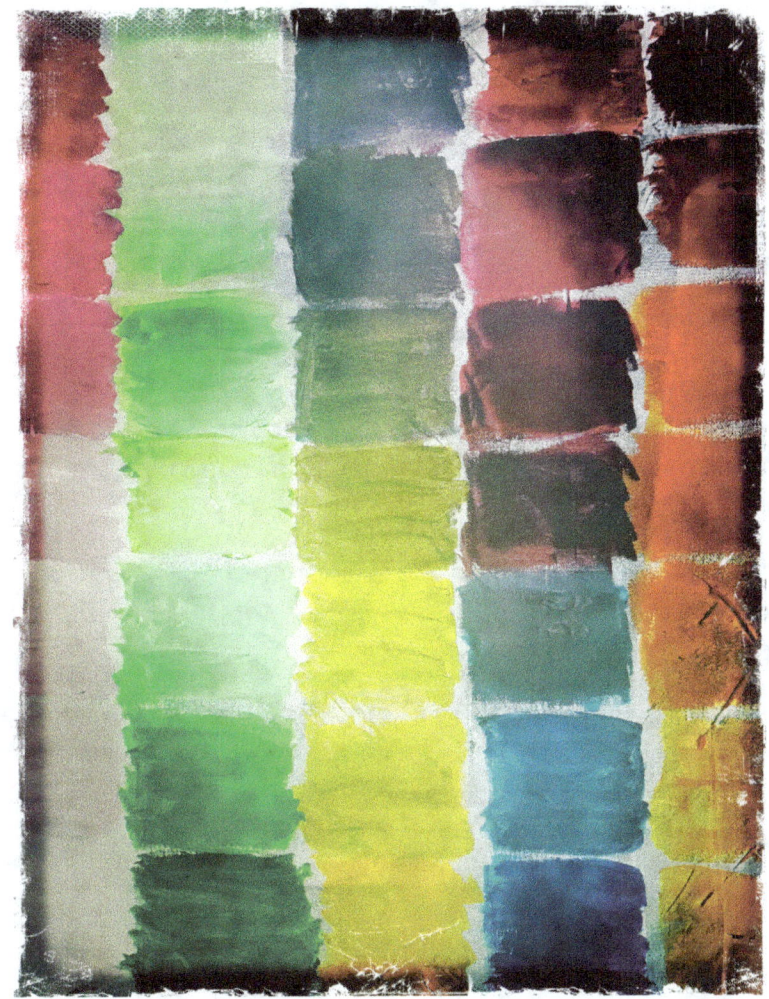

I encourage you to spend some time during your Abundance Painting Practice playing with the colors. Mix many different shades of your favorite color, for example. There is no end to the shades of color you can create!

You can mix infinite shades of red and blue, starting with red and adding a little bit of blue, then a little more, and more... and then you get to PURPLE!

You can also mix OPPOSITE COLORS. These are my favorite. If you look at this color mandala, you can see that the opposite colors are RED and GREEN, PURPLE and YELLOW, ORANGE and BLUE. When you add just a bit of the opposite color into a color, i.e. a bit of orange into blue, you get an "earthy" shade of that color.

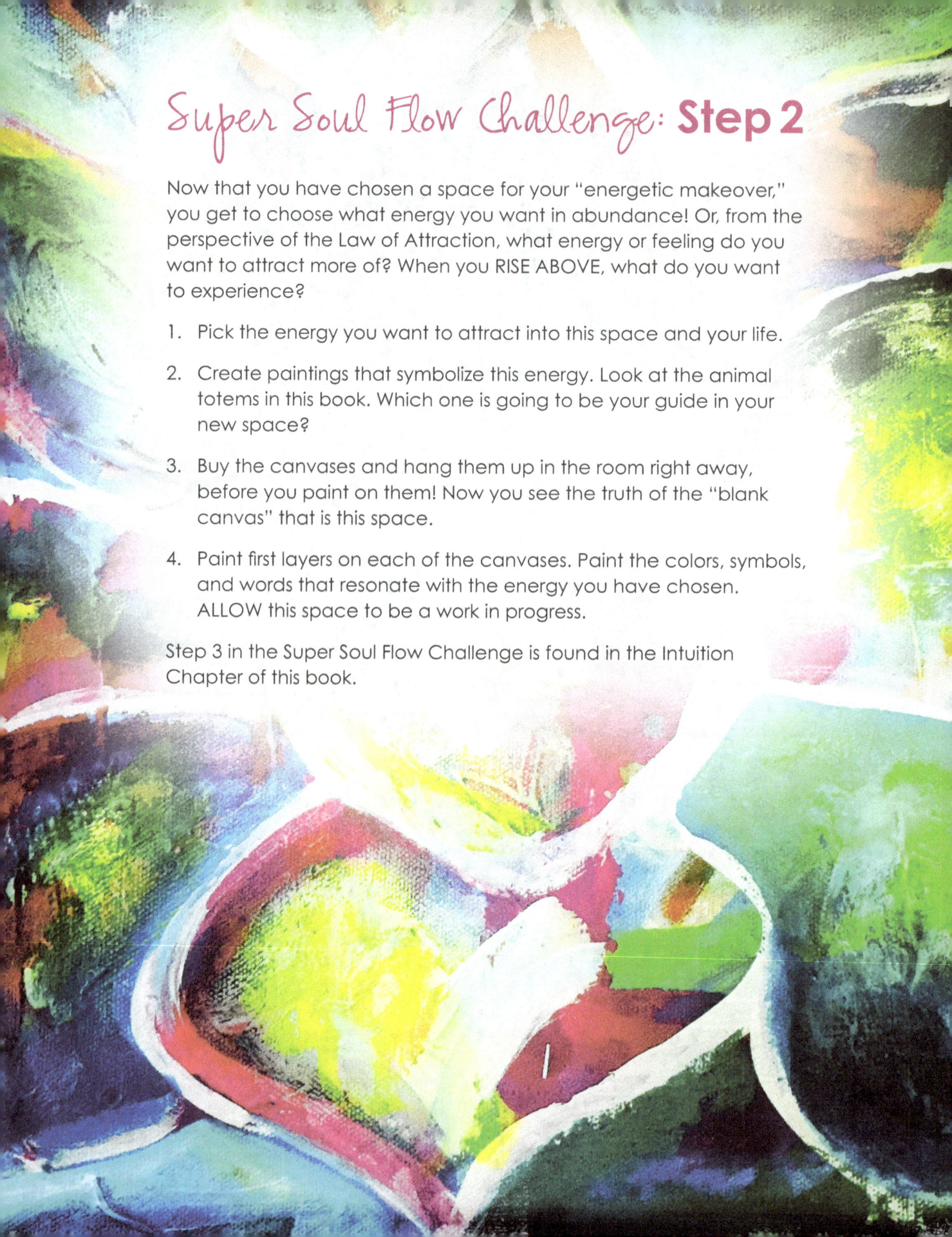

# Super Soul Flow Challenge: Step 2

Now that you have chosen a space for your "energetic makeover," you get to choose what energy you want in abundance! Or, from the perspective of the Law of Attraction, what energy or feeling do you want to attract more of? When you RISE ABOVE, what do you want to experience?

1.  Pick the energy you want to attract into this space and your life.

2.  Create paintings that symbolize this energy. Look at the animal totems in this book. Which one is going to be your guide in your new space?

3.  Buy the canvases and hang them up in the room right away, before you paint on them! Now you see the truth of the "blank canvas" that is this space.

4.  Paint first layers on each of the canvases. Paint the colors, symbols, and words that resonate with the energy you have chosen. ALLOW this space to be a work in progress.

Step 3 in the Super Soul Flow Challenge is found in the Intuition Chapter of this book.

One of the ways we connect to the energy of ABUNDANCE is by using the design principle of REPETITION. Simply repeat a shape or color over and over to connect with the infinite ways you can repeat that shape on the canvas.

I am also inviting you in this chapter to paint the symbol of the LOTUS flower, another symbol of abundance. It is the energy of the abundance of spirit, the abundance available to all of us through our Highest Self perspective. It is a traditional symbol of enlightenment and how life's "muck" is ultimately here to nourish our BLOOM!

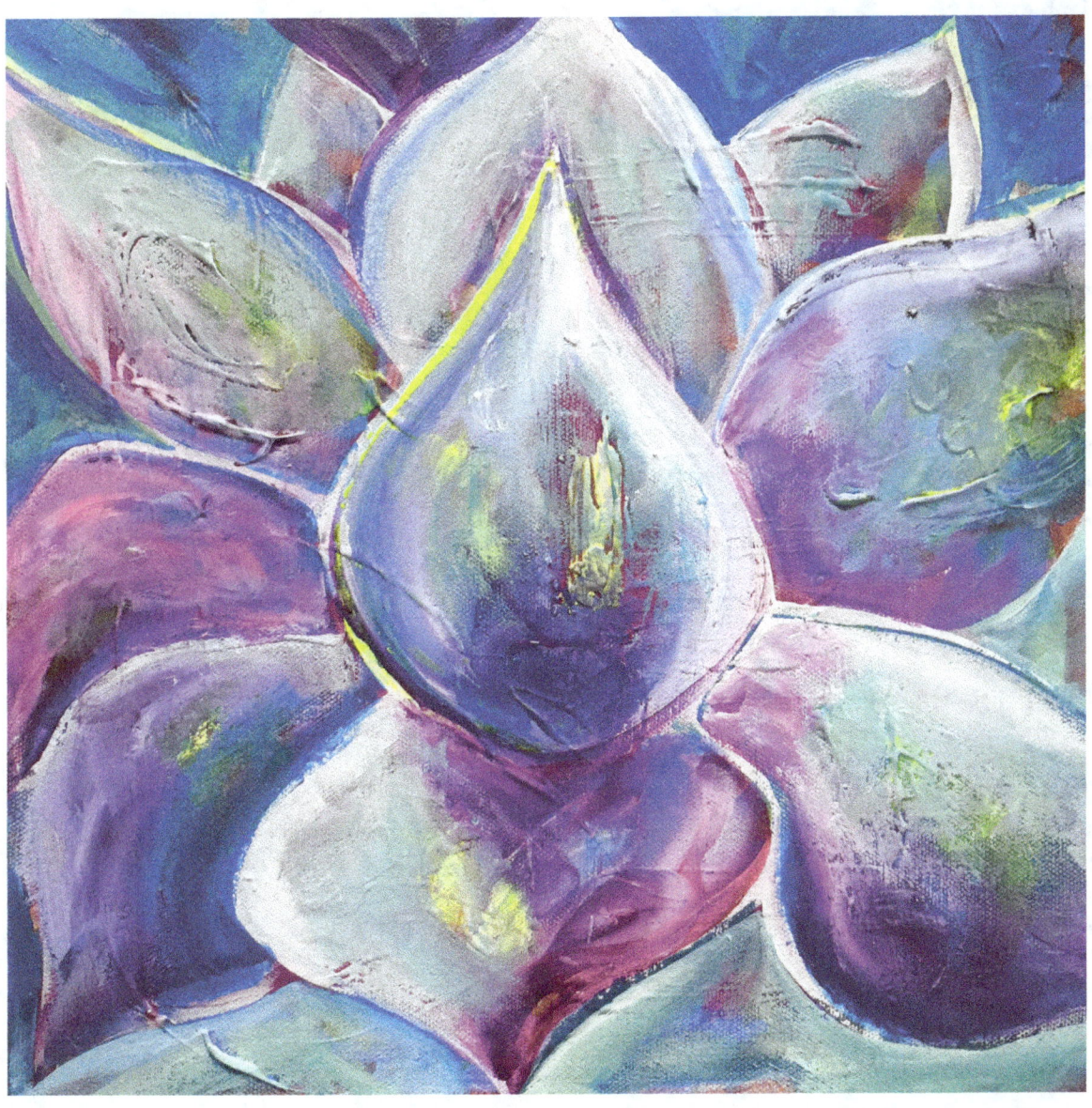

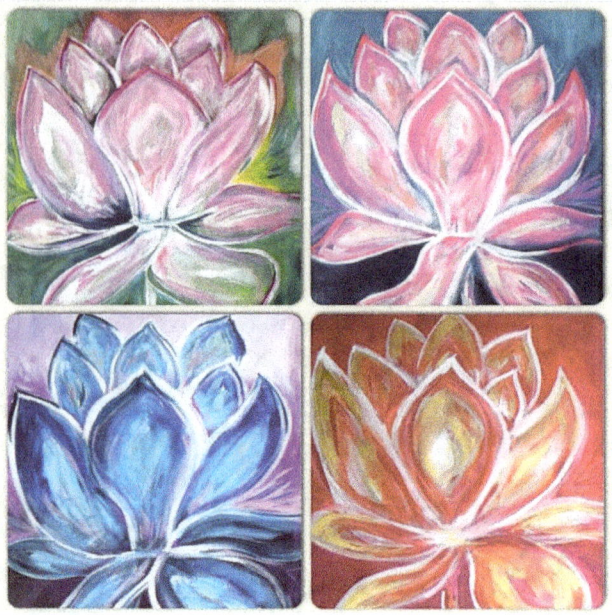

These lotus paintings were created by the most amazing Estelle Thomson, a Creatively Fit Coach, yogini, and overall goddess! Learn more about Estelle at www.estellethomson.com.

Other symbols of abundance are:

- Rabbit
- Buffalo
- Ankh
- Fish
- Turkey
- Waterfalls
- The Empress card in the Tarot deck
- The planet Jupiter

There are an abundance of symbols to create the energy of abundance!

Create a renewed intention to spend time weekly in your new Painting Practice. There are an abundance of ways you can find more time to do so. "What are all the ways I can...?" is a fabulous way to get the answers that will serve you.

Enjoy your abundance!

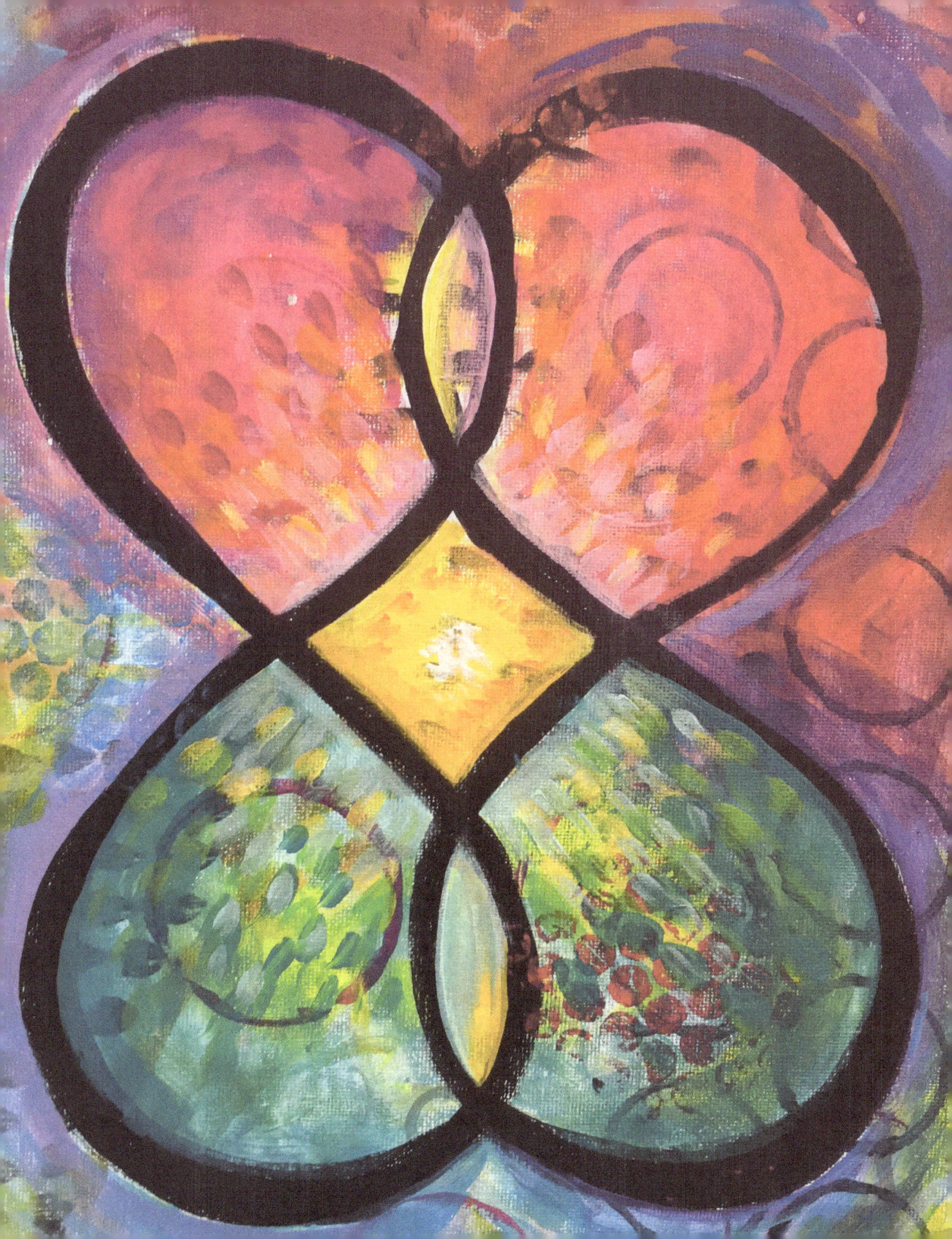

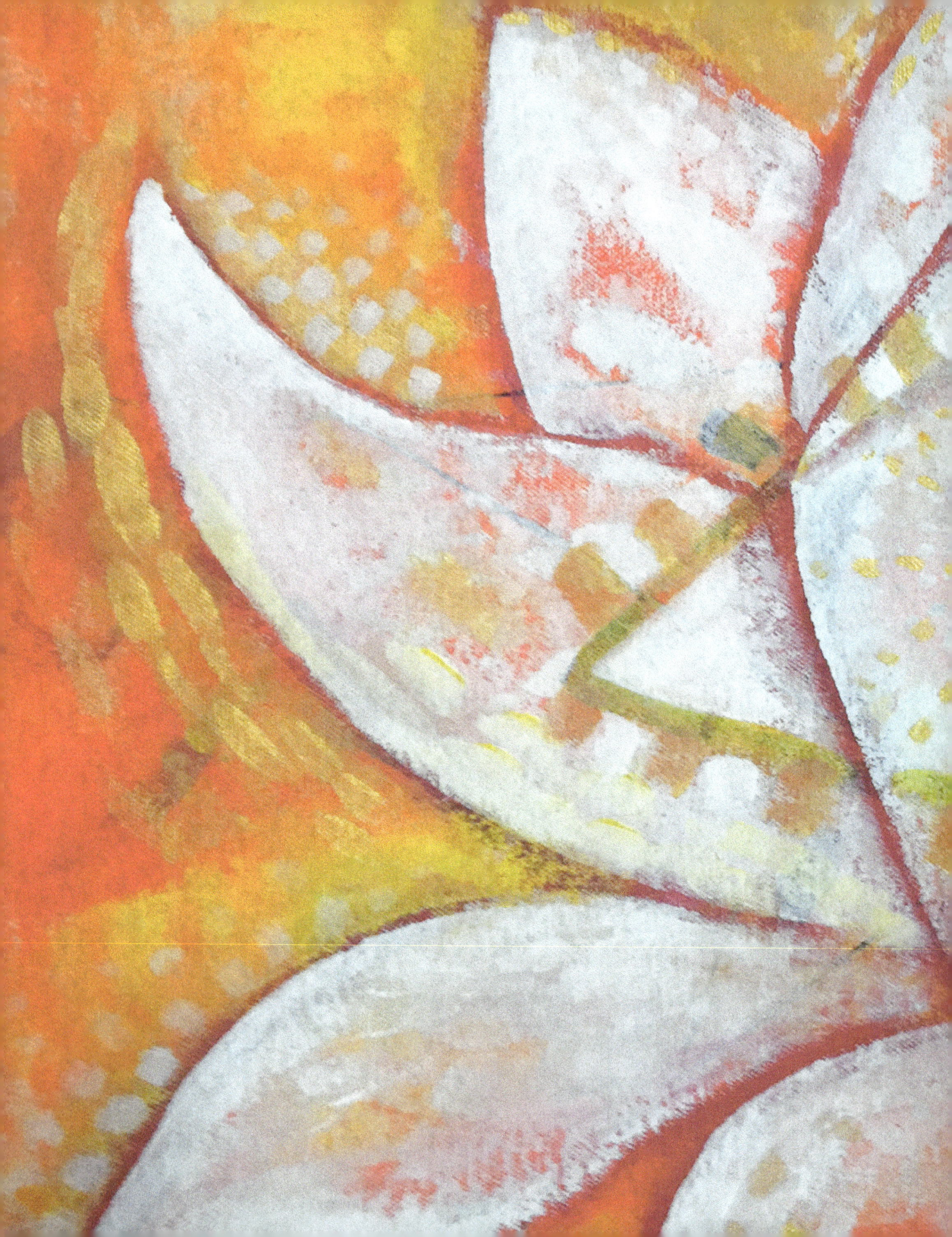

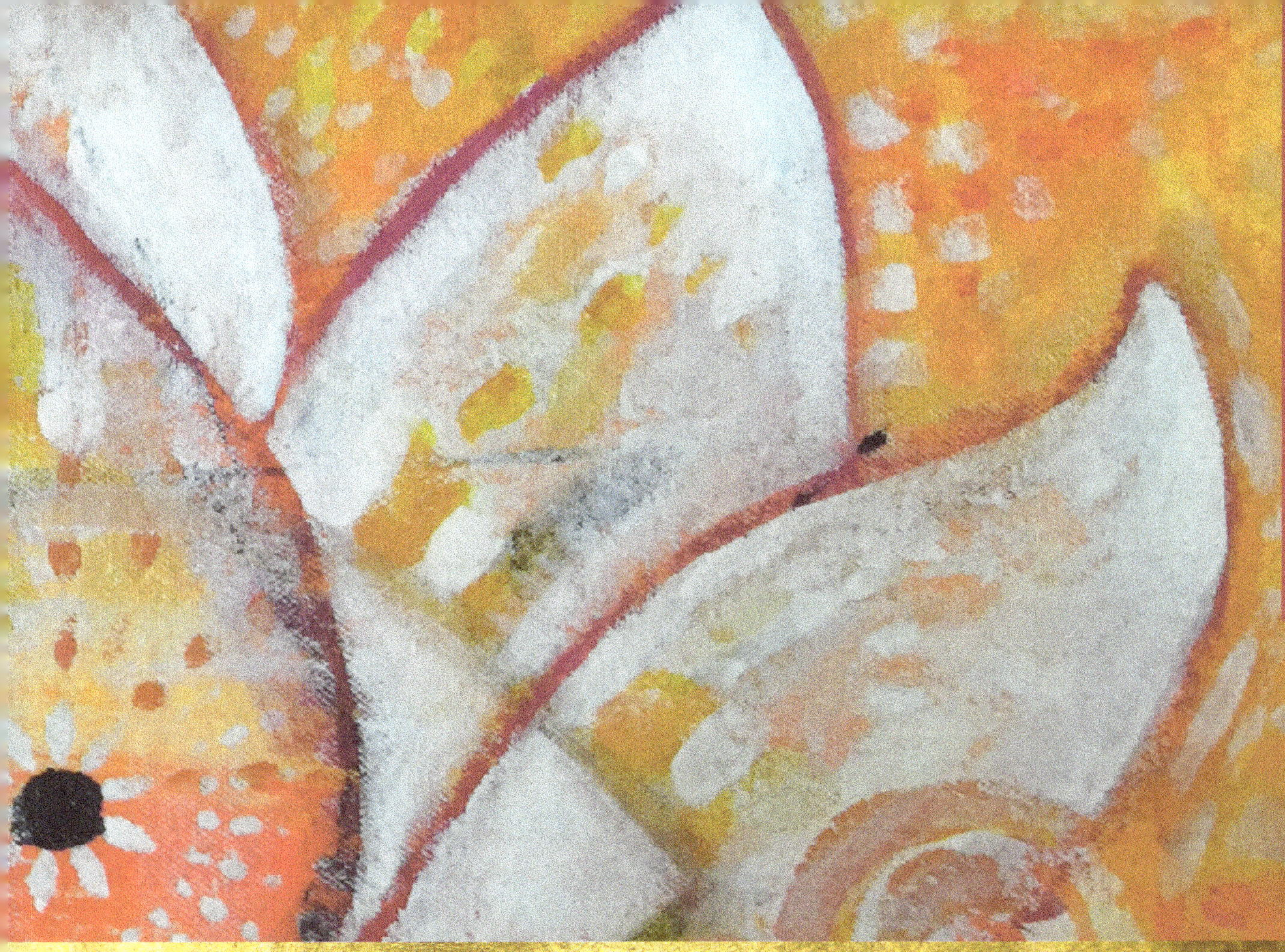

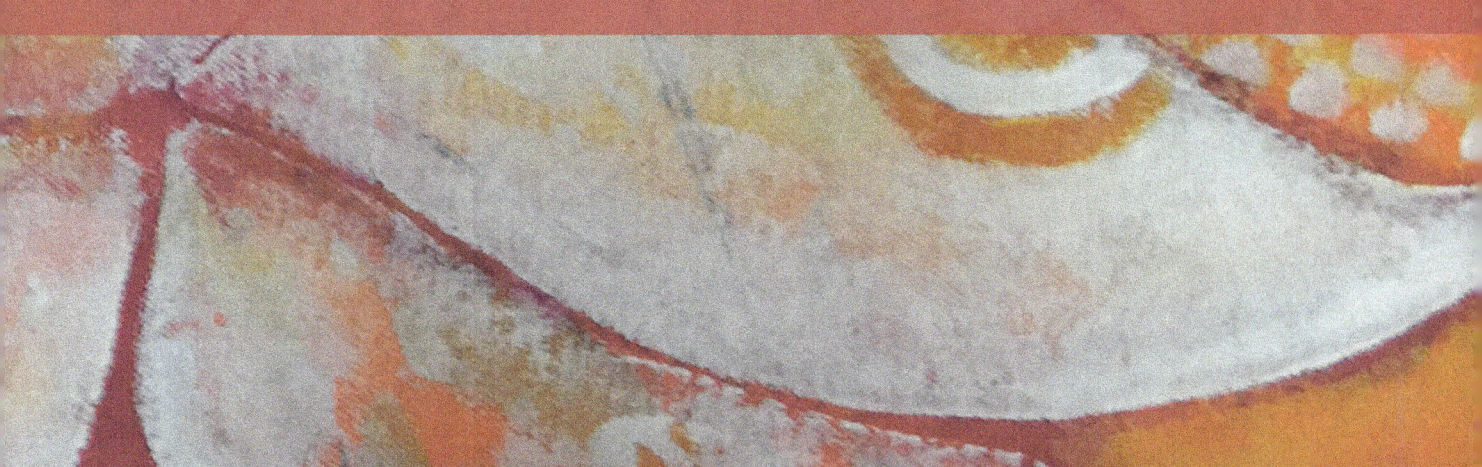

**Super Soul Flow**

# Fearlessness

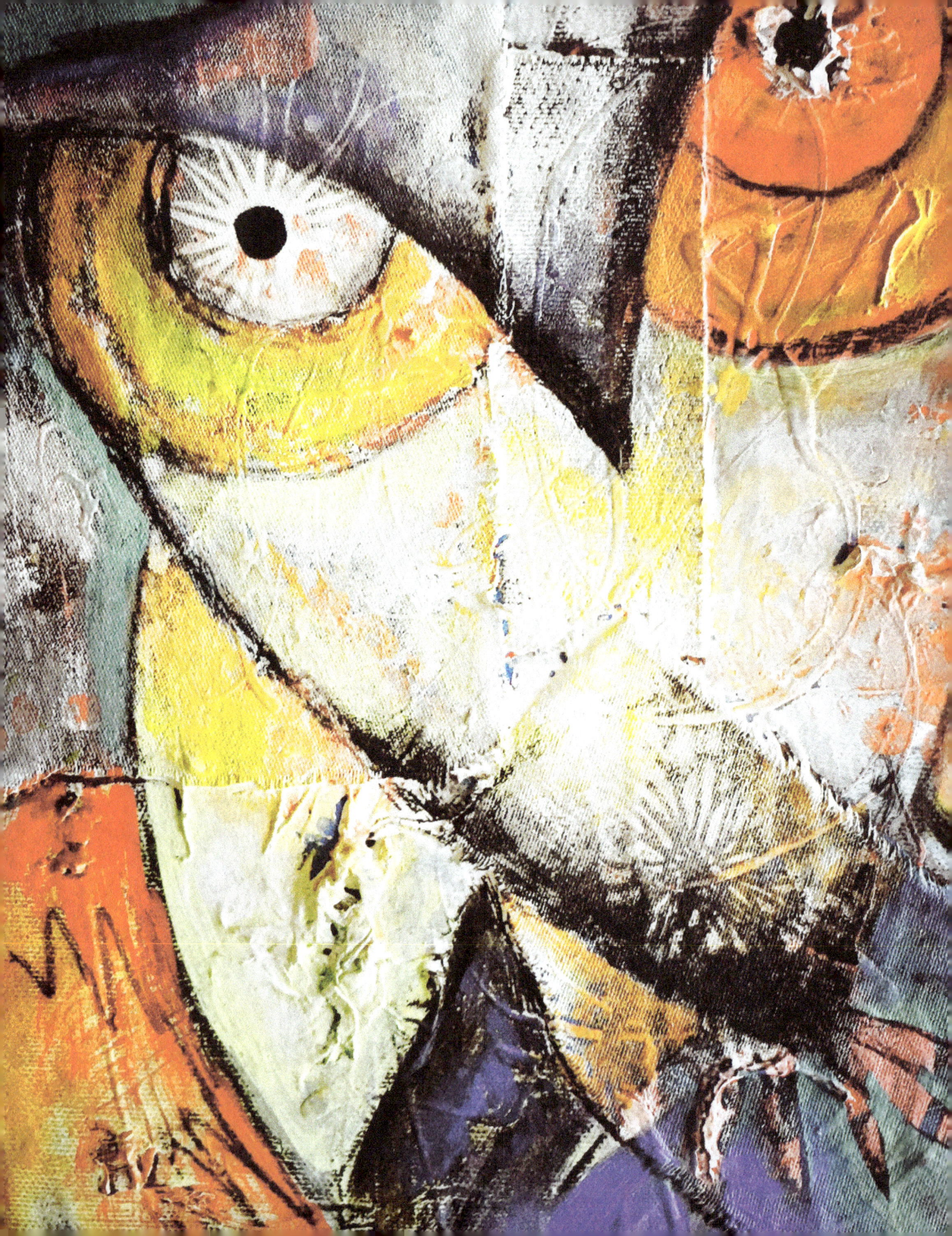

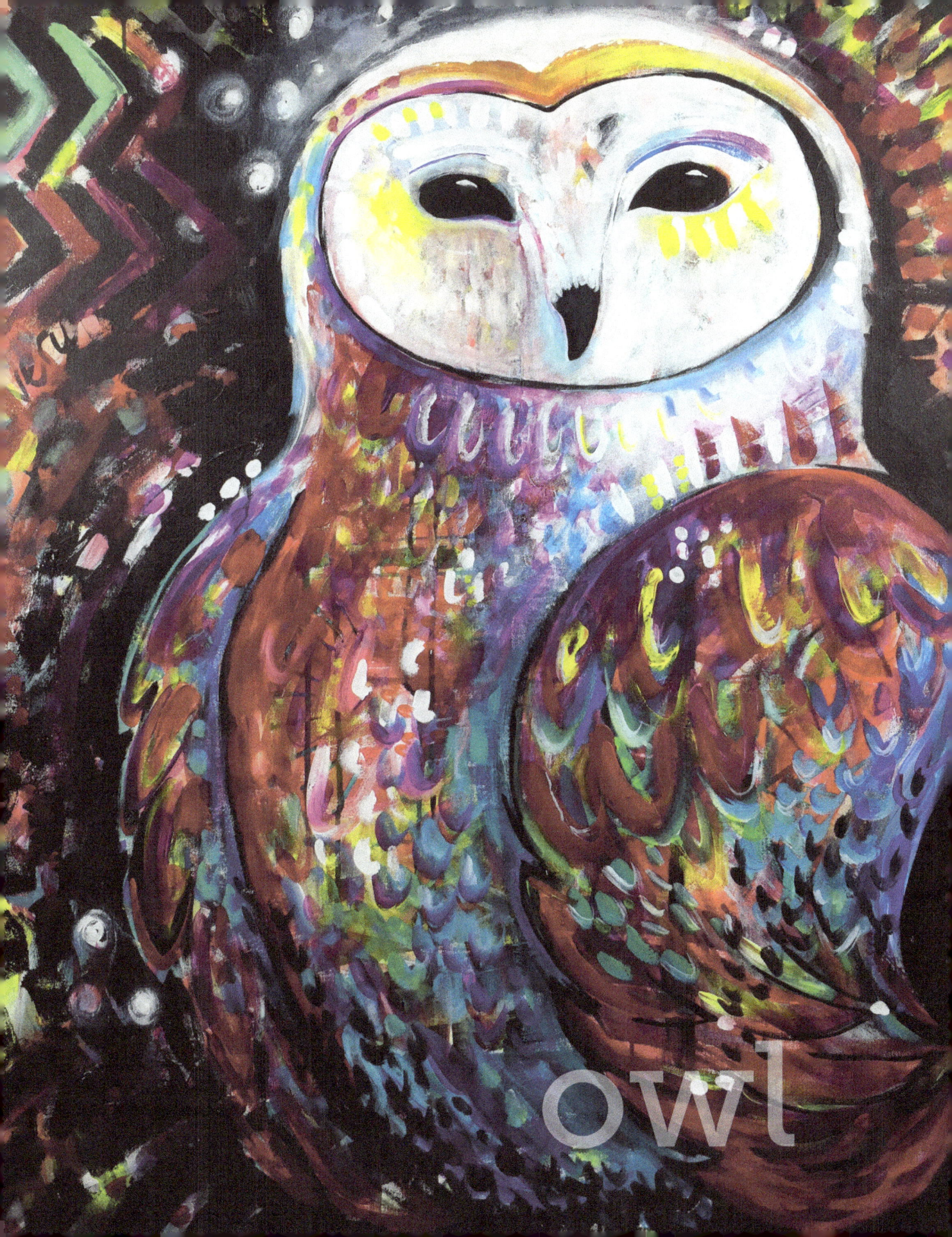

owl

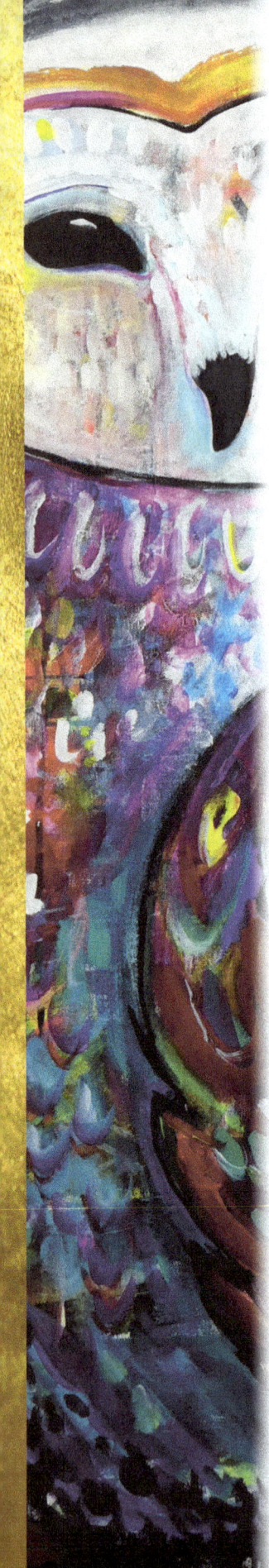

# owl

*In 2009 I was inspired by owls I saw on a computer skin in a gift shop. So I painted an owl… and another. I painted owls for two years straight. At first, I thought, "I must be going through my 'Owl Period'!" Then, when I would try to paint something else and I found myself, once again, painting an owl, I thought, "Why would anyone want to paint anything BUT an owl?!" I seriously could ONLY paint owls. There are people around the world, thanks to Facebook, that will never see an owl again without thinking of me. My "Owl Phase" was so pervasive.*

*It took a year of this before a series of ah-ha's and Google searches led me to the thought, "Maybe there is a REASON I am painting owls."*

*That was the beginning.*

*The first truth the OWL illuminated for me was that WHAT you paint is significant and that the image is alive with its own energy. I would never paint a painting again that was not a conversation with my Highest Self. The magic had arrived within the talons of the OWL.*

Can I lend you my eyes, because I can see things in the dark that no one else can see?

Can I lend you my eyes, to illuminate for you the fears that are holding you back?

Can I lend you my eyes, and transmute that which you have judged about yourself to be bad or wrong or scary into your personal power, strength and wisdom?

I am wise... I know ALL of you because I see into your darkness.

I am wise... I know your fears are your greatest teachers.

I am wise... I know what promise is waiting for you on the other side of your shadow.

Allow me to guide your path out of your underworld.

I have come to lend you my illumination, my focus, and my wisdom, that you might truly SEE the whole potential you can claim as yours.

You have survived your lessons and now is time to bathe in the light of your beginning.

You are a huntress of the truth, a beacon of light, a guide for others.

Follow me now into the world only YOU can illuminate.

A'Ho.

Once you become fearless, life becomes limitless.
~UNKNOWN

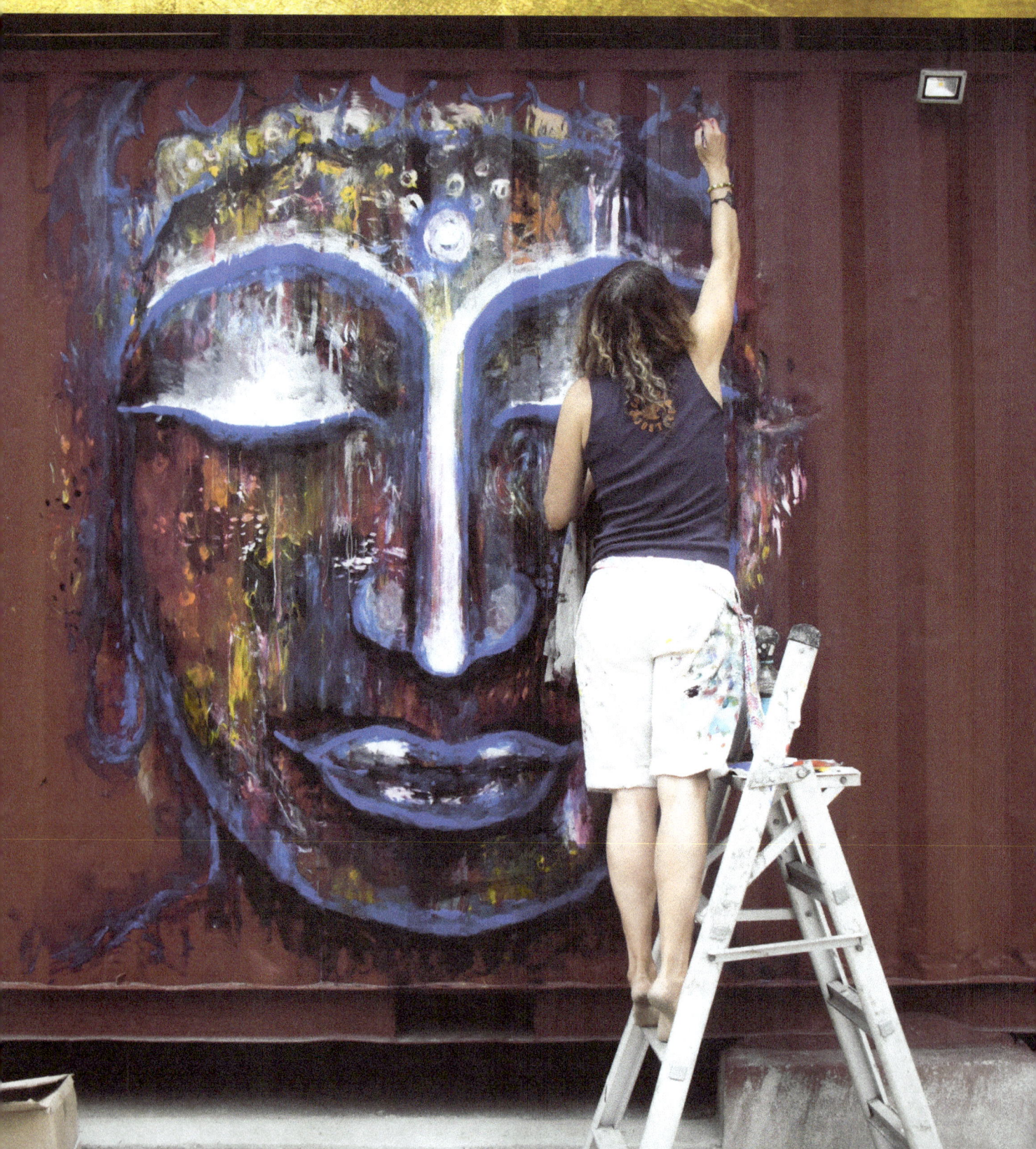

# You are going on a journey now.

Ready to engage your most amazing imagination and enter into an imagined reality that will place all your fears and dreams in divine perspective?

Take three deep breaths.

Focus your attention on where you are on this planet right now. Feel your body. Feel your clothes on your skin. Feel your breath raise your chest and lower it.

Now, picture where you are now from a bird's-eye view.

Do you have it?

Now zoom up. With each inhale, imagine you are levitating, rising like a balloon.

Now you are looking down on your entire town.

10,000 feet up… 30,000 feet up (like you are in a plane)… 5 miles up… until you are looking down on planet earth, a small green and blue marble.

Try to see yourself down on earth, sitting in your home. Take a deep inhale. Way, way down there, you are somewhere, sitting, reading this book. You are super small, right?

Now close your eyes and FEEL what you feel up there, in all that wide, open space. Close your eyes and take deep breaths. Feel the boundlessness and the lightness of being.

Do you feel your body start to tingle, as your cells merge with the infinite space, the stars and planets spinning in space around you?

Is there anything beyond your reach here? Is there anything that could possibly lie outside of the field of possibility? Now send that energy down into your physical self, like a stream of silver light.

**Did you feel the expansiveness?** There were no limitations, no boundaries, only potential. When you started to come back, did it feel almost impossible? How can you fit all of THIS ENERGY into that itty bitty body?

Next, follow your breath back down, down, down... back to your body. Deep breath. Feel yourself in the chair. Deep breath. Wiggle your toes. Deep breath. Open your eyes.

From this perspective, you can feel the tremendous contrast between that eternal, infinite reality and your limited physical reality. From this perspective, you can open up to pure fearlessness.

Read how much this excerpt from Andrew Harvey's book, *The Direct Path*, resonates with the journey we just experienced:

> *We undertake the tremendous journey of return to Origin (the infinite space we just visited) not to vanish into Origin or simply rest in its peace and glory, but to be infused with its sacred passion and power and become so saturated with its energy and love that we can "reenter" reality and become agents with and in God of a massive transformation of all the conditions of Creation. In other words, we are created by the Divine to participate with it in its "plan" of bringing the whole of the Creation consciously into the glory of its eternal being.*

Spending time in this expansive perspective, this eagle's-eye (or should we say astronaut's-eye) view, can help to create new proportions around your feelings of fear or resistance. Maybe that thing that you have wanted to do but doubted you could is not such a scary thing after all?

Let's unpack fearlessness by starting with fear.

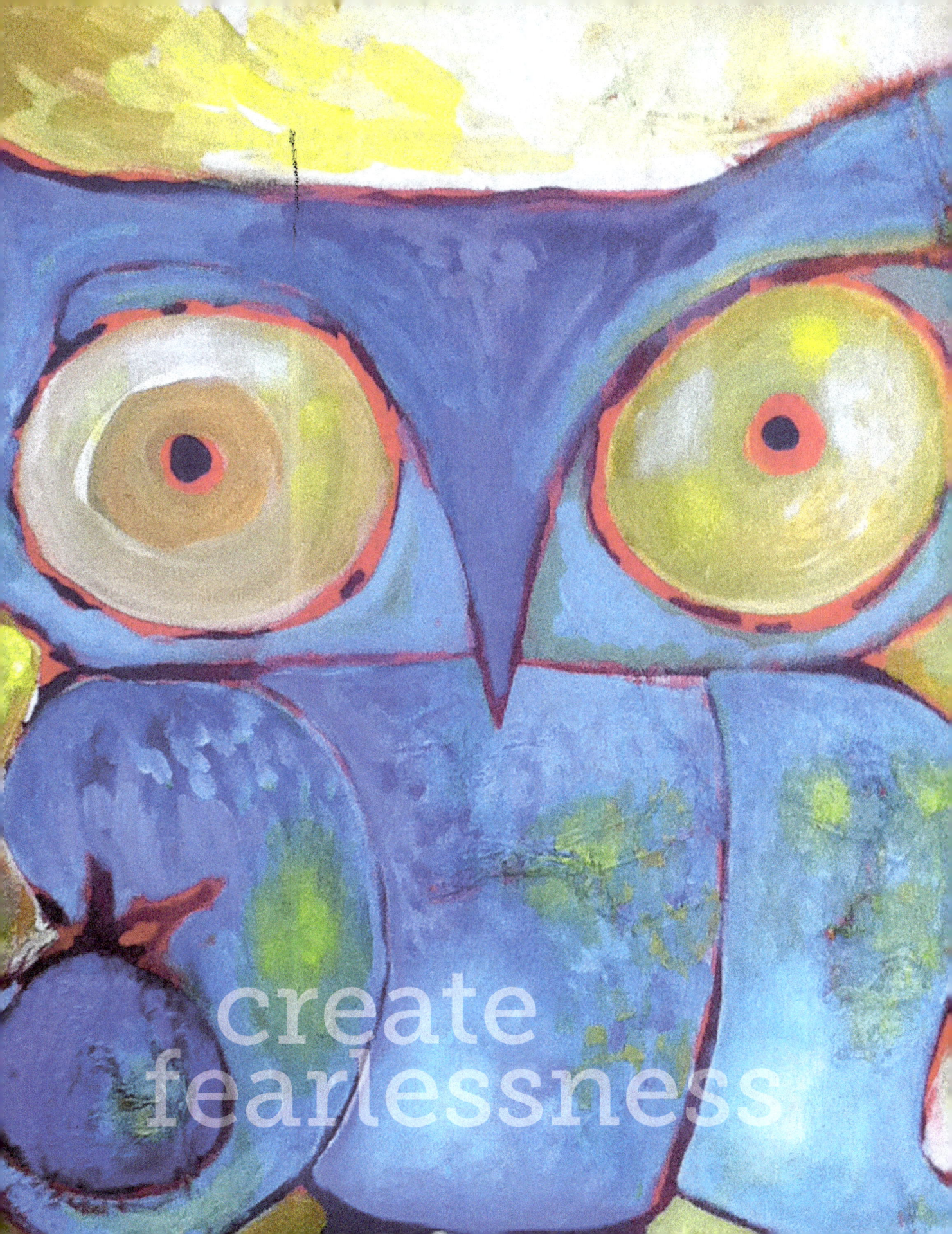
create
fearlessness

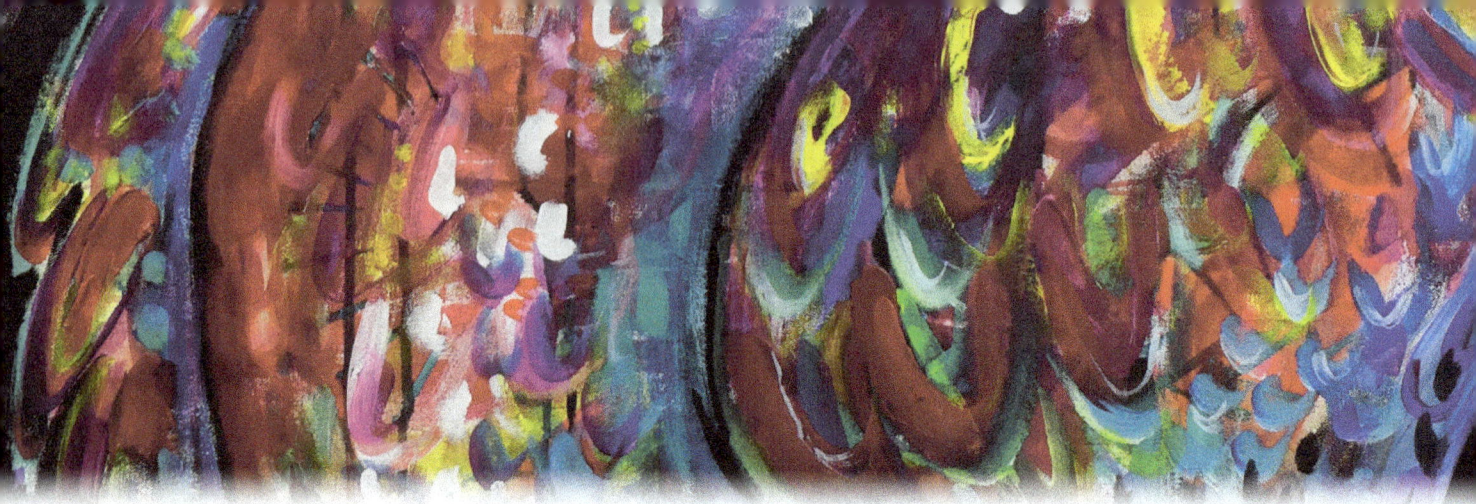

*It's not the thing itself that holds the power to hurt or save us, but the quality of awareness we bring to it.*

~THE MANDALA OF BEING BY RICHARD MOSS

We are back to our mantra, "I AM the sole creator of my experience."

How can we create a different awareness around that thing or situation that is triggering fear for us and RISE ABOVE the fear holding us back?

In the book *Power vs. Force*, David Hawkins writes:

> *There is great freedom in the realization that I 'have' a body and a mind, rather than I 'am' my body or mind. Once the fear of death is transcended, life becomes a transformed experience because that particular fear underlies all others. Few people know what it is to live without fear—but beyond fear lies joy, as the meaning and purpose of existence becomes transparent.*

What are your attachments? Maybe it is not about letting go as much as creating a new awareness around them.

Sometimes the process of being "good" or "perfect" demands being bad or imperfect. This is the nature of living in a non-dual reality.

EVERYTHING is here to serve you. Fear isn't bad, it's just a part of the experience.

*The cave you fear to enter holds the treasure you seek.*

~JOSEPH CAMPBELL

The dark "cave" is not a place to avoid. It's a place to approach with awareness and the wide open "Eye of Fearlessness" (you will hear about that in the painting section) so you can see the truth of your situation and not let stories and illusions stop you from claiming your "treasure."

*There is nothing that can be taken away from you. That which can be taken away from you is not worth keeping, and that which cannot be taken away from you, why should one be afraid of its being taken away? You cannot lose your real treasure.*

~OSHO

The real treasure? That which we are all seeking? The Holy Grail? It is YOU. The FULL YOU. The most authentic, most fearless and free YOU! Let's practice BEING that energy at the canvas...

# Creating the Energy of FEARLESSNESS

The painting below was created in a Super Soul Flow workshop with my family of Creatively Fit Coaches.

At least 15 of them contributed to this painting over the course of an hour. The final image and symbol of fearlessness was what I now refer to as the EYE OF FEARLESSNESS.

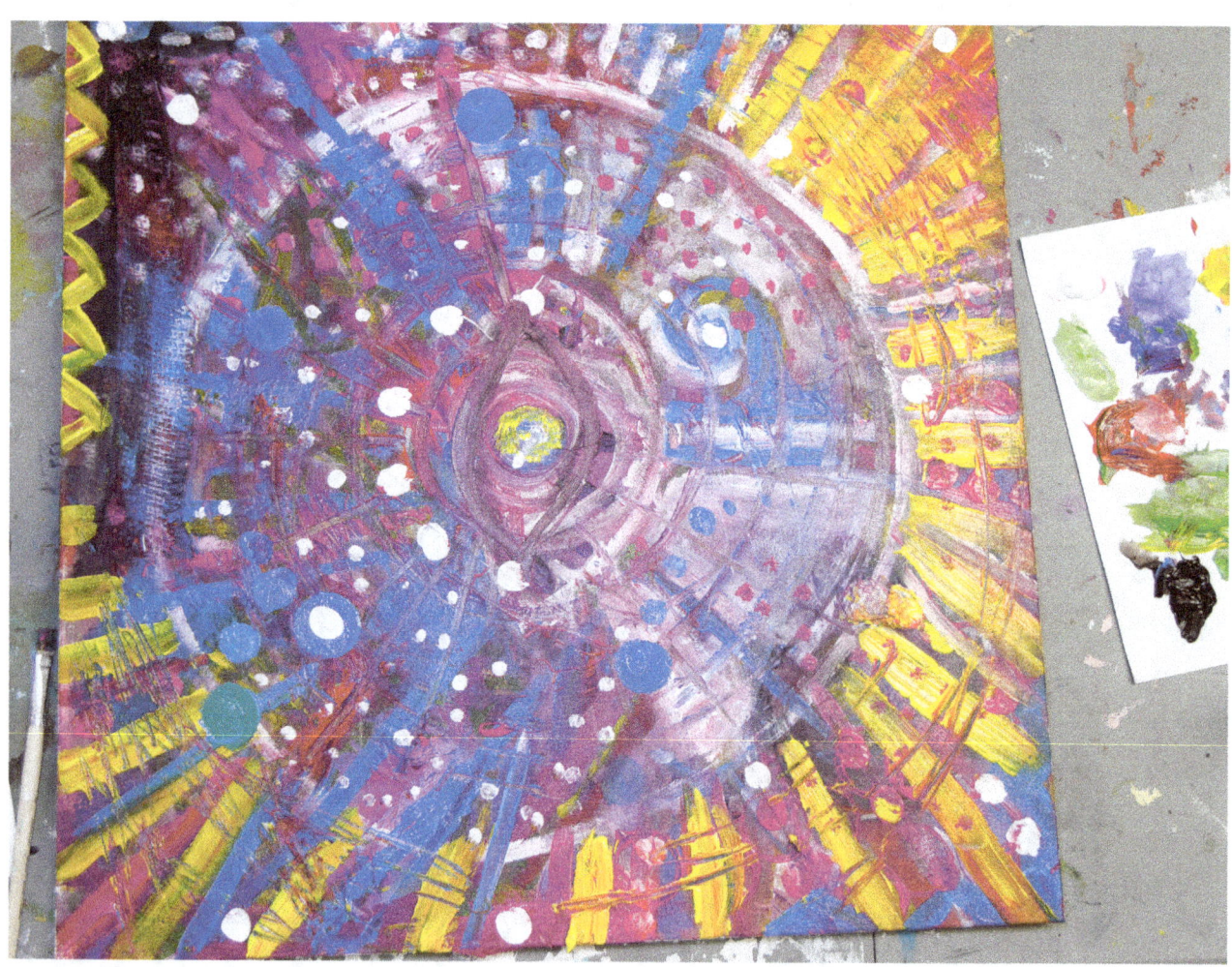

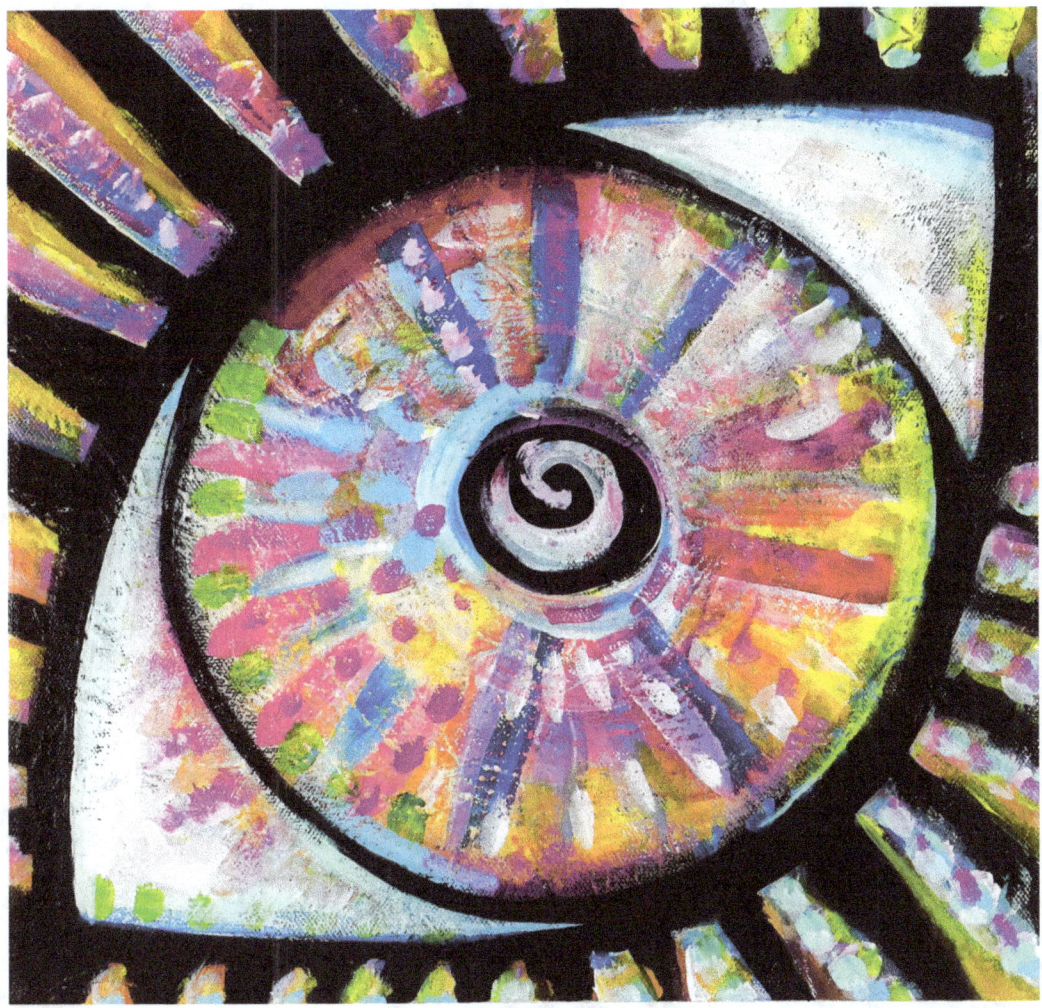

In the course of the five minutes after viewing this painting complete— as you see it above—I had waves of insights and ah-ha's around the nature of fearlessness and what I can do to cultivate this energy.

This EYE is WIDE open. It is so open that it has no right side up or down. It is simply always OPEN.

If you have your eyes WIDE open, seeing things for what they really are, with the truth of whatever situation or thing in clear view, you can't be afraid.

Fear only can exist in the shadows, in the unknowing, in the assumptions or ignorance. Because the TRUTH inherent at the foundation of it all is that "everything is working out perfectly." There is ONLY love. Fear, stress, worry, insecurity... all pass away with this physical body. All that is left is love.

From that space what do we have to fear?!

The EYE of FEARLESSNESS will help you to see the truth, to see things as they REALLY are, without the filters of our personal stories, limiting beliefs and societal pressures. Invite it in by engaging it on the canvas and see what insight it brings to you.

This is one thing I love about our Personal Painting Practice—it creates the time and SPACE for us to sink into and integrate the teachings of the symbols we choose to create. We can sit here and read about and think about this symbol, but how much more powerfully will it speak to you as you engage it by CREATING it yourself onto your Meditation Canvas?

When I was shooting the video lessons for the Super Soul Flow Online Program, I invited my friend Adele to join me. She had her own fearlessness experience with her OWL painting. As we were creating the video and talking, I noticed how cute Adele's owl was and how it seemed kind of squished down into the bottom half of the canvas.

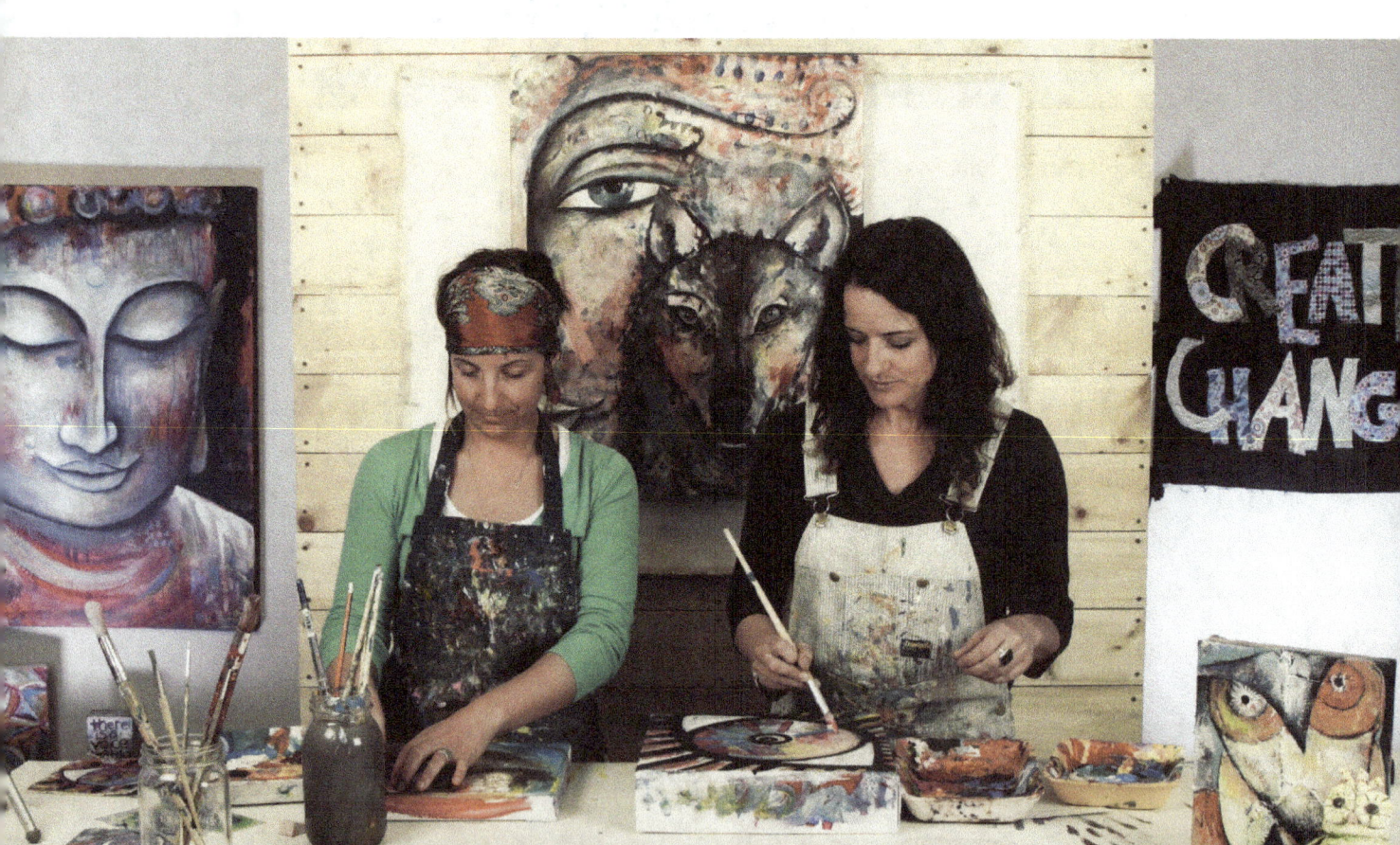

Then, minutes later, when I looked over, she had added the owl's crown. I was startled by the power of the change she had created. The crown was what made this owl fearless! The crown is symbolic of our connection to the divine. SO with our own connection to the divine, we can also step into the energy of fearlessness!

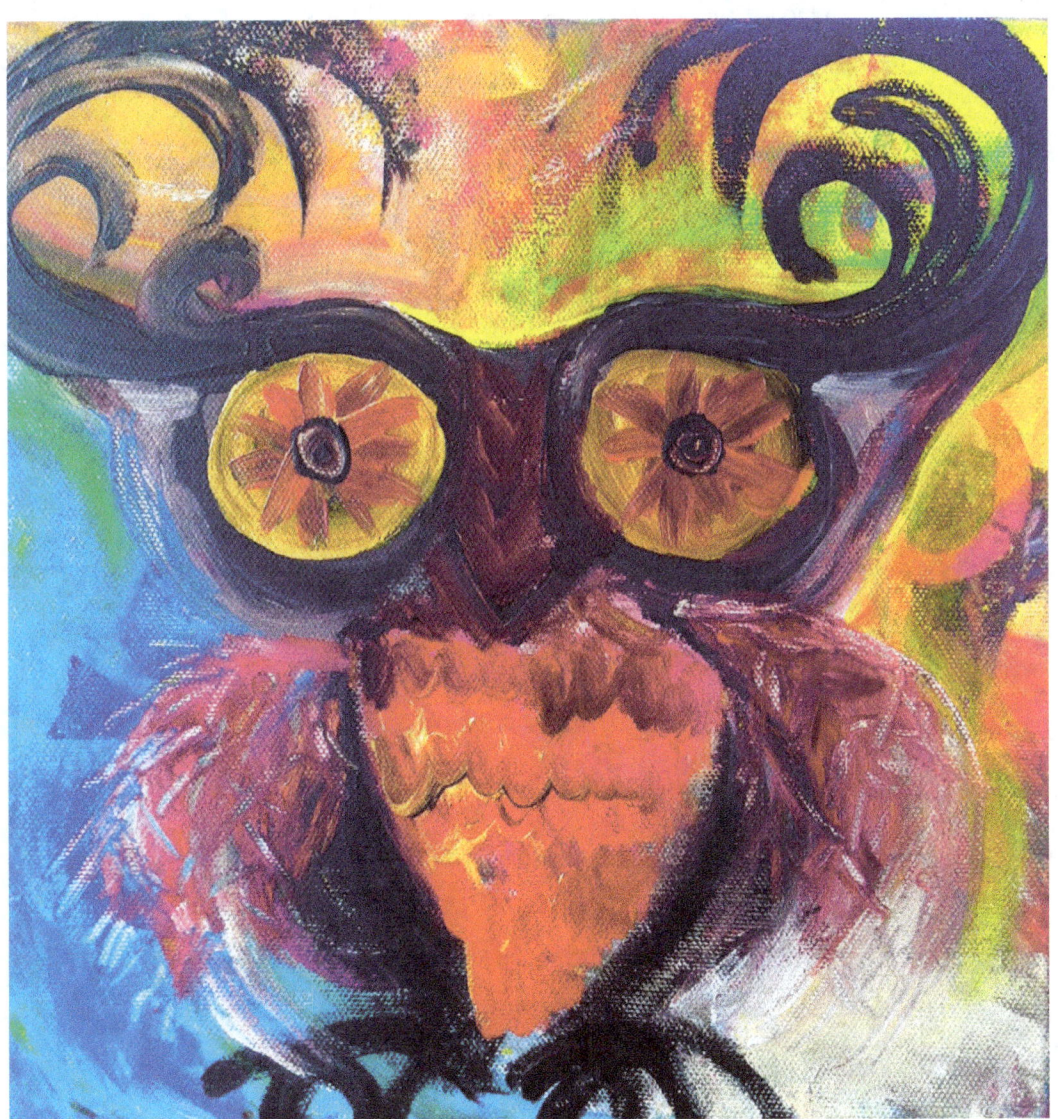

In Chinese culture the tiger is a symbol of fearlessness. In the Thoth Tarot deck the Princess of Wands is the embodiment of fearlessness, holding the tiger by the tail and in her other hand her sun wand—illuminating the truth for her, no doubt.

I invite you to paint your own EYE of FEARLESSNESS and then invite in another symbol that speaks to you in a similar manner.

The image on the opposite page is s a West African Adinkra symbol for COURAGE. It is part of my line of ARTual Sacred Symbol Stencils so I have engaged with it a lot over the last couple of years.

Ultimately, courage involves the heart. It is the mind trying to protect us from the unknown and keep us safe in the familiar.

**Fear keeps us small. We are constantly attracting to ourselves opportunities to expand. It is fear that makes us pass up those opportunities. What might shift for you if you created more of a balance between fear and fearlessness?**

Thank you all for accepting the invitation to expand! I am honored to be your muse in this journey.

Go paint!

Namasté.

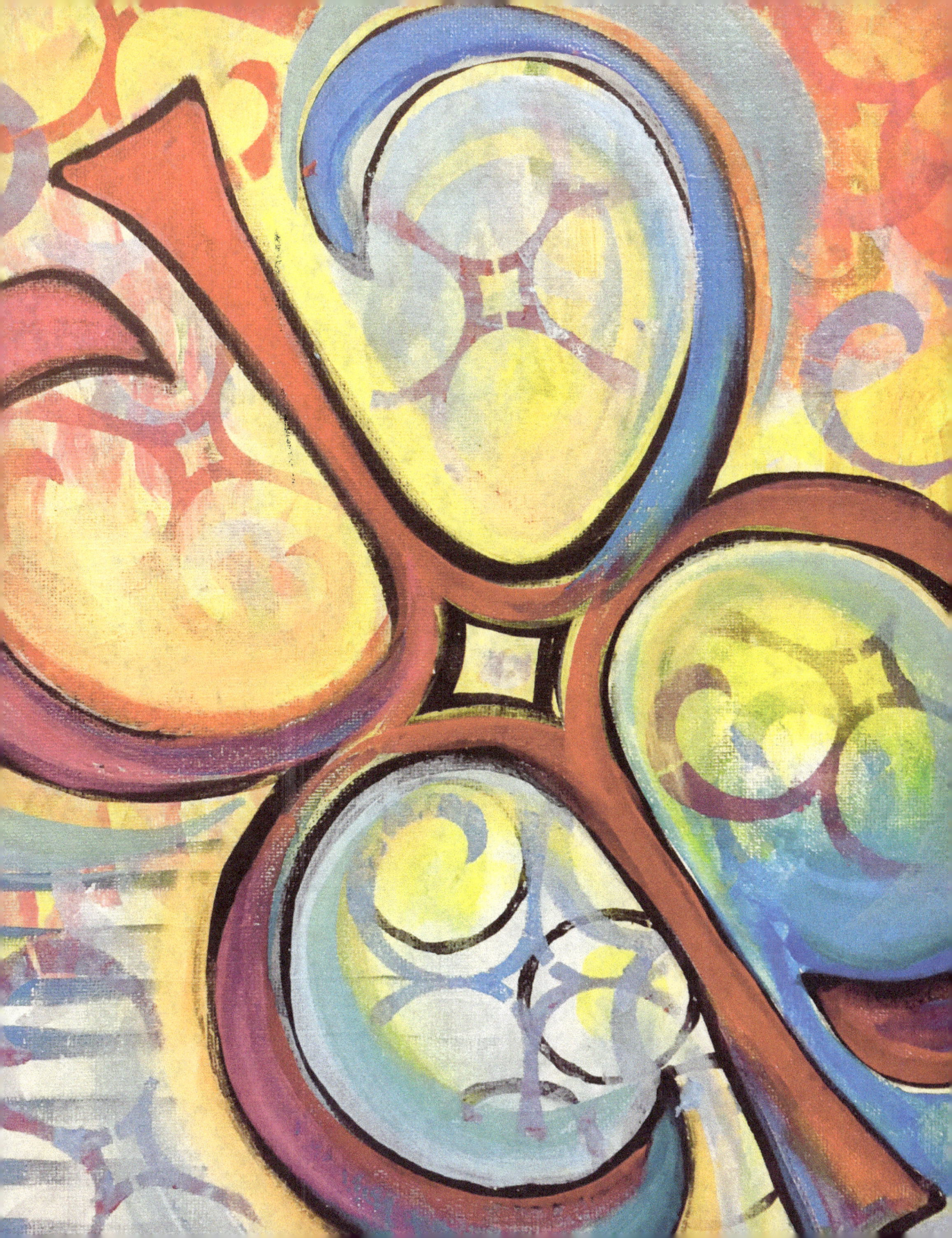

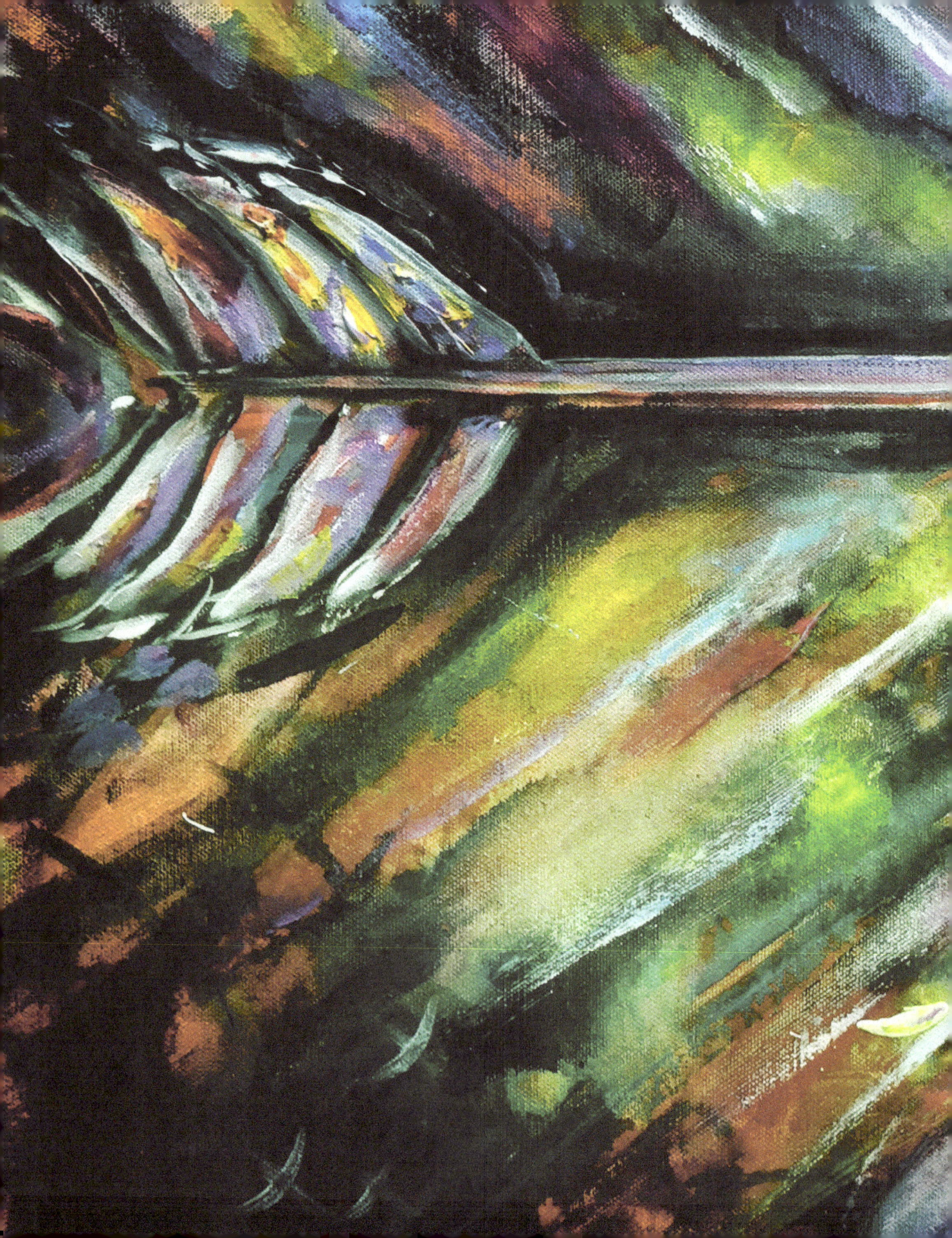

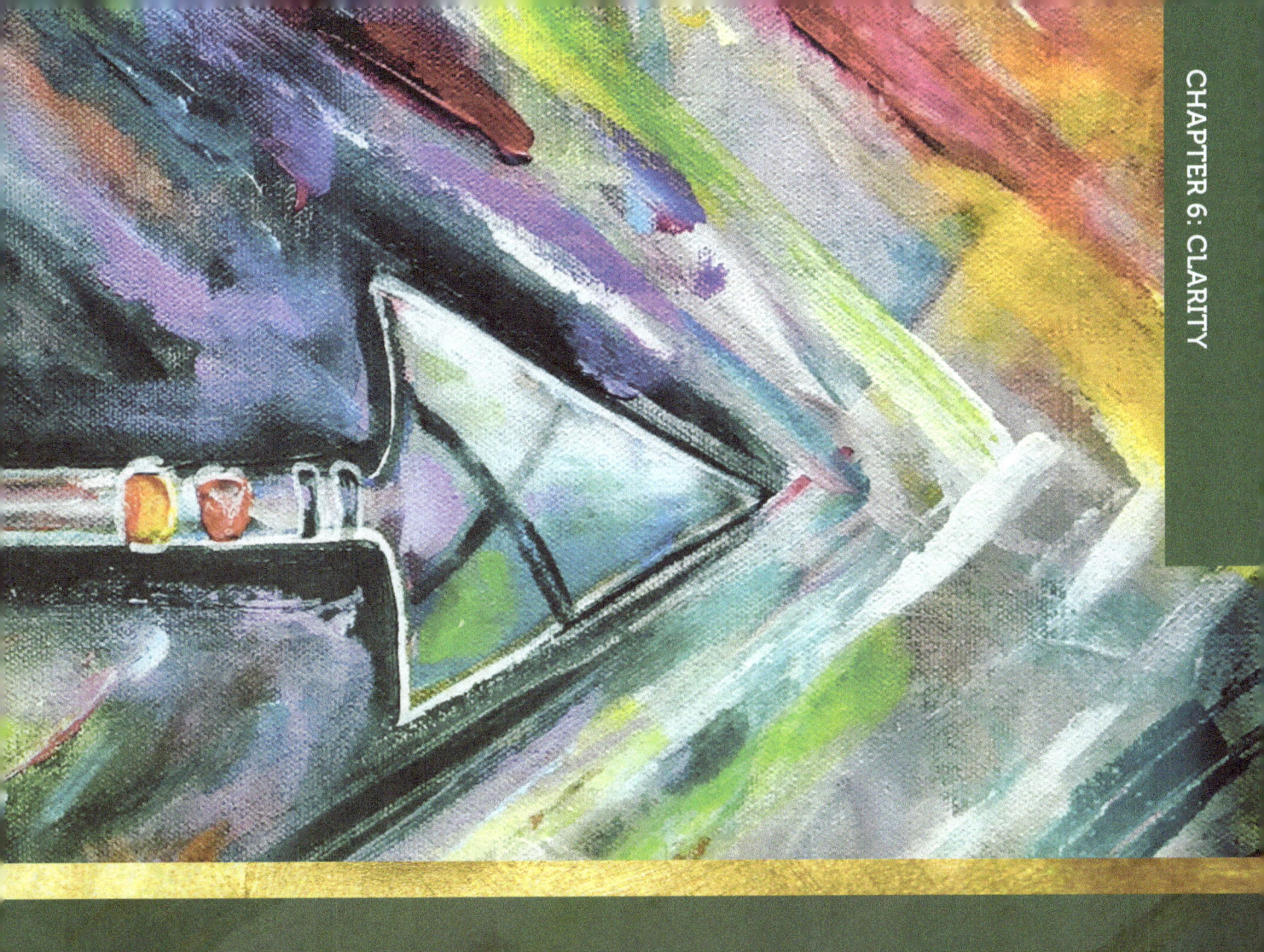

# Super Soul Flow
## Clarity

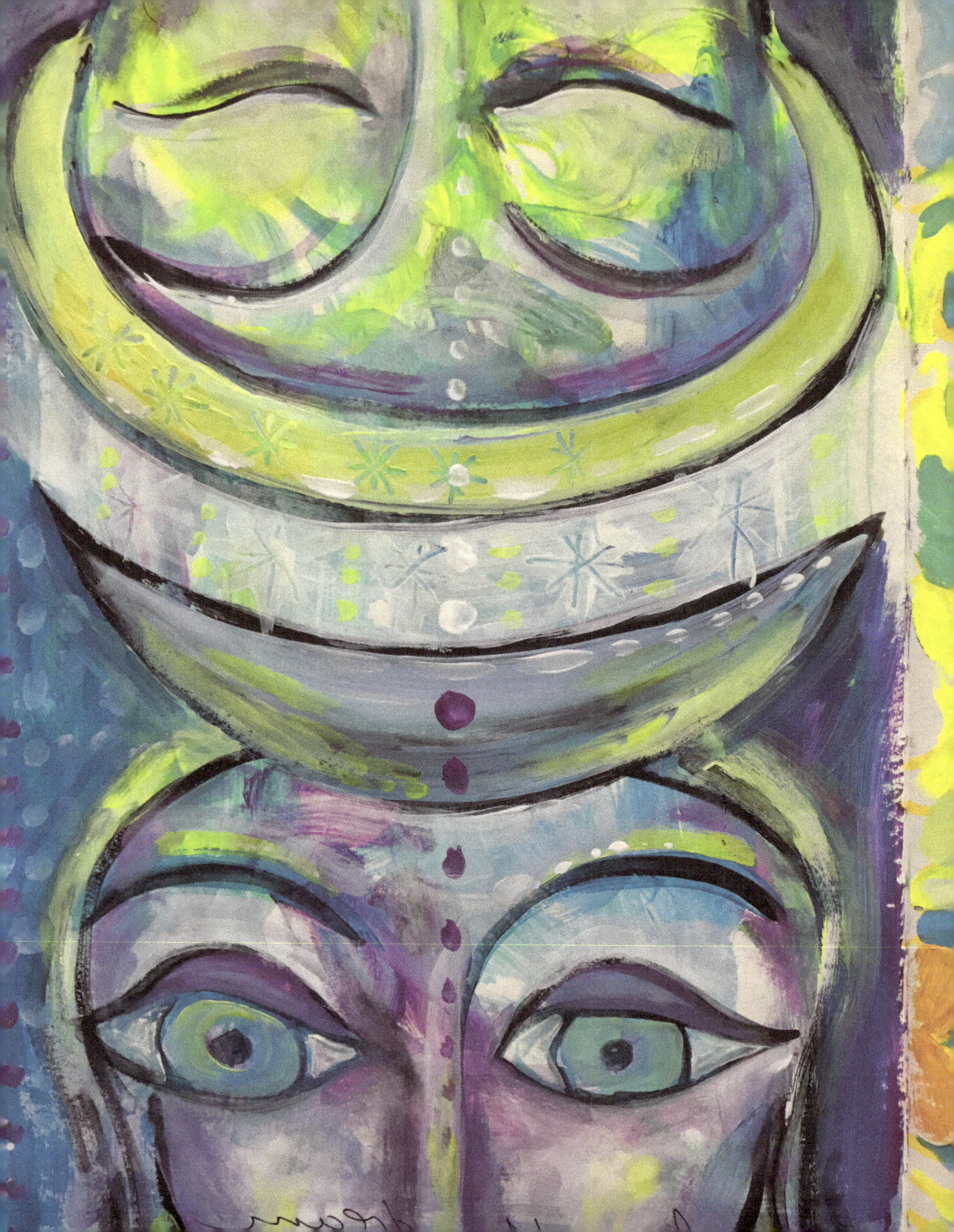

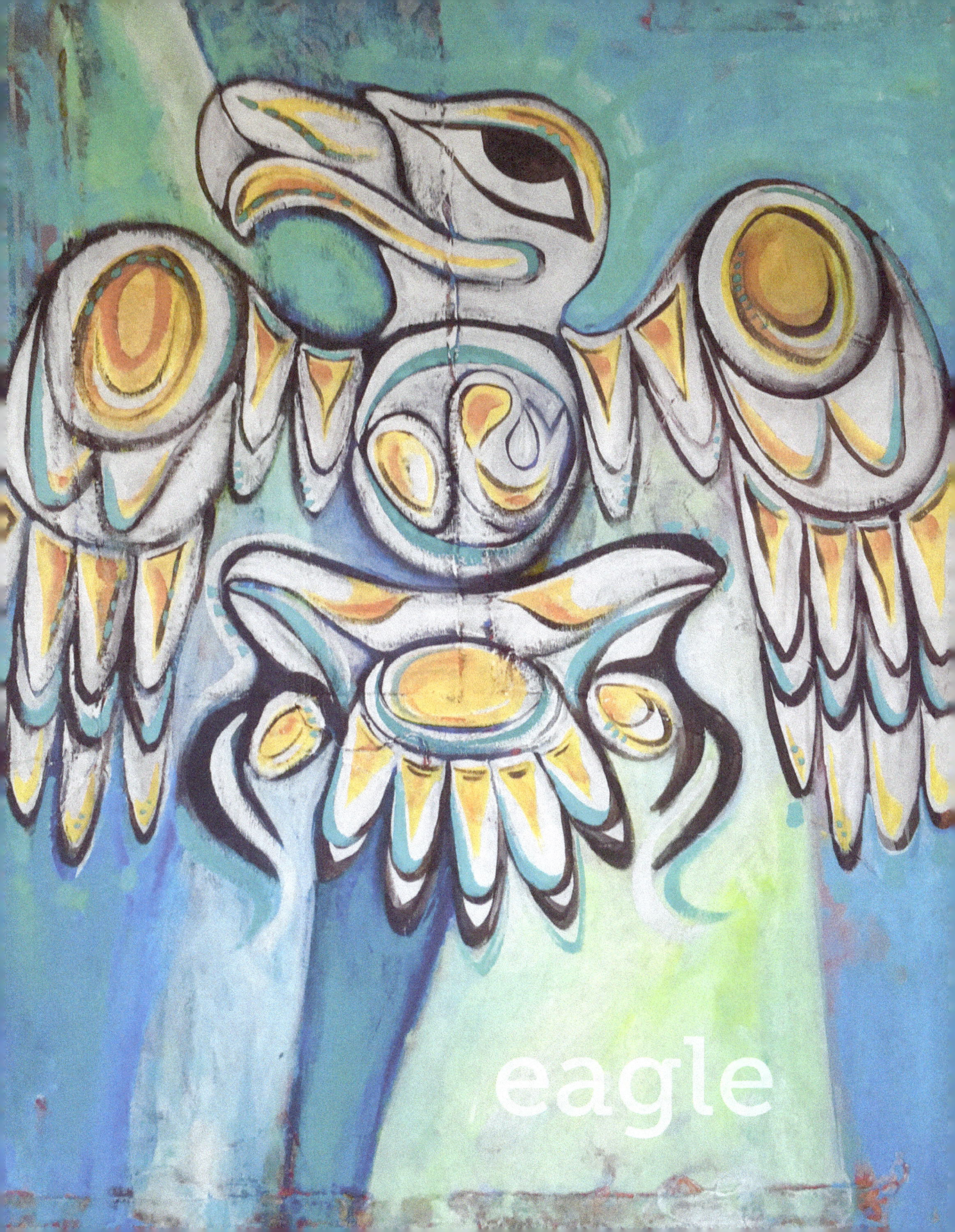

eagle

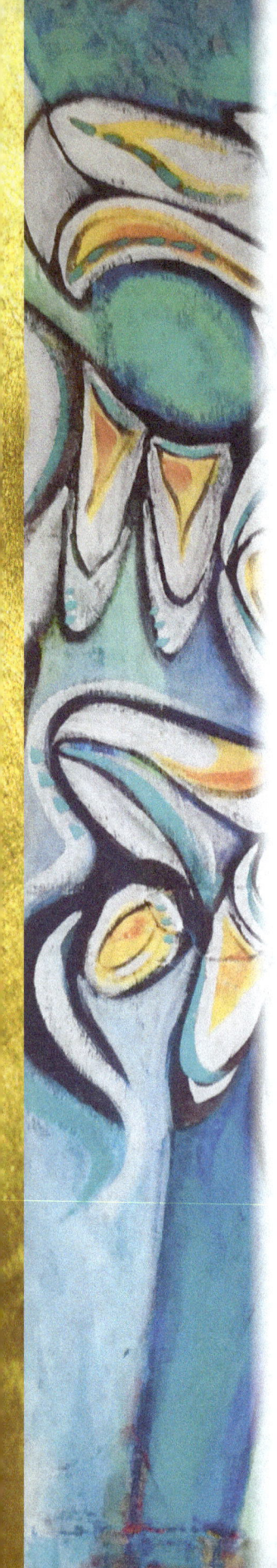

# eagle

*My wish is that the mantra "rise above" becomes powerful medicine for you. Our modern lifestyle can get so overly hectic, over-scheduled, and complicated that it demands this energy of detachment and distance to balance the details that swirl around us each day.*

*I often imagine EAGLE lifting me off the ground. I'm laying right on top of the eagle, arms extended out over his wings, looking down as we soar to great heights. I close my eyes and imagine rising above the day-to-day and reconnecting to my eagle's-eye perspective. From this distance, priorities become clearer, my soul's voice comes through stronger, and I can cut the cords of responsibility or worry that have felt heavy. Allow EAGLE to lift you up and over whatever is challenging you today.*

I close my eyes and breathe deeply.

As I exhale, I imagine the world around me melting away.

Away goes the to-do lists.
Away goes the worries.
Away goes the mail, the bills, the piles of paper.

Inhale… exhale…

I am standing in a meadow.
Open, green, lush.
Mountains frame in the horizon.

A gentle breeze blows through
my hair.

Inhale… exhale…

Eagle comes to me.
I hear his wings.
I sense him circling above me,
sinking lower and lower.
In a moment, I am enveloped by
Eagle's wings.
I am placed on his back and we rise
above the landscape.
We are one.
We fly.
We soar.

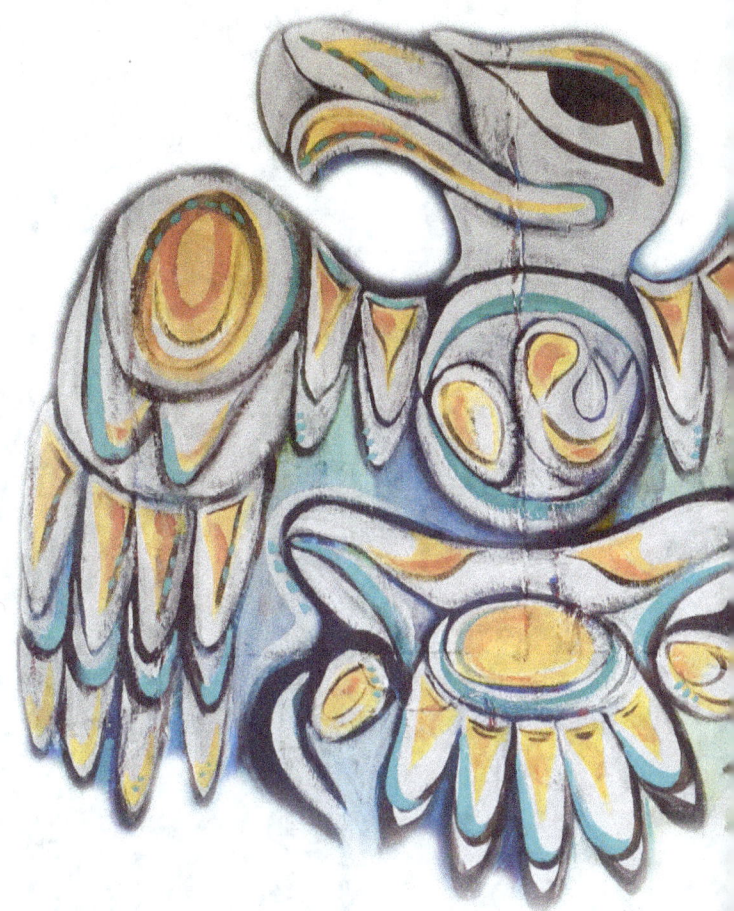

From this distance, life's clarity is
restored. I can see what is important, and the details fall away.

Eagle guides me higher.
The light washes away any worries or doubts and infuses my being
with deep knowing, wisdom, truth…

The wind blows away the chatter—everything but the present
moment.

The sun illuminates the expansiveness of the space all around me,
my fluidity in motion.

Eagle and I soar into light and possibility, my vision and heart restored
along my highest path.

Together we RISE ABOVE.

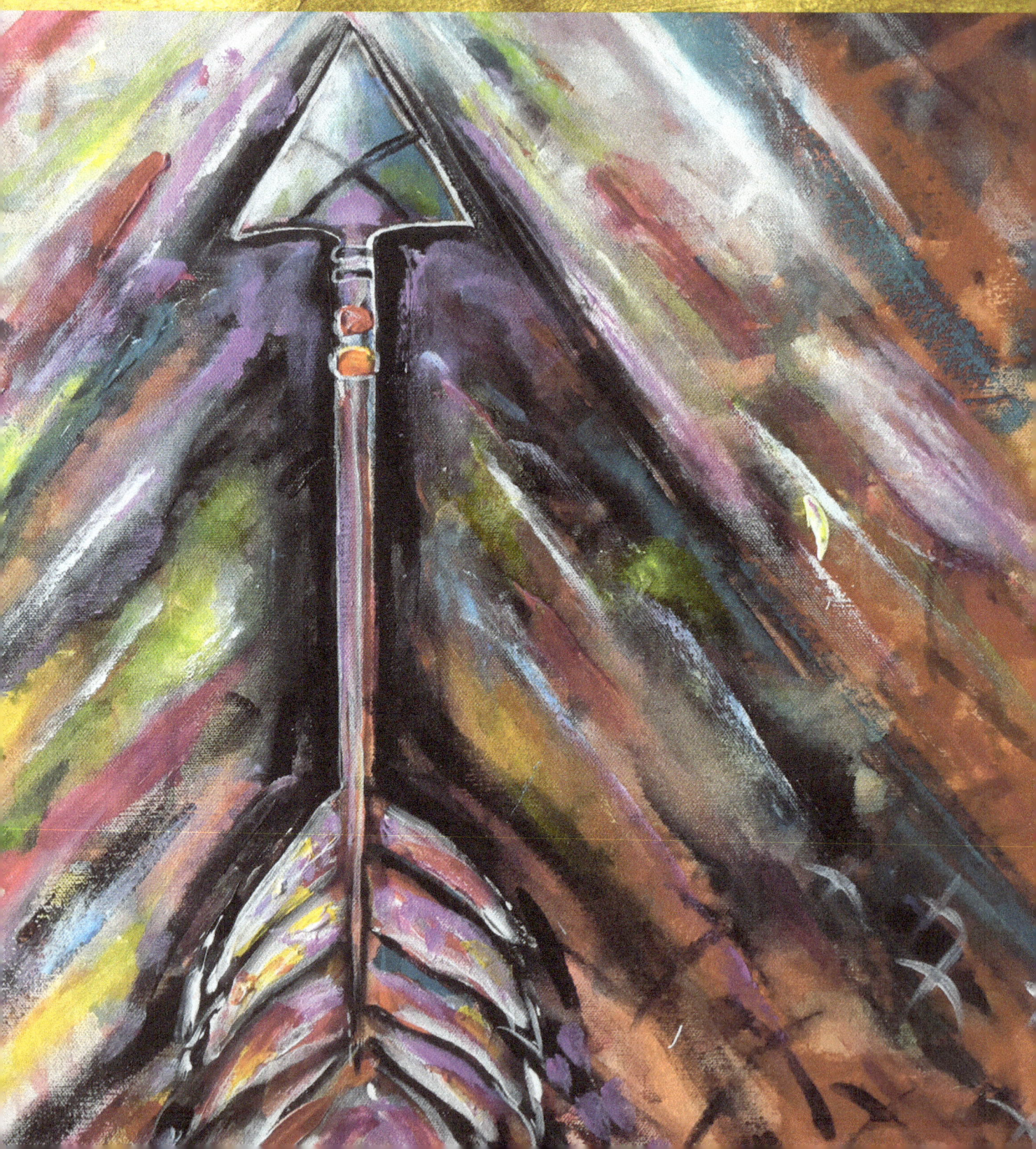

# Would you like to create more CLARITY in your life?

Clarity creates clear vision, clear direction, and peace of mind. When we worry or stress, it is because we do not have clarity. Any change you want to create in your life will happen exponentially when you have clarity around what you really want.

Let me introduce you to the "Clarity Session." This is a practice that I, and my Creatively Fit Coaches, love to facilitate for our clients. You can do it for yourself right now. You are going to create THREE "Imagination Goals," creating clarity to replace whatever confusion or discord you have been experiencing up until now.

You will choose three things that you worry about the most, identify the limiting belief, create a new belief, and then, turn them around into magical dreams of the future, a future that YOU are about to step into... NO MATTER WHAT!

Imagination is our internal paintbrush of possibility. Many of us have not been taught how to create the images of what we want in our minds. Without awareness and without clarity, you can be creating images and scenarios in your mind that DO NOT serve you.

Imagination is what connects our visible world, the physical, to the invisible world, the energetic. Have you been taught that your imagination is one of your super powers?

I wasn't.

**In this chapter, I am going to share with you a way to strap rocket boosters to your dreams and desires through the healing power of imagination and symbols.**

*The more time we spend imagining the possibilities that we want in our life—more financial abundance, fulfilling relationships and connection, more opportunities—the greater chance we have of bringing them into reality.*

What I know I tend to do, without mindfulness, is imagine what I DON'T want to happen. That looks like worries. When I worry, I am choosing to focus on what I don't want to happen. Why would I ever do that?! Do you find yourself imagining the worst-case scenario in your mind rather than the best case?

An important step in this process is identifying the LIMITING BELIEF that is at the root of our dissatisfaction. Without digging this up by the roots, we will continue to be hindered by this subconscious thought we have accepted as truth somewhere along the way.

For example, I have had, up until my own Clarity Session, a limiting belief that "I am not good with numbers." It used to cause me to worry if I could handle my growing business.

What can get you stuck in the treadmill of a limiting belief is the energy of the word at the core of your limiting belief. The word itself has baggage.

For me, just hearing, saying or thinking the word NUMBERS sends waves of negative beliefs through me. But when I attach a SYMBOL to my NEW belief, my mind is able to bypass the limiting belief that is triggered by the word because the symbol has no baggage.

I will share the process below, but the symbol my soul gave me through my Soul Scribble exercise to reinforce my NEW BELIEF that "I love the energy of numbers," was the BALLOON. I asked myself, "What do balloons symbolize?"

"Birthdays."

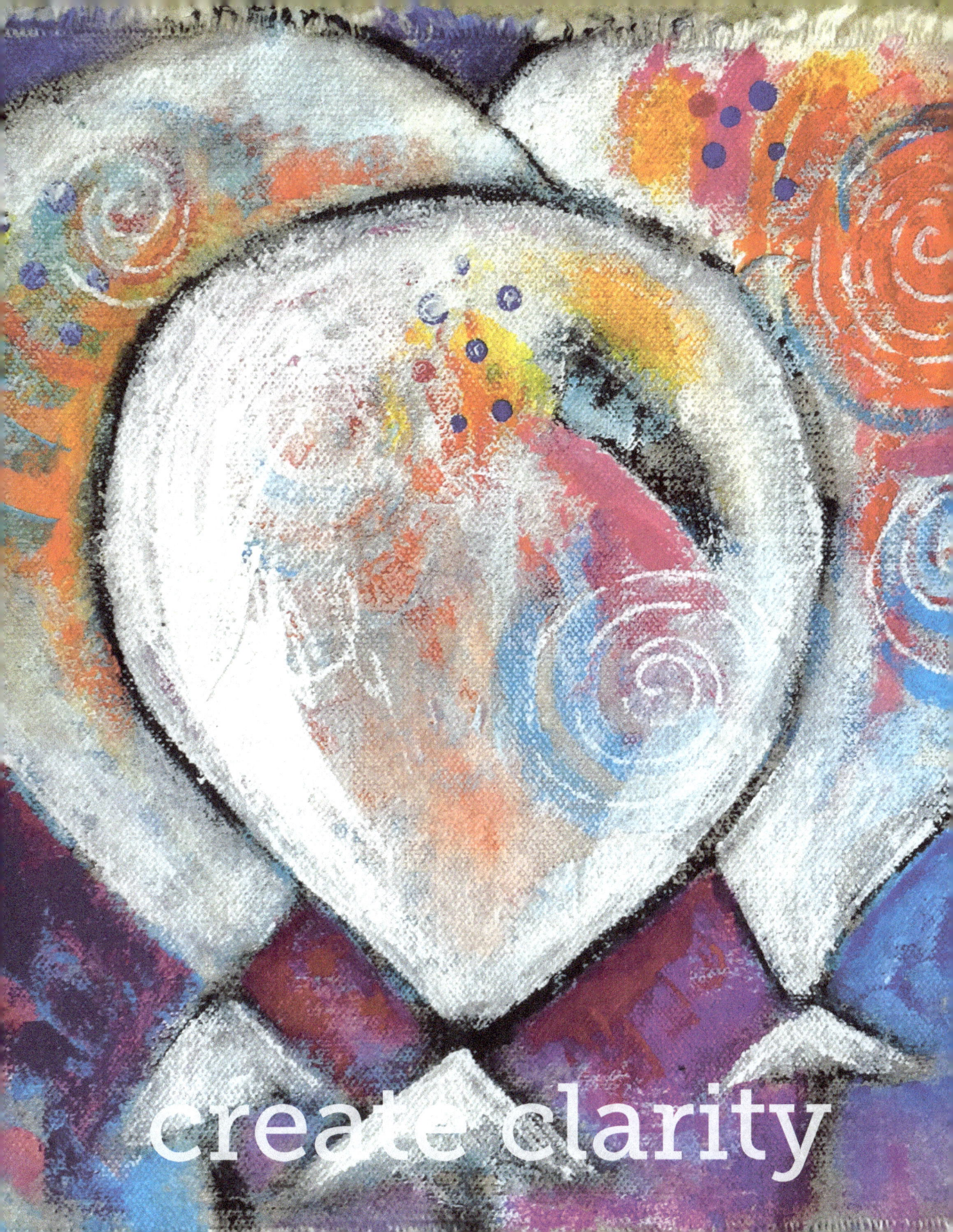

create clarity

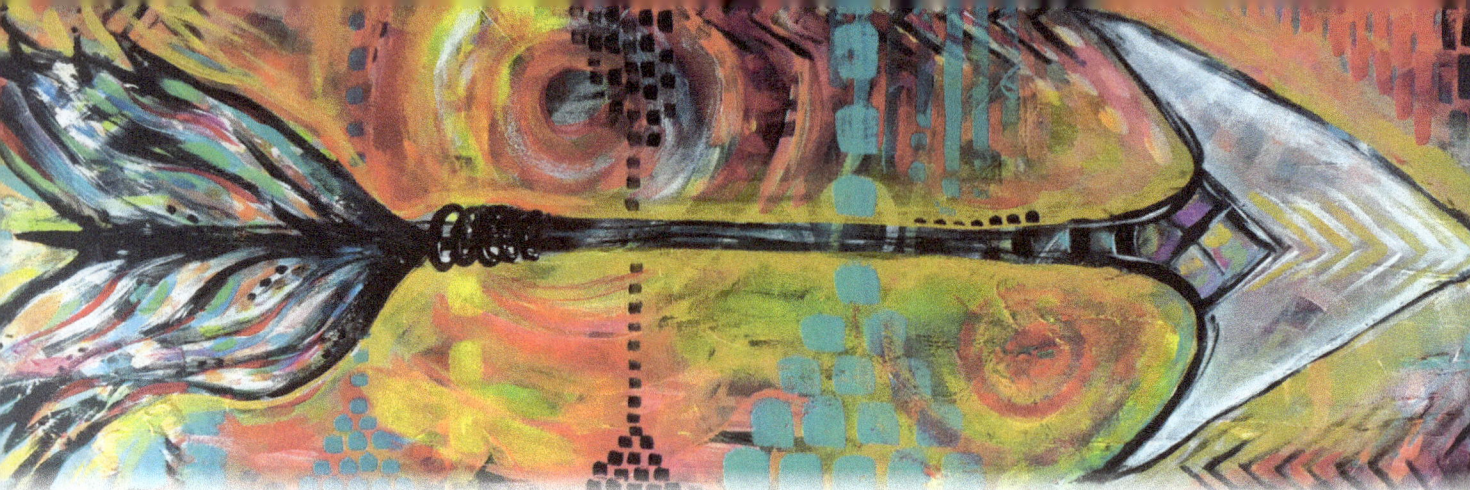

"Wow!" I have ALWAYS loved the numbers of my birthday! I am born on the first day of July. The message I got from my soul was that I have ALWAYS loved the energy of numbers, ever since I was old enough to know my birthday. NOW I have an entirely new energy and confidence around my ability to grow my business into bigger and bigger numbers!

To give you even more examples, I am going to take a leap and share with you the three parts of my life, from the Spring of 2014, that I wanted to imagine being different.

## But first, maybe these are some of your imaginings...

"I really want a partner that makes me feel good about myself, who celebrates my passions, BUT... I am stuck financially, my friends will hate me if I leave this relationship, what would I do on my own?"

"I really want to be in great physical shape, BUT I can't give up eating those things I love. I have tried before and always ended up back here, and I will never be able to look the way I want..."

"I really want to grow my business, BUT I can never get all the details together professionally. I am really not even qualified. There is so much competition already, and I probably wouldn't be that great at it, anyway..."

## Why do we allow our minds to trap us where we don't want to be when we are here to explore possibility?

*There's a thought form on earth that whatever resides in the realm of imagination is "not real" or "made up." Those who belittle the workings of the imagination are limiting themselves to a purely physical-based existence.*

~DL ZETA, *THE FUTURE IS NOW*

Here are my personal imaginations:

### IMAGINATION GOAL #1

I am a regular keynote speaker to thousands alongside widely recognized leaders in the spiritual, creative, and self-realization arenas.

**LIMITING BELIEF:** I am not famous enough or a good enough speaker.

**NEW BELIEF:** I have spoken in front of thousands of people and my passion for personal creativity always takes over and is infectious.

### IMAGINATION GOAL #2

My three kids are happy, healthy, and wise. They have been able to witness their mom and dad at their best even through a divorce. In other words, I no longer worry about "screwing them up" and I choose to imagine the future I desire for them.

**LIMITING BELIEF:** Divorce screws up kids.

**NEW BELIEF:** My kids will be more emotionally intelligent and more consciously loved by both of their parents because of our divorce.

### IMAGINATION GOAL #3

I am making smart financial decisions and am creating new products and value for others around personal creativity and ritual. I am building my own home, complete with art studio teaching space and many guest quarters, in a gorgeous area where I see both water and mountains from my back porch and can walk out my door to hike for hours and hours.

**LIMITING BELIEF:** I do not have enough business sense, enough number sense, or desire to focus on money.

**NEW BELIEF:** I have been in business for over 20 years, I am passionate about serving others, and I love the energy of numbers.

Your turn.

1. Pick the three things you worry about the most and write out your NEW "Imagination Goal," and what you WANT to happen.

2. Write down your limiting belief and your new belief around your Imagination Goal. If you get stuck with either of these, proceed to the next step, the Soul Scribble, and come back to it later.

## Now, you can create your own Soul Scribbles.

1. In your journal, or any blank piece of paper, do a quick 3-second scribble with your eyes closed. This should really take only 3 seconds. If you scribble too long you end up with too many scribbles. You want space on the paper to create the symbol of your NEW belief!

2. What does the scribble make you think of? What do you see in the scribble? Spin the paper around until you see something. Know that your left brain is very likely saying things like, "See you are so bad at this you can't even see anything in the scribble." Politely let your logical mind know that it can take a well-deserved rest and that you are calling in your right brain now because this is its territory.

Following are some examples from my scribble drawings.

### IMAGINATION GOAL #1

Let me share with you why this is so magical! Remember my goal to speak in front of thousands?

Seven months after I created this Soul Scribble, I returned from Awesomeness Fest having joined an intensive, year-long coaching mentorship with Lisa

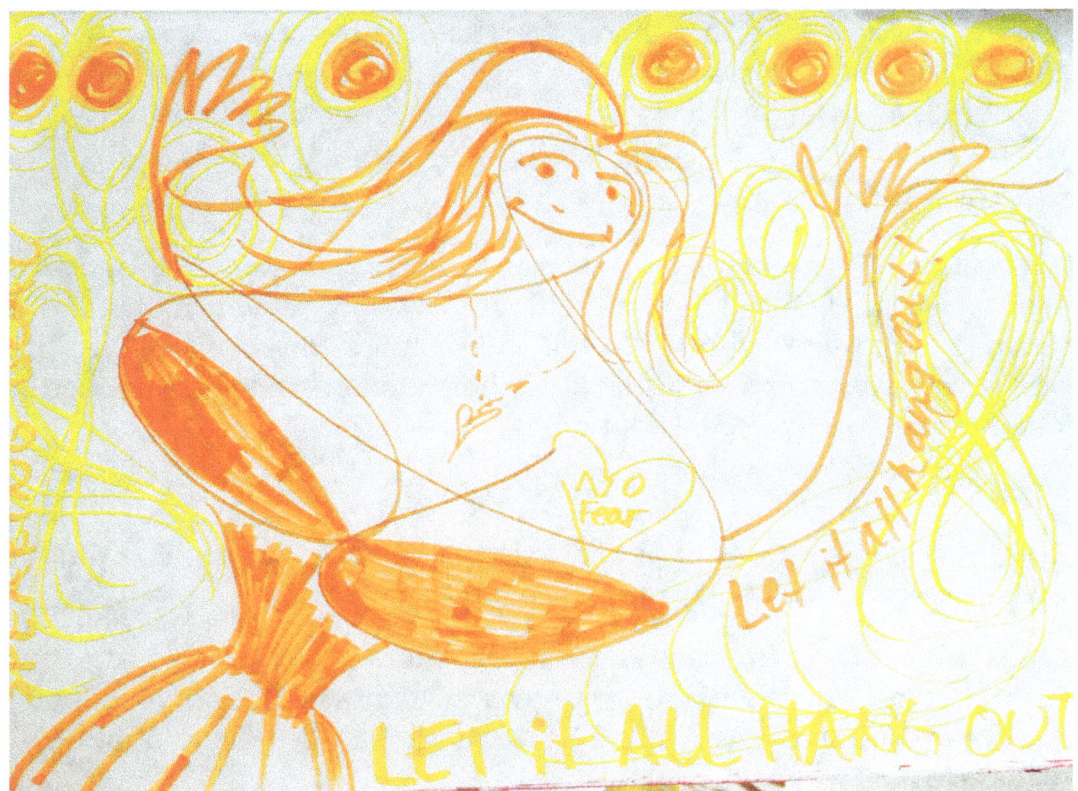

Nichols. Lisa is ALL about giving it her all, especially on stage as one of the world's top motivational speakers! I was about to be learning from the queen of "Let it all hang out!" in the speaking world. My soul knew this was coming all along—my logical mind simply had to catch up.

## IMAGINATION GOAL #2

This gave me such peace of mind.

My kids WILL learn and grow into beautiful "butterflies" but I need to allow them their own timing! My vision of my children's growth into emotional intelligence is as natural as a caterpillar evolving into a butterfly, but it takes time. Do you know that if you try to help a butterfly and spare it all that hard work of breaking out of its cocoon that it will in fact

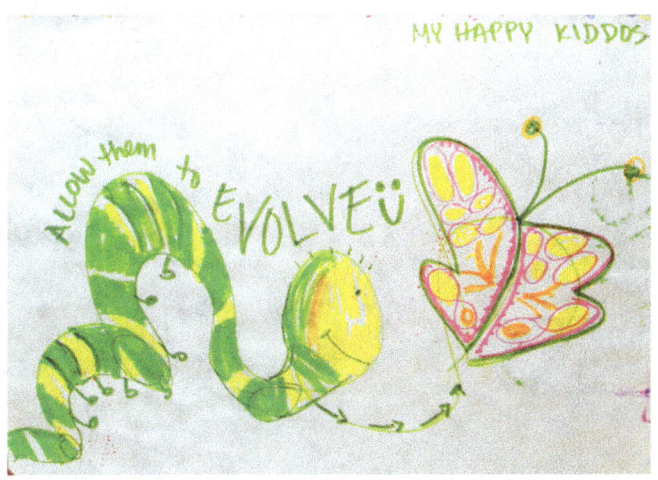

emerge fully developed and beautiful, but it will never be able to fly? It needs to develop its strength in the process of freeing itself from the cocoon. Sometimes the struggle and time IS the medicine. Phew!

## IMAGINATION GOAL #3

This scribble REALLY taught me a precious truth. Financial independence is really about FREEDOM! The balloon (another balloon, mind you) also spoke to me saying: "When you keep your vibration HIGH, you will rise above any rocky roads (and be able to help others over their own), and into the blue sky of personal freedom!

BOOM!

Create space for yourself to get honest about what is worrying you. Start with one. Now, is that REALLY what you are worried about?

For example, one of my clients told me that she was worried about her teenage son. Understandable. Whenever the worry includes another person go an extra step to ask yourself, "What am I REALLY worried about in relation to me?"

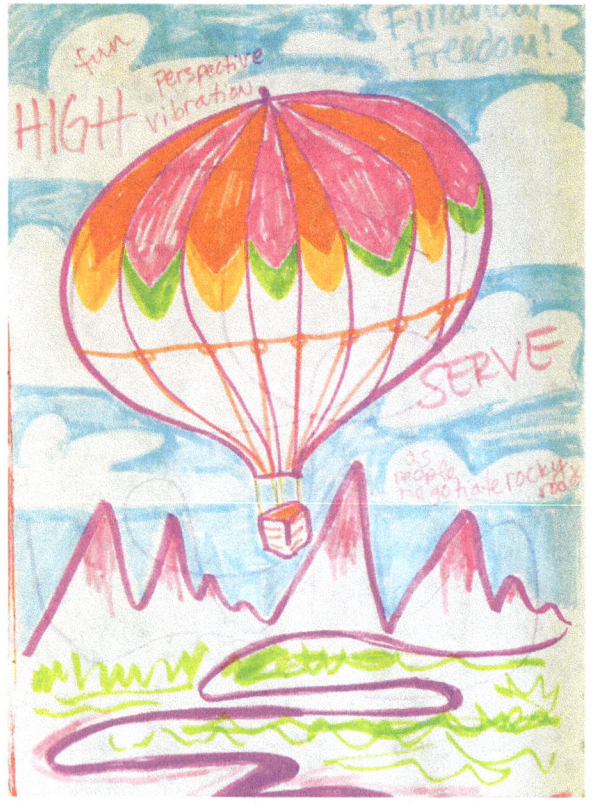

We can't control others, only ourselves. What came out is that she was really worried about not being a "good mother." Once that was out, we could create a new belief around why she is such a great "21st Century Mother." She was comparing her mothering to an old story around what makes a good mom. With her new clarity around how she was actually better preparing her son for our modern world, she was able to give herself, and her son, *space* to learn and grow without the need to control.

Her Soul Scribble showed her an image of planets orbiting around outer space. It gave her an "eagle's-eye" perspective from which she could create peace.

**Once you have your REAL worry, then you can either choose to create a new belief OR draw a Soul Scribble and ask it to illuminate the new belief for you.**

Another client was worried about having to go back into the corporate world if her own business did not succeed. We realized that she was not so worried about re-entering the corporate world—she had loved that job—as she was worried about having to go back and admit that she had "failed." The Soul Scribble showed her a big "&" symbol.

The "&" encouraged her that she did not have just two choices—fail or succeed, corporate or entrepreneurship. There were infinite (there was also an infinity sign in her Soul Scribble) ways she could expand her business AND failure is inevitable for any of us pursuing a level of personal or professional success. What do we know about failure? Everyone does it, and the most successful people have failed the most!

Now, she can imagine her infinite "&" whenever she gets worried and that shifts her imagination power to all the ways she can create what she desires.

*Symbols have NO baggage, so call in a symbol for each of your worries and allow your inner landscape to create rose-colored images of all the fun and joy you have ahead!*

# Creating the Energy of CLARITY

During your Personal Painting Practice for CLARITY you can paint a symbol from your Clarity Session, or create a symbol for clarity itself.

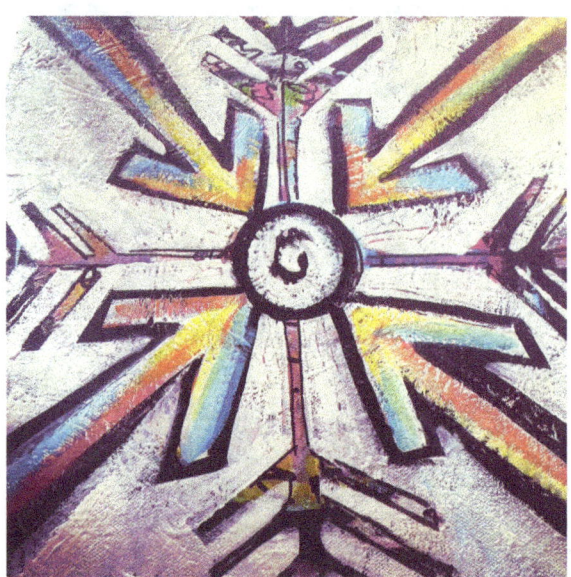

This is the symbol that I created, inspired by the energy of clarity. It's blasting out the energy of CLARITY!

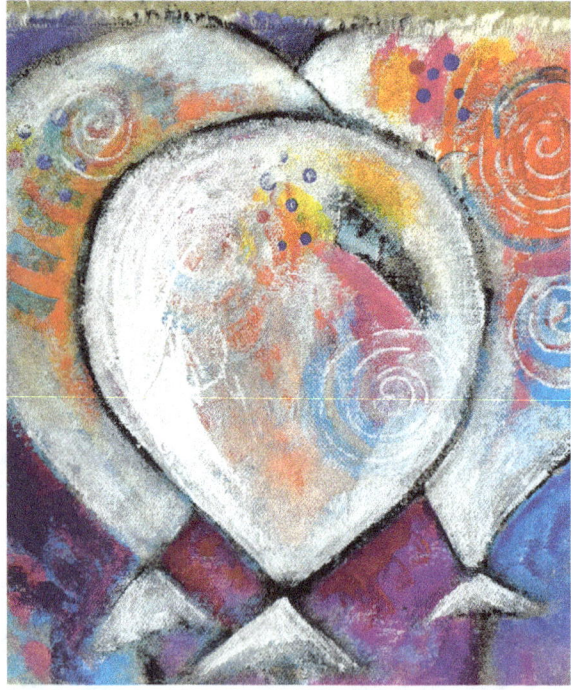

This is the painting I created to create energy and intention around my NEW BELIEF, "I love the energy of numbers."

Clarity has been a predominant theme for many of us lately.

ARROWS are everywhere, as are images of the FOX.

The arrow was my personal symbol for 2014 because my soul kept urging me, "Tell me what you WANT." That was not comfortable for me. I would rather express gratitude than want. However, when we are doing our soul's work, it is dependent on our personal will and we will experience radical shifts when we channel our soul's FLOW in a specific direction.

The Nez Perce Native American tribe, who lived where I now live in Oregon, were famous for their arrows. An arrow was never shot without careful focus, clarity, and determination.

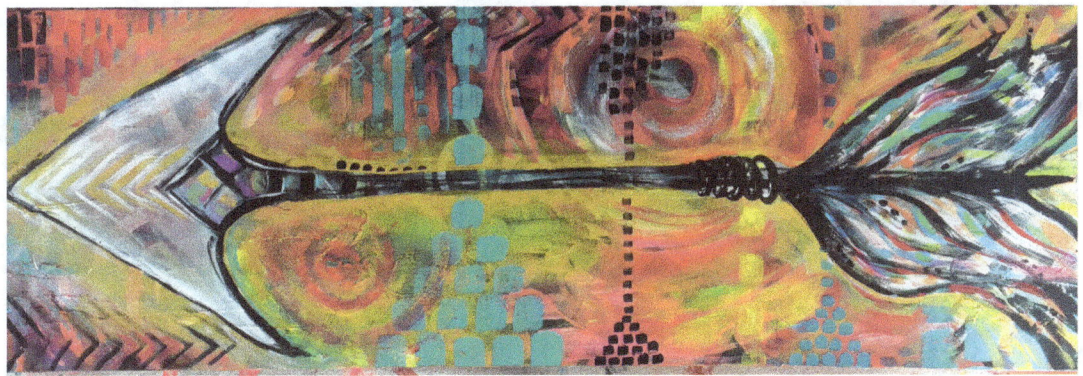

Likewise, the fox points its body like an arrow when it gets it prey in sight.

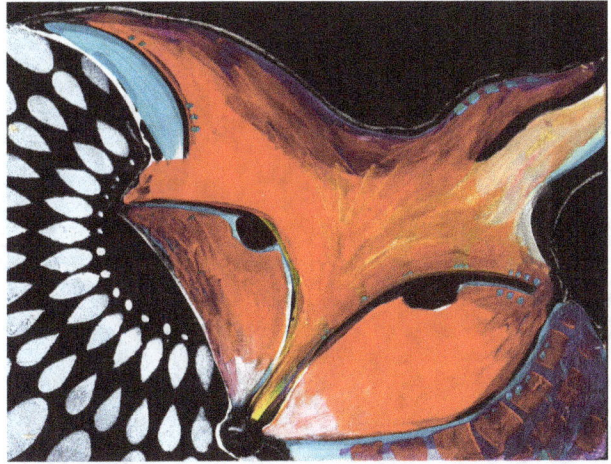

What is your canvas wanting to express to create CLARITY in the art that is your life? Paint on!

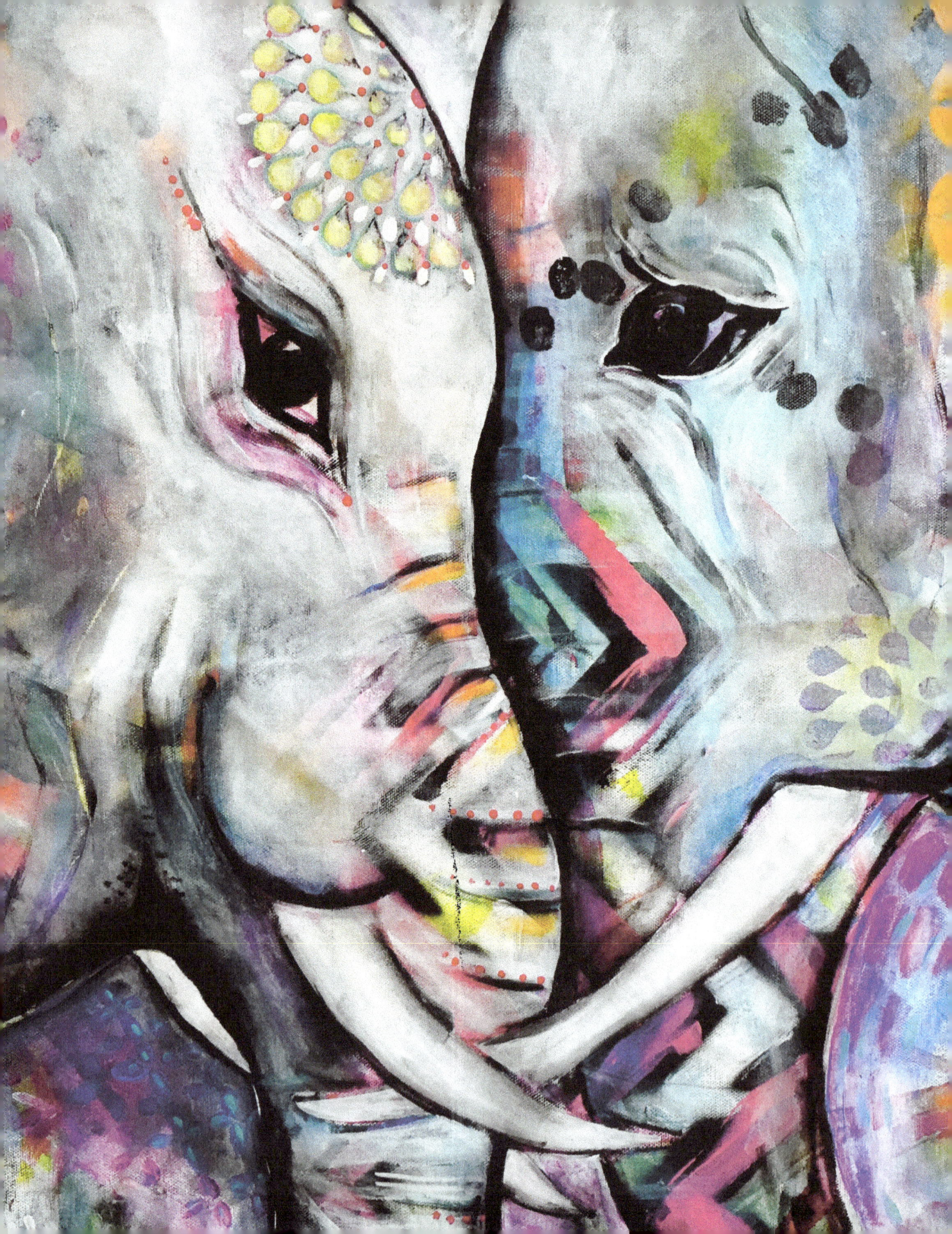

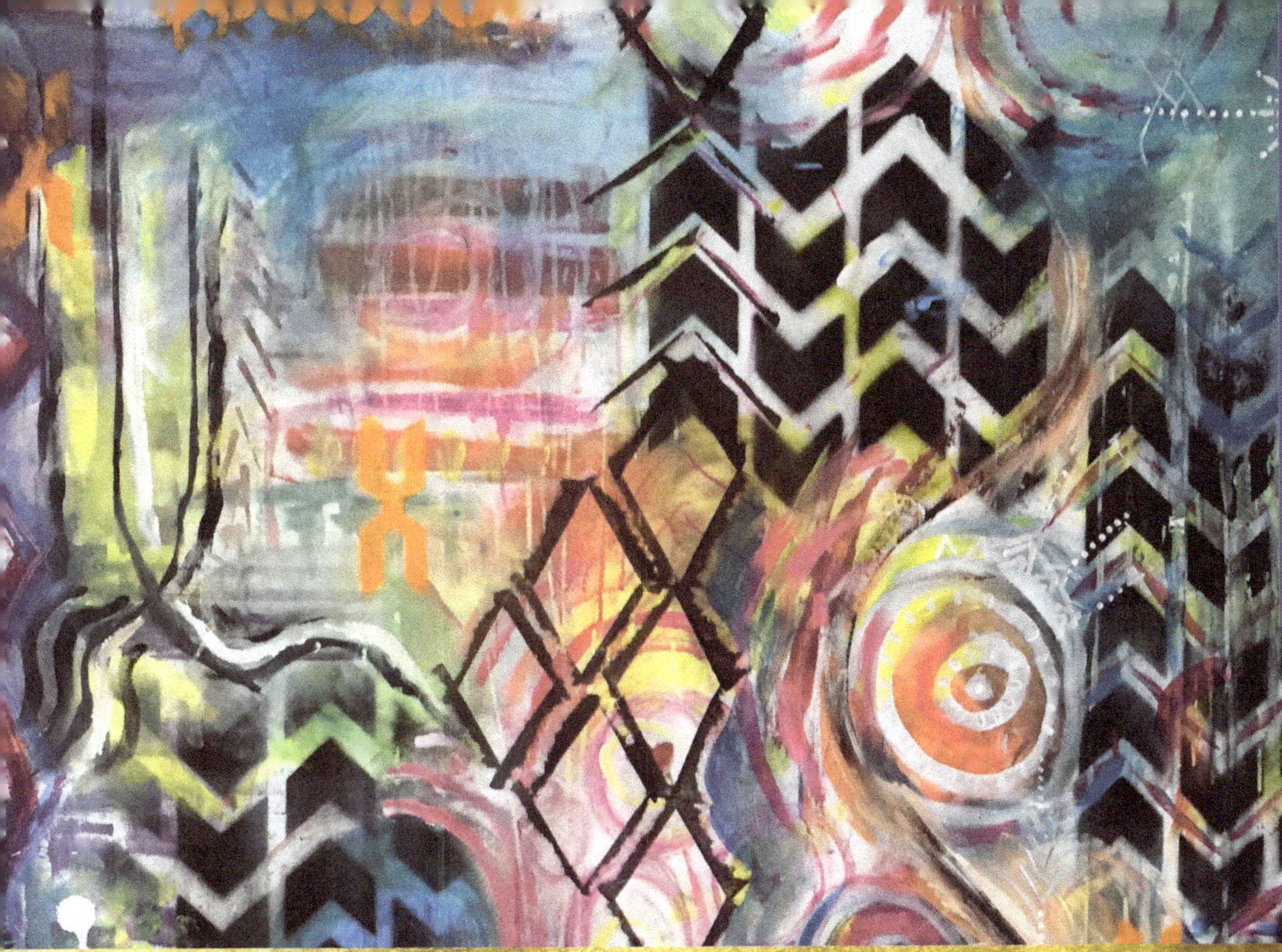

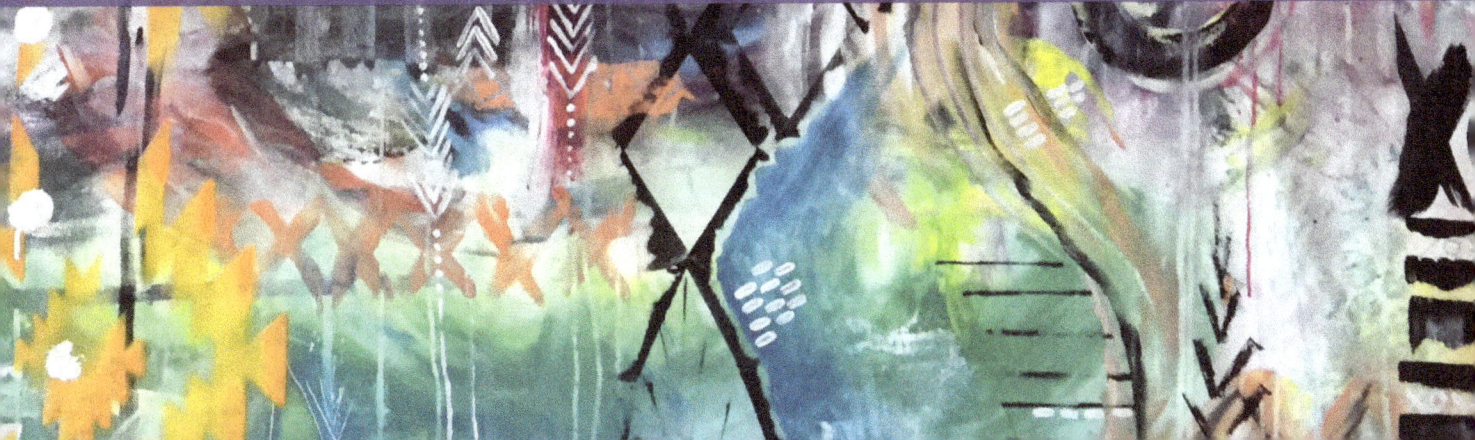

Super Soul Flow

*Intuition*

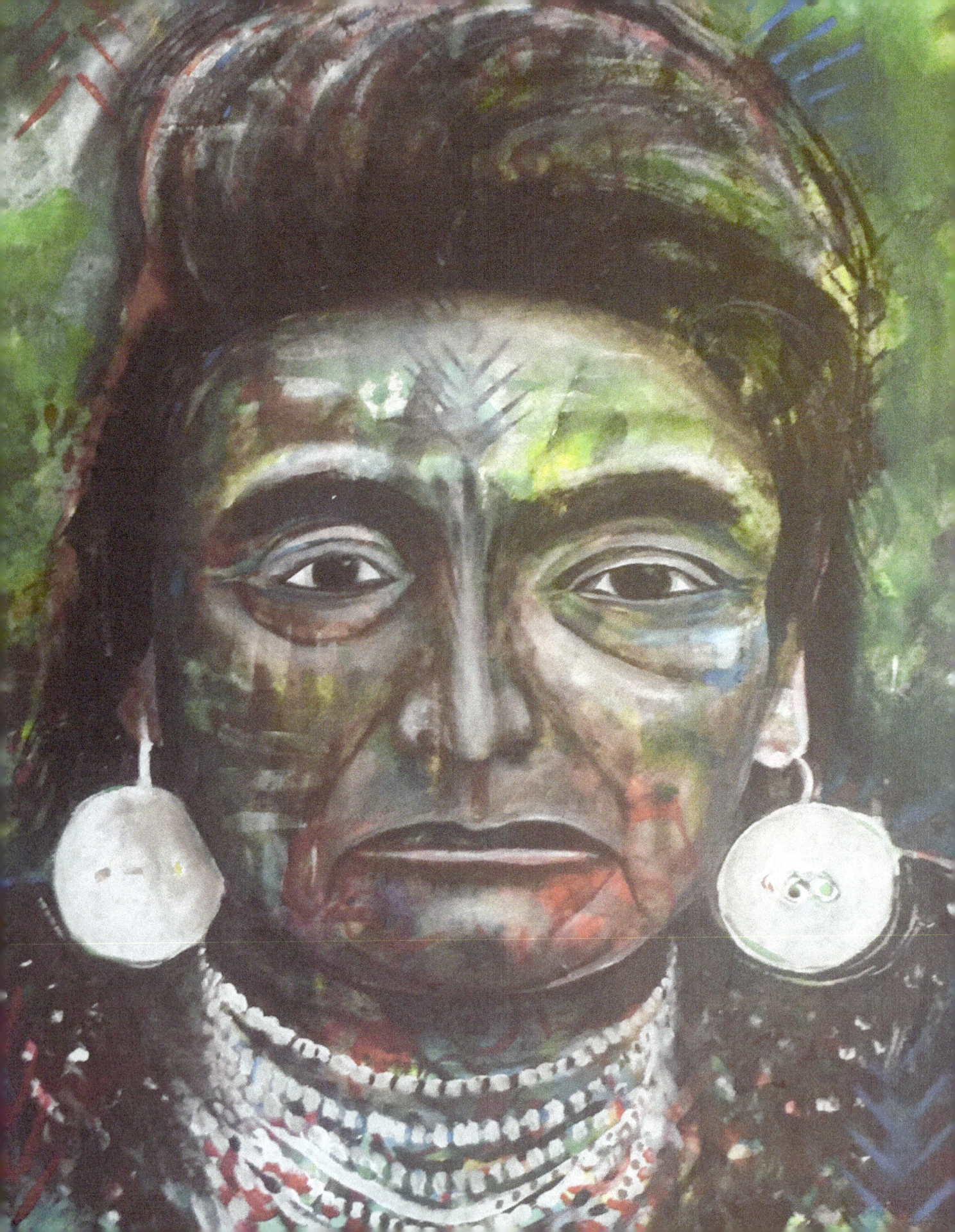

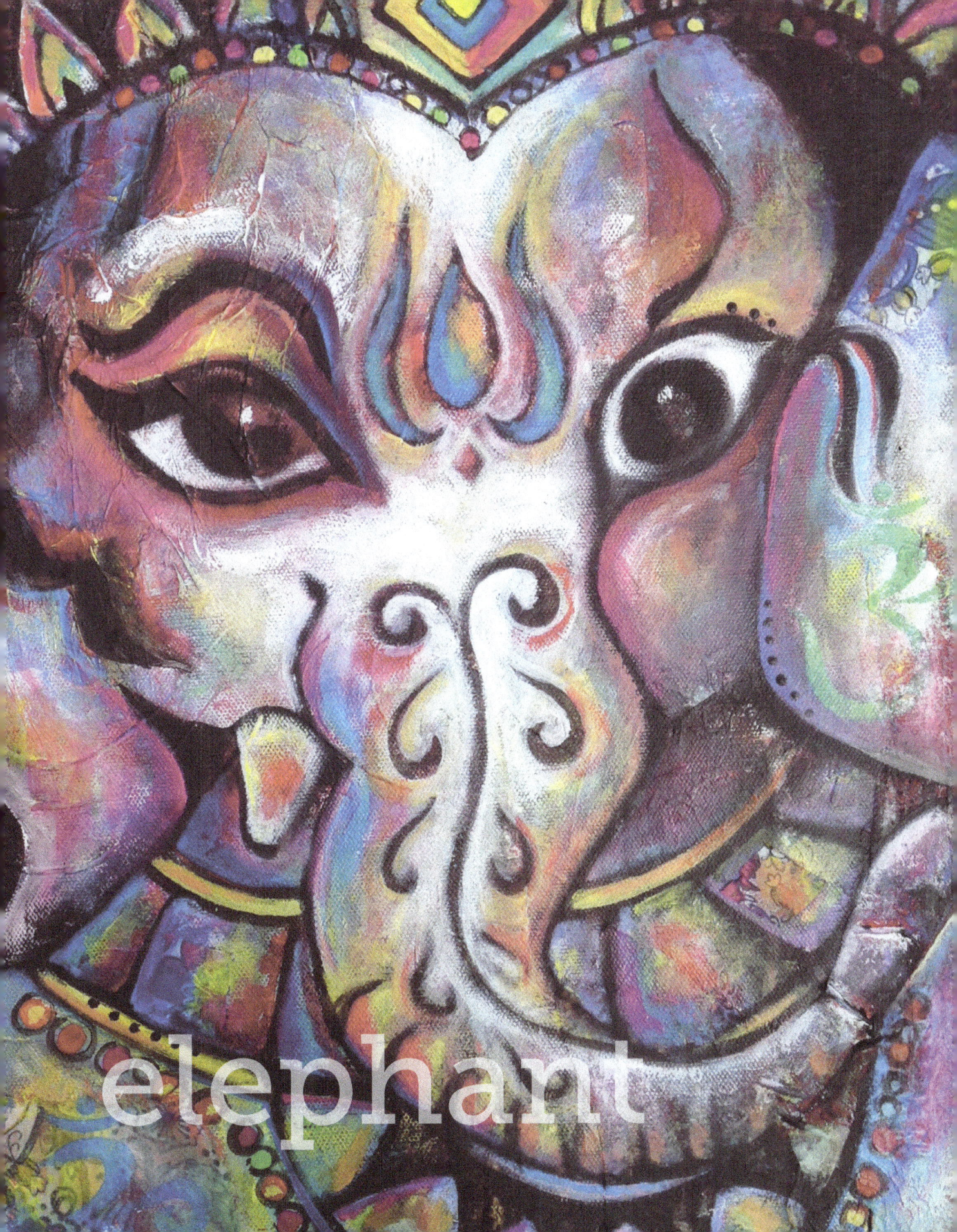
elephant

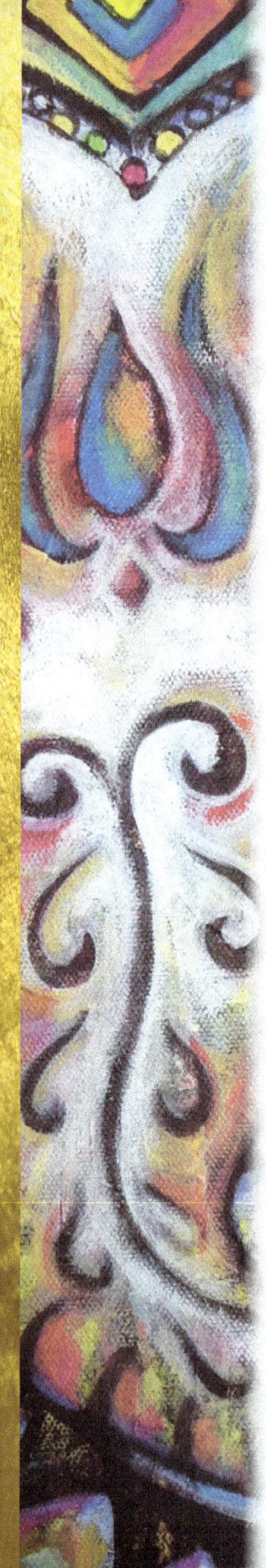

# elephant

*Mother Elephant, come to me and lend me your strength. Lend me your big love, your intuitive wisdom. Help me to bulldoze through the obstacles in front of me and to honor my highest path, my truest calling.*

*Elephants embody divine feminine love and wisdom. They are representative of the element of Earth, helping you to ground your resolve, your devotion, and inspiration into the soil of manifestation.*

*Mother Elephant gives you permission to TAKE UP SPACE. Allow your voice, your ideas, your dreams to rumble into the awareness of those around you, commanding their attention and respect. Elephant trumpets her celebration of your deep intuitive wisdom. Speak your truth into the crowd with the same resolve.*

*Painting elephants always lends me magic and courage. She creates space for my ideas to make their way out of the ethers and into my presence. The largest mammal on our planet wants to lend you her vast energy.*

SAWUBONA!
I see you

Everyday
Elephants walk thousand-year-old
paths
Embodiment of the Feminine
Our Divine Mother

Holding love on Mother Earth
Your rumbles care
Our lives are touched by
Your Unconditional Love

You teach us how to Love
That we are Self Love
That we are connected
That we belong

You bring me to Presence
to I AM

~Antonella Bargione, Creatively Fit
Coach and heART healer,
www.antonellabargione.com

*"I see you" is a Zulu greeting—
an invitation to a deep witnessing
and presence.*

*I call intuition cosmic fishing. You feel a nibble, then you've got to hook the fish..*
~BUCKMINSTER FULLER

Would you feel even more loved, safe, and supported if you knew you were being guided in each moment to the spaces, places, and people that would serve your highest and greatest good in each moment?

Would you take bolder action in your business or personal life if you had ultimate confidence that the words you would need to speak would flow through you effortlessly and the perfect wisdom for each situation would "come to mind" without any effort?

Have you ever said any of the following?

"Here is a random thought..." or

"This may sound crazy, but..." or

"I don't know why, but I feel..."

Your intuition is a voice within, a part of your being, that exists to perfectly balance your logical mind (so it is not logical) and to guide you along your master path—your highest personal expression in this lifetime.

However, this voice is subtle, often overlooked or discounted, and seldom honored by the "powers that be." And this is all about to change.

**The invitation right now is to tune into the ways your soul is whispering to you every step of your journey. It is like learning a new language. Your logical mind speaks one language; your intuitive mind speaks another.**

For example, your intuitive mind LOVES these words by Deepak Chopra from the book, *Reinventing the Body, Resurrecting the Soul, How to Create a New You:*

> *Your body is boundless. It is channeling the energy, creativity and intelligence of the entire universe.*

At this moment, the universe is listening through your ears, seeing through your eyes, experiencing through your brain. Your purpose for being here is to allow the universe to evolve. Your intuitive mind "gets this" and your logical mind will likely resist these words.

Let's explore three different ways you register INTUITION:

- Feeling
- Synchronicities and Coincidences
- Dreams and Imagination

## Feeling

Your feelings are the best portal to access your intuitive wisdom. Feelings really exist—you don't think and THEN feel. Feelings happen spontaneously and represent an unfiltered, higher perspective—a perspective not dependent on the logical mind, your past experience, or fears of the future.

Feelings are truth.

> *Your body's whole purpose is to join the visible and the invisible realms, and intelligence isn't the only force that wants to express itself through you. So do creativity, truth, beauty and love. To have a breakthrough, you must consciously connect with the invisible forces that are everywhere around you… urging you to go beyond your old conditioning.*
>
> *~Deepak Chopra*

*The Law of Attraction* explains how feeling and intuition are interconnected. Your soul communicates to you very clearly—if you understand its language.

This soul-level '…communication takes many different forms. It may come to you in the form of a clear, vivid thought, but in all cases, it comes to you in the form of emotion. Before you emerged, you set forth an agreement that communication with your Inner Being would exist. And it was agreed that it would be a feeling, one that could not be missed, rather than a stimulation of thought or an offering of words that could be missed."

Tapping into your feelings is easier when you spend time bringing yourself present and into stillness with your Personal Painting Practice. Take a time out and ask yourself these questions.

**QUESTIONS:**

1. How does each choice I am looking at feel? Really sink into the vision of each scenario that is be presented in front of you. What are the feelings that arise? Where do you feel them? Stomach? Heart?

2. Where is the energy? Which choice gets me the most excited, or the most scared? Where do I feel anticipation, nervousness? Is this feeling here to guide me in another direction or bring me present, wake me up, to prepare me to cross a threshold?

3. What do I *really* want right now? Deep desires and longings are often divinely placed to motivate you in a certain direction. It doesn't always feel comfortable because that is the desire of your logical mind.

## Synchronicities & Coincidences

*There are no coincidences.*

We all know this statement. But can you really accept that this is true? What will it take to open up even more to embracing the part of you that is infinite and energetic? Once you do you can FEEL into the future and follow the prompts you are being given through synchronicities and coincidences.

Your intuition is the part of you that literally can see the future.

The Global Consciousness Project actually registered a change in human consciousness around the events of 9/11 in the moments, even the hours, before the tragedy happened. A National Geographic article by Patrick J. Kiger, published ten years after the attack, reports a noticeable surge in energy. That's intuition!

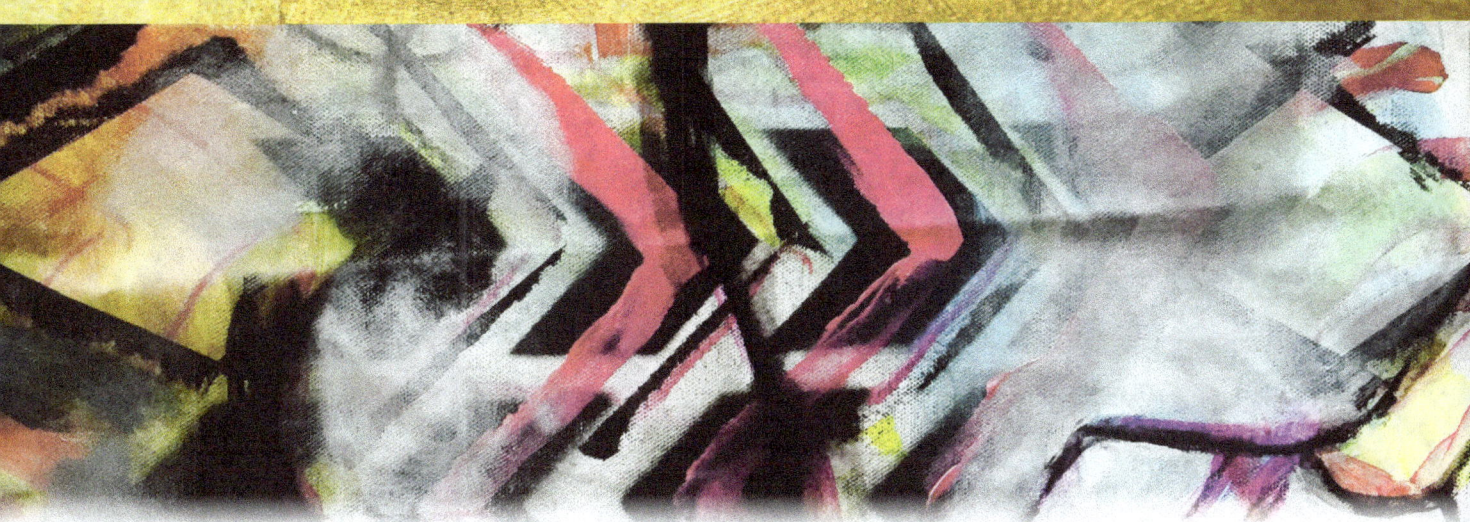

You pick up on feelings, intuition, and guidance BEFORE events in your life manifest in the physical, linear reality.

When I decided to open a wine bar with my art center partner in 2004, with three kids under the age of six and a tight budget, it was because of a flash of understanding I received clear as day: "The wine bar is what leads to my published book." It became clear quickly that I had, in that moment, remembered my future.

That was exactly what happened, although I don't recommend opening restaurants to get book deals. I signed my book deal within two years of that intuitive thought! These kinds of "synchronicities" can offer you invaluable insight into your highest course of action.

Anything repeated just twice is a message. Have you ever said, "I am seeing _____ all over the place all of a sudden"? Or have you had two or more people mention the same thing "randomly" to you? Pay attention.

Next time someone "randomly crosses your mind" reach out to them (whether you are thinking about a particular question or they simply float into your mind while you are driving, walking, doing the dishes...). There is absolutely a reason they are coming to your mind. Give them a call!

Ask your soul for a clue to help you decide or gain clarity in the next 24 hours and then pay attention to what happens.

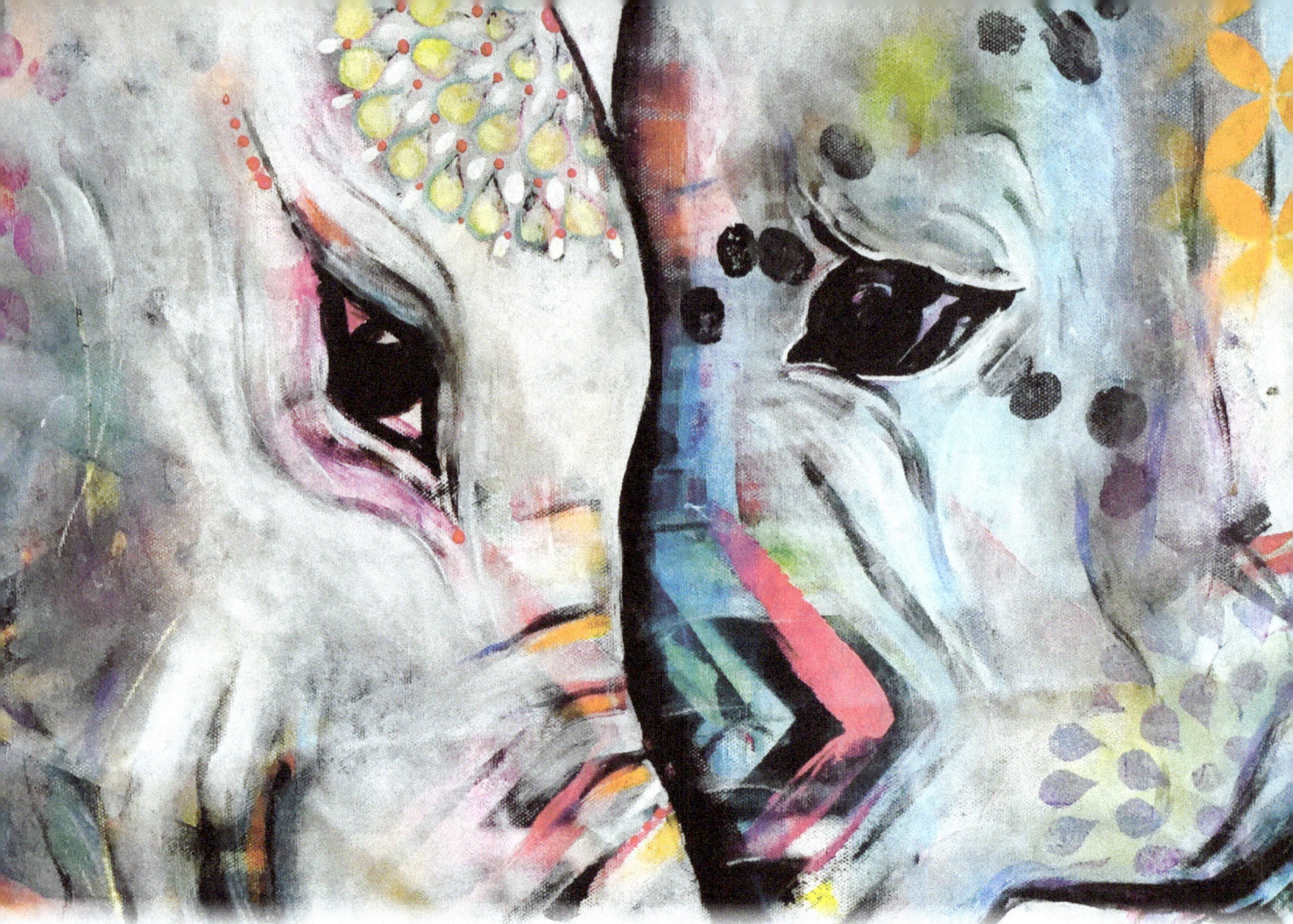

When I received a long, passionate email from a woman in Nigeria asking me if I had an "African branch" and imploring me to help the women of Nigeria, I knew to wait 24 hours to respond.

My left brain (ego) immediately thought, "Ha! A branch? We've got no business helping women in Nigeria." Your left brain wants to keep you safe in the known, remember?

Within 24 hours, in my county of only 7,000 people in Northeast Oregon, TWO people "randomly" brought up Nigeria to me! As a result, I paid attention to the email. That email became the spark that ignited my entire Creatively Fit Coaching Certification Program that now has over 200 trained coaches all over the world!

## Dreams & Imagination

A seer is a dreamer who has mastered the dream, who has learned to see. Artist, dreamer, messenger, seer—there are so many ways to name you. I prefer to call you an artist because your whole creation is a masterpiece of art.

~DON JOSE RUIZ, *THE FIFTH AGREEMENT*

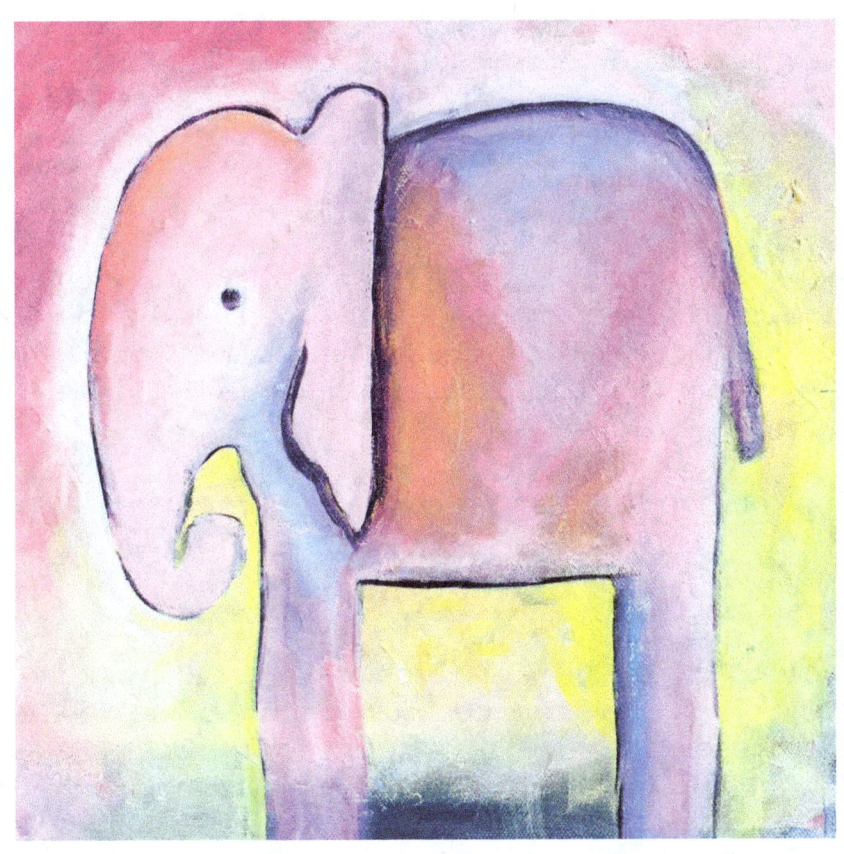

Personally, I understand that my sleeping dreams can be the "monkey mind" dreams, the "teaching dreams" and, my favorite, the lucid dreams where I am clearly being shown new steps to take in my life. The message becomes crystal clear as I share the dream with someone else verbally or write it out in my journal. Waking dreams are when you catch your mind wandering to something totally unrelated to whatever you are doing. These "day dreams" can share guidance with you, too.

Do you have a hard time remembering your dreams? Ask to remember them each night before bed and keep a journal handy to record any glimpses. You can strengthen your dream-remembering muscle!

In the spring of 2011, just before moving to Oregon, I had a very lucid dream in which I was sitting with one of my Creatively Fit Coaches explaining that we now prescribed symbols to our clients to help them to align with new levels of self-confidence and belief around whatever they wanted in their life. Four months later I started painting sacred symbols for my own guidance and everything has changed since then!

I now have a line of ARTual Sacred Symbol Stencils, this book, and a reservoir of teaching and experiences around connecting you to divine guidance through sacred symbols. All of that was seeded in my consciousness in that one dream!

## Imagination is our internal paintbrush of possibility.

Imagination is one of your Super Powers. The question is whether you choose to use this power for "good" or "evil". Do you use your precious imagination to picture or worry about what you DON'T want to happen? Or do you choose to focus your imaginative powers in the direction of WHAT YOU WANT?

With both dreams and imagination, it is important to understand what quantum physicists have proven, "The brain does not distinguish between real and imagined events."

What do you worry about? As we explored in the Clarity chapter, instead of focusing on the worst-case scenarios, what are all the ways you can spend time sending energy to creating images in your mind around what you most DESIRE to happen in that situation? Imagine THAT! Imagine what you want to happen in as much detail as possible. Today during your Personal Painting Practice, bathe yourself in the energy of your BEST-case scenario visions!

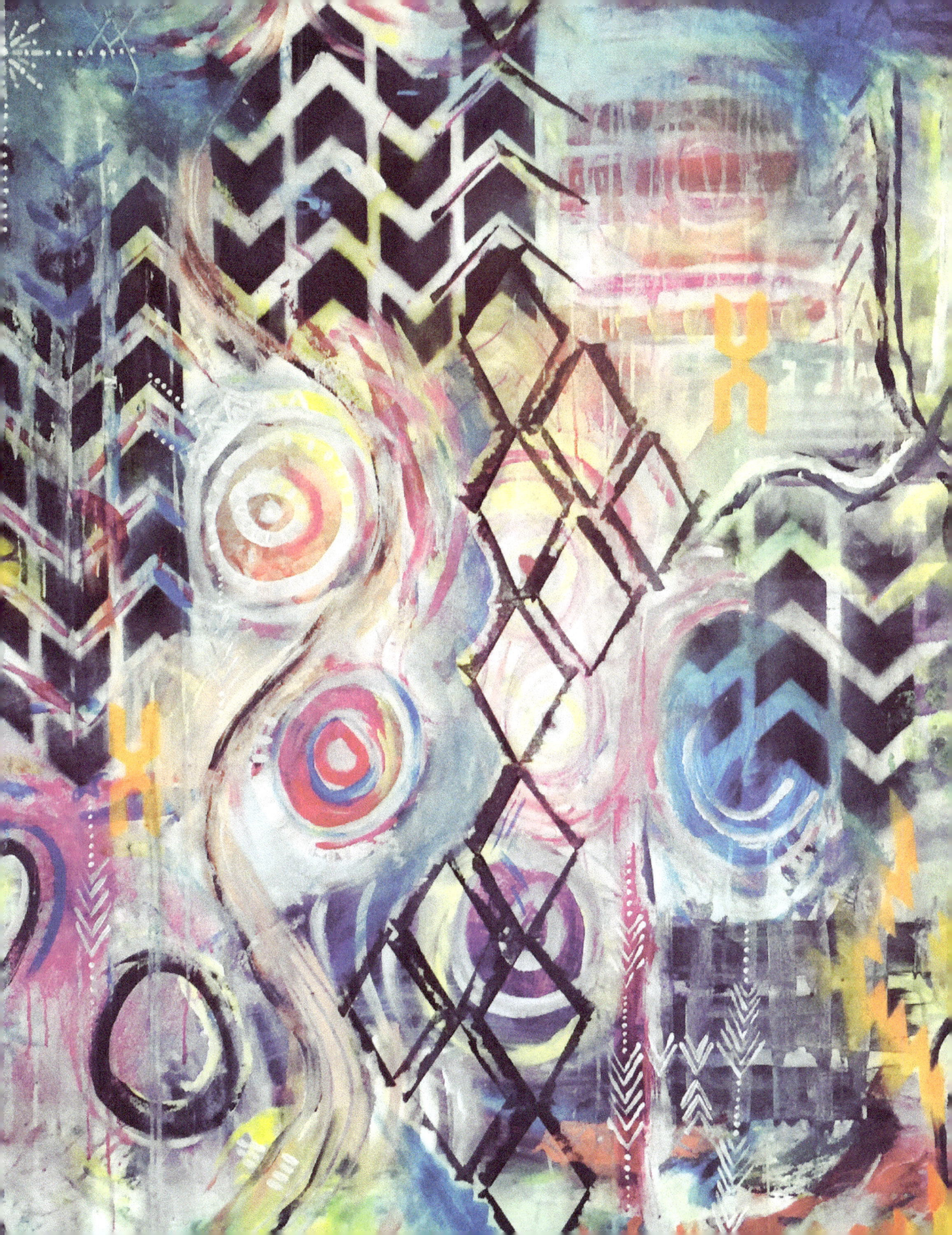

# Creating the Energy of INTUITION

**To create more SPACE for your intuitive voice, you'll paint an ELEPHANT and/or the most powerful sacred symbol of the TRIPLE SPIRAL.**

Everyone loves elephants! Painting them is even more fun.

Why are elephants a powerful symbol of intuition? An elephant never forgets! That statement that we have all heard many times truly illuminates the intuitive nature of these magical beings.

Have you heard the story of Lawrence Anthony, aka The Elephant Whisperer, whose death was mourned by a herd of elephants he had healed years before? (www.beliefnet.com)

TWO herds of elephants that had been released from Anthony's elephant sanctuary over one and a half years earlier, traveled an estimated twelve hours to his rural home in the vast Thula Thula reserve in South Africa, just a couple of days after he died. How did the elephants know? What inspired these elephants to circle around Anthony's home and spend two days there to honor their hero? It can only be explained on an intuitive level.

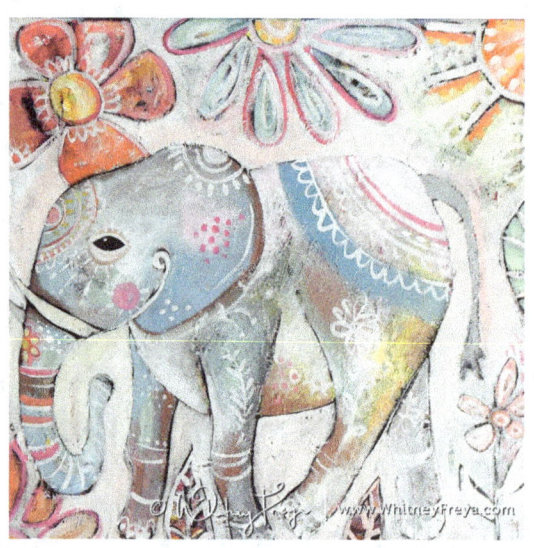

Allow elephant energy to permeate your consciousness as you paint today during your Personal Painting Practice. Here is some inspiration…

Remember, it is the LAYERS that create such interest and movement in your paintings. The more sessions you spend at your canvas, adding to your elephant painting, the deeper both the physical experience and the intuitive experience will travel.

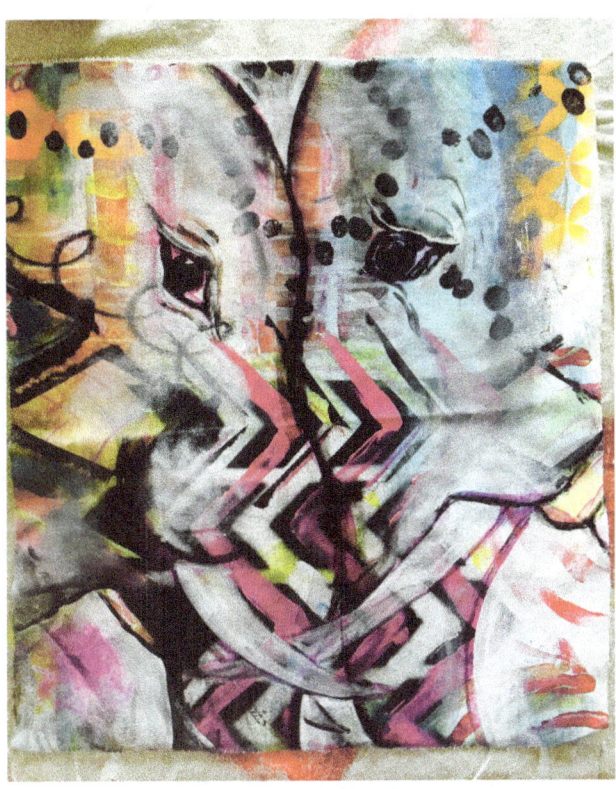

In this painting you can really see how the first layer of FUN is showing through and complimenting the final design.

Here, I painted a triple spiral and then an elephant appeared from within the spirals! LOVED that!

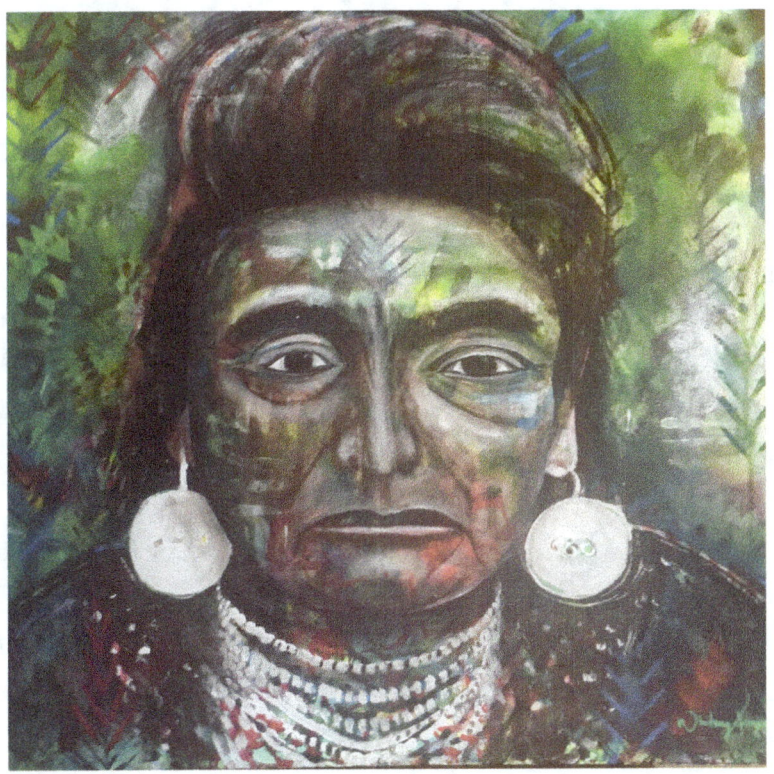

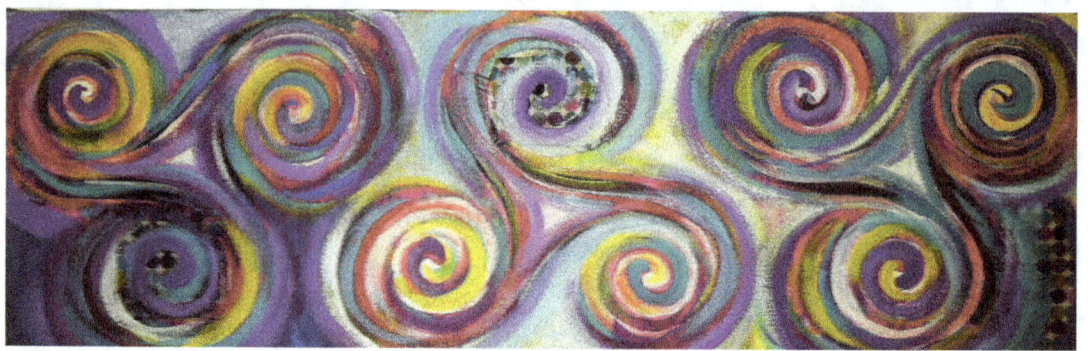

The triple spiral is an ancient symbol, carved into the stone walls of a cave in Newgrange, Ireland dedicated to the Goddess thousands of years ago. I imagine myself in the center, with these three infinite, energetic arms spiraling out into the Universe gathering to me whatever guidance or insight will serve me.

As you paint, send out your own spiral energy with clear intentions around what you desire to attract into your life experience.

What I know without a doubt is that the more you paint, the more intuitive you become, both in painting and in living.

I believe that when people become "better" at painting, they really become more intuitive. You learn to trust that initial urge to reach for the blue or paint that particular curve onto the canvas, rather than thinking... wondering what to do... worrying that you are doing it wrong.

Painting intuitively, your brush skips across the canvas, touching down without conscious thought, to create the change it desires on your canvas.

As you connect to this feeling of intuitive action on your canvas, you will find yourself receiving its wisdom and guidance in your day-to-day reality.

## It is the ACTION of painting that creates new neural pathways—to the often latent recesses of your mind.

Simply spending time at the canvas, in the present moment, and connected to your Creator Self, will absolutely increase your intuitive abilities.

I can't wait to see your elephants and spirals!

# Super Soul Flow Challenge: Step 3

How is your new space evolving? Imagine that it will never finish. It will be a continuous flow of new beginnings. As you create and then attract the energy you choose into your space, life will expand accordingly. Then, the time will come when a new feeling or energy is calling to you and you can begin the process again. For example, I painted on top of several of my previously completed paintings after I chose to become single again—as I adjusted to my new life and stepped up to new and different thresholds.

1. Get excited to experience how your paintings can shift your experience in your space.

2. Resist the urge to judge or quantify your paintings and progress. "What do I want to create right now?" That is the best question.

3. Bring this "layer" of your Super Soul Flow Challenge to a level of "completion." Add final touches to each painting. Maybe as time passes, and your paintings hang on the wall at whatever stage, you are called to paint new colors, or add a symbol, to fall in love with it even more.

4. Look at your "before" picture and take a step back to appreciate how your space feels different with its energetic makeover.

5. Share your images of your new space with me on social media or connect at **whitneyfreya.com.**

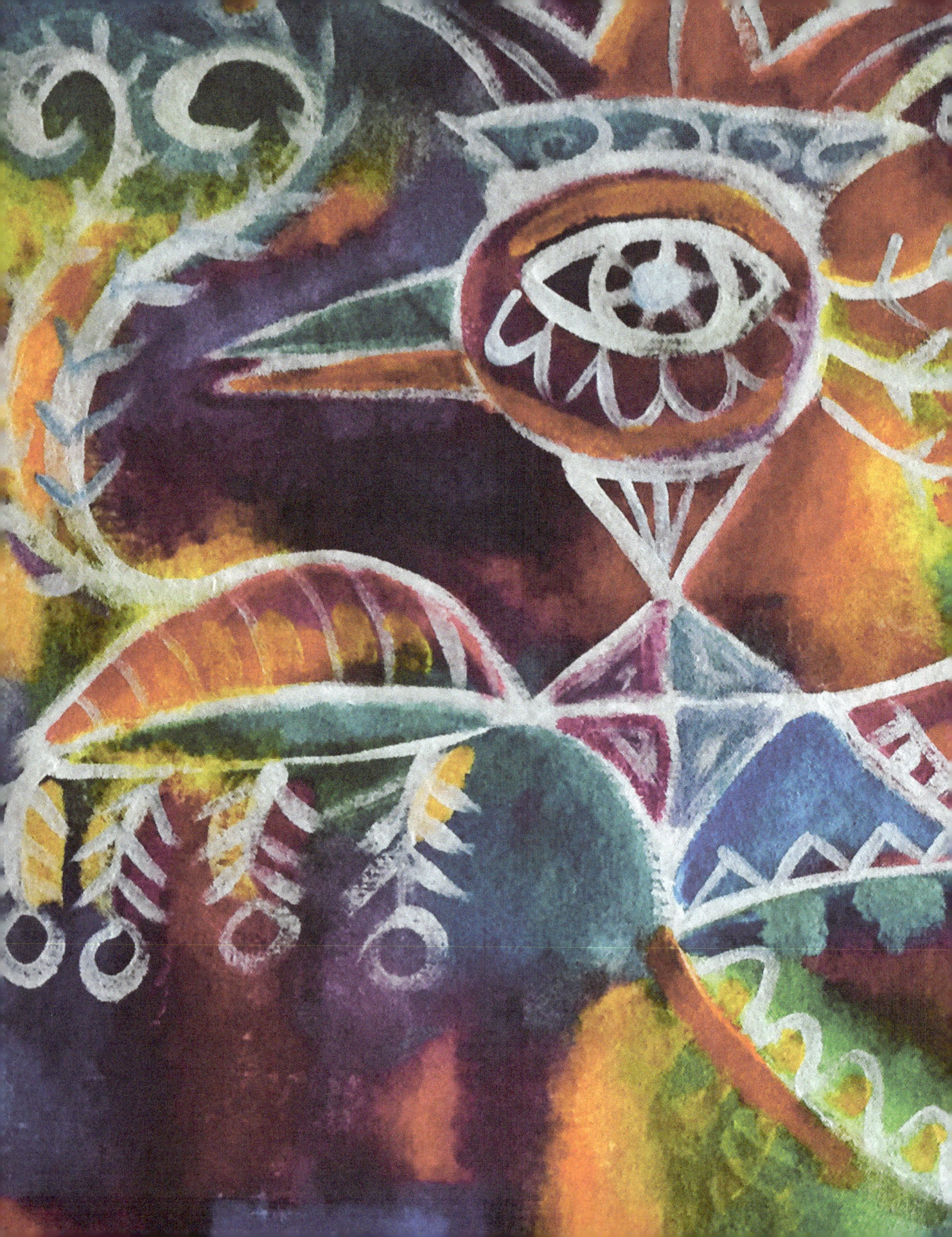

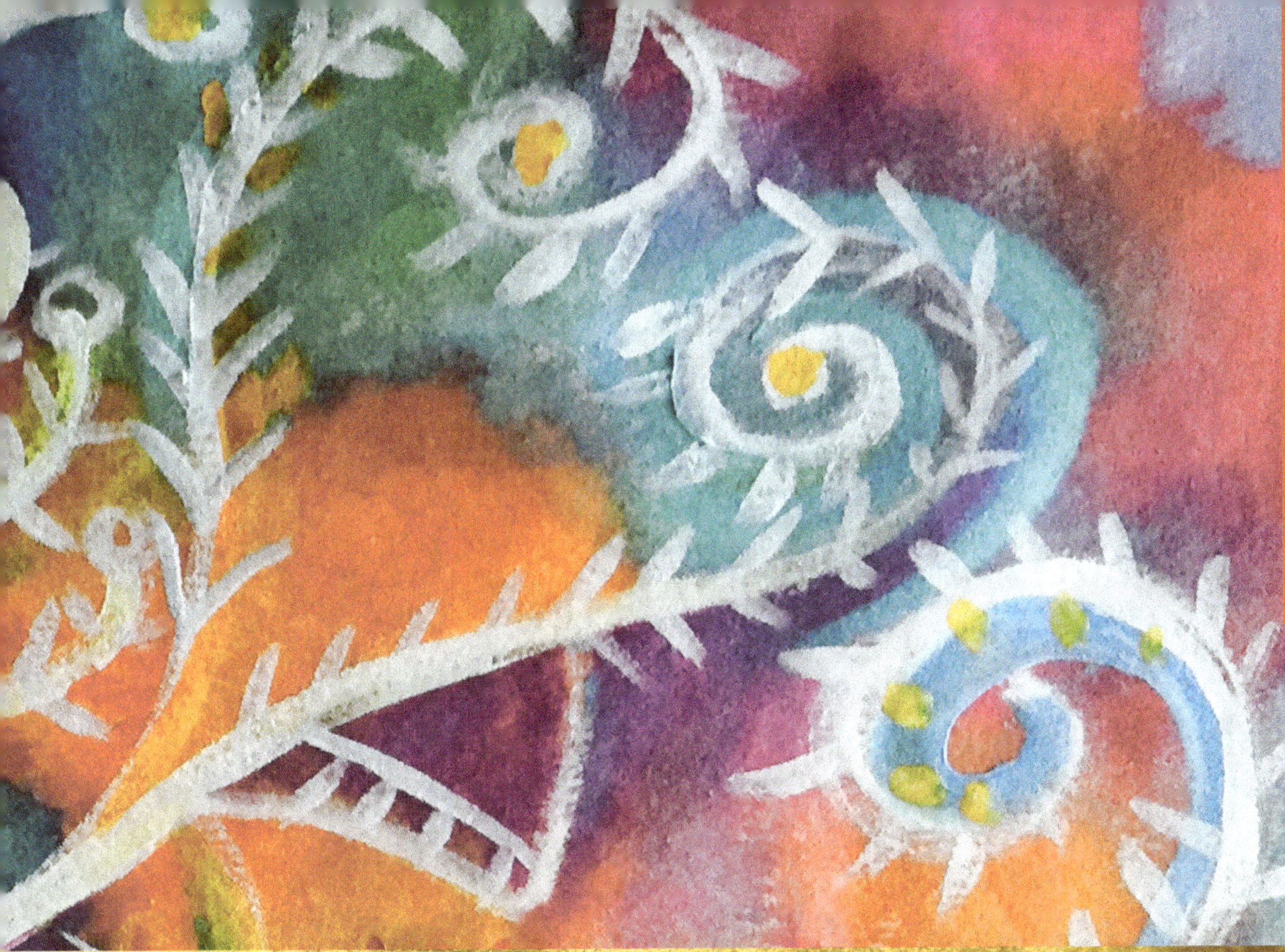

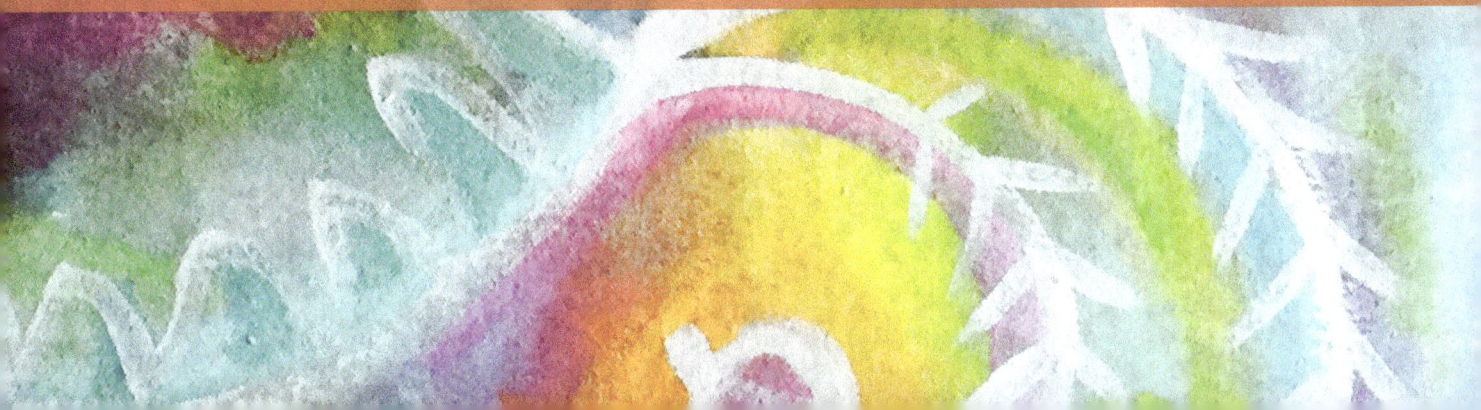

Super Soul Flow

*Spaciousness*

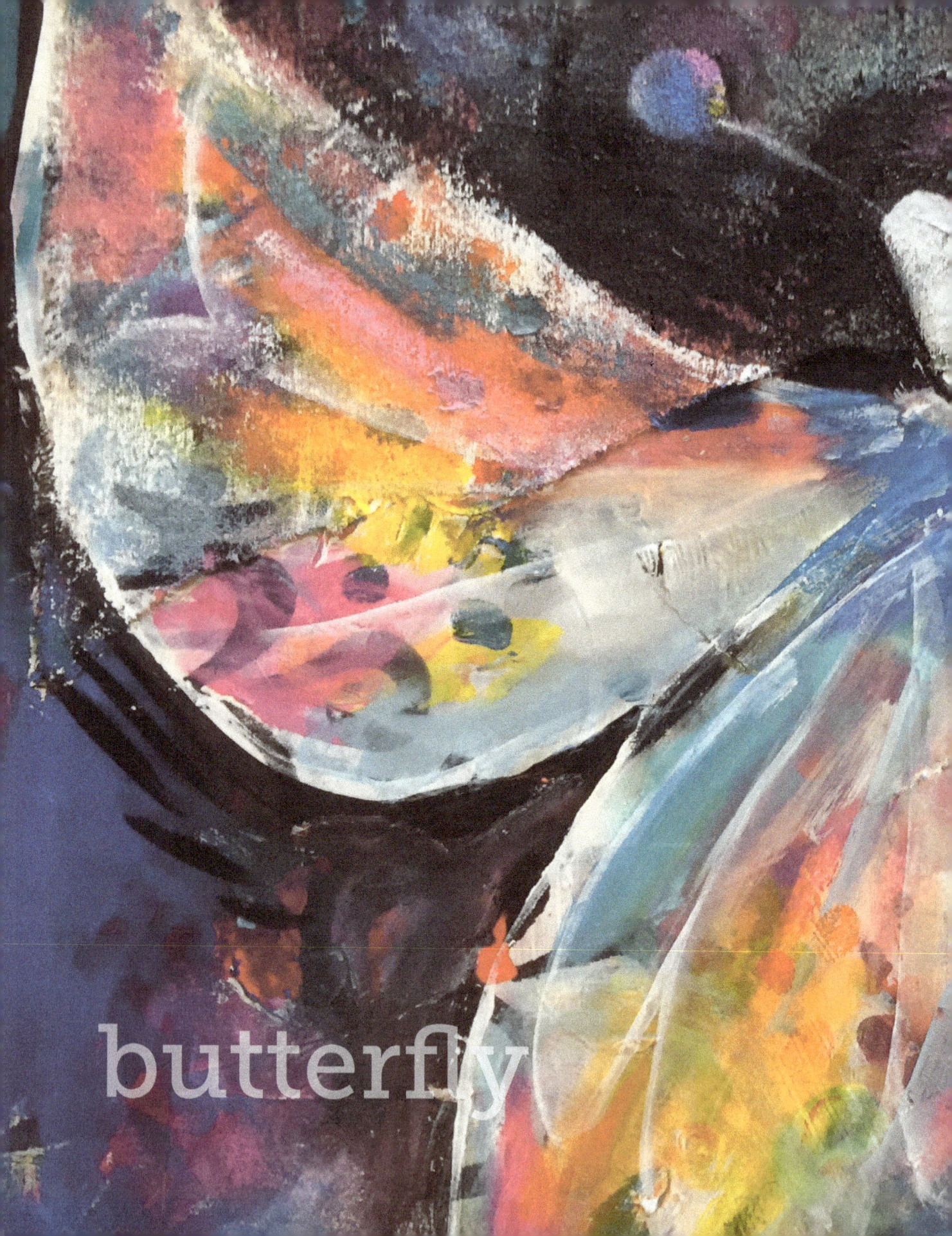

butterfly

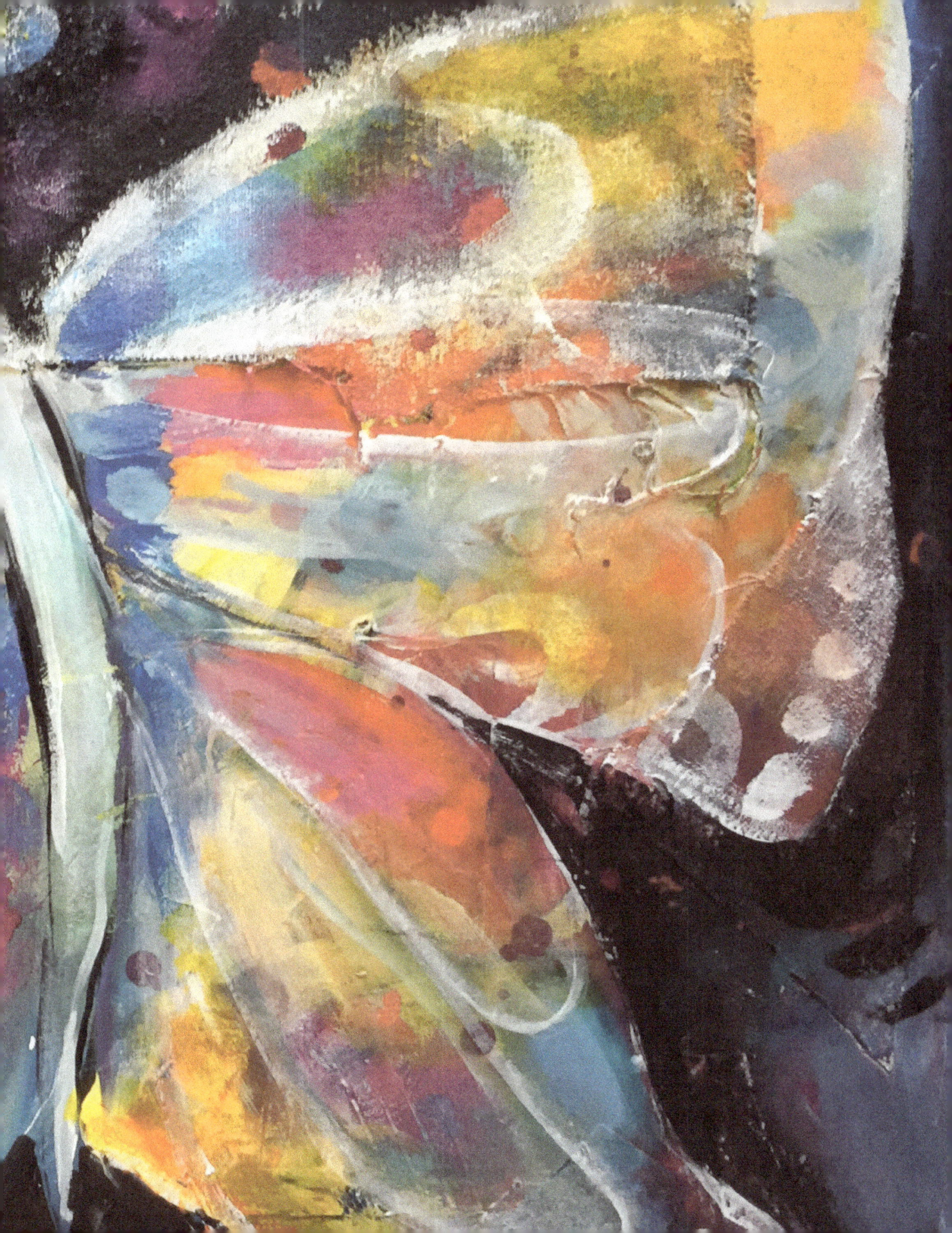

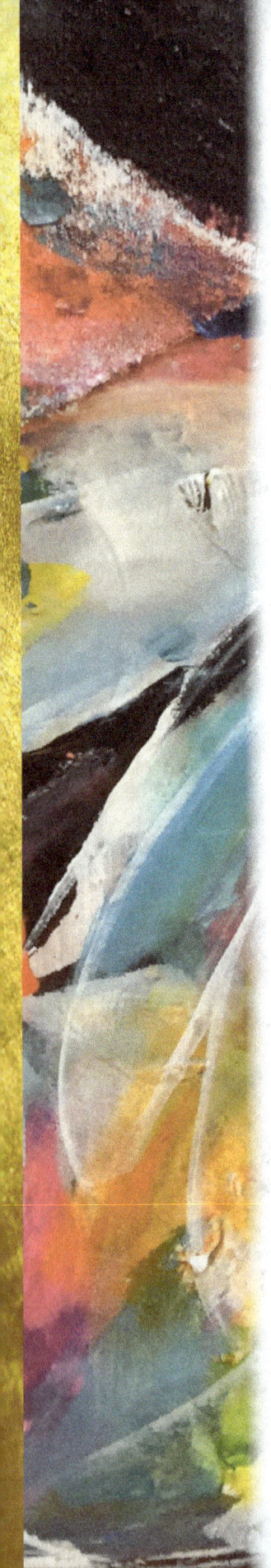

# butterfly

*Butterflies never seem to be in a hurry. Their flight is almost skipping, lightly bouncing through the sky, exploring each colorful blossom or inviting leaf. They don't zoom from plant to plant, they meander. Butterfly encourages you to enjoy the journey and to take your time.*

*My favorite lesson from the butterfly is the relationship between divine timing and its basic survival. In the final stages of development within the cocoon, butterfly flexes its wings over and over, gradually breaking free of the cocoon. However arduous a task it may be to break through the hundreds— or thousands—of silken threads in which it is encapsulated, its greatest reward would never be realized if it skipped any of this process. It can only fly because of the time spent in struggle to liberate itself from the cocoon. The struggle is what strengthens its wings SO that it can fly.*

*Likewise, butterfly is here to reassure you that within your struggles is the beginning of your next opportunity to RISE ABOVE!*

My soul sent me a muse today

to sprinkle some magic into my routine.

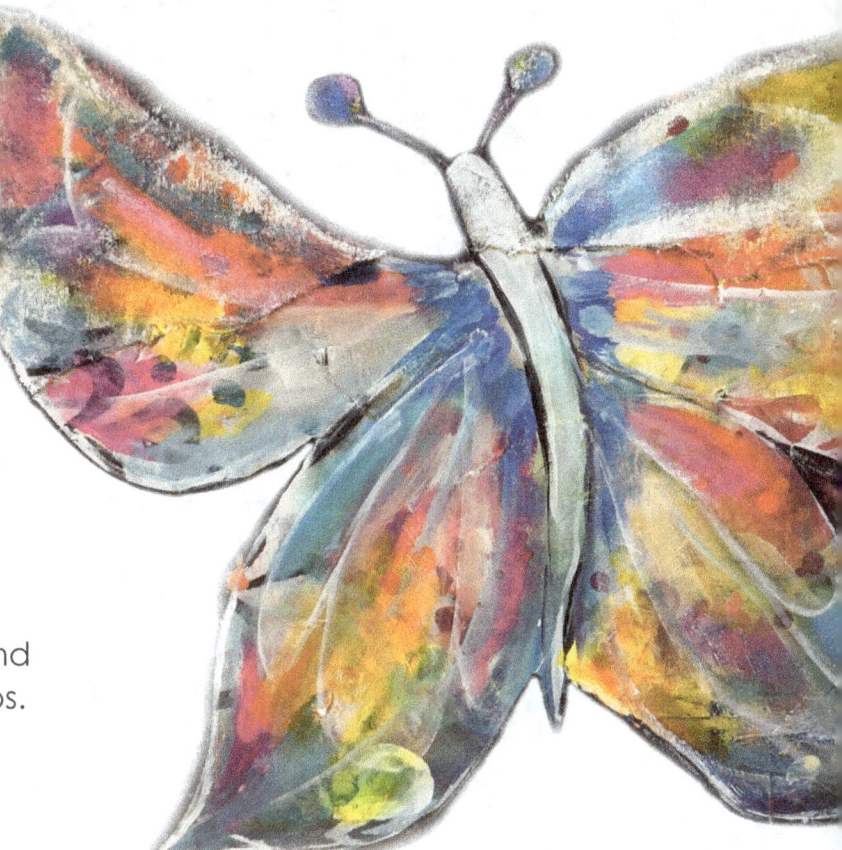

My muse bounced into my awareness, light as a feather...

as colorful as a rainbow.

Light sparkled around her.

Her wings danced with the wind and bubbled with the sundrops.

So delicate.

So free.

Her flight captured my imagination.

I wished for iridescent wings and a boundless landscape.

She whispered to me...

Within the simplest moments are infinite reservoirs of light and love.

New magic waiting to bloom into my life.

The flight of the butterfly entrancing my imagination to new heights.

Together we RISE ABOVE.

Let's get creative with time. I invite you to open up your consciousness to a new story around time. Instead of feeling limited by a lack of time, or rushed through time, or expecting time to proceed in a predictable matter, let's embrace a "right brain" version of time, one that is morphic and creative.

In ancient Greece they had two words for time: *chronos* and *kairos*. **Chronos** referred to linear time, the definition of time to which we are accustomed. **Kairos** is the word they used to describe "ah-ha" time, those moments within which we get lost in a state of flow, inspiration, or pure presence.

Both versions of time are as real as the other and can dance with each other in the art that is your life. As the sole creator of your experience, you get to choose which will serve you best in any given moment.

Let's dive into a new current of reality around time in order to create a new sense of spaciousness in your life, relieve some of the stress caused by the busy, hustle-bustle of chronos time, and create new opportunities for your personal flow and expansion.

## Cyclical Time

Kairos time is cyclical.

Think about it. Everything in our natural world cycles. Our planet spins around its axis as it cycles around the sun. Seasons cycle through each year. In our parks, gardens and open spaces, growth is followed by death, regeneration and rebirth. The tides, women's bodies, and the moon follow a cycle. We are surrounded and immersed in a cyclical environment, within which we desperately try to keep the machine of our lives operating in a predictable, linear pattern.

We beat ourselves up for not doing things every day or every week. So many of us get stuck, never creating a vision in our minds into reality, because our process doesn't evolve in a linear pattern. We skip a day or two, and we believe all is lost.

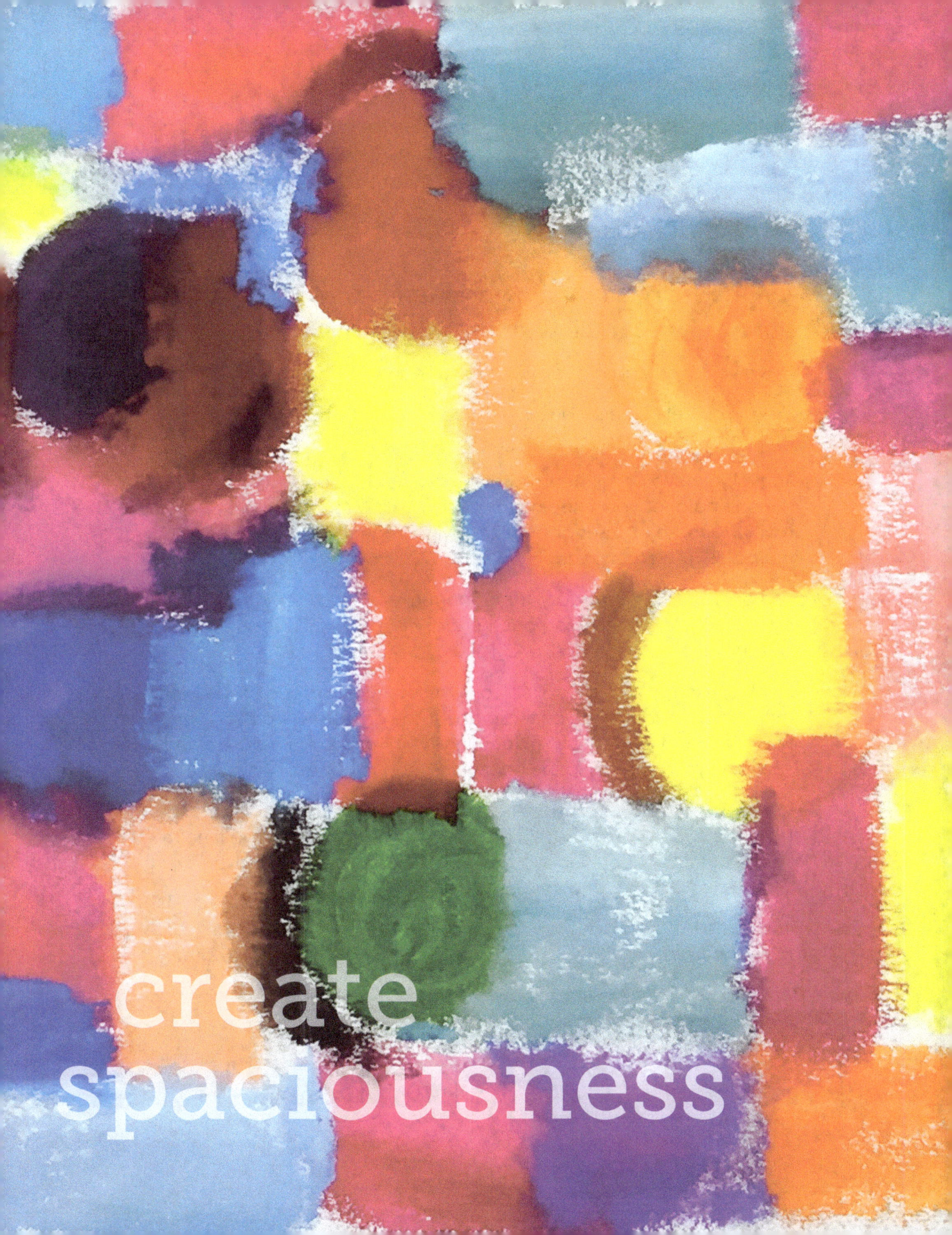

create
spaciousness

**We tell ourselves we are behind, off track, or blocked.**

We create expectations that if we are to be successful at losing weight, developing a new skill, creating a project or nurturing any new practice we must do "it" every day, or within a certain time frame. But that goes against the nature of time—it is cyclical! And kairos time is dependable but not predictable. You can't schedule it but you can invite it in.

## Let me share a couple of examples that illustrate how creative we can be with time and spaciousness.

Have you ever read a book that was a "can't-put-downer"?

When you get immersed in such a book you find yourself finding all kinds of time to read, right?

You might have been meaning to read this or that book for months, but *this* one catches your imagination and you can't seem to pull yourself away. All those excuses about not having enough time to read melt away as you devour each page.

You did two things to create the opportunity to read. You created space by not spending time doing another activity, and you became totally present and lost in the story. Magic!

Another example is a typical day or two before a big vacation. How much more productive are you on those days? You can get a week's worth of work done in a day by, again, focusing in on the present moment and only spending your time doing the necessary, most important activities.

What about those days and weeks when you are in the throes of a new, passionate relationship? Isn't it amazing how you can find the time to spend together when your days before were already full to overflowing with to-do's and have-to's?

You could call it time management, but I prefer to call it time bending—or "Can't-put-downer Time," "Vacation Prep Time," or "New Love Time!"

Are you with me? Are you ready to create a new story around time and invite in more feelings of spaciousness?

*YOU are a Time Bender!*

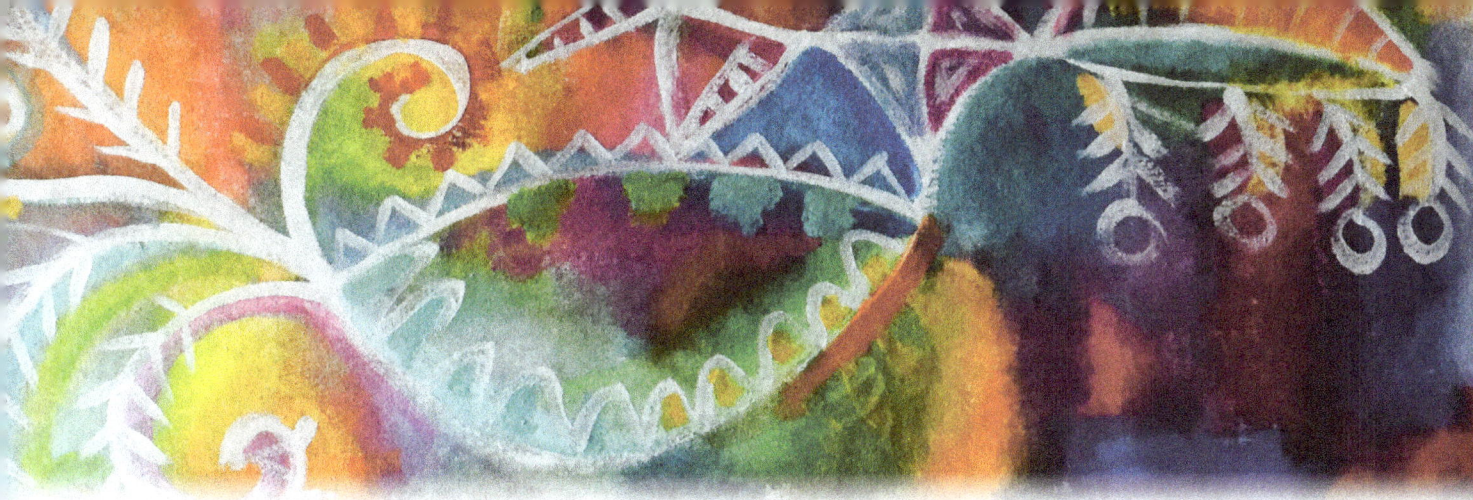

I do recommend starting with my #1 top Time Bender practice and proceeding accordingly. Each practice will become easier and easier as you rediscover your time bending power.

Overarching each of these practices is the power of being present. You know how to create the energy of presence at your Meditation Canvas. Take a moment now to acknowledge the value of the present moment and your ability to access that state when it serves you best. If you are not present, you are inherently sending your awareness to the past or future.

Our past and future are also invaluable energies. But they are not meant to dominate our consciousness. These three Time Bending practices will empower your present-moment awareness:

1.   Start your day with activities that give you energy.

2.   Decide that you have enough time.

3.   Learn "Segment Intending" as taught by Abraham Hicks.

## Time Bending Tip 1: Starting Your Day

This is pretty simple… simple, but maybe not easy.

Imagine that the first hour of your day is like immersing yourself in a pool of liquid energy. This energy can be golden, glowing, luminescent, infused with scents of jasmine and lavender. Then, for the rest of your day, you are left dripping and glowing with this same liquid energy.

Or…

This pool of liquid energy could be thick, dense, opaque, devoid of any scent at all, or worse. This is the energy you might pick up by spending the first hour of your day checking emails, trolling Facebook mindlessly, or worrying about your future. You feel like you are being productive, but in essence you are zapping your precious life force and cloaking yourself in this energy, carrying it around for the rest of the day.

**How you start your day, the energy pool you immerse yourself in for those first 15 minutes to an hour, will permeate every step you take for the rest of the day. That does not mean that a day can't "get better," but as a Life Artist, you achieve a new level of energetic discernment.**

Starting your day reading, being, or doing positive, rejuvenating, supportive, creative, or inspiring elements will create tremendous change in how the rest of your day evolves.

The classic excuse that I give myself is, "I don't have time to start my day doing that. There is just too much going on today."

Sometimes that voice wins. That's ok.

AND what I have also experienced on those days when I defy my logical mind and proceed with my hike or painting time is that I am that much more focused, present, and effective the rest of the day. Things just seem to fall into place, the perfect ideas flow into my consciousness, the ah-ha's happen, and I simply feel fabulous.

JUST FOR TOMORROW...

How are you going to start your day?

Do you want to set the alarm 15 or 30 minutes earlier?

What do you want to have set out before you go to bed to increase the odds of you spending your precious first moments of the day immersed in that golden, glowing, luminous pool of energy?

Do that.

Meditate.

Read words that expand and inspire.

Paint.

Doodle.

Take a walk.

Pick flowers.

## Time Bending Tip 2: You Are Already There

YOU get to decide that you have all the time you need.

Our inner dialogue around time illuminates for us another way that we can allow our super power of imagination to suck the energy out of us.

I imagine that you have at least one thing, job, task, project..., that is causing you to worry that you won't have enough time. You may be thinking, "I am SO behind." It could be writing a newsletter, planting the garden, getting to the gym, planning the trip, creating the business plan, studying for an exam, fixing up the guest room for visitors arriving soon...

Do you have one?

Now, do you spend more time imagining it completed, ticked off the list, successfully turned in or in working order? OR do you allow your imagination to paint images of not getting it done, being late, or having to abandon the project?

There are two steps to harness your power and decide that you are already there:

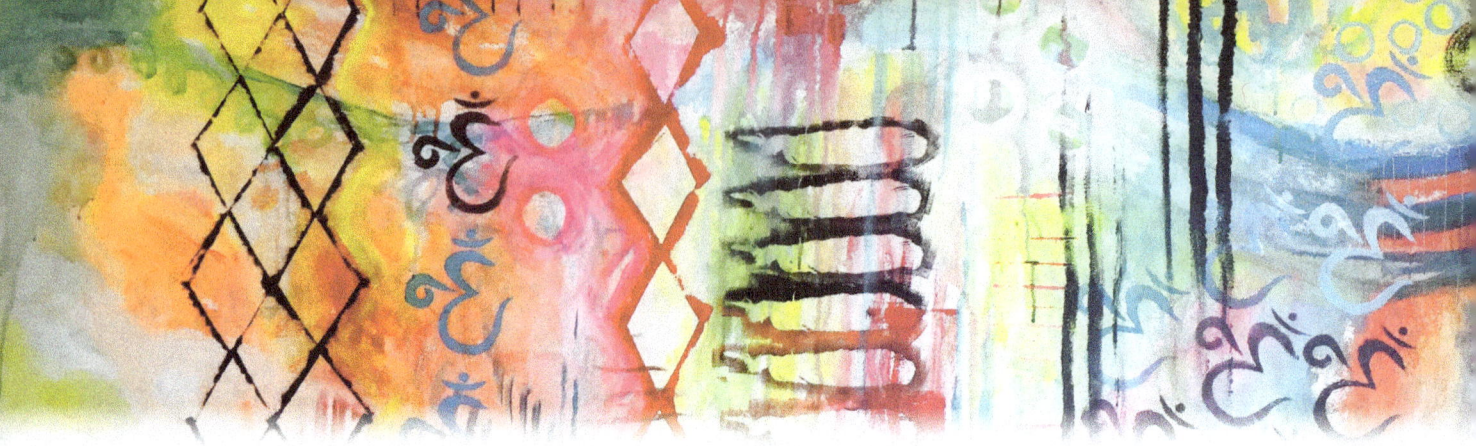

1. Decide that you have all the time you need. You want to eliminate any doubt that you won't have time.

2. Remember that time cycles. Replace expectations of the task happening in an orderly, linear fashion with confidence that the cycle of time will, eventually, come around to present to you just the right amount of time, energy and focus that you need.

## Decide

Coaching hundreds of people through my online programs, I have witnessed the pervasive tendency that exists to dwell on feelings of "being behind" or "getting off track."

*Worrying that you won't have enough time is a choice.*

Deciding that, no matter what, you are going to cross the "finish line" is also a choice and just as viable an option.

Instead of worrying about whether or not you are going to "get it done" you can DECIDE that you will get done and get CURIOUS about how that is going to happen.

You are sending the message to your soul that you KNOW you are going to complete whatever "it" is, maybe you just don't know how. The difference is that you have decided that you will get it done AND have opened up to ALL THE WAYS you are going to make that happen. You have left no room for doubt. There are no "*If* I get enough time…" only a non-negotiable vision in your mind of you across the "finish line."

So, what can you STOP worrying about right now and, instead, create an iron-clad vision of you FEELING the feeling of being finished, complete, or across the threshold?

Again, I believe we can feel "off track" or behind because of unrealistic expectations around our time proceeding in a regular, linear pattern.

Imagine that the time you have spent away from whatever task or activity has simply been the wheel of time on the upswing, AND it is inevitably coming back around to dip back into the energy of that activity or commitment.

For example, maybe you LOVE to be outdoors, hiking, biking, and camping. However, in the winter and colder months you are not able to be outside as much. When summer arrives again, the season cycles back around, and you immerse yourself in nature as much as your schedule allows. You understand that summer is your opportunity and that it too will cycle away again. Do you beat yourself up in January, when it is snowy and icy, that you are not camping up in the mountains? Probably not.

The cycle of seasons is obvious. You get that.

Now, open up to a new awareness of other cycles in your life. Your time painting may be more cyclical than linear too. Your commitment to your yoga practice may have cycles. Allow the time away from whatever activity to inform and inspire what you WANT.

When I start thinking, "I haven't painted in a while" I know that means that I am coming up on a painting cycle.

The presence of the awareness that I have not painted recently lets me know that I WANT to paint. Rather than beat myself up about not painting, I focus in on the fact that I WANT to paint and let that energy inspire my next action.

Be kind to yourself. Embrace the cycles.

## Time Bending Tip 3: Segment Intending

Segment Intending is when you get super intentional within small pockets of time. The opposite is the intention you have for the year, the summer, or your life. Segment intending is about bringing yourself totally present and setting your intention for right now, or JUST this morning. It is about allowing all of the moving parts of your life, all the details, dreams, commitments, and ideas to filter down into just this moment. What do I want RIGHT NOW? Set that intention and allow everything else to fall away.

## How easy is it to get overwhelmed these days?

In the state of feeling overwhelmed, our minds are all over the place. You may feel like a ball in a pinball machine. Or maybe it feels like the current of the immense ocean is pulling you out, away from any sense of grounding or stability. From that place, we are not in our power. We are not sending a clear message, nor are we able to receive a clear message. We are not in Super Soul Flow.

When we bring our power of intention into just this moment, this afternoon, this meeting, we focus ALL of our energy, desire, and intuition into THAT moment. Then, we are in our power. Then, we are sending a clear message to our soul, the Universe, this IS WHAT I WANT.

In planning your day, with all of the myriad of tasks and to-do list items, how can you set specific intentions for:

1.  My first hour of the day,

2.  The time between breakfast and lunch,

3.  The afternoon,

4.  Evening,

5.  Before bed?

To begin, take it one step at a time. Right now, set an intention for just the next hour of your day. Maybe your intention is to relax, connect with a good friend, finish writing the chapter, plan dinner, or get creative and paint. Then, detach from the mental chatter, the monkey mind, and focus in on JUST that intention. Do you feel the spaciousness? Can you breathe a sigh of relief?

We can't do EVERYTHING all the time. Do we have a lot going on? Heck yeah! Does thinking about all the things you can't get around to in the moment, in the moment, serve you? No.

Do what you are doing with all of your attention and heart and you will create so much more magic, beauty and peace. When that "segment" is done, let it go, and set your next intention.

Before you begin your Personal Painting Practice around SPACIOUSNESS, please enjoy the following meditation:

> You are forever. You are that which cannot be defined. You are that which cannot be held back or imprisoned. It is only through your perceptions of the limits that are in place that you can be enslaved to the constructs of your mind... Step back and expand until you cannot feel a sense of the confines of your body. Become space. All passes through you.
>
> Now you can see, know and feel the ALL of Spirit. Leave the realm of ordinary senses and become the All of it. This is where you will find peace. The more often you do this, the better you become until you realize you can shift your reality completely. Now create what you want in alignment with divine. Create from spaciousness—silence and expansion is consciousness.
>
> Bring this forward. Become the great creatrix. Practice the art of becoming spaciousness. Go there often and bring back wisdom. It will come naturally because you are exposing yourself to consciousness. Connect to Source and you will receive the wisdom and the knowing of how to manifest a new earth.
>
> ~**SHONAGH HOME,** AUTHOR OF *IX CHEL WISDOM,*
> *7 TEACHINGS FROM THE MAYAN SACRED FEMININE*

Now, we paint SPACIOUSNESS!

The following is, of course, a prompt, a suggestion. Ask yourself the question, "How can I paint spaciousness?" For me it led to thoughts around blurring the edges, the lines, the boundaries of time. Instead of thinking of "chunks" of time, how can I expand the fields and play with the edges?

# Creating the Energy of SPACIOUSNESS

"Chunks of time" is what this first layer (below) inspires for me.

Then, I sought to blend the edges with color, layering thin shades of color over the lines and in between the chunks.

What is the opposite of spaciousness for you? That may inspire an image. Maybe it is feeling boxed in, regimented, limited, tight, or closed? Paint that. Then, create spaciousness.

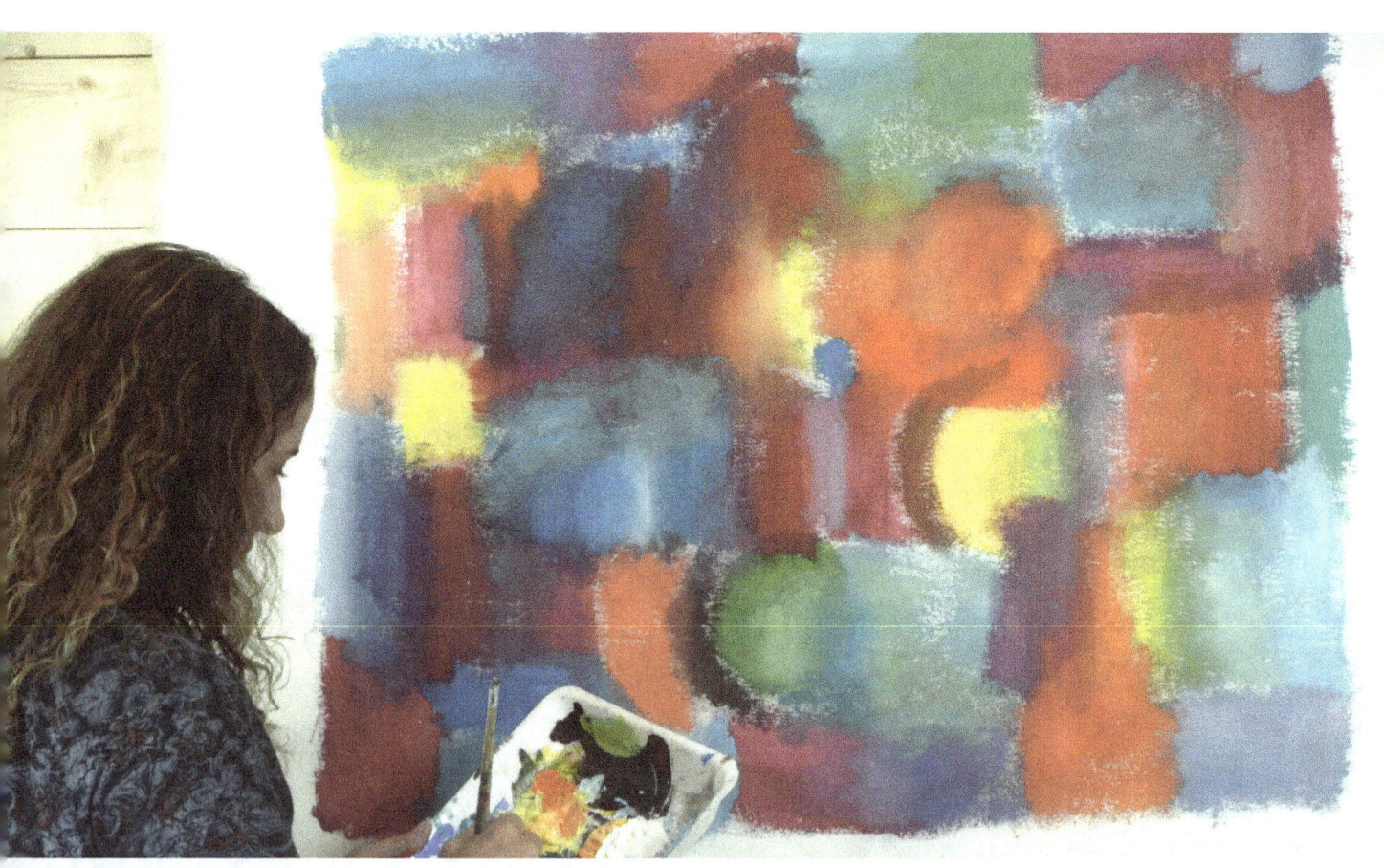

I painted this bird, inspired by a "mascot" of sorts, at the iconic restaurant *Nepenthe* in Big Sur, California. It is a magical bird that flies through… spaciousness. Maybe it also flies through time, through the veil to the other side.

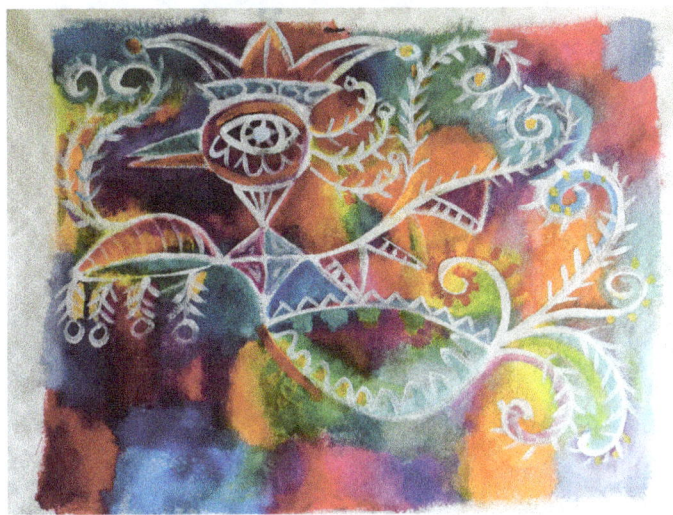

Below is this same bird I painted on one of the sheds at the ranch where I lived in Oregon until summer of 2012. I LOVED painting it so BIG!

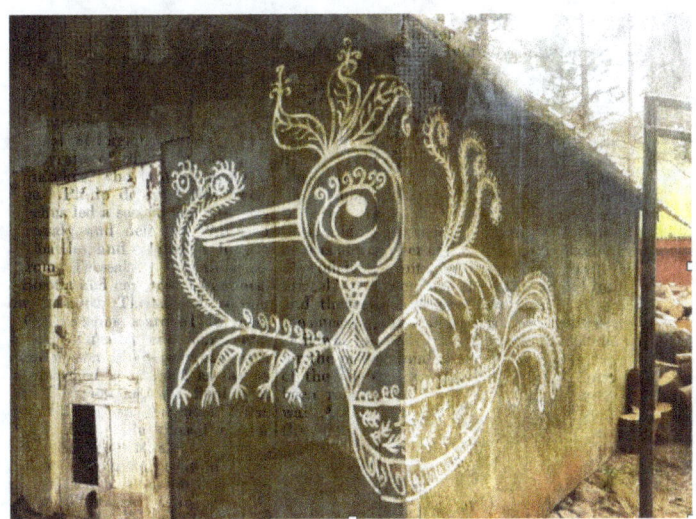

Maybe SPACIOUSNESS wants to be painted really BIG! Does it inspire you to get out into some spacious, wide open spaces in nature? Maybe you could paint spaciousness in an open park or field or forest?

I can't wait to see your paintings that create the energy of spaciousness for YOU!

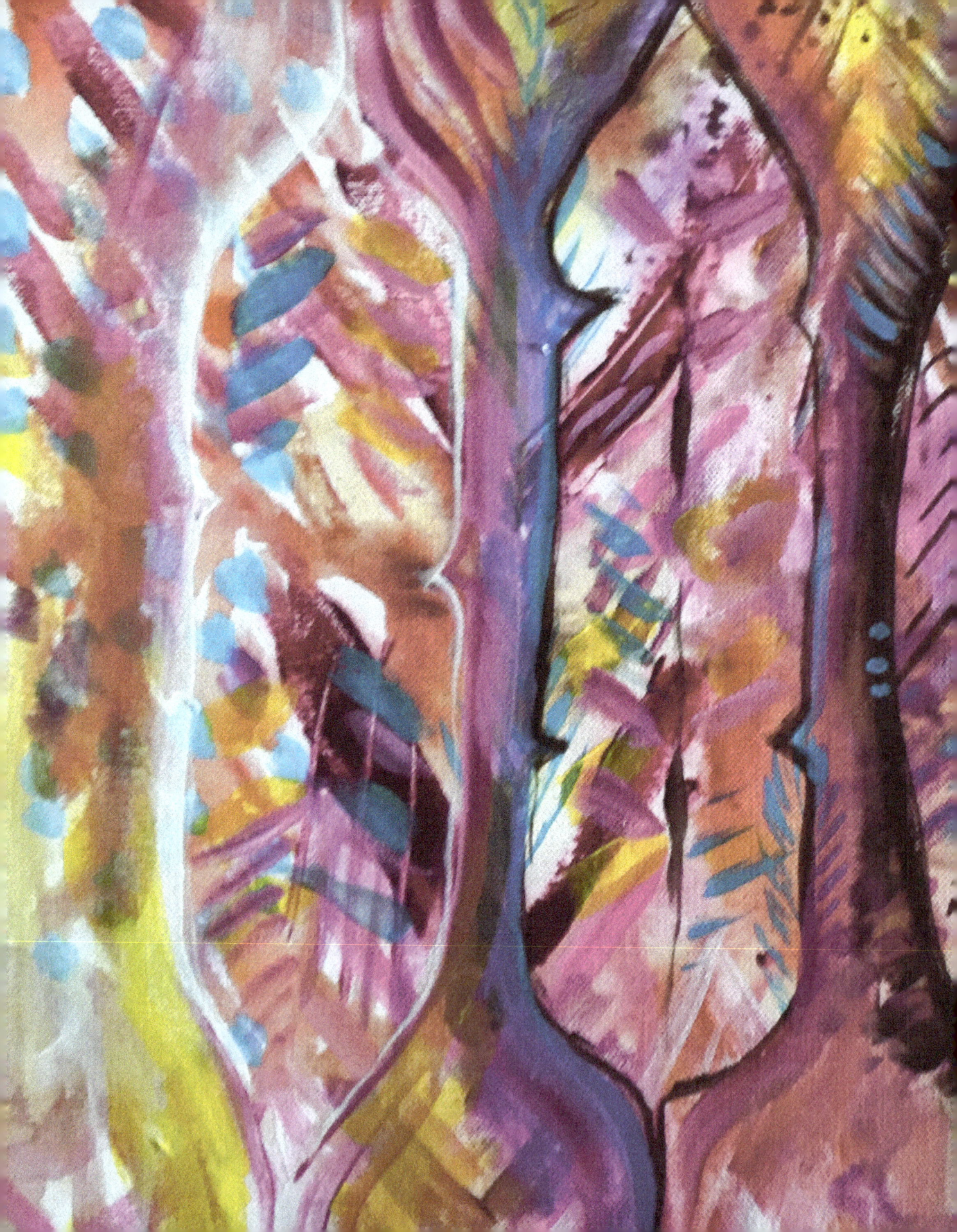

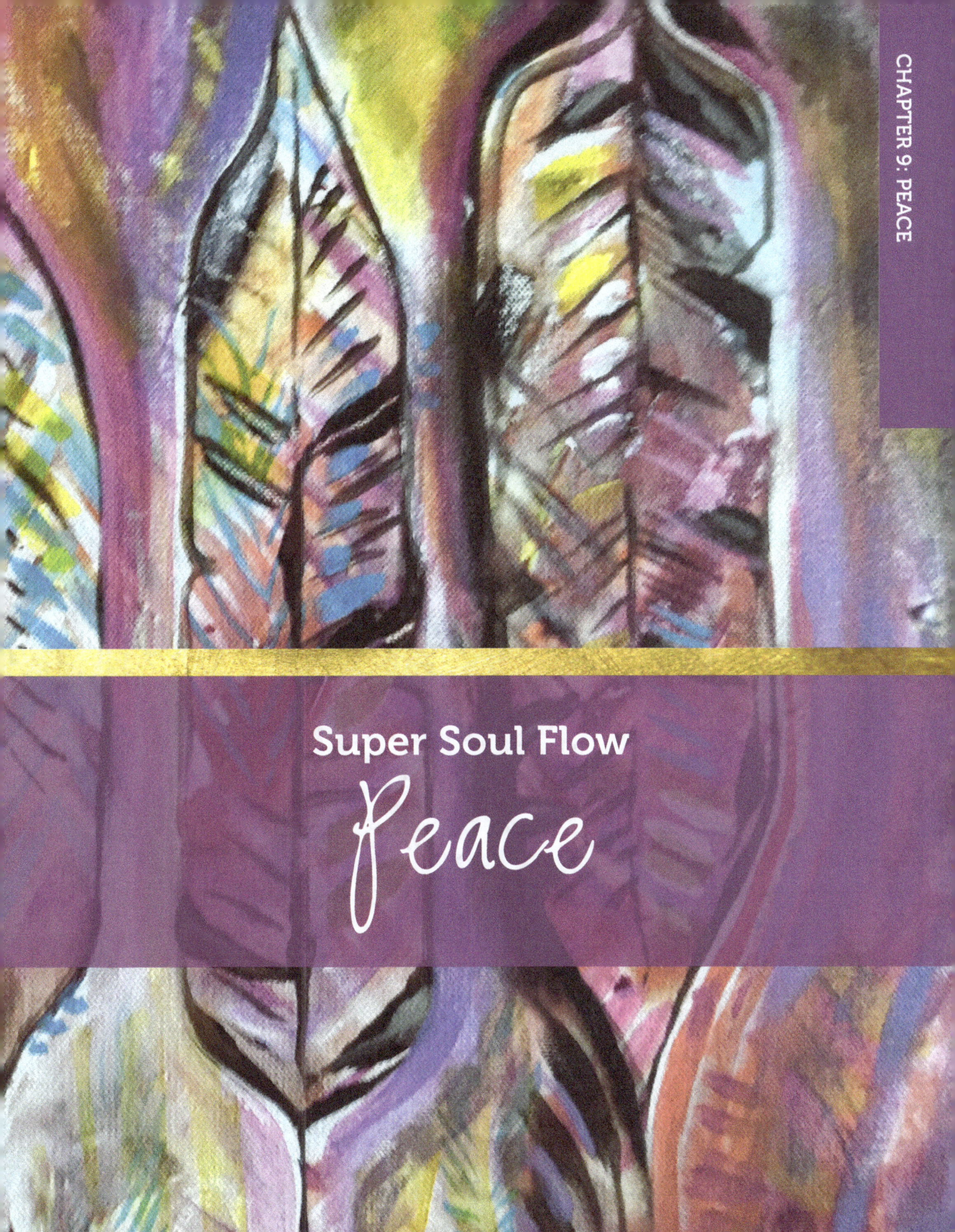

Super Soul Flow

*Peace*

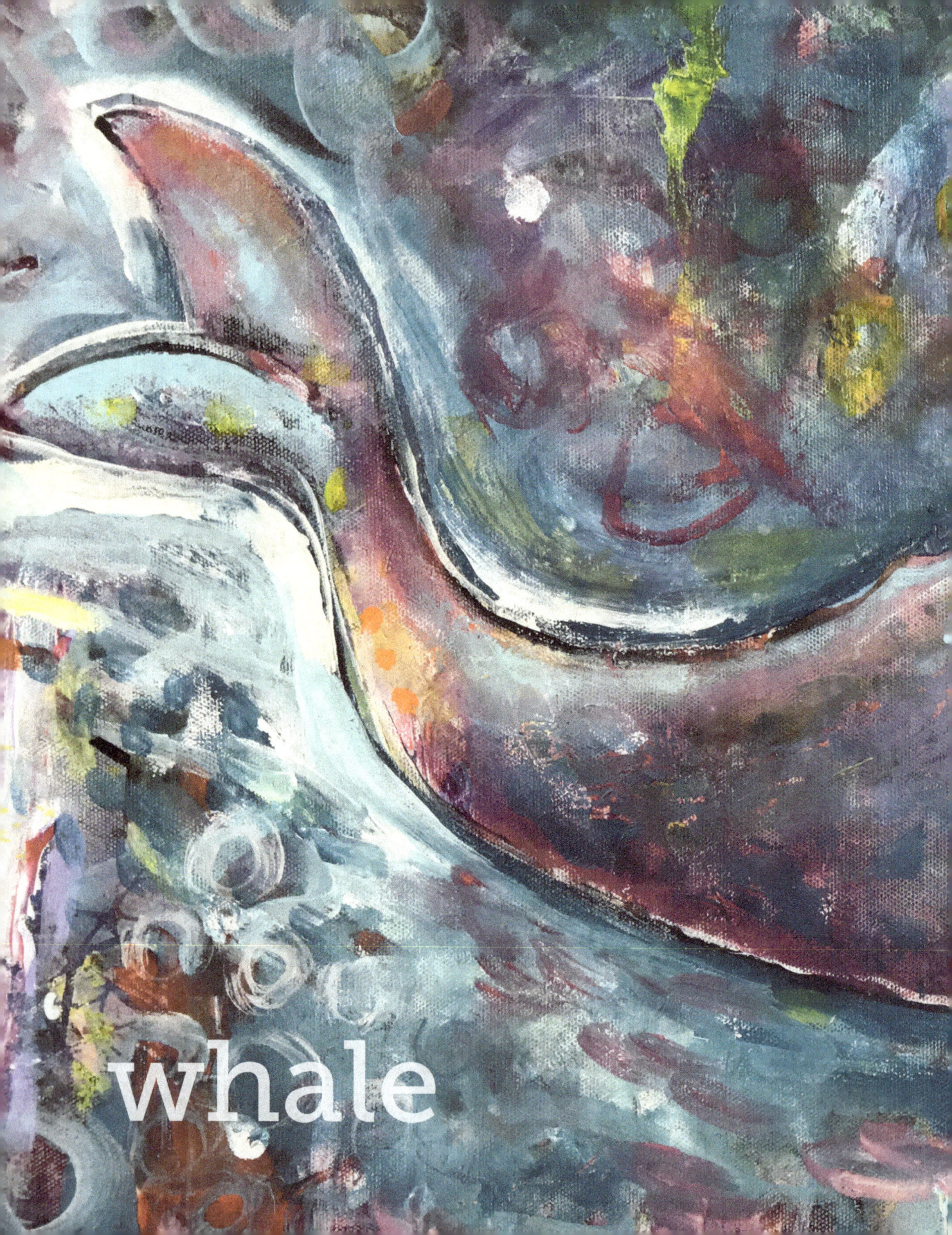

whale

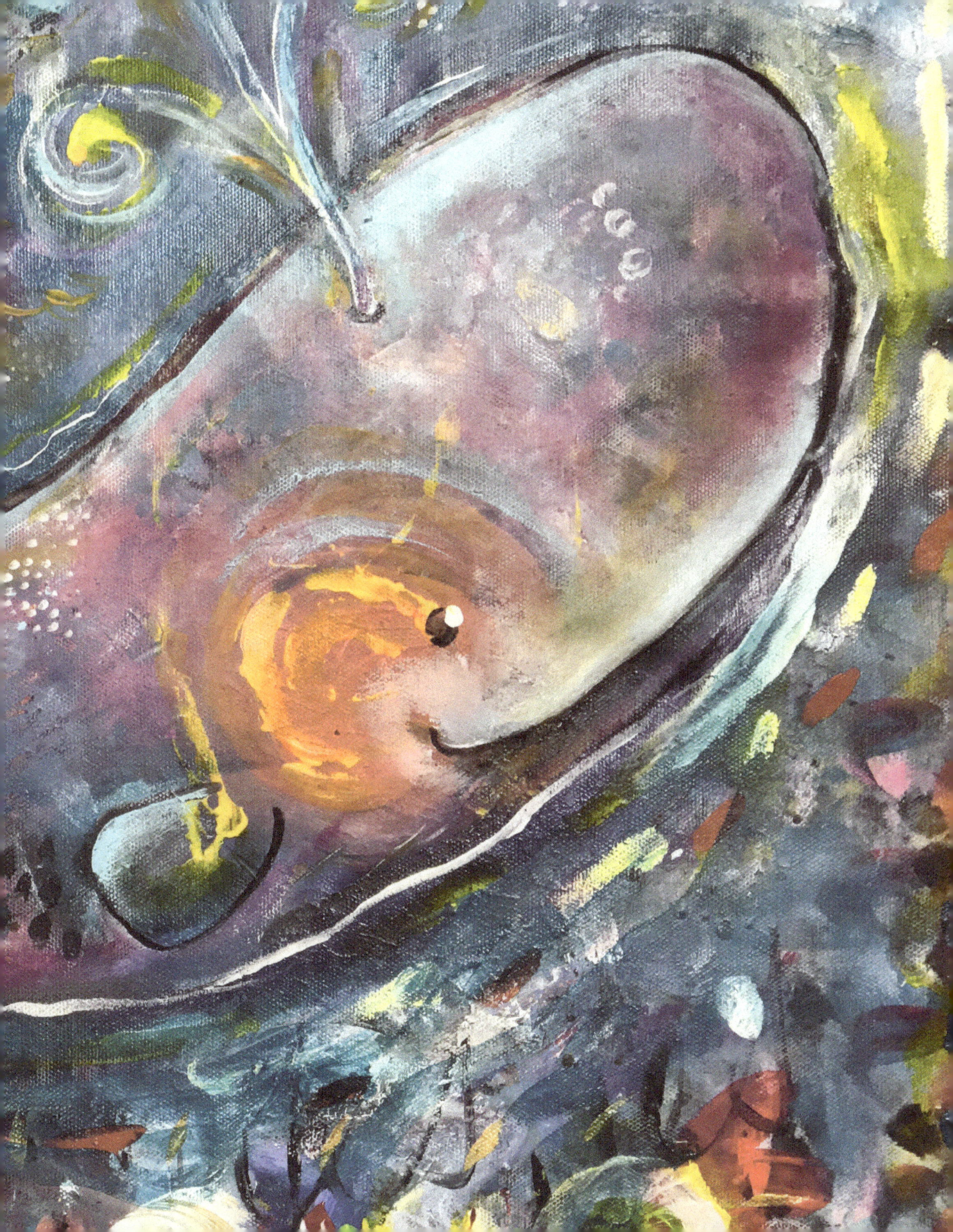

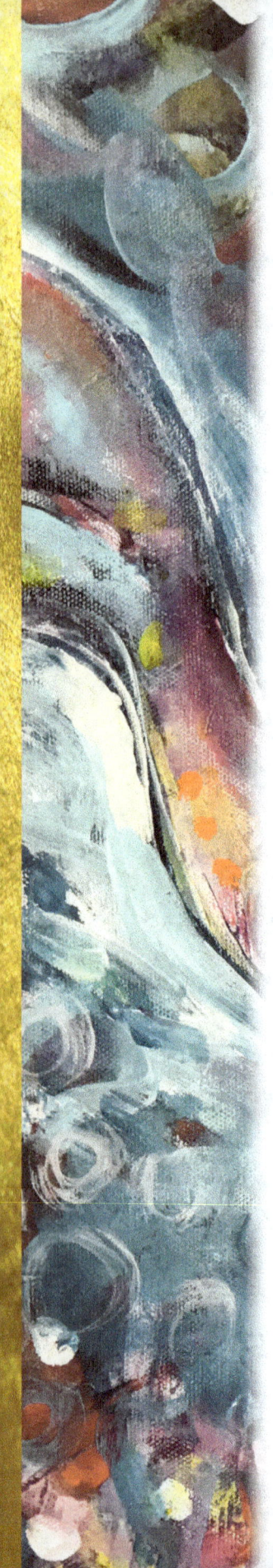

# whale

*Close your eyes. Connect to your whale. Feel the weight of the water, pressing all around you. Sink into the waters. Feel the buoyancy of your being… you are at home in the depths. You flow. Take a deep breath and feel your entire whale body as it undulates through the currents.*

*Whale offers you everything you need to embrace life as it is and feel peace, even when surrounded by the unknown. Whale guides you to new emotional depths and supports you as you process overwhelming emotions.*

*Whale is the Queen of the ocean, the element of water, what lies underneath the surface in our lives. She teaches you how to transform emotional disturbances into portals and new levels of inner peace.*

*Shallow breathing equals shallow thoughts. Deep breathing equals deep thoughts. Take in a deep, expansive breath as you breach the surface of your emotional waters and then dive deep with the power, the creativity and the wisdom whale brings you. You got this. Peace.*

I drift off to sleep. Gently floating further and further away from any worries or fears.

I immerse myself in my dreamtime, calling me into new reservoirs of divine guidance and inspired insight.

I go underneath the surface of my day-to-day:
… the to-do lists,
… the should-do lists,
… the business of maintaining this physical world.

I remember my flow.
I remember the totality of EVERYTHING I have to offer my world.
I remember the wisdom that allows me to navigate the emotional waters that can threaten to overwhelm and drown me.

I feel how big I am.
I feel the power in each undulation.
I feel the energy flow all around me.
I feel enough.

Whale lends me her sight.
She guides me to new depths, where the emotional realm serves me and informs me.
I see how small I can perceive my being, next to the massiveness also available to me.
I am one with the currents.
I am a master of the unseen.
I know only openness, expansiveness, and freedom.
Peace.
Flow.
Breath.
Whale.

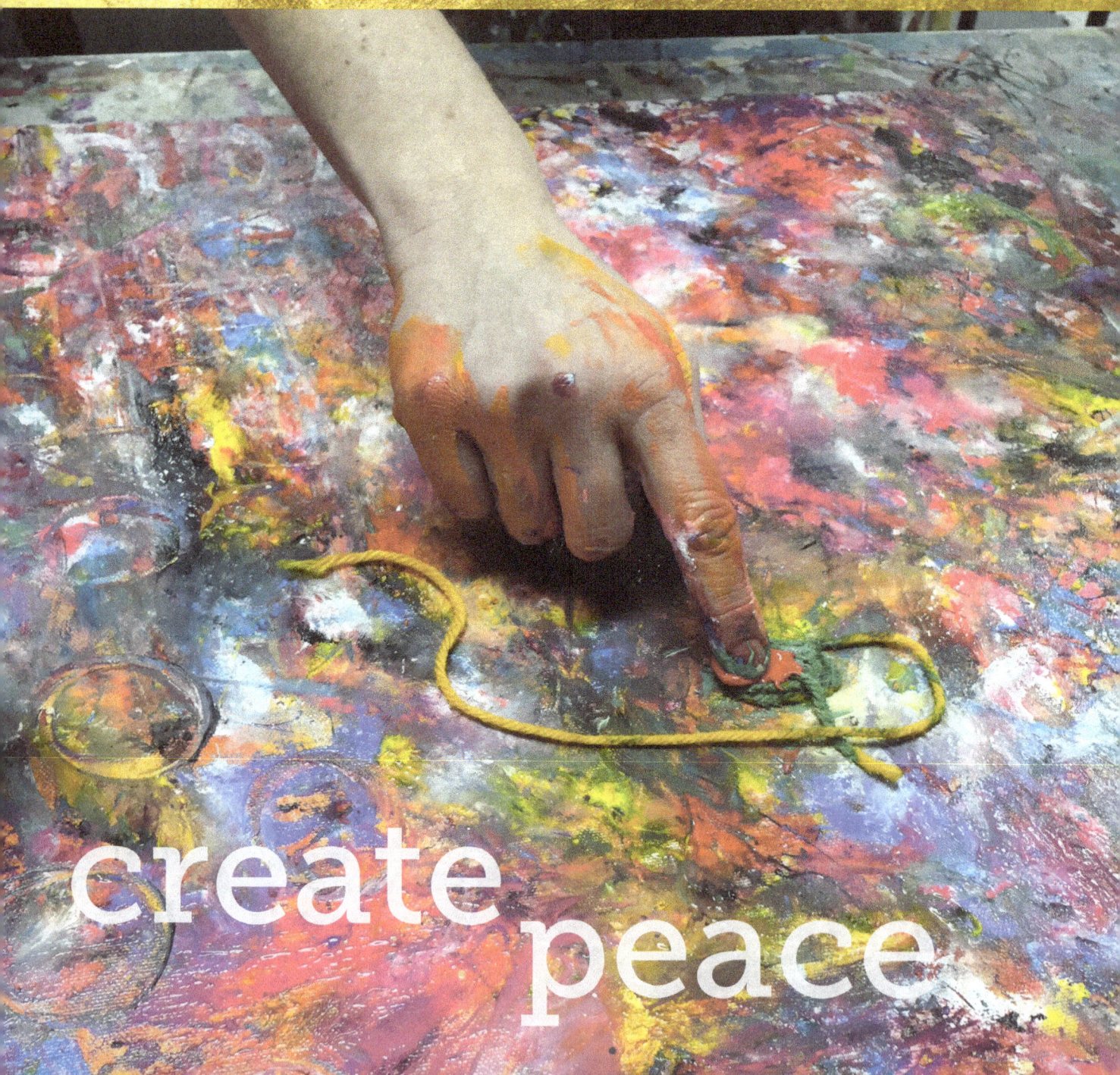

Ego says, 'Once everything falls into place, I'll feel peace.' Spirit says, 'Find your peace, and then everything will fall into place.'

~MARIANNE WILLIAMSON

create
peace

# Peace, man.

Look at this word: PEACE. It almost feels overused, certainly underutilized. For many, it is a lifetime goal or the inspiration for our life's work. Today, let's bring this small yet powerful word down into this moment and create a new energy and a new perspective.

When you feel at peace, do you feel connected, secure, and safe? Or alone, individual, and vulnerable?

It is easier to create the energy of peace when you are feeling connected with the greater world, community, or family around you. You feel intimately a part of your environment, home, work, or school—supported and safe.

In this chapter, you are going to explore a new way to expand into MORE energy and MORE peace.

## The Four Elements

The four elements—air, fire, water and earth—are the traditional, Native American guardians of our physical world. They dance together to create everything we see, touch, eat, grow, and build.

At their most primal level, each element helps to sustain our physical life on this planet. AIR is what we breathe; FIRE keeps us warm, heats our food and protects us; WATER sustains and nourishes our bodies; and EARTH is at the foundation of everything. Each element has power that can be both sustaining and threatening. Tornadoes, forest fires, tidal waves, and earthquakes all reflect the transformative and destructive power that these elements hold.

Likewise, the four elements live in each of our physical bodies. AIR is the oxygen in our lungs and blood; FIRE is the synapses firing in our minds; WATER makes up the majority of our physical bodies; and EARTH is the bones, flesh and muscle that houses the entire system, just as in the physical world outside of our bodies.

In the interest of creating more of the energy of PEACE, you are now invited to embrace the elemental nature of both our inner and outer landscapes. You are going to get to create elemental altars in your home and paint a symbol that can embody the four elements and weave their energies into the art that is your life.

## How can the four elements help me to create PEACE?

Connecting to the four elements weaves your mind, body and soul into the fabric of the entire planet Earth. Instead of feeling alone, helpless, or scared, you can summon up the powers from within and all around you.

Connect to the breath, the wind, the air that carries every vibration.

Embrace the fire of your own sacred spark, the transformational force that burns away what no longer serves.

Dive into the purifying waters and allow them to support you under the surface of the visible world and guide you into the infinite depths of your invisible world.

Sink into the steady ground, the unlimited growth and manifesting power of earth.

*Creating your own home elemental altars is a magical way to ground yourself in a deeper sense of connection and receptivity. It is simple to do and can be an ongoing and collaborative process!*

One Christmas I pulled a small model bird nest out of my stocking. It was a gift from my kids. They said, "It's for your Earth altar!" Too funny!

Your elemental altars may just look like a decorative arrangement to most people. But you, and your other magical friends, will know better.

Follow these simple instructions to start creating your own home elemental altars.

- Identify the spaces for each of your altars.

- The Native American placement that I follow is AIR = east (sunrise), FIRE = south (hottest side of your home), WATER = west (sunset, cooling), EARTH = north (dark).

- If you have a special room in your home that is all yours—an office, meditation space, etc.—you can set up the altars in each direction of that one room. OR you can place them throughout your house. My fire altar is the windowsill above the kitchen sink, as an example.

- Place a candle in each of the spaces. You can get creative with the candle holders for each element. For example, a large shell can make a great candle holder for your water altar.

- Look around your home for the first object for each of your altars. Examples follow in the images below. Your altars can expand with time and you will attract to you, or rediscover, objects that are perfect for each direction. You will be surprised, or not, when a friend gives you a "random" gift that you immediately recognize as the next offering to one of your altars. You can research all the ways you can anoint, bless, and create a relationship with your altars. My intention is to make it easy for you to begin to create a new relationship with the elements to support and expand your Super Soul Flow.

## AIR ALTAR

Here is an image of my AIR altar on my bedside table. AIR is about communication, our mental realm, intelligence and the power of intention. The white swan feather in the top right corner is supported by a wish jar (a symbol of intention). There are multiple owls, reflective of air and flight. The Eye of Horus and the Goddess Nut in front of the Buddha are both ancient symbols connected to air. Nut embodies the sky and the Eye of Horus symbolizes our intuitive intelligence. The Himalayan white salt lamp reminds me of the light waves traveling through the air and the cubic crystal in front of it is a yellow calcite crystal that is beneficial in connecting our emotional and mental bodies.

At my air altar I express gratitude for my ability to communicate my truth to so many people. I ask for clarity and for help spreading my message of creative hope and possibility. I take deep breaths and connect to the air that has circled our Mother Earth and been breathed in and out by my human, animal AND plant family. I sense how boundless the dimension of air is and connect to the spaciousness available to me.

Resist the temptation to "make it perfect." Instead, set the intention to create a new, more expansive and peaceful relationship with your GREATER surroundings through the elements.

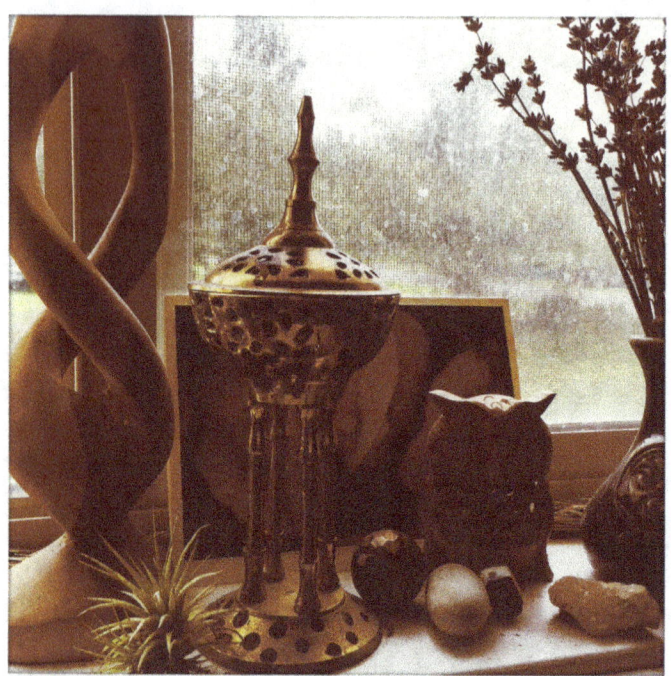

## FIRE ALTAR

Besides the element of fire, this altar is also about the energy of inspiration—what gets you fired up? There are stones that are specifically connected to the fire element, including Tiger's Eye (the faceted, round stone pictured here next to the incense burner). The incense burner is from Dubai, and burns really hot! The infinity sign sculpture speaks to me, like rising smoke, of my connection at each moment to the higher realms. The air plant is there because it can thrive without earth or water (and I liked the spiky leaves). Owls, and all birds, have a solar element because they can soar closer to the sun than those of us without wings. And owls have been such a huge source of inspiration and motivation for me over the years. The candle holder in this altar is from Italy, a place full of fiery energy.

When I visit this altar I am thankful for the "fire in my belly." I am so grateful to have passion as a predominant fuel in my life. I thank it for keeping me warm, heating my food, and helping me to burn away and transform those elements in the art that is my life that no longer serve me.

There is no "right" or "wrong" in the creation of these altars when you come with a sincere intention to communicate with the elements. If an item inspires a connection with a certain element for YOU, that is perfect!

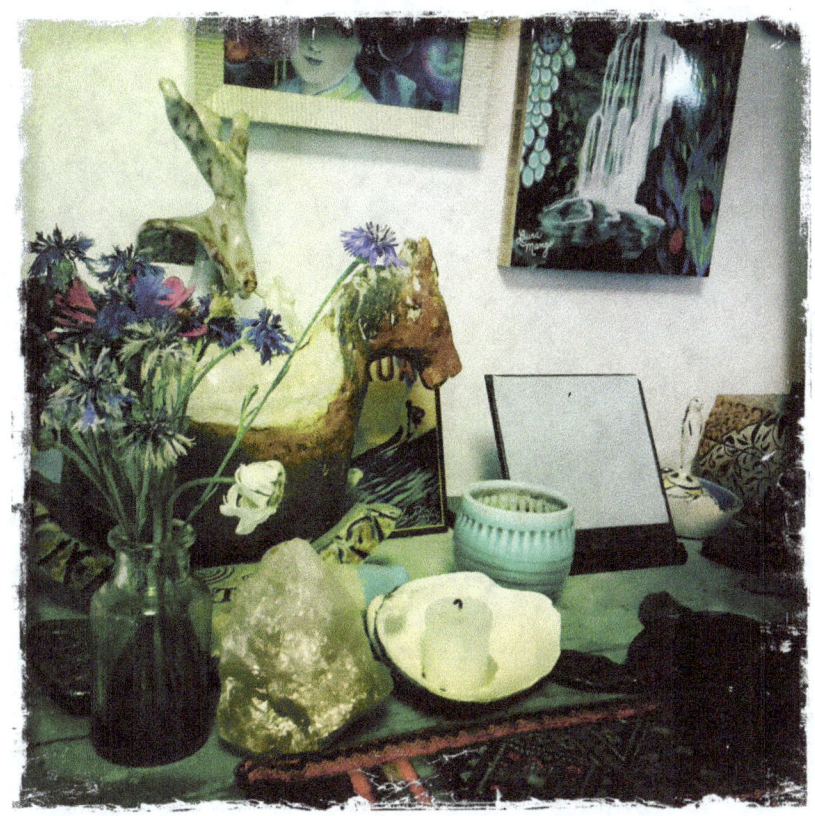

## WATER ALTAR

This altar is my favorite, which is no surprise since I am a water sign and have always loved the water, going with the flow, and immersive experiences. WATER is about emotions, so the crystal closest to the bottom left corner of the photo is a rose quartz, for the heart chakra. The candle is in a shell from the Oregon coast. The clay piece falling off the bottom right corner of the photo is a sea turtle my oldest daughter created years ago. The clay sculpture in the top left is a teapot! When I come to the altar for my morning ritual, I make my mark with water on the Buddha Board that is there in the back. The entire altar is on a sea-blue old dresser, and the image of the waterfall is from an artist I met in Hawaii.

At my water altar, I express gratitude for the ability to receive and flow with my emotions, without getting tossed about. I ask for emotional intelligence and wisdom. I visualize riding the waves of life, rather than getting hammered into the sand. I am grateful that my life has led me underneath the "surface" into the subtle realms of life on this planet.

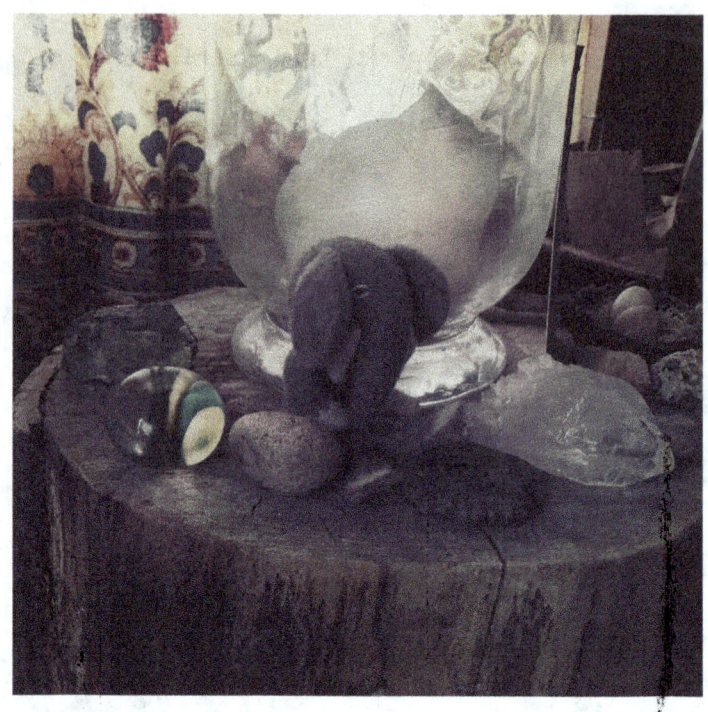

## EARTH ALTAR

I love this tree stump upon which my ELEPHANT, an animal totem associated with Earth energy, gets to live. The jade disc to the right of the elephant (finger puppet!) is a symbol of Earth. The rocks are all from hikes around my home in Oregon, reminding me of my deep connection to this particular part of Mother Earth.

I share with Earth my gratitude for the ability to manifest change, growth, and expansion in my life. I thank Earth for the support, the solid ground under my feet, and its continued support. I plant "seeds" of ideas, experiences, or opportunities that I want to manifest and connect to the vast resources that lie within our Earth's crust that are available to me at any time.

More vital to connecting to the elements than anything is a sincere desire to honor and respect the WHOLE of your physical experience here on Earth. When you sincerely examine how each of these elements speaks to you and manifests into your life and, then, express those things, you will feel your energy expand and your feelings of peace grow.

Have fun creating your elemental altars.

# *Creating the Energy of Peace*

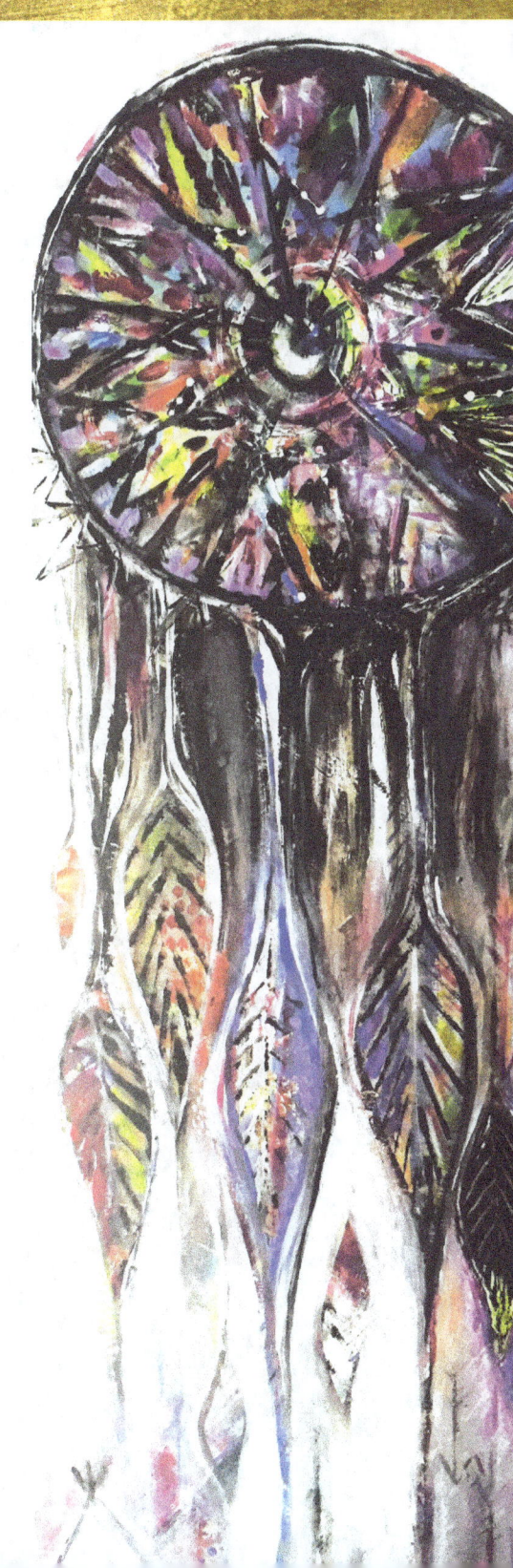

**To expand further upon the indigenous wisdom of the Native American Tribes, we will paint a dream catcher to symbolize our energy of peace and interconnection with the seen and unseen.**

I love this question, "Are you a dream catcher?" What are all the ways we can honor our dreams and manifest them into our reality? How much more peace would we experience with a heightened consciousness around our infinite potential and collaborative relationship with our Soul and the entire physical world around us?

When you start painting your dream catcher, and the mandala at the top, you can divide it into the four directions and create layers of symbols for each element into your painting.

You can intentionally create four feathers, one for each element. Or allow the feathers to appear as you are so inspired.

In my latest dream catchers, I have used a large mandala stencil to begin the top mandala.

## Step 1

You can paint your DREAM right onto the canvas. Using black paint, I created this DREAM catcher to hold my largest vision for a creatively empowered world.

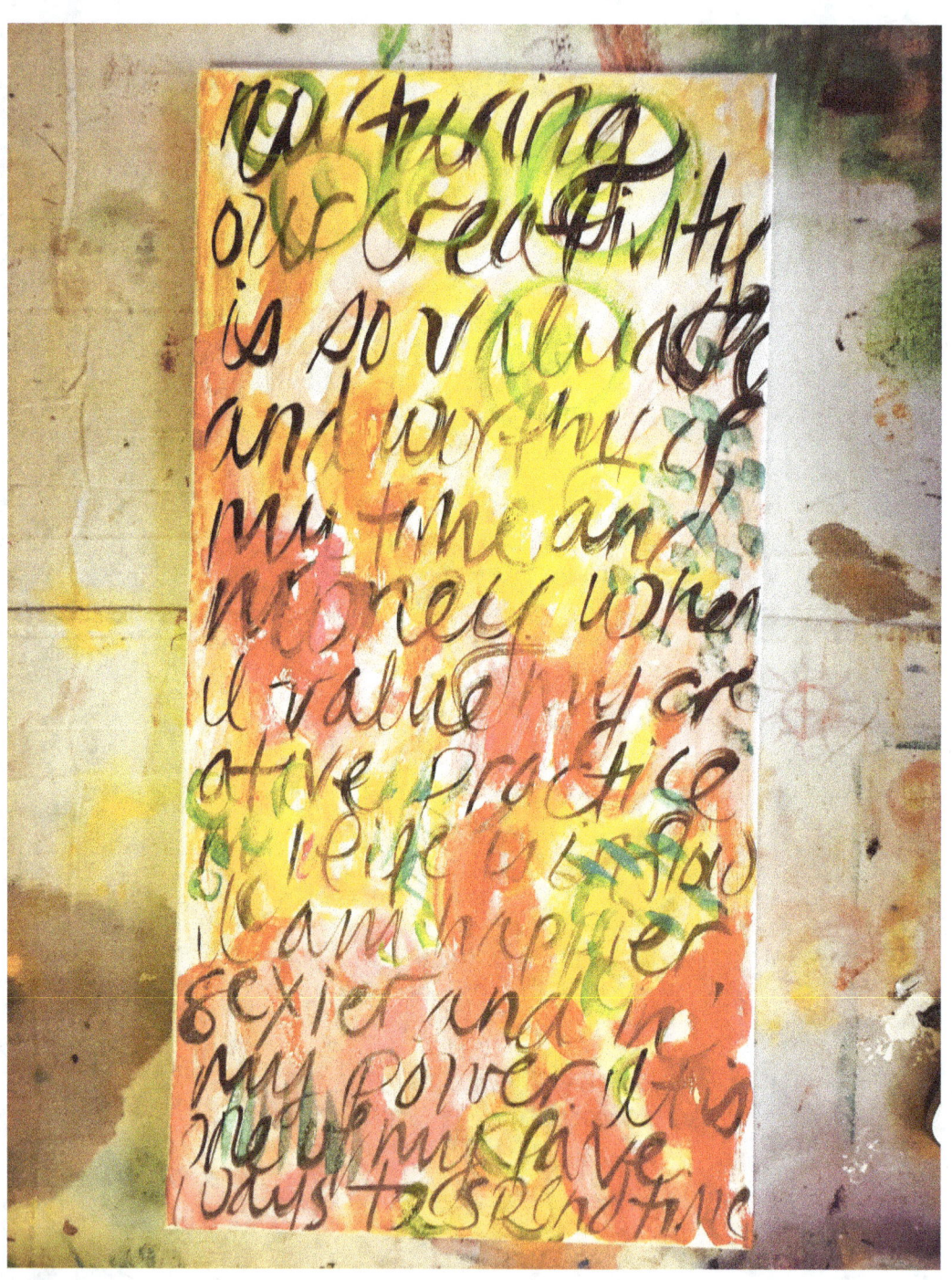

## Step 2

This is where you play!

I am somewhat conscious of the idea that the mandala shape will be at the top of the page (the spirals) and the feathers will be toward the bottom (the chevron shapes).

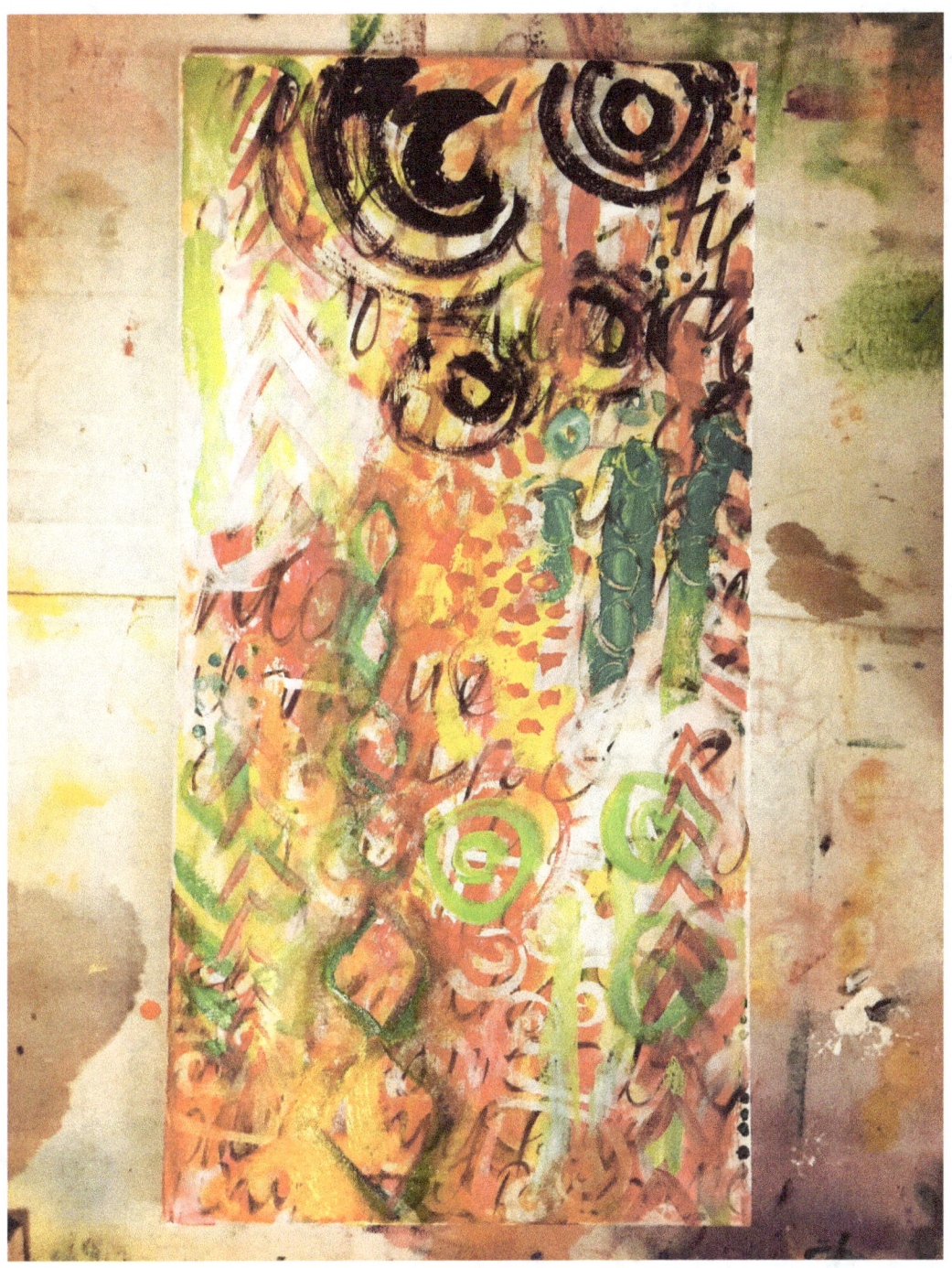

## Step 3

Create the mandala at the top of the canvas (it can be the full circle, or just half) and the feathers hanging down.

I got to use some fun feather stencils in this dream catcher!

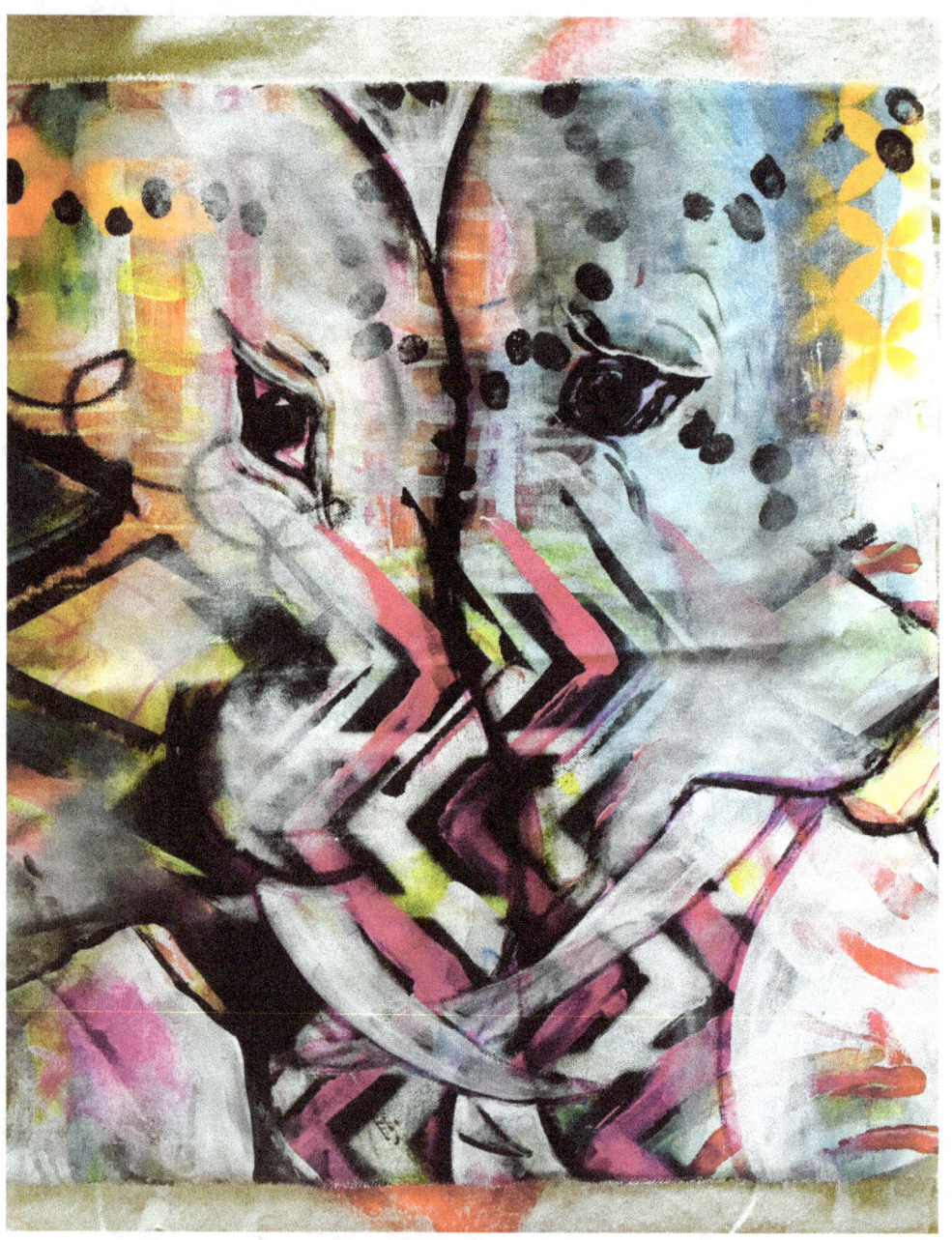

# Final Image

Can you see how the more you play and make your mark, the more fun the image becomes?

DREAMS are FUN and often include layers and layers of activity, intention, action and belief. With each brush stroke, paint your dreams into your reality!

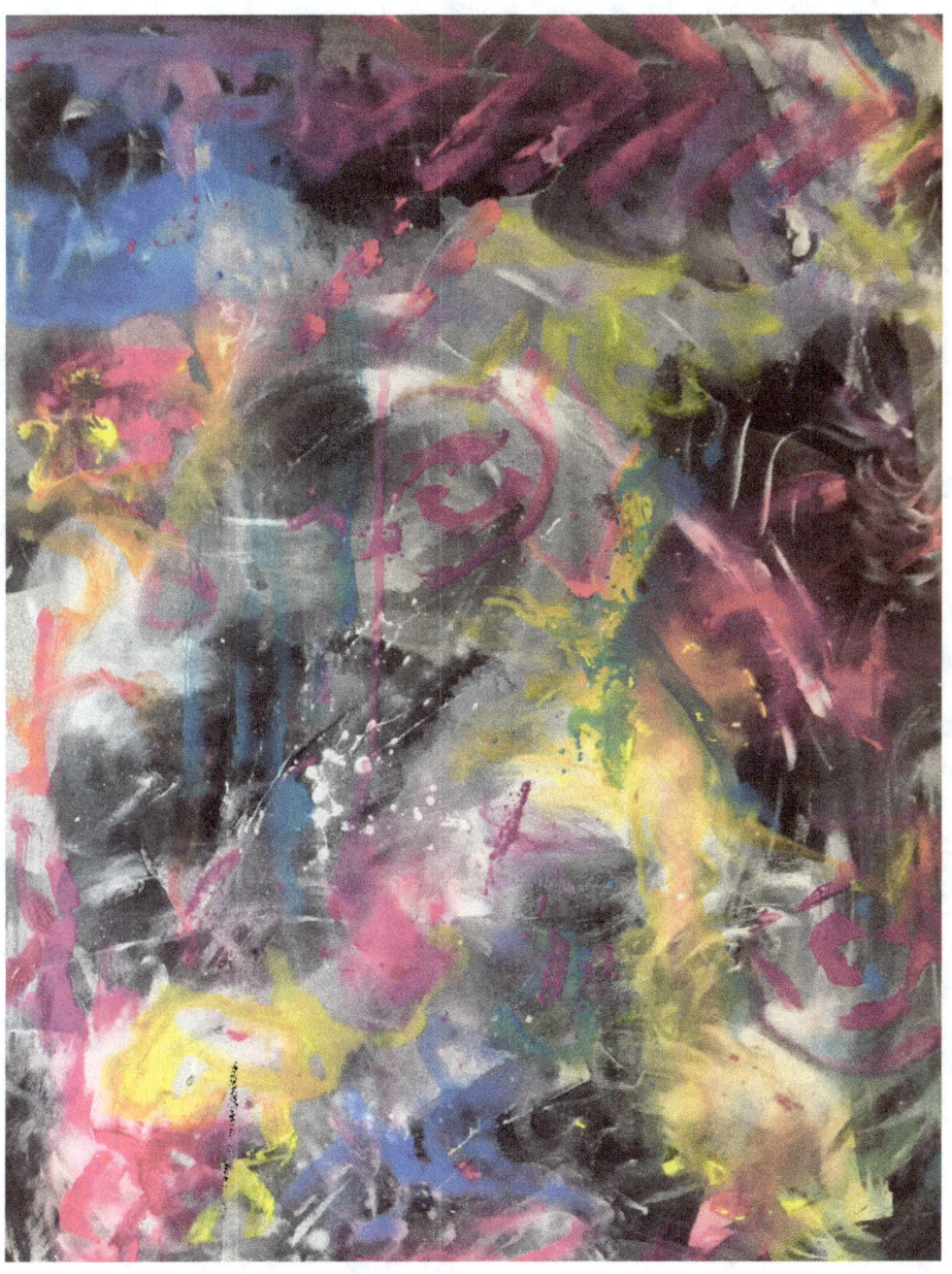

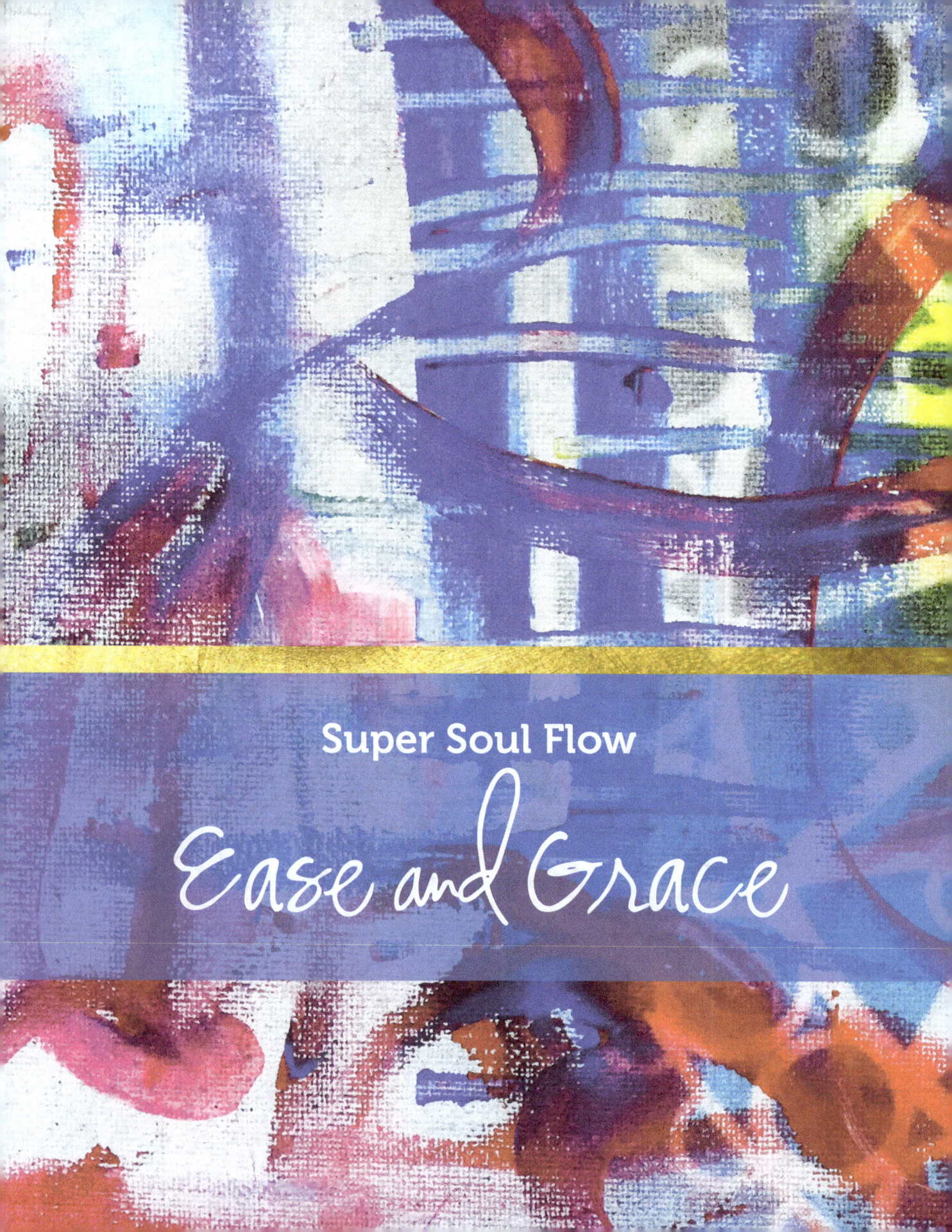

Super Soul Flow

Ease and Grace

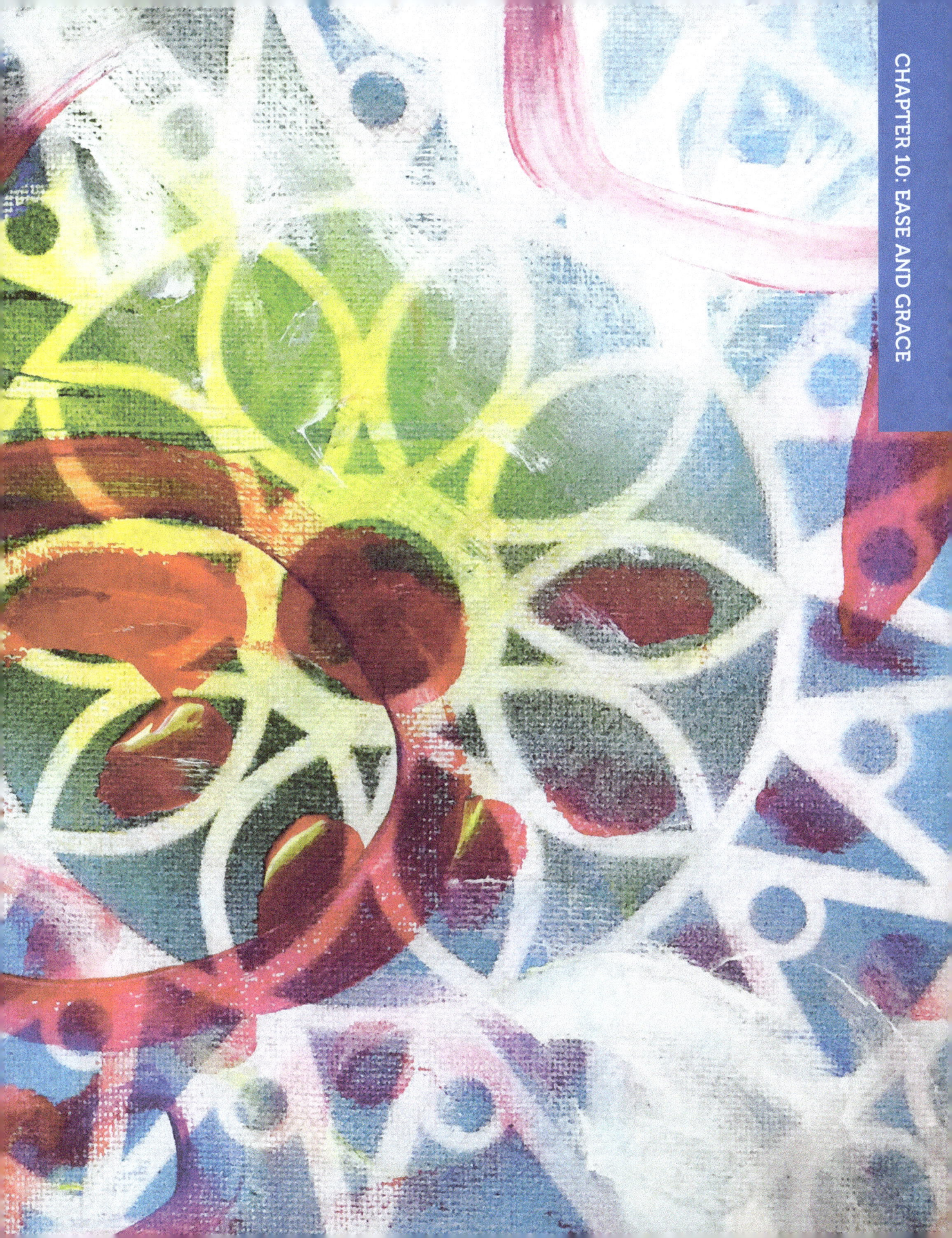

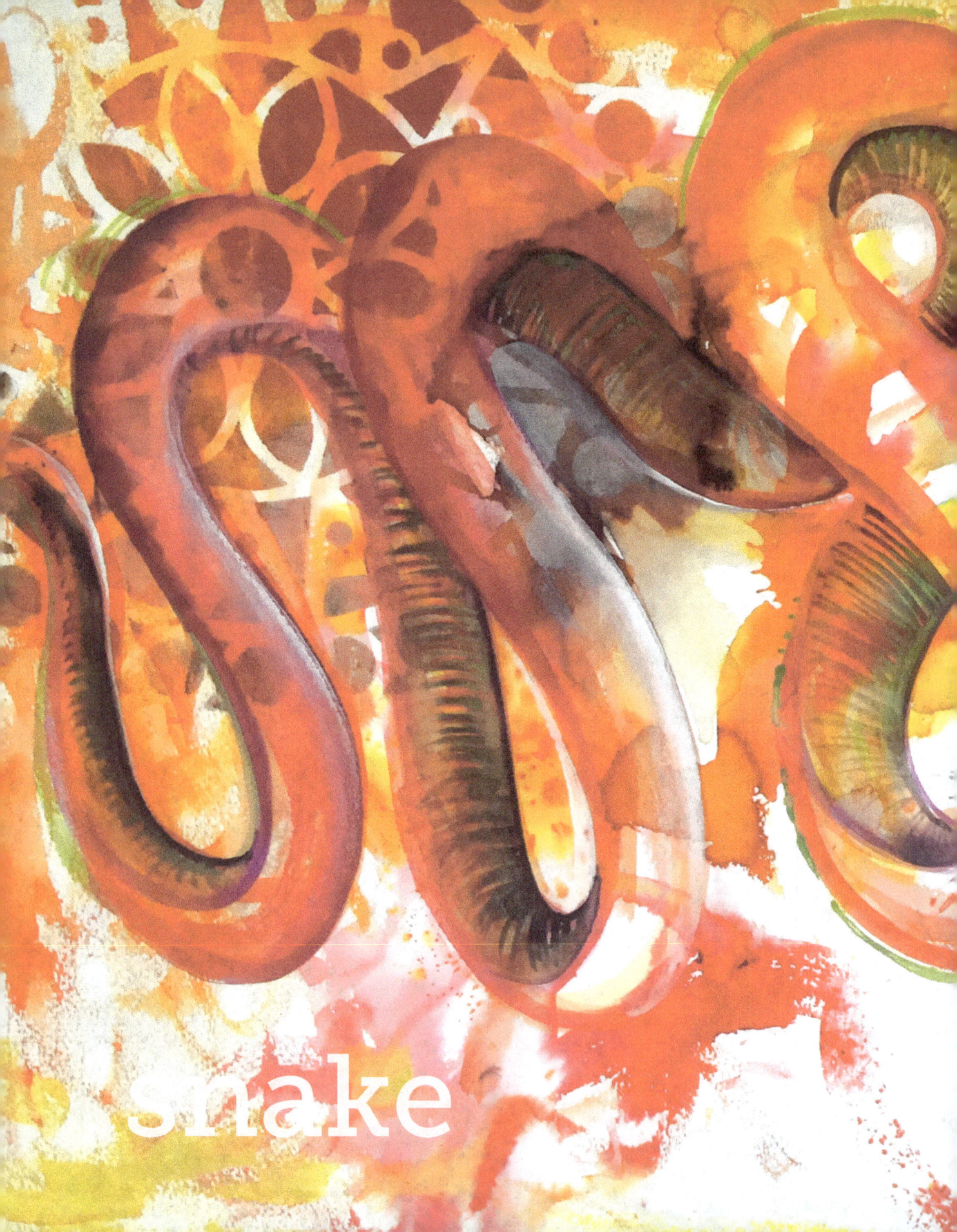

snake

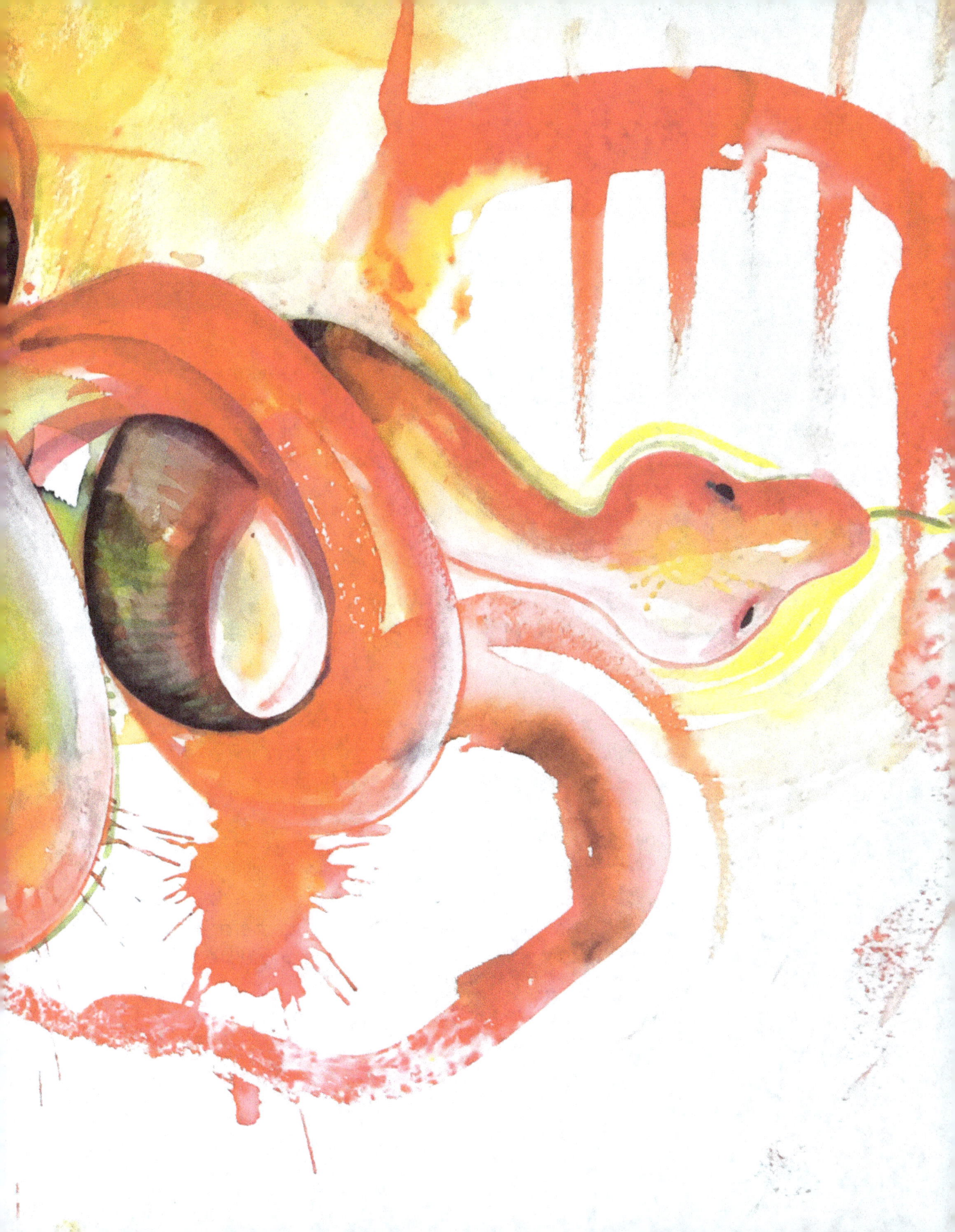

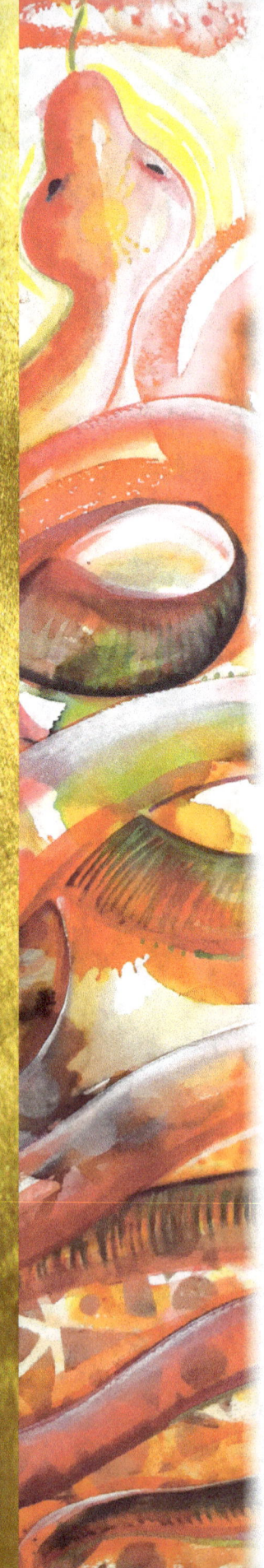

# snake

*When I created the red snake painting you see in this chapter, I was given so much insight into how our own spiritual journey mirrors that of the snake.*

*For many, snakes are still viewed as vile, evil, repulsive, gross, scary, deadly creatures. We've been largely programmed to look at them through this lens, from the Genesis Bible story to Indiana Jones in Raiders of the Lost Ark, "Snakes... why did it have to be snakes?"*

*As you expand the circle of your spiritual journey, you inevitably come across the snake as a symbol of spiritual awakening. From this perspective, "snake medicine" is amongst the most powerful and most desired energies.*

*Kundalini is seen as the spiritual life force that lies coiled at your spine. When you have a Kundalini Awakening the spiritual life force energy zings up your spine, the "snake" uncoiling and shooting upward.*

*Your relationship with the snake, I would like to suggest, is reflective of where you are in your own spiritual awakening. There is no right or wrong here, just an "is." As a global consciousness, when we shift from perceiving the snake as villainous to the snake as divine life force energy, we will also shift from a world based in fear to one based in love. Bring on the snake medicine!*

You volunteered to play this role, didn't you?

You agreed to humble yourself and slither on your belly, no legs, no wings…

You allowed us to villainize you and reject you…

You understood the meandering journey of Spirit.
You are not fear,

You are love.

You are not the enemy,

You are our guide.

You promise that as we choose to look at our own shadow, we will also be given illumination.

You protect us as we risk the shift from judgment to acceptance, from rejection to embrace.

Once we learn to love the scariest, slithering, vile, monstrous side of ourselves, so can we prepare for the awakening of our truth.

Everything exists under the law of love.

Nothing exists outside the boundaries of love.

Love your enemy… they are love in disguise.

Embrace your "snake," for it is the portal into your next level of personal freedom!

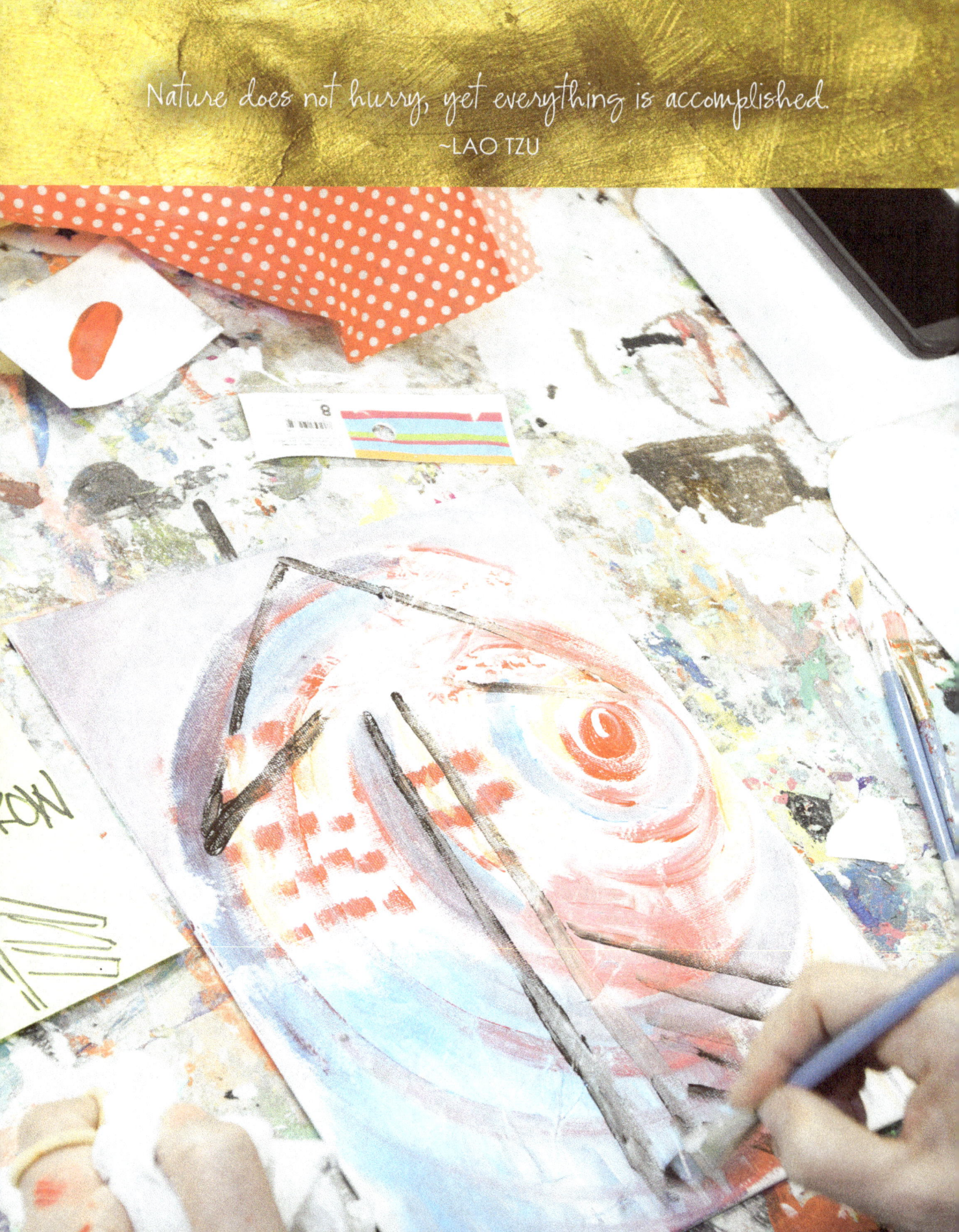

Nature does not hurry, yet everything is accomplished.
~LAO TZU

I'll never forget Margaret. She was a little girl who attended my summer art camps. I knew her between the ages of 5 and 9. She was a powerful and beautifully willful child.

One morning upon arrival I guided her back to the purple room, where the rest of the group had initiated a new project. She refused to participate. She would not even enter the room. I had other things to attend to at that moment and the art instructor had at least 12 other kids who were following directions quite nicely, albeit still up to their elbows in paint and glue. We really wanted Margaret to cooperate and join the herd.

She wouldn't have it.

I thought briefly about forcing her or threatening to call her mother (who was a force of nature in her own right). And then some words of wisdom entered my consciousness, "Don't turn it into a battle of wills."

I pulled a chair out into the hallway.

I handed Margaret her sketch pad.

I said, "Here, you can draw whatever you want until you are ready to join the group."

"Ok." That was all she said.

With a hopeful look exchanged with the instructor, I made my way back to my administrative station at the helm of the ship that was my art center. Ten minutes later I peeked around the corner. Margaret had moved her chair into the room and was happily interacting and creating with the rest of the group.

Ease and grace.

# What are all the ways you can create ease and grace?

Is it about being in a state of allowance?

… acceptance?

… gratitude?

… receiving?

… humility?

Imagine how each of these energies comes into play.

How much time do you spend in the opposite energy, banging your head against a wall or willfully trying to force something that simply won't budge?

The age of struggle and force is over. That is the good news.

Literally, in the story of humankind, the chapter we created so that we could experience struggle, force, and the "no-pain-no-gain" energies is over. We are still left with some residue from that consciousness, but today we can gratefully expect and ask for ease and grace. If it is not "flowing," stop pushing.

What do you do when something isn't working?

You wait.

You redirect your attention.

You accept the "wholeness" of the situation, the parts you like and don't like.

You trust in perfect timing.

When you have your "Super Soul Flow" on, you will experience an abundance of ease and grace.

When you are able to spend more and more time in present-moment awareness, without being distracted by what just happened in the past or worrying about what might or might not happen that night or the next day, you will experience more ease and grace.

Sound too good to be true?

Let's try it.

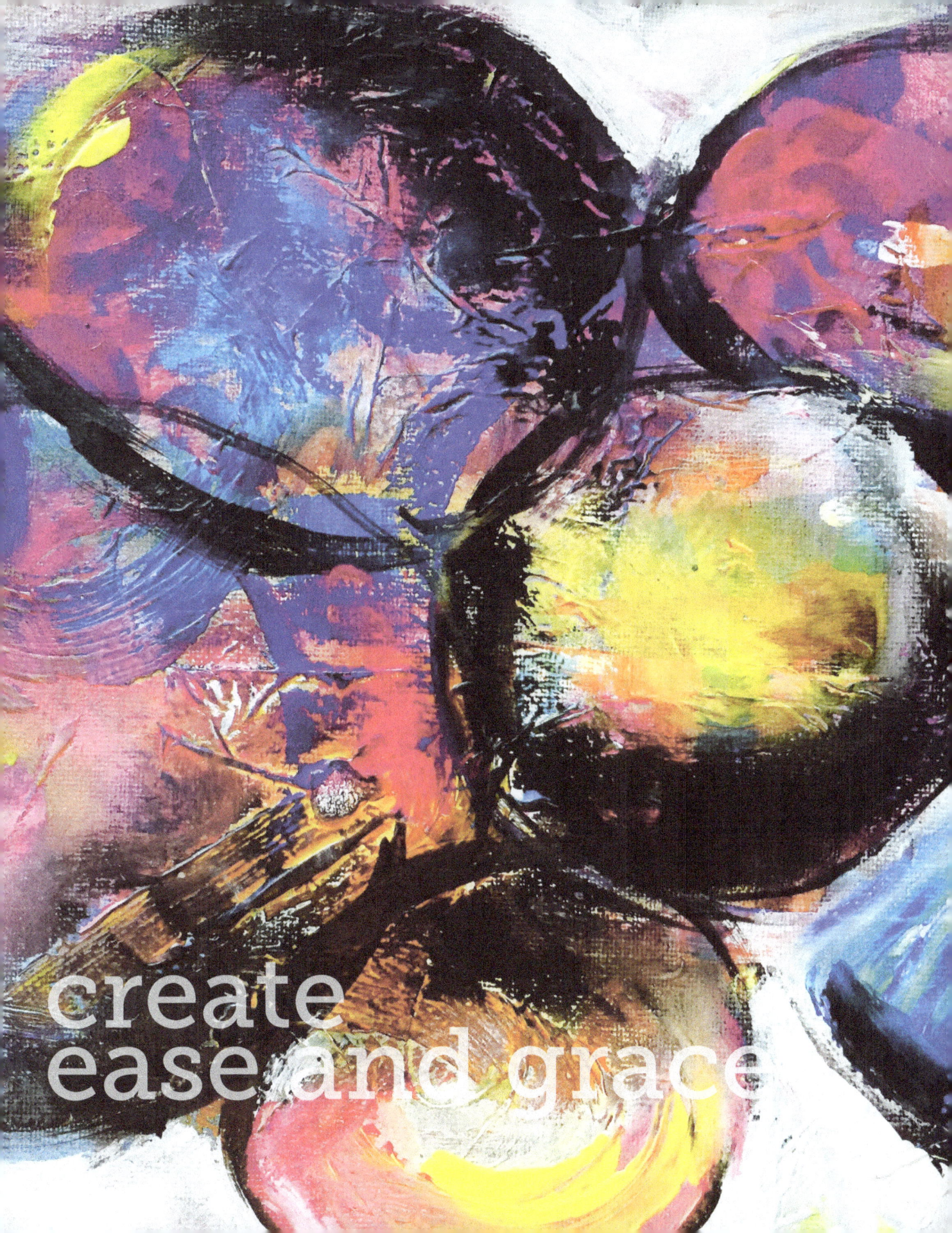

create
ease and grace

# If there is another statement I hear more than, "I can't even draw a straight line," it is "I have to figure it out."

What if you didn't?

What if you could allow the answer or insight to simply appear with ease and grace? Recently, one of my Creatively Fit Coaches shared on a call that she had to "figure out" whether or not she was going to open an art studio of her own. What sprung to mind, with ease and grace, were these three tips on how to NOT figure it out.

As I looked back over my notes after the call I thought, "That is a blog post!" Later, on my hike, thinking about what my content might be for my next Super Soul Flow chapter on ease and grace, it hit me! It was those same three tips! Ease and grace was being perfectly revealed to me! I didn't have to figure anything out. It just landed. I SO love that!

By the way, when that happens for you, which it will, don't question it. Act on whatever has been delivered to you with ease and grace. Resist the urge to confirm, hash it out, and research. At least take the first step in that direction and feel it out. You will most likely experience another wave of ease and grace. Let it flow, baby!

Without further ado…

## 3 Tools for Inviting in Ease and Grace

### 1. Remembering Your Future

Does this sound impossible? Ok, fun!

First, do this for me: Think about what you did yesterday. Do you remember? What did you do last night? Who did you spend time with yesterday? Remember that conversation. Where were you? What were you wearing? Was it rainy or sunny outside? Got it? Good. You are now remembering your past.

Next, think about what you are going to do after you are done reading this. Maybe you are going to bed? Are you going to make coffee? Get in the car to go to the store? Pick up the kids? Whatever is absolutely next on your agenda, imagine that you are already doing it. Imagine

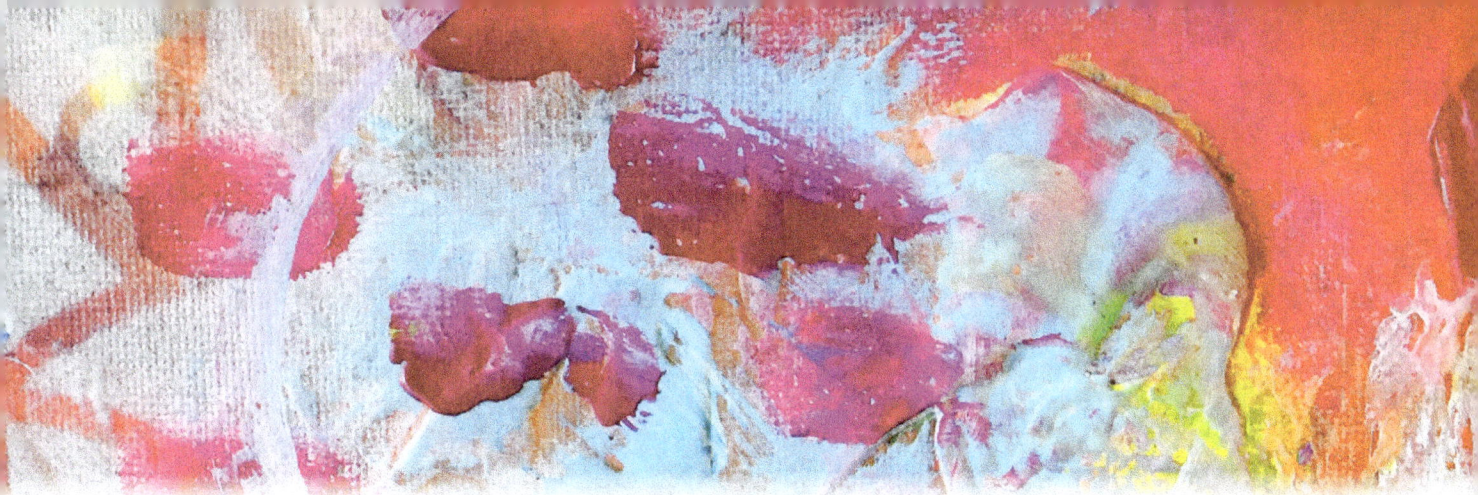

getting in the car, pulling back the covers, putting the water on to boil... Can you see it? What are you wearing in this next part of your day? How much time do you have? Are you going to be rushed? Do you have a vision in your mind of what you are going to be doing, say, 30 minutes from now? Take yourself there.

You have just remembered your future. You have painted pictures in your mind of what you will be doing in the future, based on our linear perspective of time. Perfect.

Now, let's get a bit more crafty!

I want you to think of something that you COULD do tonight (or tomorrow night if you are reading this before bed) that you probably WOULDN'T do if you didn't make a serious effort. What is that thing that you have been meaning to do? It is something that is TOTALLY doable, but you would be prone to putting off again if you didn't really commit to it right now.

Got it?

Imagine yourself doing that thing tonight. When I did this with a client, she shared that she had been meaning to do the next lesson in an online course for WEEKS! She agreed that it was possible for her to do it that night and that she would probably put it off again otherwise.

I asked her what she was going to be wearing. She had her slippers on, her comfy sweat pants and her favorite sweater.

Where is she sitting? *In the big, upholstered chair next to the computer table.*

What else is around you? *A floor lamp, a cup of tea, and my art journal.*

Where is everyone else? *Kids are in bed and hubby is reading.*

Now we are ready. She just remembered her future. I suggested to her that when she was there that she could think back to our conversation and conjure up a bit of déja vu energy.

And that night, she did exactly that. Magic!

Now you do it. What are you going to do tonight? It could be a short activity or longer...

Is it a bubble bath, painting with the kids, clearing out that junk drawer, organizing the laundry room, or indulging in a good book?

This is practice.

NOW, when you are trying to "figure something out" you know how to remember your future. Pick one option, then the other. Imagine yourself in each scenario. What are you doing? Wearing? Feeling? Who are you with? Where are you? What else is there?

Which option feels the most familiar? Which one feels the most comfortable? Do any of the options create a reaction in your mind like, "Oh yeah! That's what I do!"?

There you go!

AND, you can take the information you gather from this exercise and move on to tip #2. They all FLOW together, of course!

## 2. Ask Your Body

"Does this option/choice/idea feel LIGHT and EXPANSIVE or HEAVY?"

This is really all you need to ask your body.

If this feels like a stretch for you, allow me to suggest a simple exercise.

Think of a super fun time you have had recently. Or think of someone you love tremendously. Close your eyes. Check into your body. Does it feel heavy or light and expansive? *LIGHT and EXPANSIVE.*

Now think of a big chore you have to do that you have been putting off. Taxes? Fixing the gutters? Organizing that big closet? Close your eyes. How does that feel? Heavy or light and expansive? *HEAVY.*

When you have a decision to make and your logical mind has made its perspective known, take a moment, close your eyes and ask your body.

I was taught that your body and the feelings you feel come directly from your Highest Self—your soul. You can choose to count on these feelings completely.

Practice with small questions first.

One evening, a client shared that she had received a last-minute invitation to a concert. Normally, she would have said no because she had to work the next day and she hadn't planned on going out that evening. However, this time she checked in with her body, and it felt so light and expansive that she decided to go.

She was thrilled! She had a wonderful time and met someone who could help her with a new project she had been mulling over. What a difference it had made for her to process the decision differently!

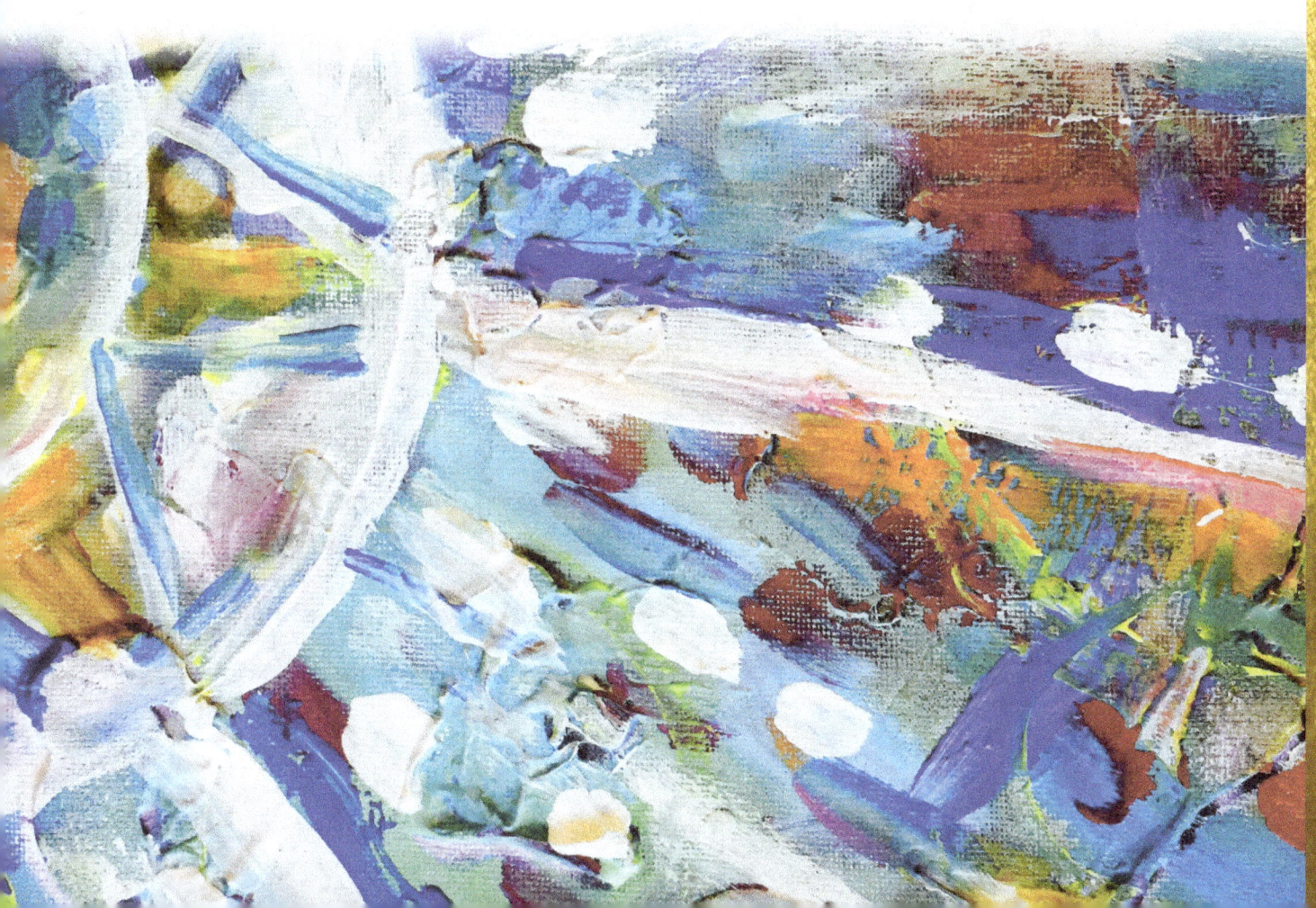

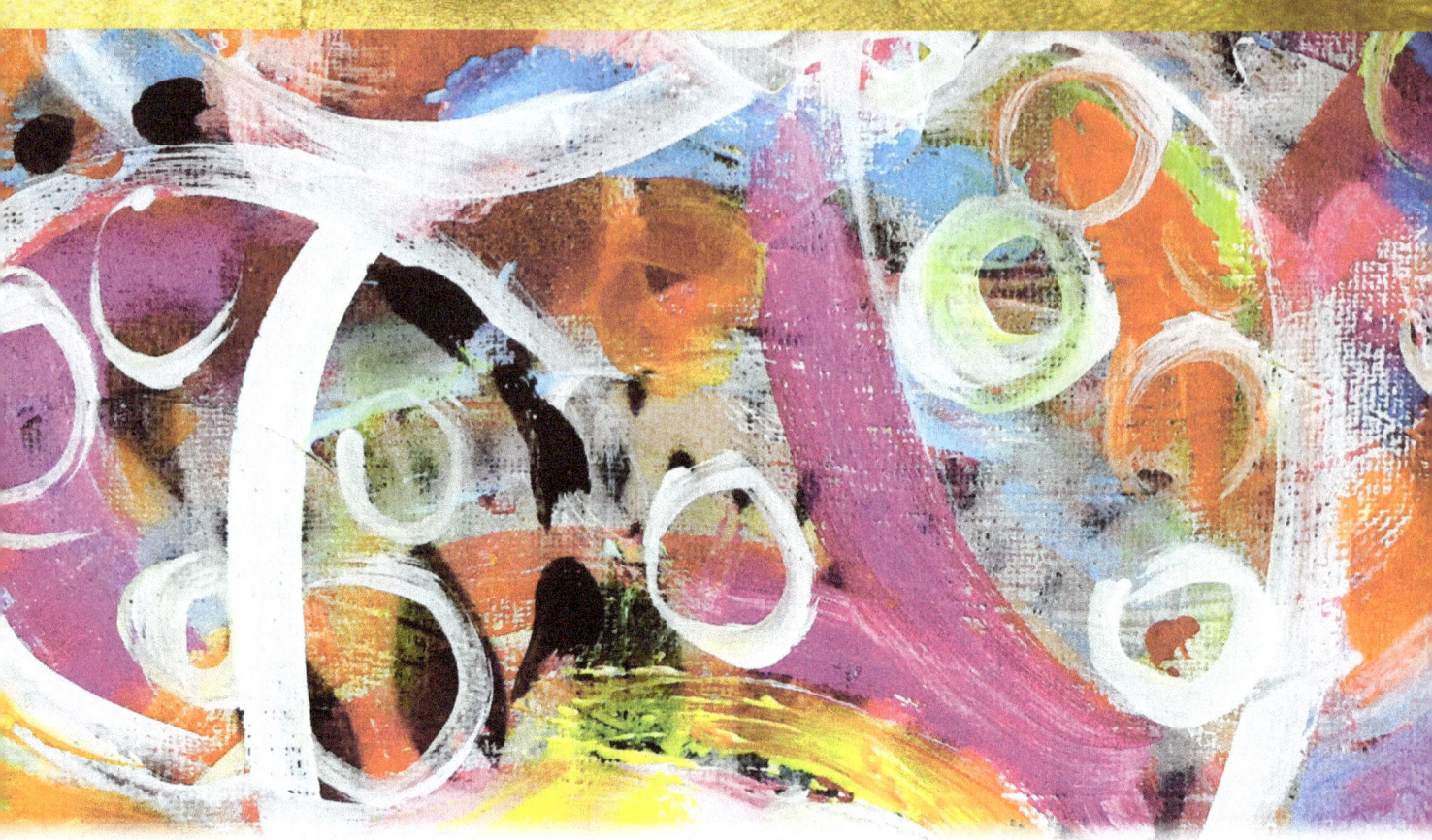

### 3. Look for the Clues

In the teachings and musings around quantum physics, there is the idea that if anything "crosses your path" more than once, you should pay attention. When you hear something or someone mentioned twice within a short period of time (24 or 48 hours), follow the clue. When you see something for the first time and then see it again, and again... follow that clue. When someone pops into your mind repeatedly, reach out to them.

These are all "clues," or subtle promptings by your soul to guide you in a particular direction.

Usually our logical mind discounts these clues because they are NOT, well, logical. How many ah-ha's has your logical mind quickly ushered you past, distracting you with facts and figures, improbabilities and practicalities? Remember, the logical mind wants to keep you safe in your known. These "clues" are always encouraging you in a new direction.

We can thank our logical mind for its desire to keep us safe and then also recognize the contrasting wisdom of our intuitive mind—not that it does not want you safe, but for your soul, change and the unknown equal new potential!

One way that I open up to soul clues is to do the "Open-the-book-to-the-random-page" exercise after asking for insight into a question. What words catch my eye? Those words can be a clue.

These types of synchronicities and coincidences will increase the more receptive you become. The more you honor your Personal Painting Practice, the more receptive you will become.

Sometimes the clues are guiding us to a more receptive state of mind or emotional state so that when we make the decision we are choosing rather than reacting, or being more conscious and intentional rather than allowing an old story or knee-jerk reaction to make the decision for us.

*The bottom line is that we don't have to feel pressure, like we are stuck or that the world is all on our shoulders. You are a limitless being with an infinite soul who always has your highest and greatest good on the top of its list. What are all the ways you can lean into your soul's knowing even more?*

This is big magic and can create feelings of being supported and loved instead of feeling alone or blocked.

Ease and grace is something you can choose to create. You can create a receptivity, an openness, and willingness to take action rooted in a trust that ease and grace exist.

In the painting prompts that follow, I share another example of ease and grace.

# Creating the Energy of EASE and GRACE

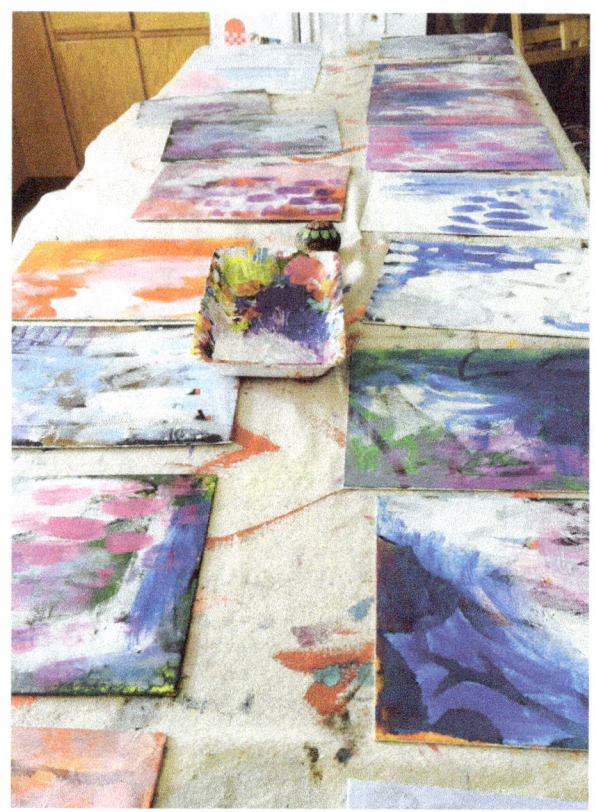

One night I got a "crazy idea" (that was my logical brain's response to my intuitive inspiration) to paint 26 paintings in the course of five days.

While I did start 26 paintings, what really happened is the foundation was laid for this chapter on ease and grace. When the time came to shoot the video lesson for the online version of this book, I realized that I had an abundance of canvases ready and waiting to help me illustrate ease and grace to you!

During your Personal Painting Practice I invite you to PLAY, diverge, and experiment on your canvas. This is reminiscent of our first FREEDOM chapter, although now you can allow an image or symbol to appear from within your brush strokes.

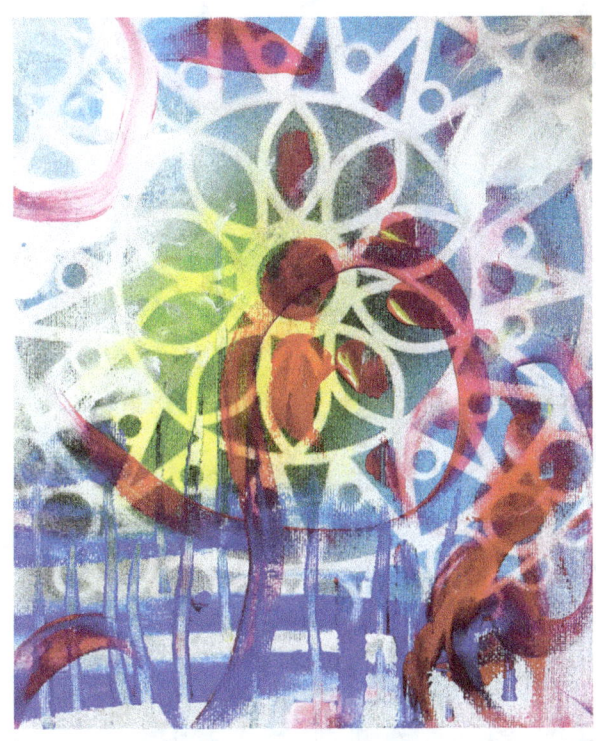

Use stencils, stamp with found objects, finger paint. Create an abundance of shapes and colors on your canvas to create space for ease and grace.

I would also encourage you to do this on more than two canvases so you can easily shift from one canvas to the other. If one canvas isn't speaking to you with ease and grace, you can shift to the next one.

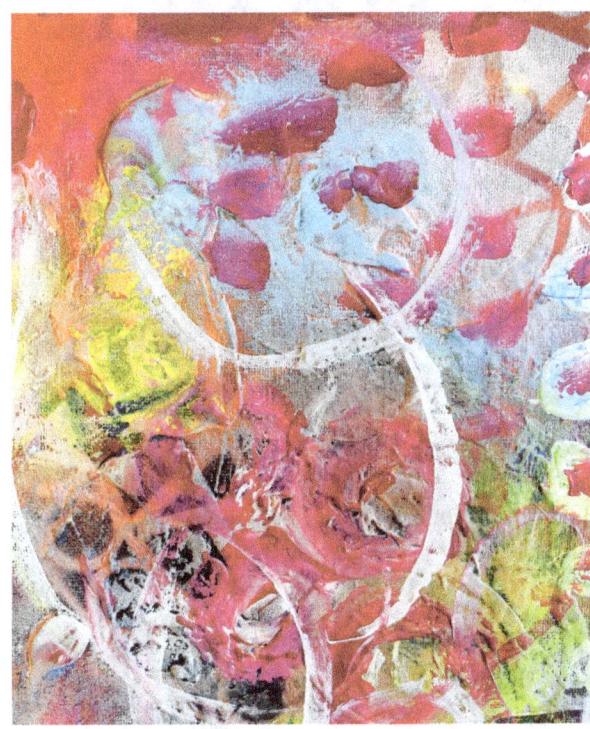

Next, scribble on your canvas. Close your eyes and move the brush around randomly. It may look like this... see the white painted line?

Allow the scribble to inspire you. "What does it make me think of?" It is about allowing the canvas to let you know what it wants to be. OR ask yourself, "What does my soul want to create through me right now?"

This is what my painted scribbles led to when I just let go and chose to create ease and grace:

A crazy face!

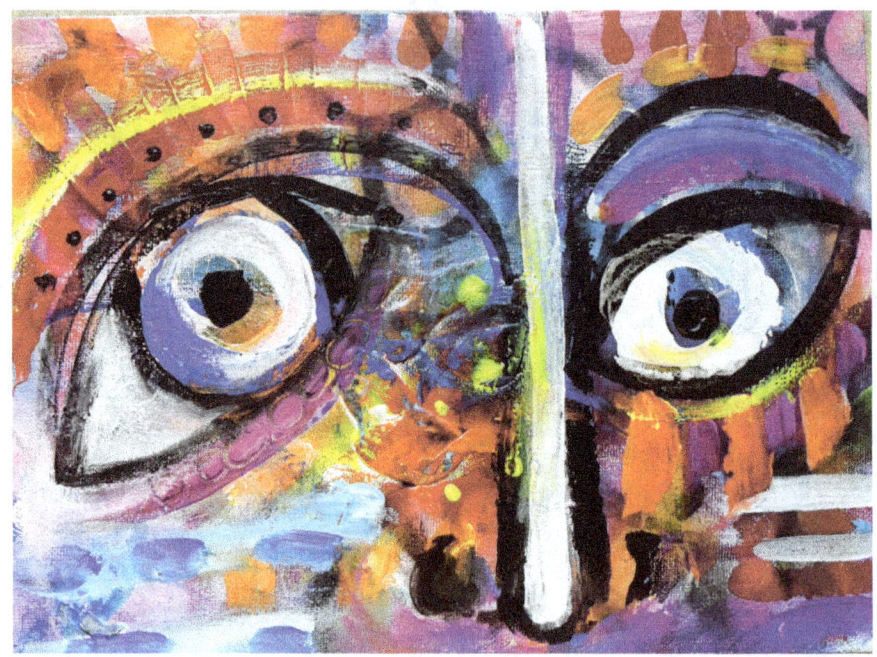

"It takes a village..."

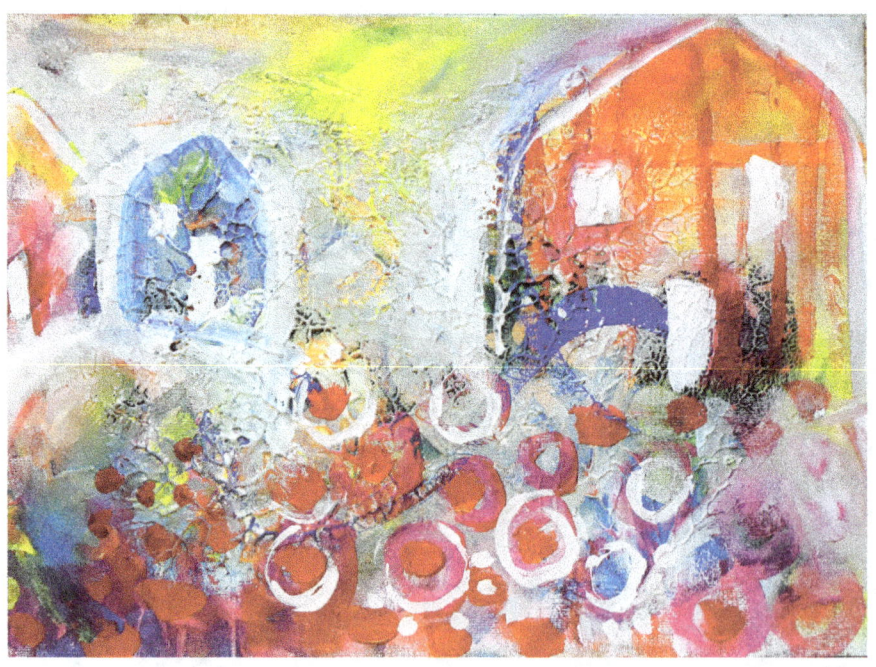

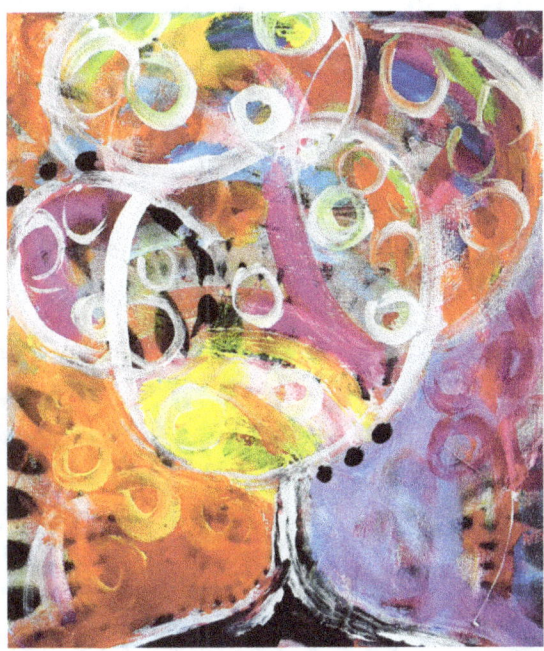

A bountiful tree, or a chalice.

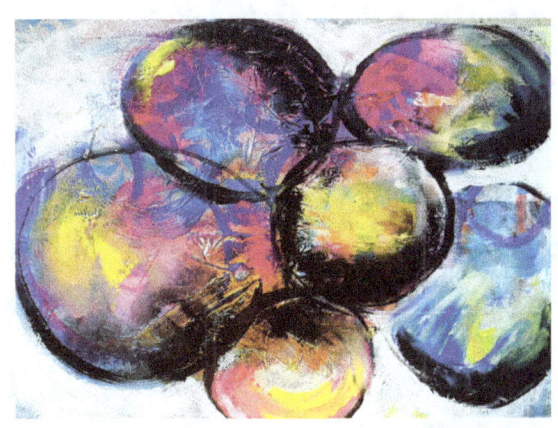

A funky flower (someone else saw portals into space!)

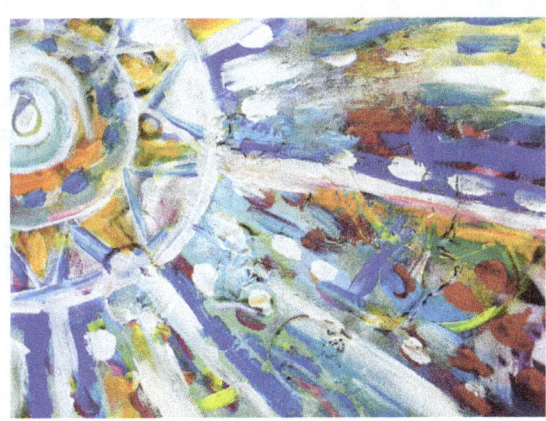

A starburst!

Finally, I had to see an owl!

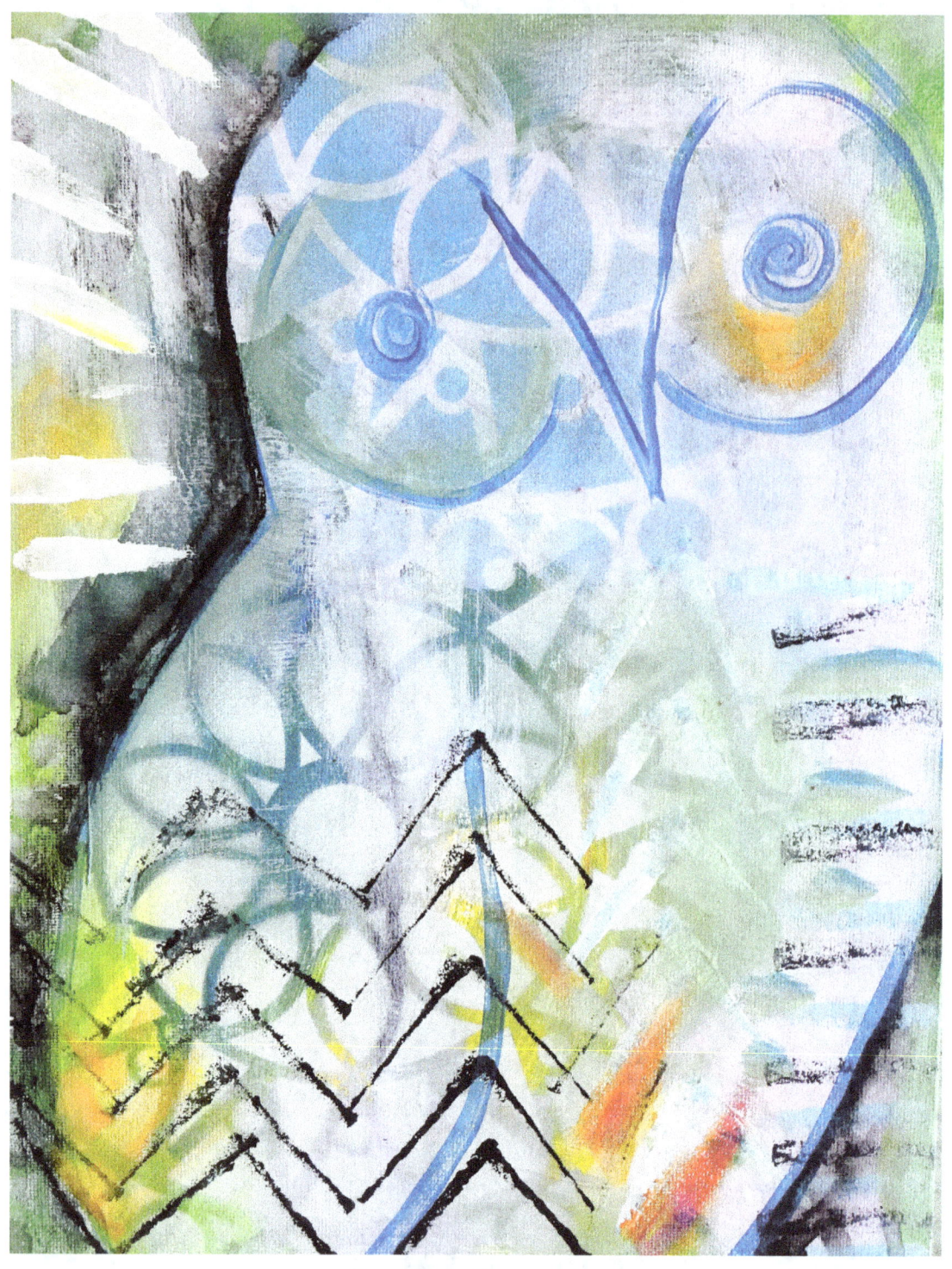

Without consciously creating ease and grace, I can put too much pressure on myself to perform, produce, or be perfect. When I intend to follow the energy of flow, ease, and grace, I open up room for the mystery—for my soul to co-create with me.

*Your Personal Painting Practice isn't about "painting right," but about creating an openness and receptivity to the subtle ways we can collaborate with our BIG self to create BIG magic!*

Who knows what might come through?! That's the adventure! Olé!

Now you can allow that energy of flow to expand beyond the canvas and into the art that is your life. Before you know it, you are trusting that you will have what you need, on every level, even when, in the moment, you can't see the order of it all.

Trust.

Be.

Create.

Open.

Flow...

Thank you for sharing your flow with me!

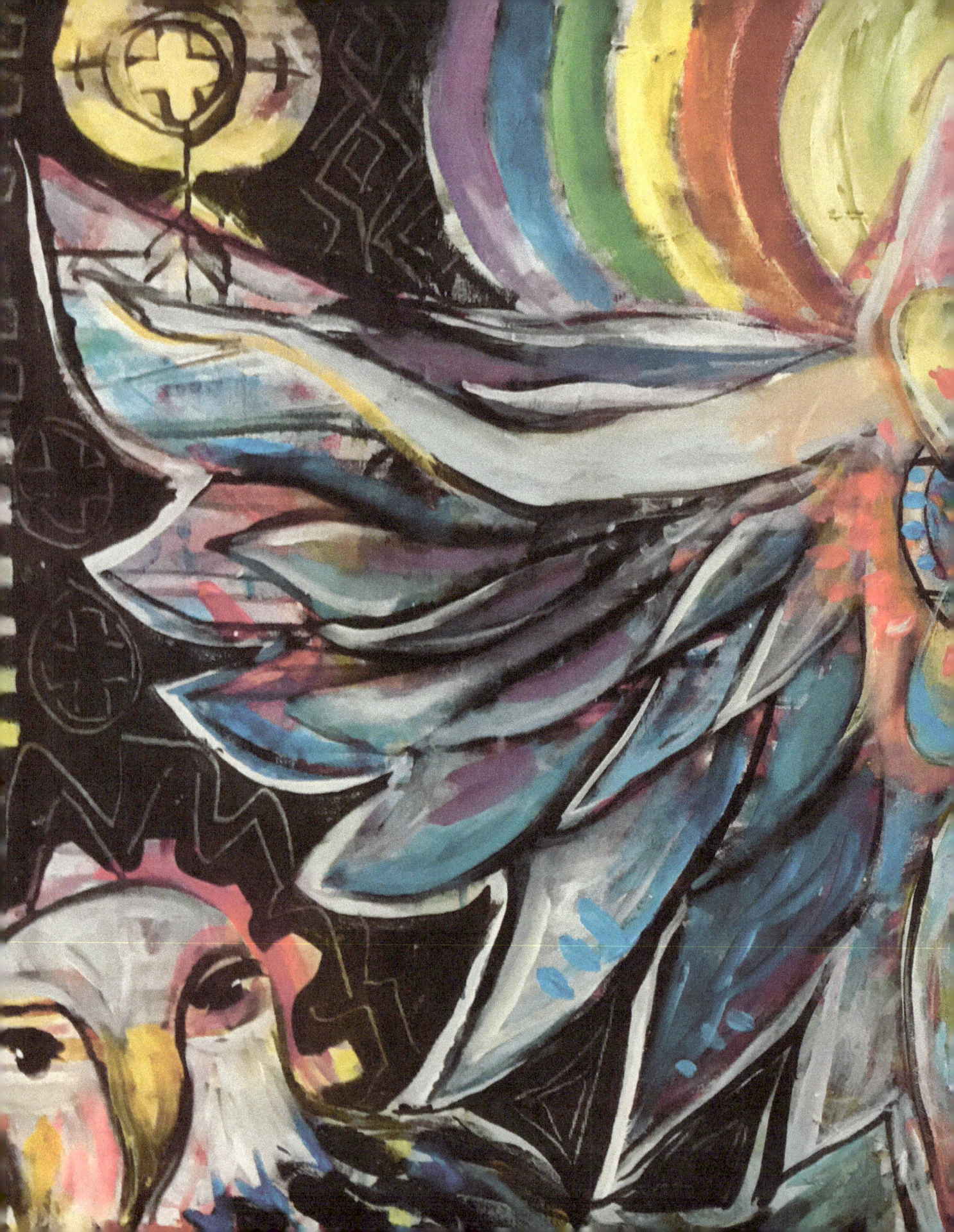

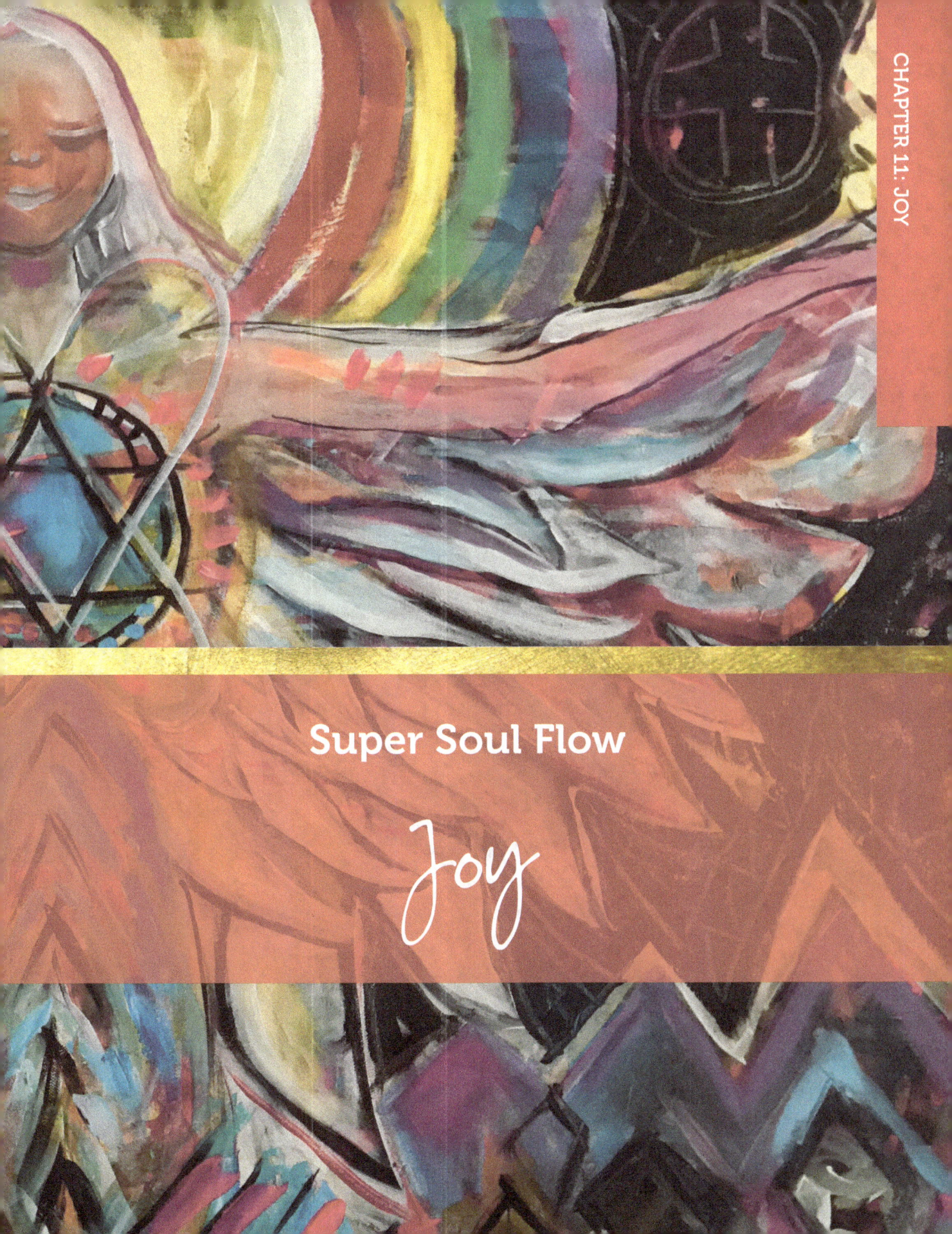

Super Soul Flow

*Joy*

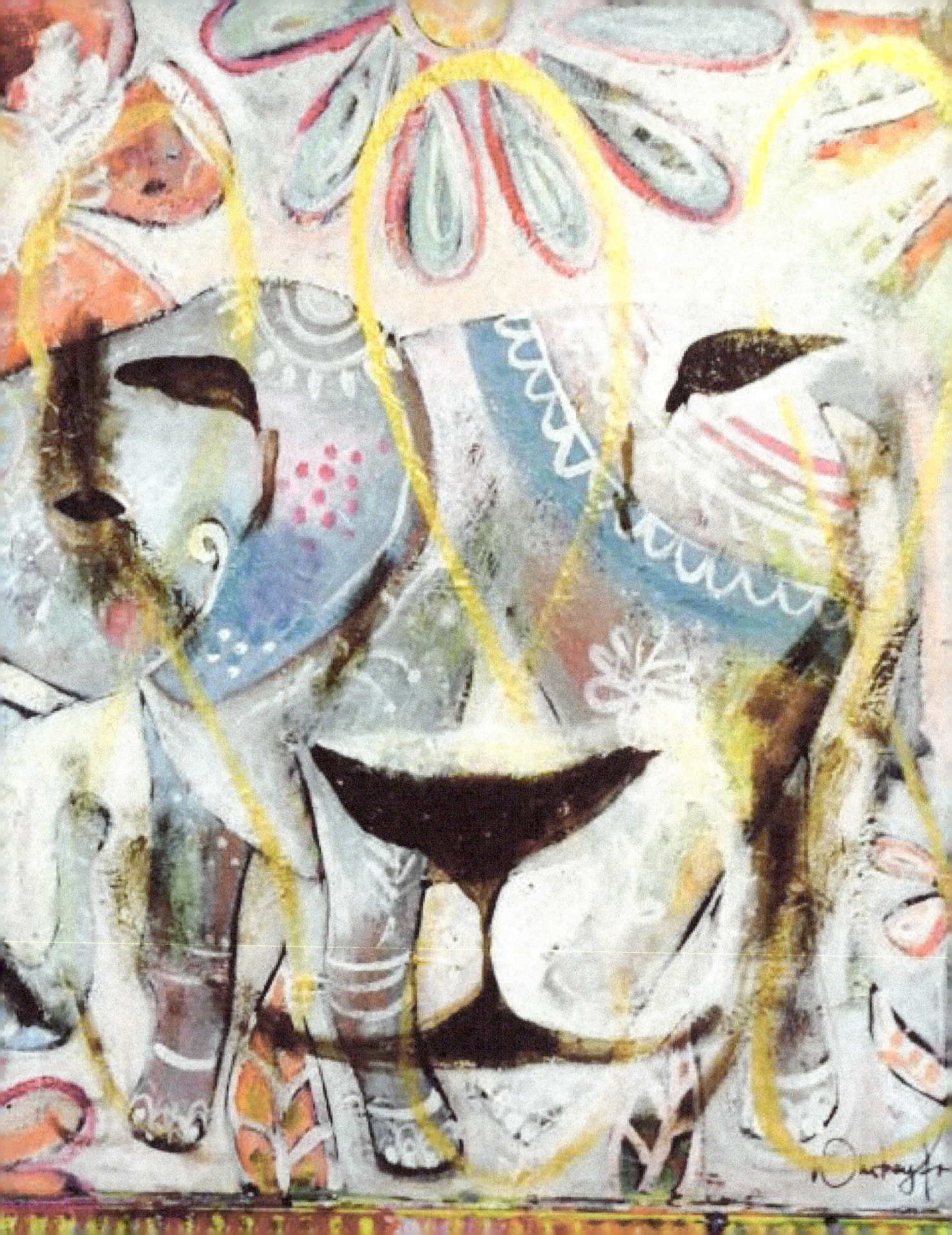

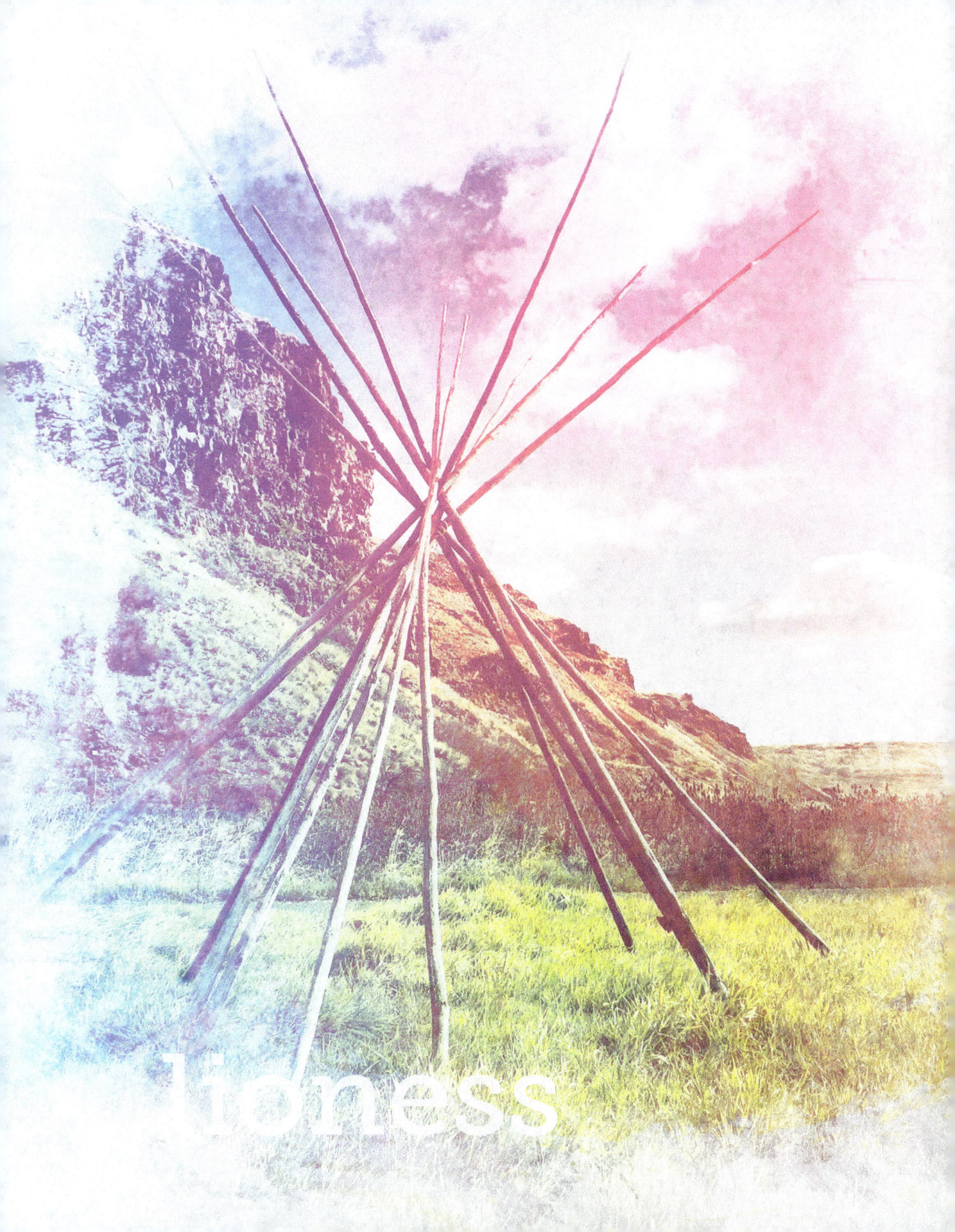

# lioness

*Joy is our birthright. It is the life pulse of the divine. And we have been raised to believe that there is such a thing as too much joy. We learned joy was reserved for special occasions, holidays, and accomplishments. People who appeared too joyful might be considered unbalanced, irresponsible, or otherwise daft.*

*As we RISE ABOVE and gain new clarity and objectivity, we get to choose, to ROARRRRRR our OWN truth into our world.*

**"I found God in myself and I loved her fiercely."**
**~Ntosake Shange**

*The lioness is the hunter, the protector. She has traditionally accompanied the Goddess and lent her strength, conviction, power, and assertiveness. She is the feminine energy that KNOWS that the pursuit and capture of JOY is one of life's greatest quests.*

*Invite lioness into your Personal Painting Practice and your life now and ask her to help you to protect those things that bring you joy, to help you hunt for more joy, and to defend your right to BE joy.*

I close my eyes, take a deep breath and call to the lioness.

I see her appear in the distance, her shoulders shifting with each step.

Closer and closer, until we merge in a golden light, and energy of joy and strength.

Together we roam and survey our dominion.
We are free.
We are strong.
We are one.

We bask in the golden sun.
She seems to bathe me in confidence, root my energies in the temple of the earth.
I breathe in the space, the openness and I feel the joy.
She asks me, "What is caging you in? What is blocking your path?"

I breathe in her golden light.

I see fences, or walls, appear to trap me, to keep me from roaming freely.

She walks toward the obstacle and I know I am to follow.

She steps right up to the edge, inhales deeply, and lets out her most primal ROARRRRRRRRRRRRRRRRRR.

Whatever is keeping you from your freedom, your joy, starts to shake.

ROARRRRRRRRRRRRRRRRR.

The stories that fenced you in. The beliefs that, block by block, hid from you what was possible, crumble and fall.

ROARRRRRRRRRRRRRRRRR.

Your lioness is here to defend your territory, to dissolve the fear, and guard you as you step bravely into your JOY.

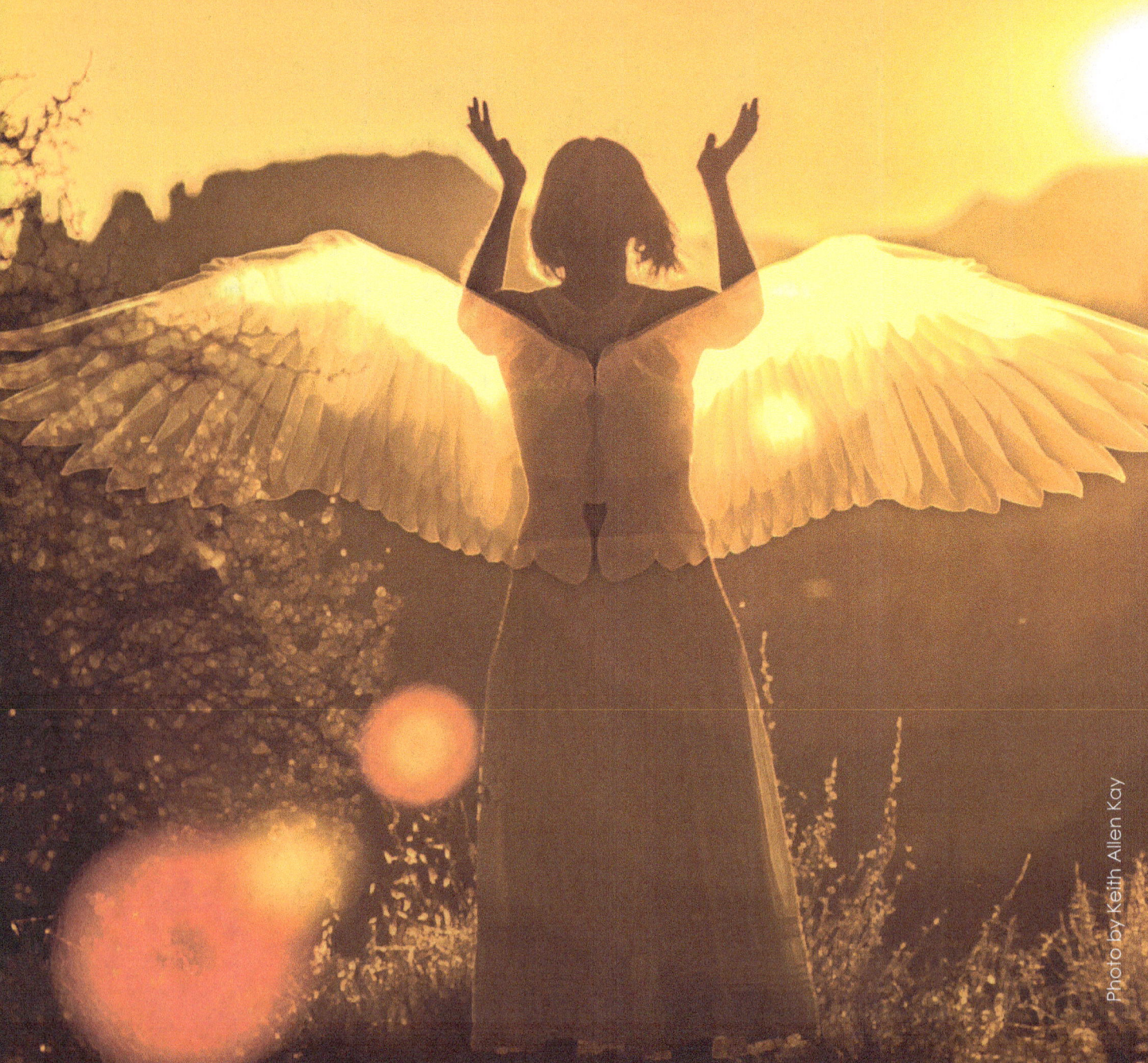

Joy is felt when you are free to create in each moment the fullest choosing of that moment. Joy is the passageway to freedom and knowledge.

~FLO CALHOUN, *I REMEMBER UNION*

Photo by Keith Allen Kay

I believe the energy of joy has been dramatically misinterpreted by our human perception. In fact, I could imagine that true joy is not even possible coming from an egocentric perspective. Why?

Because the egocentric, human, traditional perspective can only perceive itself as separate from the whole, with much to fear, and in need of protection.

That's ok. Because it has now guided YOU to this new vibration of joy.

This is the joy that comes from deep within. This is the joy that can only be known by a soul whose "person" is waking up to the infinite truth. It is when you REMEMBER UNION with your soul that you can rediscover true joy.

Boom!

You are shifting your entire perception from a human-centric focus to a soul-centric focus. You ARE an infinite being who has chosen to have THIS human experience. You chose ALL of it!

In fact, the unique challenges and heartbreaks and obstacles you have faced are ALL here to serve you. They are "lessons" that you CHOSE to come here to learn.

Are you an overachiever? Did you choose A LOT of lessons? That can only mean that you are that much more of an advanced soul. Can you imagine the feeling, the energy, of joy that your soul feels each time you learn to RISE ABOVE an experience of human drama, trauma, or disappointment?

The call, the human experience chosen by your infinite being, is to REDISCOVER JOY in spite of the human experience.

This is why the LIONESS is your animal totem for this chapter.

Joy requires strength, courage, and a level of protection as you take back your mastery. You get to ROARRRRRR in the light of defeat and failure.

What if that thing, that situation, or that handicap was... YOUR PORTAL to your truest joy?

Instead of giving away your joy to that person or that job or that situation, what if in the process of learning to LOVE whatever experience you are having you DISCOVER true joy?

Maybe it is ONLY when we remember that EVERYTHING is here to love us that we can feel and create joy! I remember hearing the Dalai Lama speak about his gratitude to the Chinese government. Whaaaaaat?

He spoke with a lightness of being about how had he not been exiled, his country oppressed, and their freedom attacked that he would never have had the opportunity to travel the world sharing his teachings, writing countless books, giving countless speeches and becoming one of, if not *the* most widely recognized spiritual leaders of our time.

Had he never adopted that perspective...

Had he chosen to instead create anger, resentment and blame... would he ever know true joy?

## Here is the GREAT news about JOY...

Now that you remember that you can choose to find joy within the challenging moments, you can also remember that when life is going great, creating positive, loving, happy experiences, your JOY-meter can really blast off the charts!

**Joy is everywhere!**

**Joy is in the shadows AND in the light.**

**Joy is in the challenges AND the breakthroughs.**

**Joy is in the mountaintop experiences AND the valleys.**

**Joy is in the calm AND the storm.**

Take a moment. This is a HUGE shift.

There is a part of you that is thinking, "Are you kidding me?! I've spent all this time feeling _____ about _____ and now you are telling me I could have chosen JOY? The 'fullest' choosing in all those moments could have included JOY?!"

Yes.

And now you are here. And now you know. So what is next?

## Joy Exercise

RISE ABOVE the human drama. This is going to be so fun! And you are going to freak some people out. Ready?

I'm just guessing there is going to be some form of human drama that will cross your path this week... a misunderstanding with a friend, a gossip session that presents itself, a situation that could lead you to complaining about something...

Someone hurts your feelings, ignores you, forgets to invite you, doesn't thank you properly… Someone will be insensitive to your situation. Someone might lie to you, cheat you, or hurt your feelings.

Instead of getting pissed off, turning to your other friends to complain about so-and-so, or feeling victimized and blaming him or her, you are going to RISE ABOVE.

You can now call in your lioness guide for courage and to protect you energetically. Allow your lioness to ground you in your moment, the moment you are going to CHOOSE to create, not a moment dictated by external factors.

Once you are grounded, strong, and in your power, you can put on your "wings" and rise above the human drama.

You are going to ask yourself, "Do I choose to participate in this human drama?"

"What am I being invited to learn here?"

"What are all the ways I can be the light in this dark situation, rather than adding to the darkness?"

"What shade of negative energy am I being given an opportunity to transmute into personal power?"

"Can I detach myself from this drama and understand that it is not about me? This person is simply on their own learning, expanding journey and I don't have to participate in their drama."

*When you do this, energetically, the drama just falls away. The drama energy has nothing to attach to in your field. AND you will feel a wave of joy as your soul sends you affirmation, through the feeling of joy, that you have just achieved mastery in this situation.*

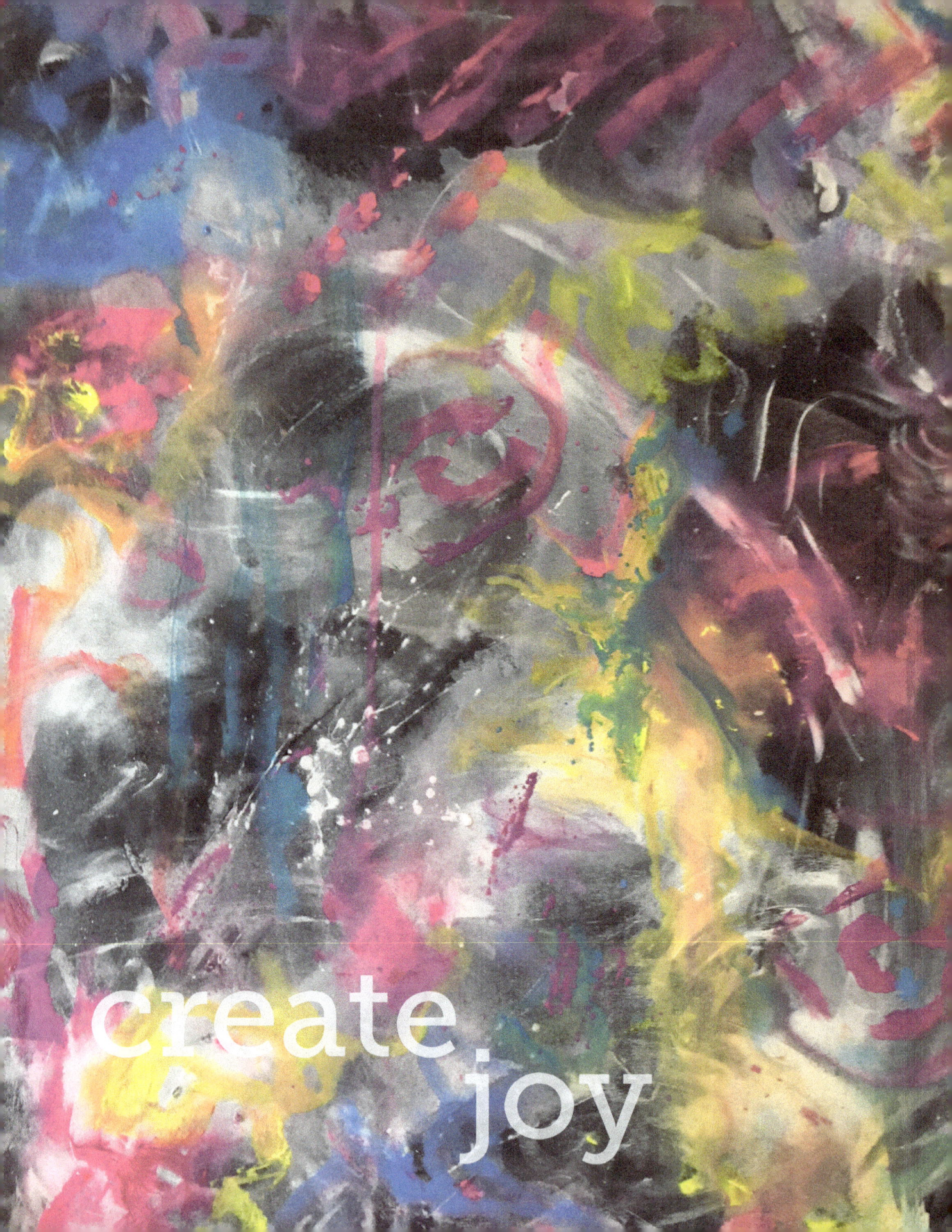

create
joy

What about when the drama finds you when you are all alone? Is it only your drama knocking on the door?

Do you find yourself passing judgment on something or someone?

Maybe you are reading the news or an email that triggers your inner critic.

Or perhaps you are playing the role of your own worst enemy and beating yourself up for not being _____ enough.

## What if that thing, that person, or this behavior of your own that you are judging is really here to hold up a mirror?

What if it is not the other person or situation that is ignorant, mis-informed, wrong, bad, stupid, clueless, insensitive, and dishonest? What if they are just holding up a mirror for you to see all the ways you are being ignorant, misin-formed, wrong, insensitive, and dishonest...?

That can be a tough pill to swallow AND it is your medicine. Your JOY med-icine. Life simply reflects back to you what you are projecting. It doesn't do that to make you wrong or reprimand you. It does that to ENLIGHTEN, ILLUMI-NATE and guide you back to your most joyful, loving self.

When you look into that mirror and open to the highest good, you enter into a space of choosing. You are the Life Artist at the "canvas" choosing what to create. Will you choose more of what you don't want or more of what you do want?

From that perspective, you can create the change you desire.

From that perspective, you become the change you want to see in your world.

From that perspective you can BE compassion. From your compassion, for yourself first, the joy can flow!

It may not make sense reading this now, but trust me. Give it a try.

The FULLEST choosing in any moment can always include joy. I so love this quote:

> *Joy is felt when you are free to create in each moment the fullest choosing of that moment. Joy is the passageway to freedom and knowledge.*

—FLO CALHOUN, *I REMEMBER UNION*

No matter what is going on in your life, if you are not choosing to add a heavy dose of joy into it, you are simply not choosing the FULLEST potential of that moment.

AND when you remember that no matter WHAT anyone else does, or no matter WHAT life circumstances are presented to you, you can always experience the energy of joy. THEN you are free! This is the passageway to freedom and knowledge.

This does not mean that 100 percent of your life is lived in a feeling of joy...

What it means is that at least 51 percent of the time you are able to create positivity over negativity. At least 51 percent of your energy is in alignment with joy. This is the tipping point; 51 percent is all your soul needs to send your infinite awareness flowing into your consciousness and to empower you to RISE ABOVE any suffering.

I am channeling Buddha here: Joy is not the absence of suffering. Joy is in the choosing, in light of the suffering.

And we miss out on the joy when we think that the suffering is wrong or bad. We are afraid we are suffering because we are wrong or bad. No.

You are a joy-creating machine BECAUSE of the contrast provided by the suffering. BECAUSE you know suffering, you can choose joy.

Let's take it to the canvas. This is where you get your wings!

Let's paint your wings. And we are not walking hesitantly up to the canvas, asking, "Pretty please can I have my wings now?"

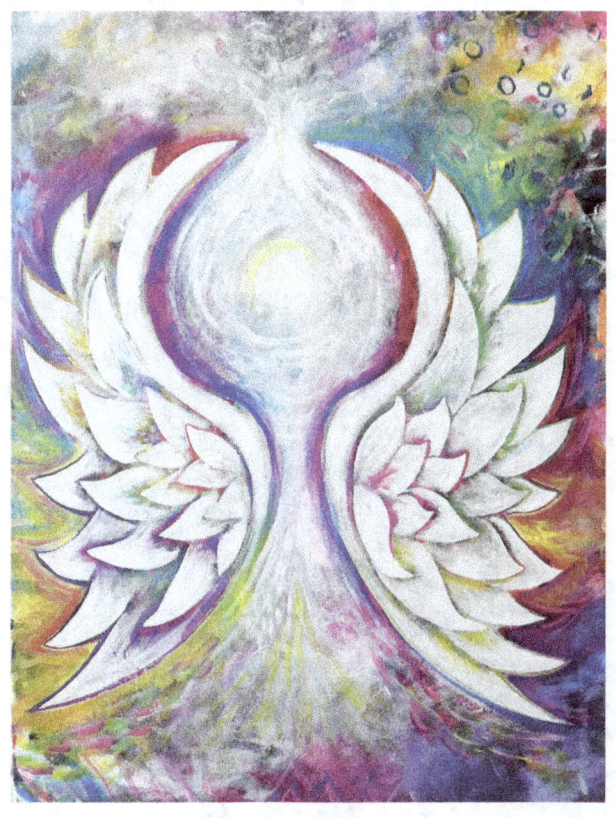

You are striding up to the canvas and ROARRRRRING into the void, "I CHOOSE JOY. I CHOOSE TO RISE ABOVE the human drama. I CHOOSE TO PROTECT FIERCELY my right to be, feel and create JOY!"

With each brushstroke, you will expand your ability to RISE ABOVE the human drama and include JOY in every aspect of your life experience. Quiet joy. Deep joy. Jump up and down joy. Every shade of joy is now available to you.

And when you forget, which you will, your wings will come to you. You will find a feather on the ground, your painting will catch your eye, a song lyric will sing about wings and flying. And you will remember.

And when you think that joy is not nearly possible in THIS situation, you will remember your wings. You will put them on. You will RISE ABOVE.

I know this because you are here reading these words. Your soul attracted you to these words today, right NOW, for a reason.

You are ready. You have earned your wings. You get them now.

Welcome home!

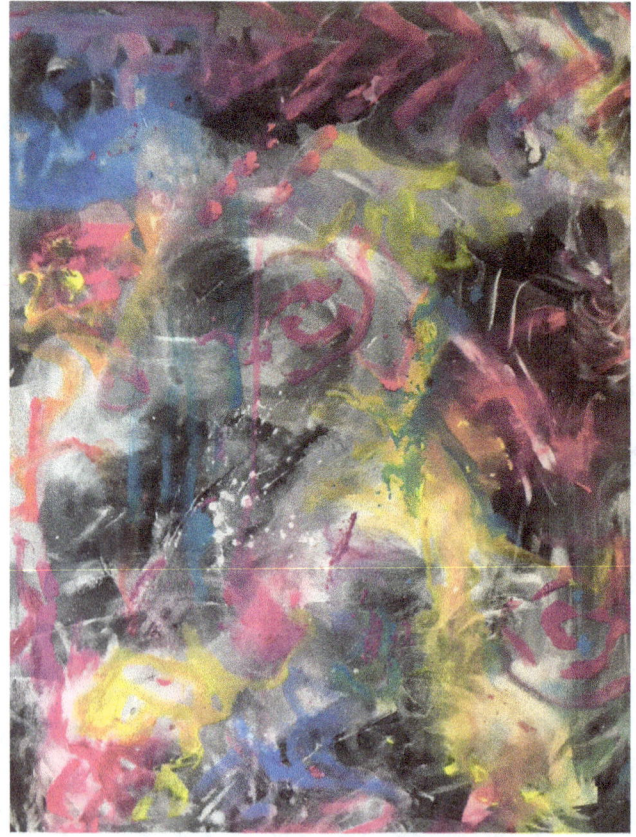

Step 1: Paint your first, fun layer, with light and dark and movement and flight!

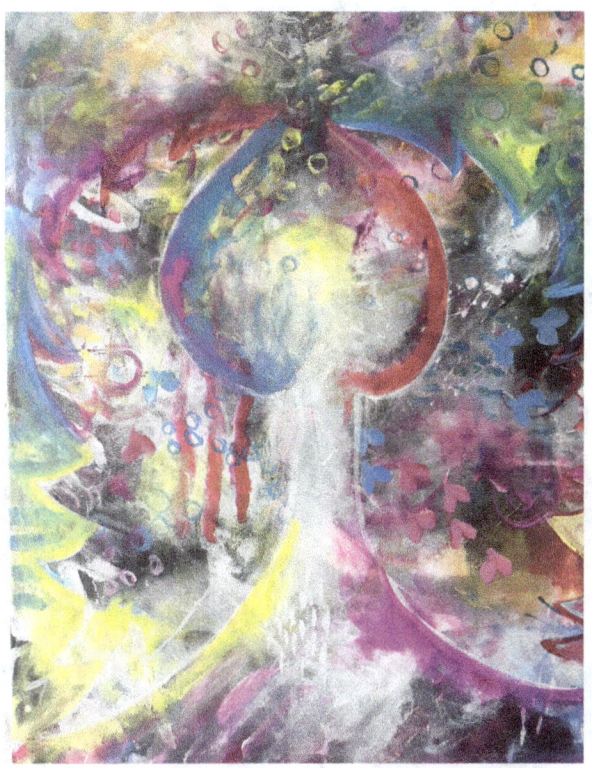

Step 2: Outline the silhouette of your wings. Merge the outline of the wings with your background by painting different colors around the outside of the wings and blending into the background.

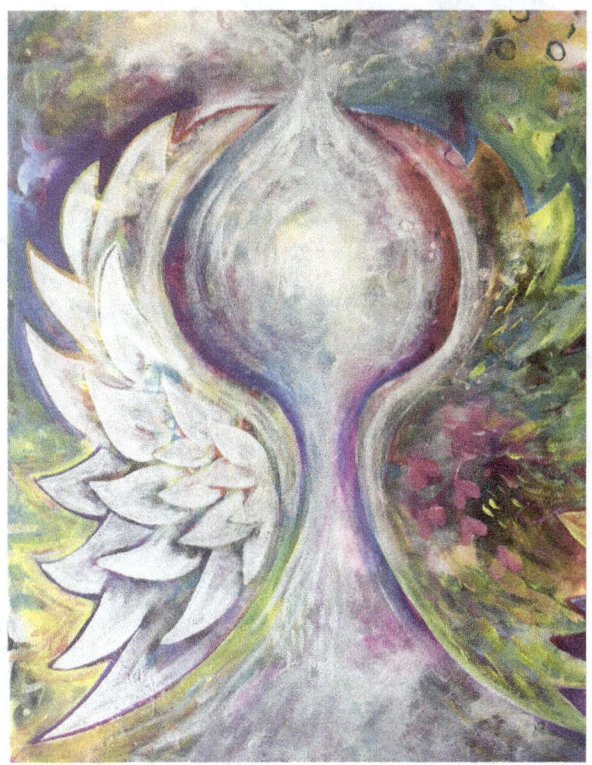

Step 3: See how I added colors and shapes into the right wing in "flow" with the shape, or movement, of the wing? Then, as you see in the left wing, I painted the feathers in starting on the inside, the smallest feathers, and worked toward the outside.

Step 4: Have FUN! Make it a sacred time! You are getting your wings!!!

Step 5: Paint more colors and contrast into the wings and around the edges of the wings.

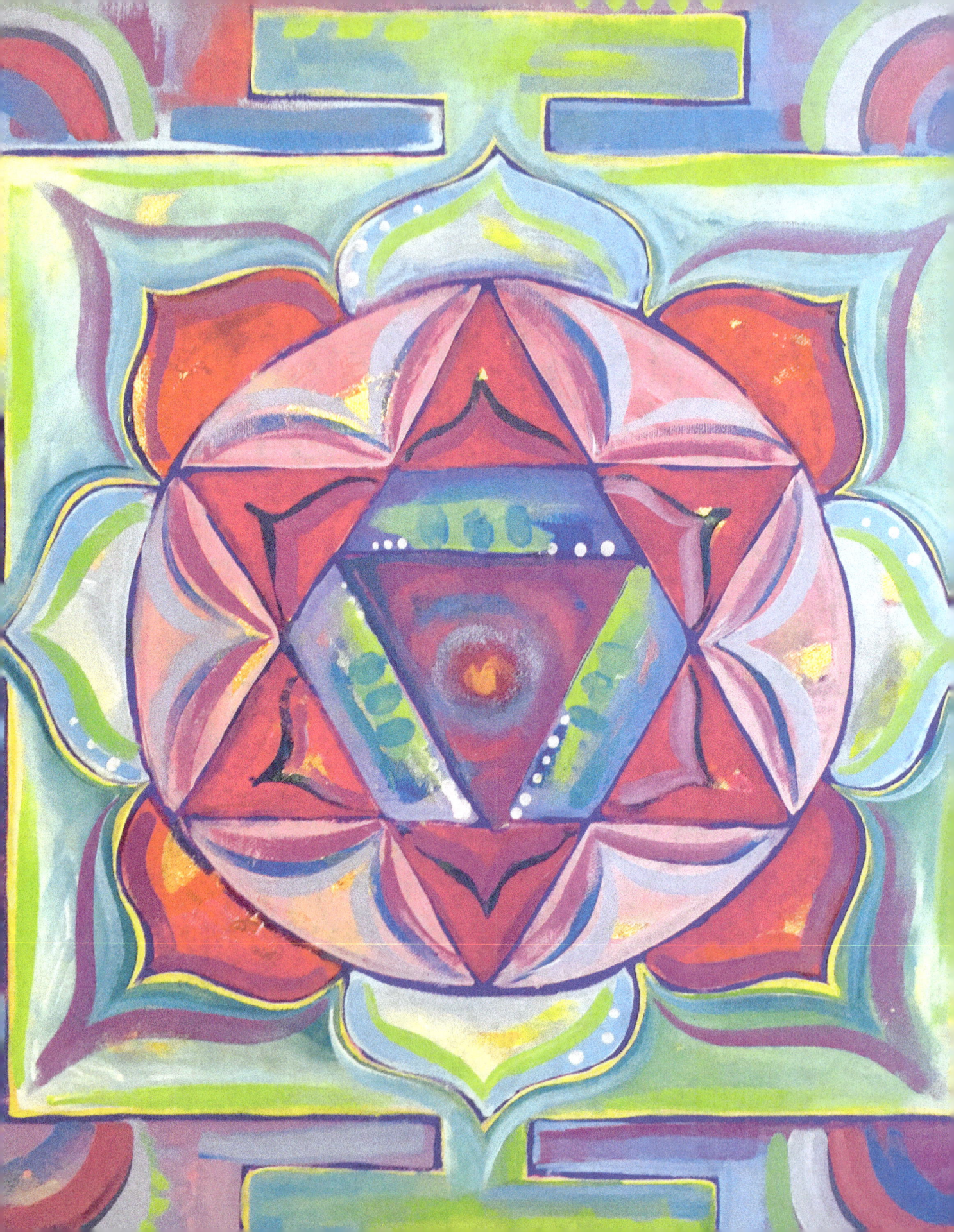

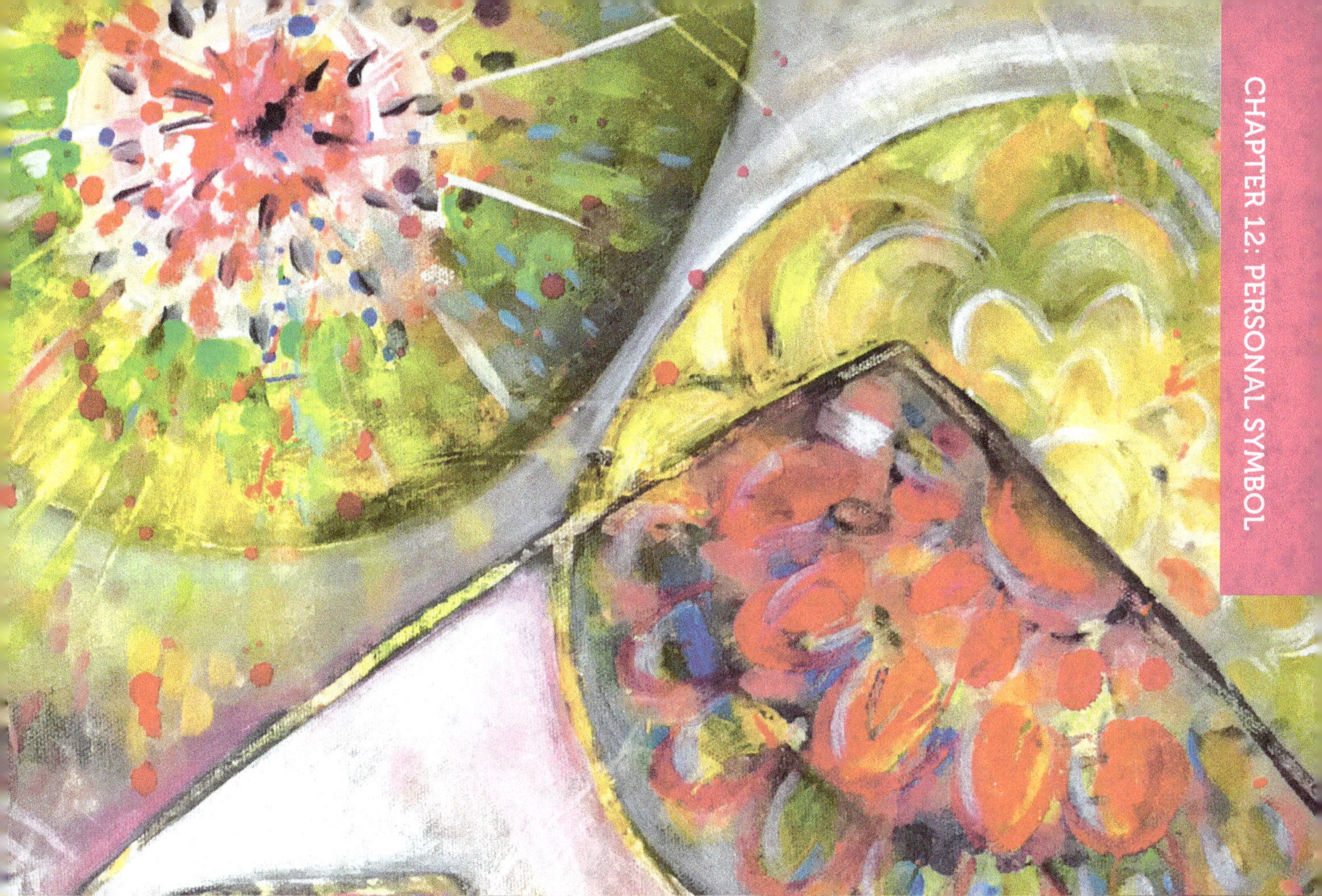

Super Soul Flow

*Personal Symbol*

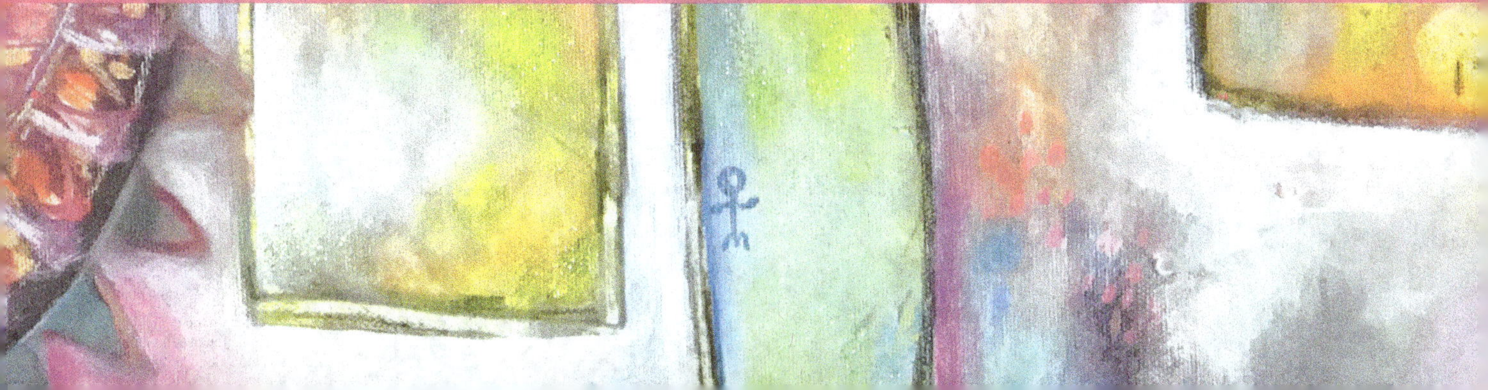

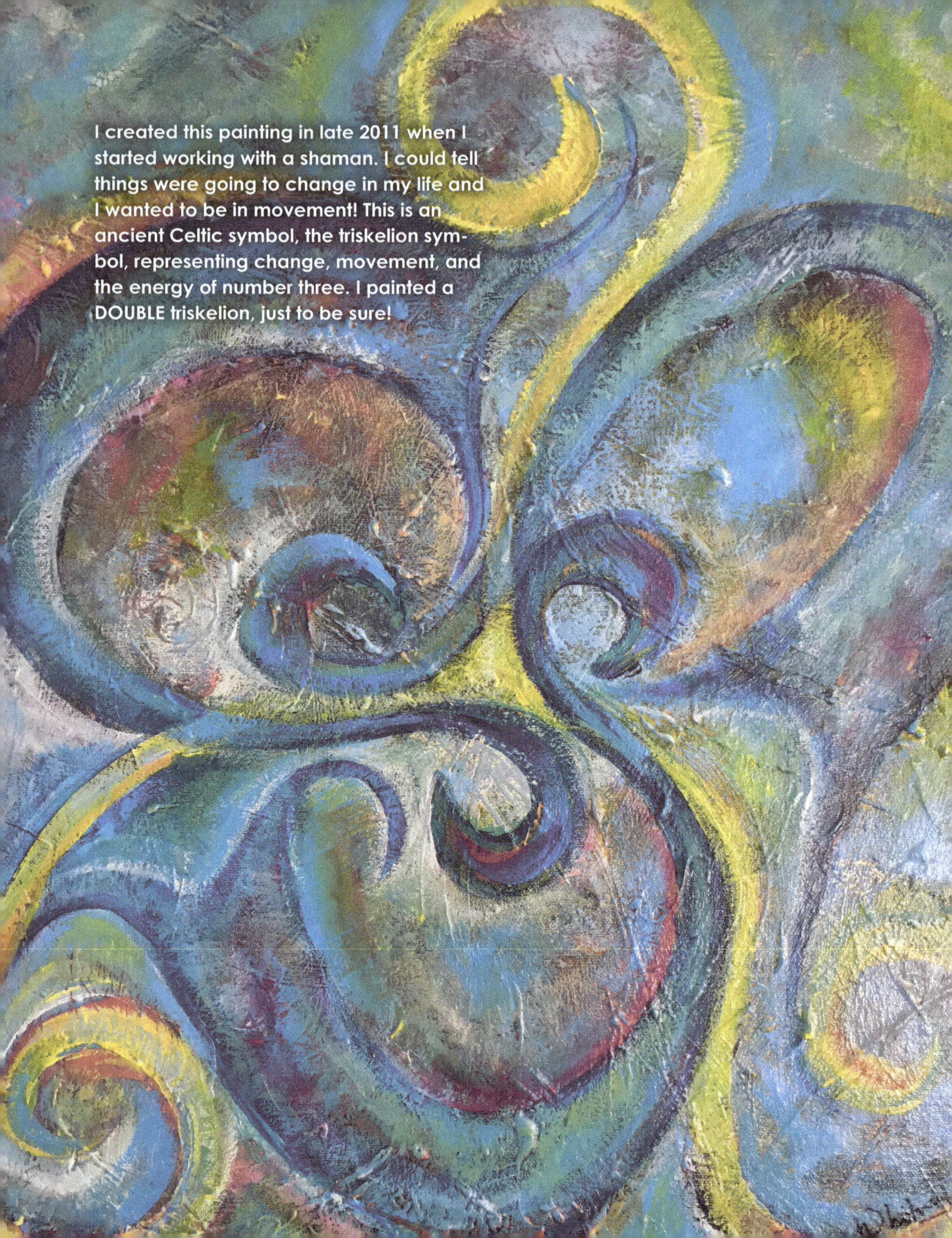

I created this painting in late 2011 when I started working with a shaman. I could tell things were going to change in my life and I wanted to be in movement! This is an ancient Celtic symbol, the triskelion symbol, representing change, movement, and the energy of number three. I painted a DOUBLE triskelion, just to be sure!

**NOW you get to exercise ALL of your creative magic. You are going to create a Personal Symbol Painting that vibrates on multiple dimensions with the truth of what you really want to experience in your life.**

This is a Painting Journey that will connect you both deeply and expansively to a NEW LEVEL of BELIEF about what is possible in your life.

Because, here is the good and the bad news: Whatever you believe, you are right.

You can WANT something, and if you do not believe it is available to you, you will never attract it into your life experience.

You can WANT to be in a passionate, expressive, fulfilling, and loving romantic relationship AND if, deep down, you don't feel worthy, you will not be successful attracting this relationship to you.

You can WANT financial freedom and abundance, AND if you do not believe you are capable or good enough to achieve that kind of success, you will be right. You will not be able to attract that "color" of success.

There are THREE SECRETS to harnessing the full potential of your infinite creative ability, and the Law of Attraction:

1.  You're not here to create STUFF. You are here to create ENERGY. The first secret is to create the FEELING, the energy, of what it is you desire.

2.  You have to BELIEVE and then take ALL STEPS FORWARD in alignment with that belief. Once you FEEL the energy of what you want, you will want to maintain that vibration as much as possible. The second secret is to know that, no matter what, this feeling and energy are absolutely, positively in your future and to take EVERY STEP in light of that soul reality.

3.  Words have baggage. Love, money, business, sex, romance, wealth… are all loaded with the energy of your experience up until now. If you want more MONEY, we have to liberate your BELIEF from the baggage you have around the word MONEY. The third secret is to use SYMBOLS to align your inner and outer truth with what you desire.

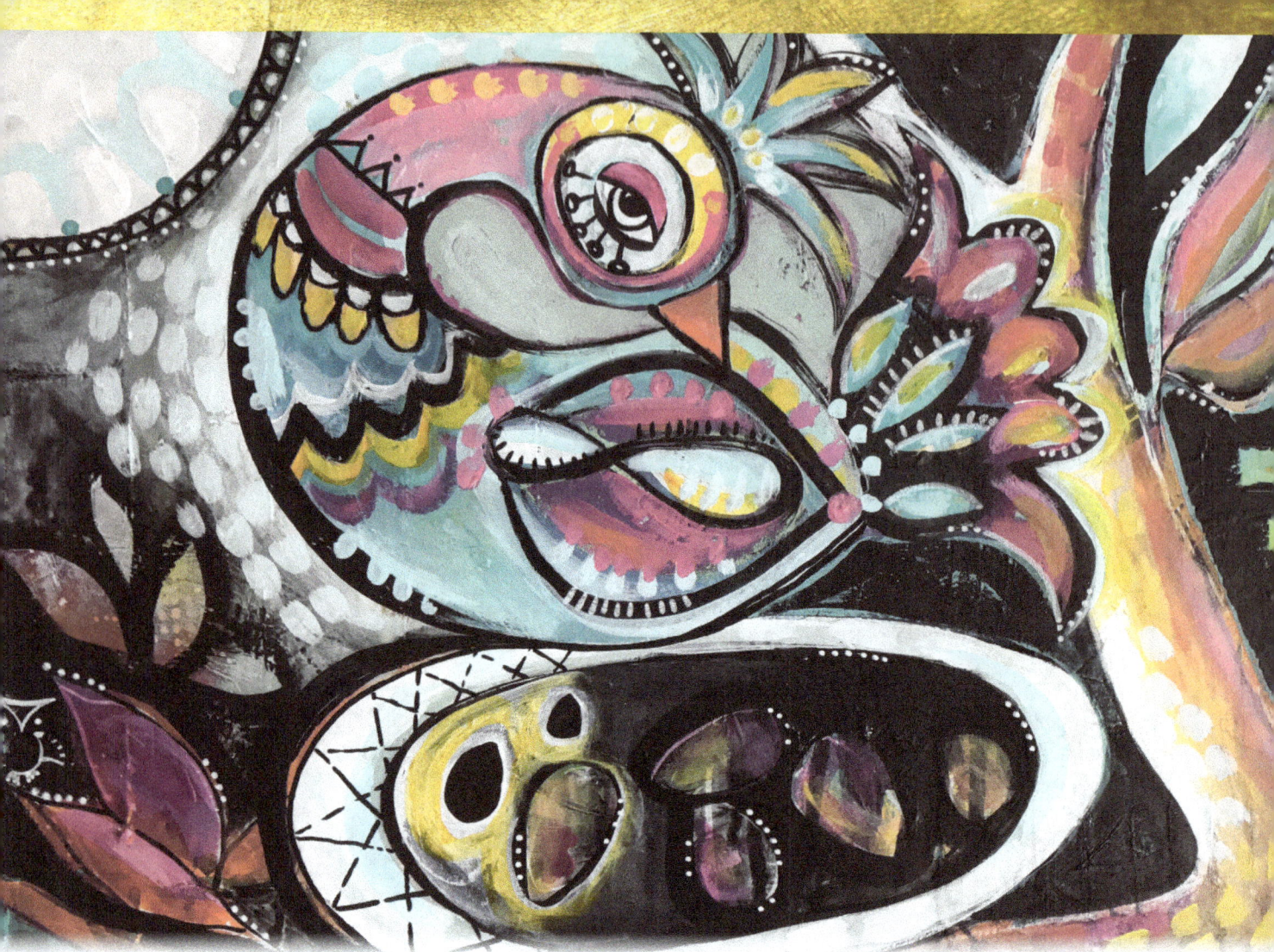

You are going to embody each of these three secrets through the experience of creating your own Personal Symbol Painting.

## The 1st Secret: The Story of The Bird & The Nest

I have strong desire to live in a collaborative, collective home, with a small group of my soul sisters, in magical Wallowa County, Oregon. My future "ARTshram" will be a creative and spiritual oasis for those of us living there and our visitors.

The way my thinking mind processes this desire is, "I want to buy property and build a unique home."

My BELIEF level, from this thinking-mind perspective, can be low. I currently rent. I left a lot of financial security when I chose to divorce, and I don't know if I could qualify for a large enough mortgage.

So, let's shift this logical belief to a FEELING and ENERGY reality.

## What is your "ARTshram"?

Do you also have lots of logical reasons why it is going to be hard for you to realize this vision? Do you worry that it will never happen?

ANYTHING you want—ARTshram, relationship, etc.—is really just energy. So let's tap into that.

Transport yourself into your future ARTshram or relationship and FEEL what it feels like.

For example, my ARTshram feels warm and welcoming. It feels safe and secure because I have my tribe there, and together we effortlessly attract whatever we need to pay the bills and whatever else we need to do. It feels open, connected to nature, and like an oasis for the world! I can close my eyes and put myself there, sitting in meditation, cooking in the open kitchen that looks out into the studio, surrounded by my community that cares for each other and collaborates effortlessly.

### The painting on the opposite page is my Personal Symbol Painting for my ARTshram.

The bird and her nest remind me that I do not have to worry about HOW my ARTshram comes into being. It is so reflective of my own inner nature, how I have always imagined living and giving, that it will naturally appear in my life. AND I already have friends come and stay with me, clients as well, and we support each other and create together. The ARTshram is already IN ME as this feeling!

The bird also radiates the energy of freedom.

The eggs are symbolic of all the potential and creativity that will hatch within the nest of the ARTshram.

Your turn… FEEL into the energy of you ALREADY living in your fulfilled desire. You begin to paint from this feeling. Under the layers of this painting are images of homes, the words "ARTshram" and all the magic juju I could ever need to create this into my reality.

You will start your Personal Symbol Painting there, with colors, symbols, and words that feel the way you are going to feel in your dream come true.

As you paint, the FINAL IMAGE (like the bird and her nest) will come to you. Stay present and open as you paint.

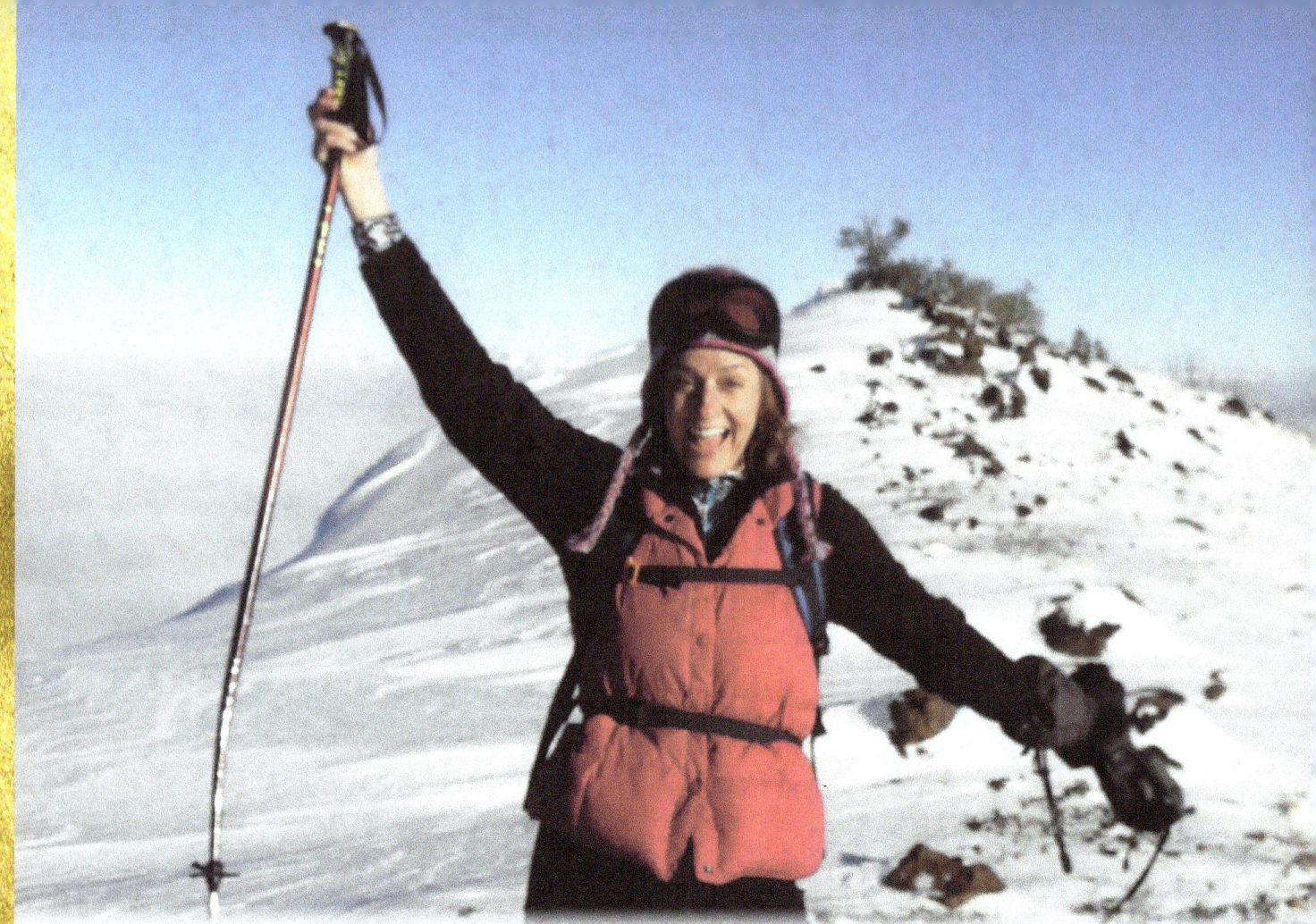

## The 2nd Secret:

## The Story of the Mountain & the Golden Boomerang

I want you to imagine that you are at the top of a mountain. From this vantage point you can see in all directions for hundreds of miles.

From this place of heightened, elevated vision, I want you to connect to your dream, your goal, your highest vision for your life in the near future, just like we did in the 1st Secret.

Now, hold out your hands. Imagine that, right before your eyes, a magical, golden boomerang appears. It is yours.

You receive the guidance, "Tell the boomerang whatever it is you want to attract into your life. What is your desire? Send your desired vision into the boomerang. Now, take a deep breath, and throw the boomerang out into the ethers. It will come back to you, with exactly what you told it you desired. You just have to wait and maintain your **BELIEF** that it WILL come back to you."

*Patience.*

Here's the tricky part that most of us forget.

You want to maintain that same "high vibration" of belief that you have at the top of the mountain.

You send your own golden boomerangs out into the ethers every day. And something else happens.

You lower your vibration.

You start to lose faith that the "boomerang" will ever come back to you.

Every time a thought like, "It will probably never work...," "I don't have enough...," "I'm not _____ enough," comes to mind, you lower yourself down the mountain a bit more.

Days go by and you don't see even a glow or a flicker of the "boomerang." So you worry. And you slip further down the mountain.

The boomerang WILL COME BACK. Guaranteed. The problem lies in the fact that you might not still be at the top of the mountain to catch it when it does.

When limiting beliefs call you to take steps down the mountain path, turn your eyes back to the skies. Keep your vibration high.

*Stay on your mountaintop. Make whatever choices are in ALIGNMENT with the TRUTH that your "boomerang" is coming back. That is the secret.*

## Free Your Mind, One Brushstroke at a Time.

You will go to your Personal Symbol Painting (you can paint as many as you like!) every time you feel yourself slipping down the "mountain."

Go back to the canvas to raise your vibration, to connect to your infinite creative self, and to RISE ABOVE the worry, doubt, and fear.

Your Personal Painting Practice will keep you on top of the mountain, so that you are there to receive your boomerang!

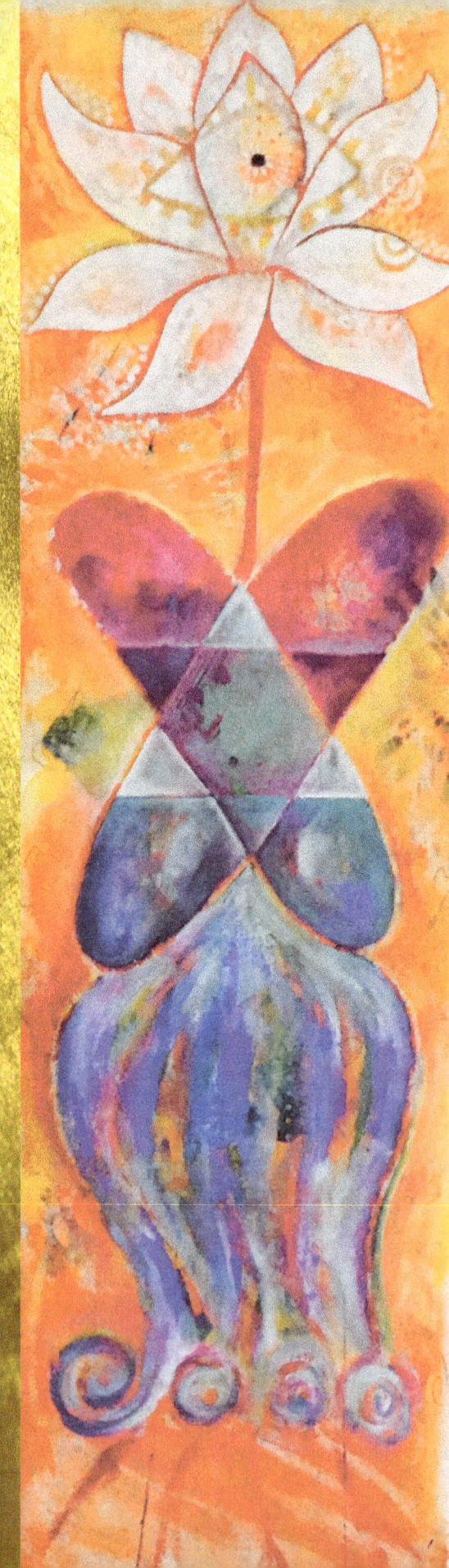

# My Favorite Symbols

Make a list here of the images, symbols or animals that have always held a special place for you OR that have been resonating with you powerfully lately.

1.

2.

3.

4.

5.

6.

7.

8.

9.

10.

## The 3rd Secret: The Story of the Best-Selling Book

The painting on the left is the Personal Symbol Painting I created to attract into my life the experience of writing a best-selling book. It hangs on my bedroom door so every day I CHOOSE to walk through the door of my belief!

When I used to say "best-selling book" there was a twinge of self-criticism. "Who are you to write a best-selling book? A bit egotistical, are we?" Those kinds of thoughts entered in.

I don't NEED a best-selling book. I'll be happy no matter what.

TRUTH.

AND there is nothing wrong with CHOOSING a reality in which I write a best-selling book. So, how to bypass those limiting beliefs and inner critics?

SYMBOLS!

I knew I wanted my **Freya "Knot"** of infinite love, as above so below, to be at the center. What I know is that my best-selling book is here to LOVE as many readers as possible!

The **waterfall** is the abundance of inspiration, hope, encouragement and excitement that YOU are receiving right now!

The **lotus** reflects the beauty that I am able to share because of the muck I have waded through IN ORDER to bloom!

And in the center of the lotus is the **EYE of FEARLESSNESS,** reminding me that it will take bold action and fearless conviction to see my vision into this reality! When I look at this painting, or imagine it in my mind's eye, I get a shower of belief around my dream.

You are currently holding my dream come true. I poured so much love into this book! You feel it, right? Thank you for sharing this book with others and giving it wings!

When I painted this house painting I had just moved into my first home that was all mine, energetically speaking. I wanted to ground in my belief that I had made the right move, becoming newly single and independent. It was scary!

This painting affirmed the magic that was all around me through the mandalas and the colors. I remember feeling a bit frustrated as the house became shades of gray. I didn't want my house to be symbolized by a dirty, grungy color. Then I realized that it was BECAUSE I lived in a house that did not entertain black-and-white thinking that the magic was alive. All shades of opinion, beliefs and expression are allowed and celebrated!

The color grey led to a major breakthrough in BELIEF for me and allowed me to RISE ABOVE the doubt and worry!

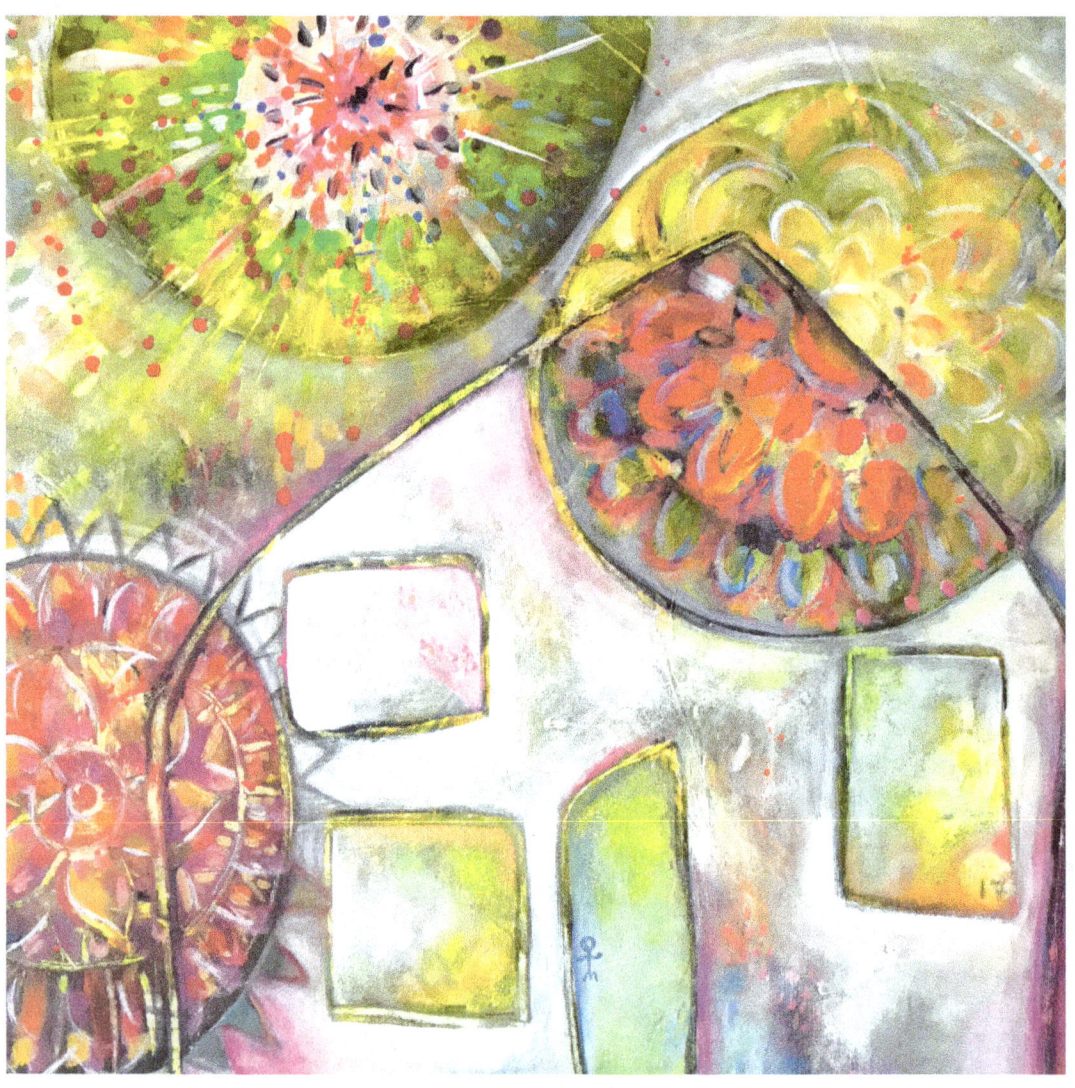

I painted this Lakshmi Yantra, an ancient symbol of abundance, to hang in the abundance and prosperity corner of my new home.

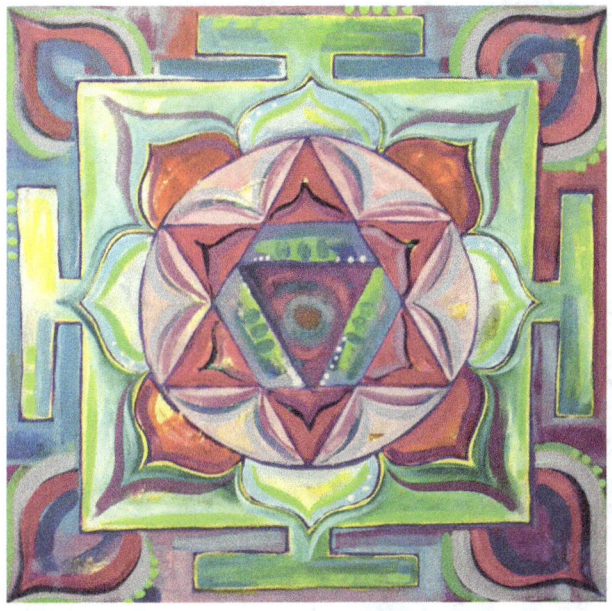

And this painting allowed me to believe fully in my personal power… as a Woman Who Runs with the Wolves!

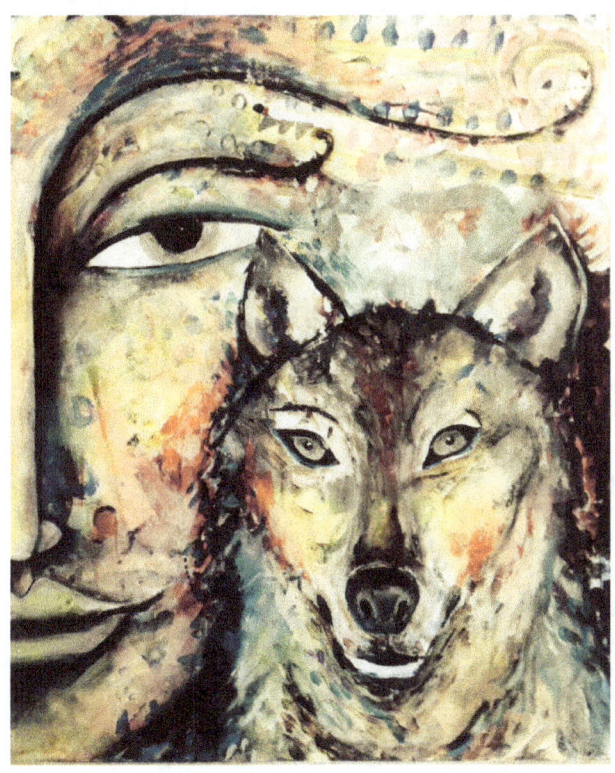

# Creating Your Personal Symbol

### TO BEGIN...

Paint the first layer with colors, symbols and affirmations that align with your desire. I painted a painting for all of us for this chapter. It is a Personal Symbol Painting as a reminder: **"I AM enough."**

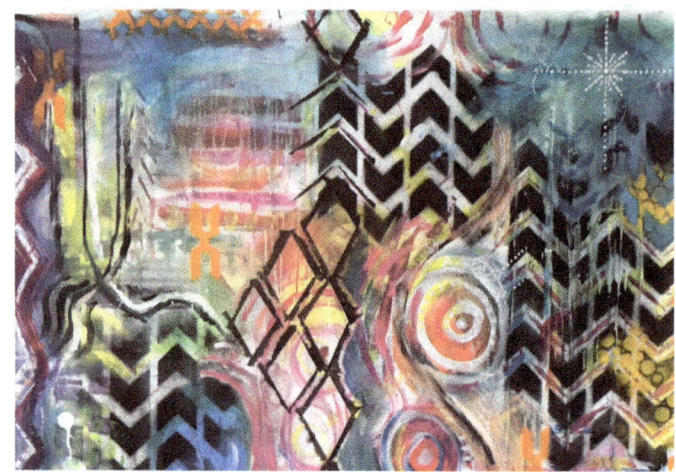

In the first layers I found myself painting circles... this reminded me that circles are a symbol of wholeness, completion and inclusion. How perfect is that for an "I AM enough" painting?!

One symbol leads to another. I added infinity symbols because when you are connected to your own infinite nature you are not able to feel unworthy, deficient in any way, or in need. Everything is available to you— everything! Infinity.

I painted the words, **I AM complete.** How often do you feel that you are lacking something, someone, some feature, ability, or knowledge? Since you are infinite, you are complete.

What came next made me chuckle, but I was obedient to the intuitive nudge. I painted a big smiley face. That is always a GREAT symbol!

The last energetic element onto our communal Personal Symbol Painting was the spiral, to illustrate the infinite nature of possibility. There is always an opening, room for expansion and growth.

## Are you excited to get your canvas going?

What is the "I AM..." statement that you are stepping into, choosing out of all the possible futures for the art that is your life?

Write it down here... or right onto your canvas.

I AM...

I AM ecstatic you are here and that you are exploring the infinite possibilities that your Creator Self has to offer you.

## NEXT STEP...

Now that you have your first layer of energy painted onto the canvas, you can open up to the symbol for your painting.

Recognize if you are putting pressure on yourself to come up with THE symbol. Instead, ask, "I am thankful to receive a sacred symbol that will serve my highest and greatest good...

... right now."

... to inspire my highest choice in this _____ situation."

... in my current career."

... to support the move I want to make."

... to support my physical health."

Where would you like to create change, clarity, and more personal power in your life right now? Now ask to receive a symbol.

If you are ready to paint right now, simply start painting to tap into that level of communication so you can receive your symbol.

You can intend to receive it in the next 48 hours, or the next week.

It will come. I'll tell you some stories of how I received some of my favorite personal symbols.

## The ARROW

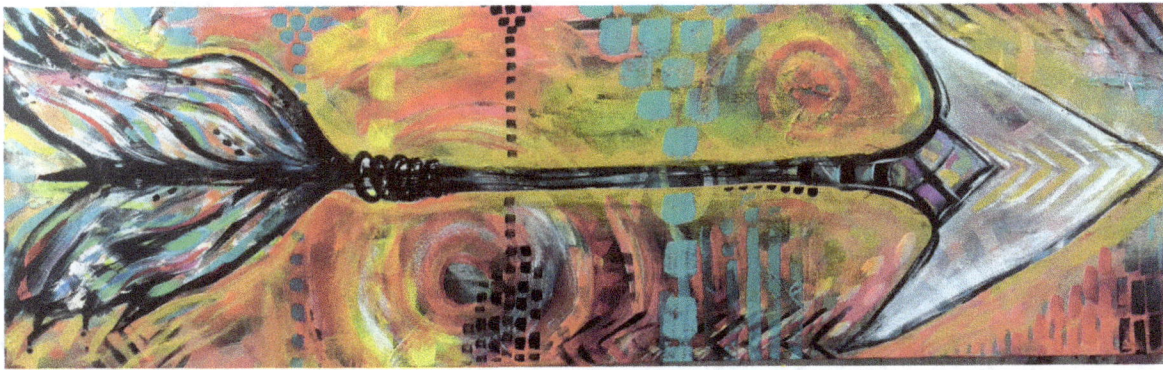

Each year, since 2014, I pick a SYMBOL for the year. I love it!

The symbols find me. I can't go looking for them. It's about setting the intention to receive a symbol, believing that you WILL receive a symbol, then opening up and allowing it to come to you.

The first thing that happens is that the symbol catches your eye. You may be shopping, on a hike, surfing the Internet… wherever you are looking around at things. It will attract you.

You may say something like, "I'm seeing arrows everywhere," or "I LOVE _____." This is your CLUE #1.

Next, it will repeat itself. You may keep seeing it, or it may pop up in a totally different context.

I remember seeing arrows everywhere and then I "happened" to read that the Nez Perce Indians were famous for their arrows and that tribes would travel hundreds of miles (in fact, their summer trading site is exactly where I live now) just to trade for one of the Wallowa Nez Perce arrows.

Not only did I read about that fact, but it also captured my attention and I imagined into it. I imagined being the new owner of a handful of Nez Perce arrows. I had traded dearly for them so I was going to use them sparingly and with tremendous focus and precision.

I was being asked to focus my desire, attention, energy, and resources in the exact direction of my desire. That way I could accelerate my progress AND my team of divine helpers would also have their marching orders!

All of those thoughts and experiences converged in a Personal Symbol. Ah-ha! The ARROW had found me.

## The Chalice

Sometimes the symbol has been on your radar for a while. It is something that has crossed your path before, and now it is coming to you at a greater frequency.

Initially, I had some resistance to the chalice because it triggers associations with "organized religion." When it continued to show up in a novel I read, *The Mists of Avalon*, and in an article somewhere, I took notice.

One time I was drawing an entire figure holding a chalice and instead of first focusing on the fun mandala headpiece or the colorful fabric, I found myself coloring in and adding details to the chalice first. That seemed out of character to me. I knew to ask, "Why am I attracted to the chalice first?"

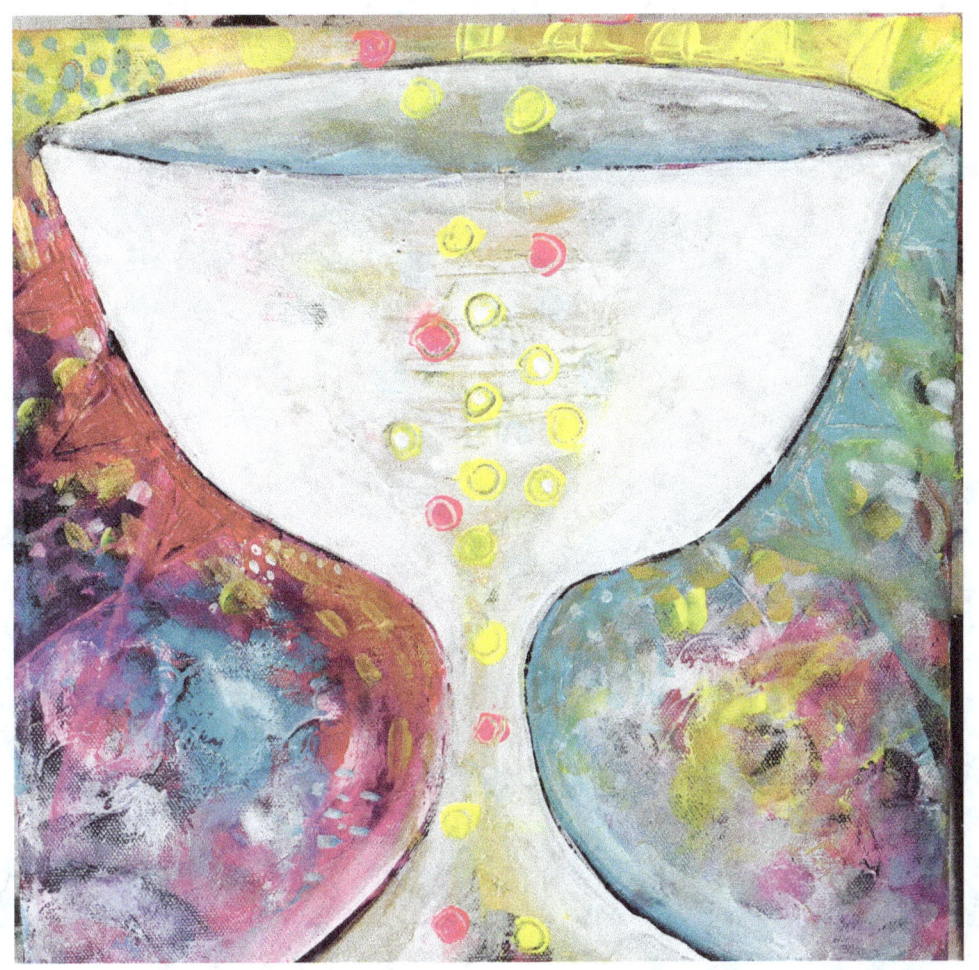

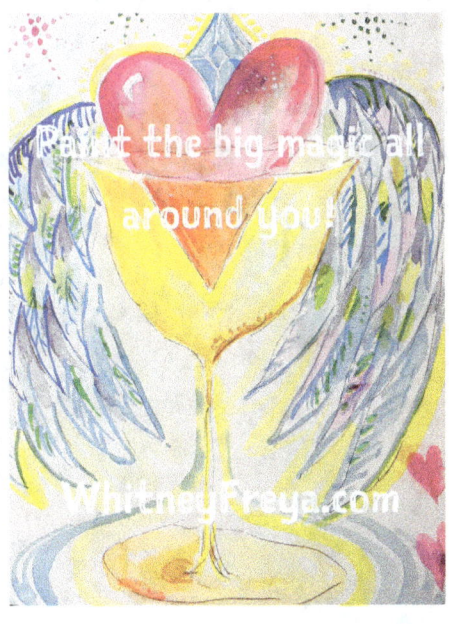

Paint the big magic all around you!

WhitneyFreya.com

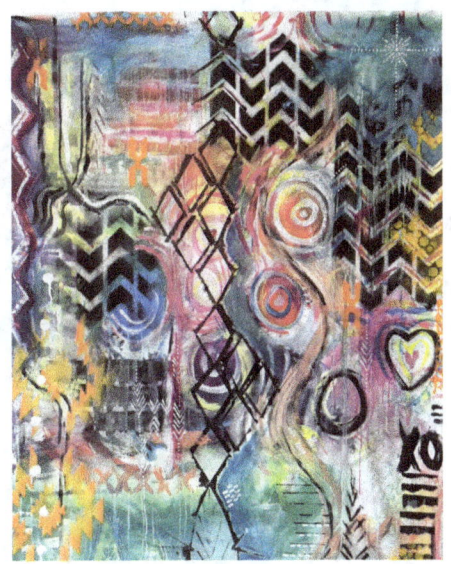

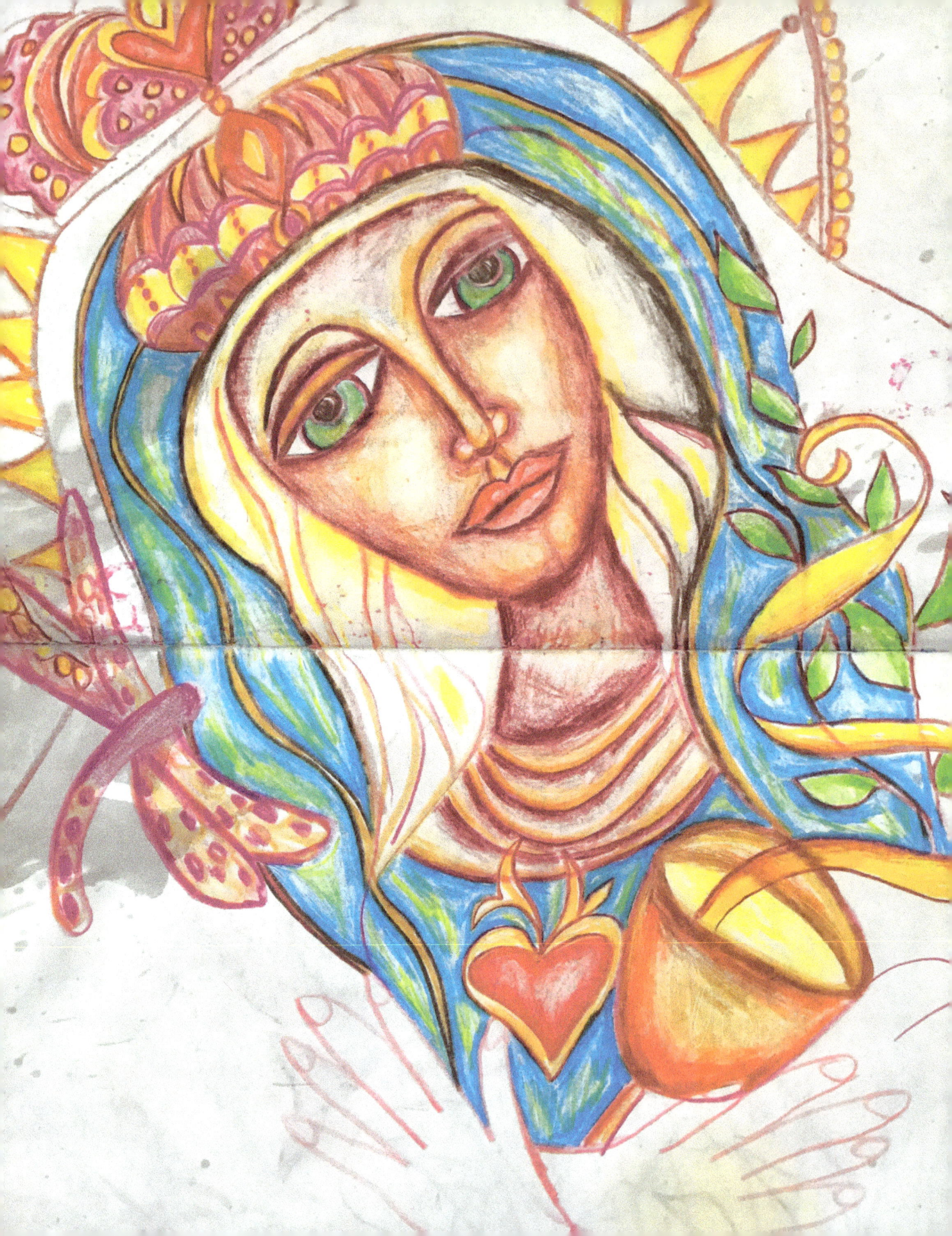

This journal entry image to the left was inspired by the artwork of Marie Howell from the Color of Woman Creative Soul Deck. (www.shilohsophiashop.com/illustrated-decks)

What came to me was insight into what might be INSIDE the chalice, the liquid that I might be drinking. The question that came to mind was, "What Kool-Aid am I drinking?"

That created clarity that I knew I wanted to be drinking the divine "Kool-Aid."

Soon after, while being interviewed on a webinar about ritual, I became instantly clear that the symbol for the guided meditation I was giving would be the chalice. It was like the chalice was speaking to me.

*Our physical bodies are the chalice into which the Divine can pour its light, love, and wisdom. Instead of trying to do it all ourselves, we can simply receive and then share from our overflow.*

Ritual helps to fill us up with the knowing, the peace, the passion, so that we can serve in this lifetime to our highest potential. Your Personal Painting Ritual is one place where you fill up your chalice.

The day after the webinar I pulled a card from the *Mayan Oracle Deck* and read:

*I have surrendered to emptiness. In the space of my open arms, a chalice forms and fills freely with the incomprehensible sweetness of abundant life force.*

Boom! This became my Personal Symbol Painting for 2016.

# The I AM Enough Symbol for this Chapter

The morning arrived for the next Super Soul Flow video shoot. I knew I was going to paint the Personal Symbol for this chapter—and I had no idea what it was going to be.

Do you ever have that feeling? *I have no idea how this is going to work...*

In that moment you can choose to get stuck in the unknowing OR get really curious about how the right information is going to find you! I prefer the latter.

After shooting the video for the first layer of the painting, I came downstairs to change clothes and "reel in" the symbol. I STILL did not know what I was going to paint. While drinking water, my eye went to a collage hanging on my kitchen cabinet. I thought, "Let's see what catches my eye…" A sea turtle! Of course!

I have multiple sea turtles in my home, at least two other paintings and a ceramic sculpture one of my kids made years ago. AND I love sea turtles. I have seen them in Hawaii and the Virgin Islands, and often slip into my *Finding Nemo* sea turtle impersonation, "Ride the current, duuuuuuude."

AND turtles have everything they need, such as their home right on their back! They have ENOUGH all the time! (angels singing in the distance)

I bounded back upstairs to paint the sea turtle that is your Personal Symbol for right now if you have yet to receive a new one. I AM enough! Yeah, you are! Even the first layer made sense with all the swirling blues!

You may want to paint a sea turtle IN ADDITION to your own Personal Symbol Painting. I am sure you will have as much fun as I did painting this magical creature. As I painted it, I imagined that I, too, was swimming in the ocean of pure potential—supported, guided and infinite. I can't wait to see your sea turtle and ALL of your Personal Symbol Paintings!

Use #RiseAbovePaintings and #SuperSoulFlow to share them with us all online. What I absolutely know to be true is that in our future, everyone will have—or at least be aware of—the value of their own personal creative practice.

*Our creative energy is our chi, our life force.
Fill yourself up at the canvas!*

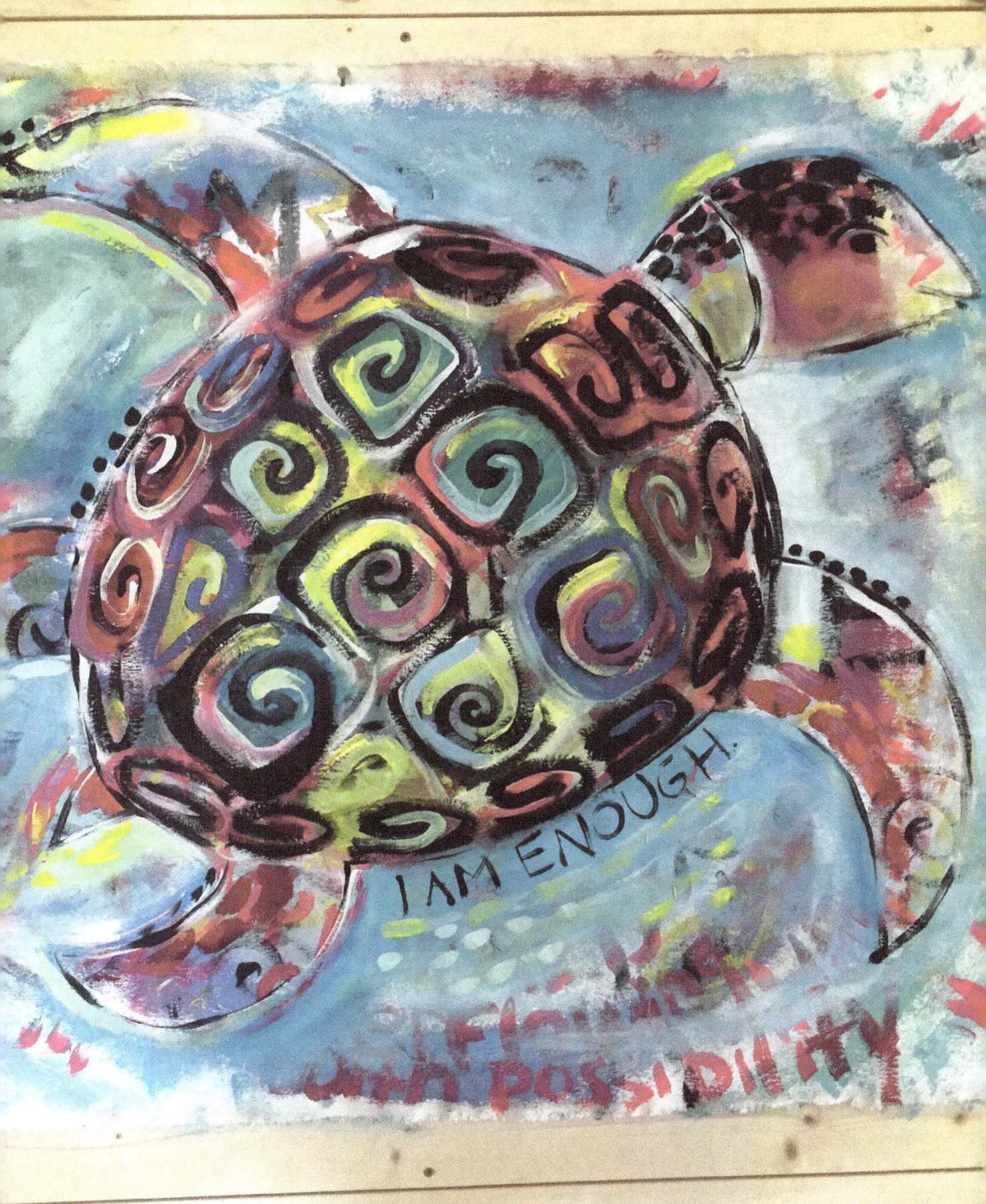

# Conclusion

My greatest wish for myself, my children, my family, my Creatively Fit Coaches, my students and clients, my friends, the kaleidoscope of souls I get to connect with, and every precious person on this planet is to be *happy.*

I believe we ARE happiness expressing itself currently in this physical reality as YOU and ME.

And BECAUSE we are so infinitely happy, we come here to play in this physical reality. We come here for the grandest game of hide and seek ever! A good game has contrast, excitement, a bit of fear, and a reward at the end.

Your Super Soul Flow self is hiding and you are the seeker.

You start the game with a handicap—to keep it interesting—that causes you to forget you even have a Super Soul Flow Self. You also start the game in a maze of limiting beliefs, stories that affirm right and wrong, good and bad, and a tendency to get stuck in the muck.

Oh! And just because we REALLY love challenging games, we each get a logical, rational mind and put it in charge.

The challenge? Free your mind, reunite with your Super Soul Flow Self and RISE ABOVE the muck!

The reward? You GET TO live on this magical, abundant, lush, sensual, radiant planet Earth, enjoying ALL of the physical plea-sures, the human interaction, the community and the adventure WHILE ALSO looking at it all from your infinite perspective.

YOU are winning the game.

YOU have connected to an inner knowing, a glowing ember of truth within, that has guided you to explore that which lies outside logic and rationality.

YOU have learned to suspend judgment and to stay open.

YOU see beauty.

YOU value happiness and peace.

YOU are not interested in the way things have always been done.

YOU are a Rainbow Warrior.

YOU are here to free your mind and RISE ABOVE life's drama, and, then, YOU are here to guide others!

The extra bonus is that once you answer the call to RISE ABOVE and feel the freedom and peace and abundance and joy that is accessible to you from that vantage point, you won't come down.

It becomes easier and easier to RISE ABOVE.

It's like a snowball growing as it rolls down the hill.

Your wings will only take you higher and higher!

And all the drama, the petty arguments, whatever mayhem is going on politically, the grudges, the feuds… they fade into nothingness as you rise.

And the souls still engaged in those conversations receive your compassion because they have yet to remember the game. Whatever their behavior, they are doing the best the can in their own pursuit of happiness, security and love.

The only way to help them is to shine your light that much brighter to illuminate what is possible for them, too.

For those of us attracted to color and imagery, who are drawn to explore what all we can create and express at the canvas, I know we are here as torchbearers. We are here to liberate ourselves and those attracted to us from the cages we have created with our should's and have-to's, our fear of judgment or making a mistake.

The canvas is where we get to recognize what has been keeping us trapped. As you created self-love, you got to recognize all the ways you are not loving to yourself. As you created the energy of abundance, you got to observe where you have unknowingly been tapping into the energy of scarcity.

Now you go to the canvas to CREATE the ENERGY that you want to attract into your life.

Now you understand the power of a symbol to communicate to the universe the energy of what you want to attract into your life, recognizing that as you create that energy onto the canvas, you are drawing this new life experience closer and closer.

Now you will go to your Meditation Canvas to raise your vibration when you are feeling overwhelmed, sad, mad, frustrated, or scared. You engage your infinitely creative spirit rather than your wounded child or your inner critic.

NOW you know how to RISE ABOVE that which has been holding you back, keeping you from taking the next step toward your highest dream for your life.

I leave you with my latest YANTRA, the feather.

May this symbol create within and around you a new lightness of being.

May this symbol inspire you to let go of the energies that have been holding you down, weighing you down with worry or stress.

May this symbol guide you, appearing just when you need it, to remind you that you CAN rise above the heaviness.

YOU can fly.

YOU have wings.

Thank you, for all the ways only YOU can shine the light of love and happiness into our world.

A'Ho.

*P.S. There is another "layer" to this Super Soul Flow experience. It is The 7-Week Super Soul Flow Meditation Course that adds an entirely new element of guided and self-guided meditation.*

*The 7-Week Super Soul Flow Meditation Course is offered by myself and my Creatively Fit Coaches in group or individual experiences.*

*It is a powerful journey to reconnect to your multi-dimensional self, and this book is the companion guide.*

*Learn more at **SuperSoulFlow.com**.*

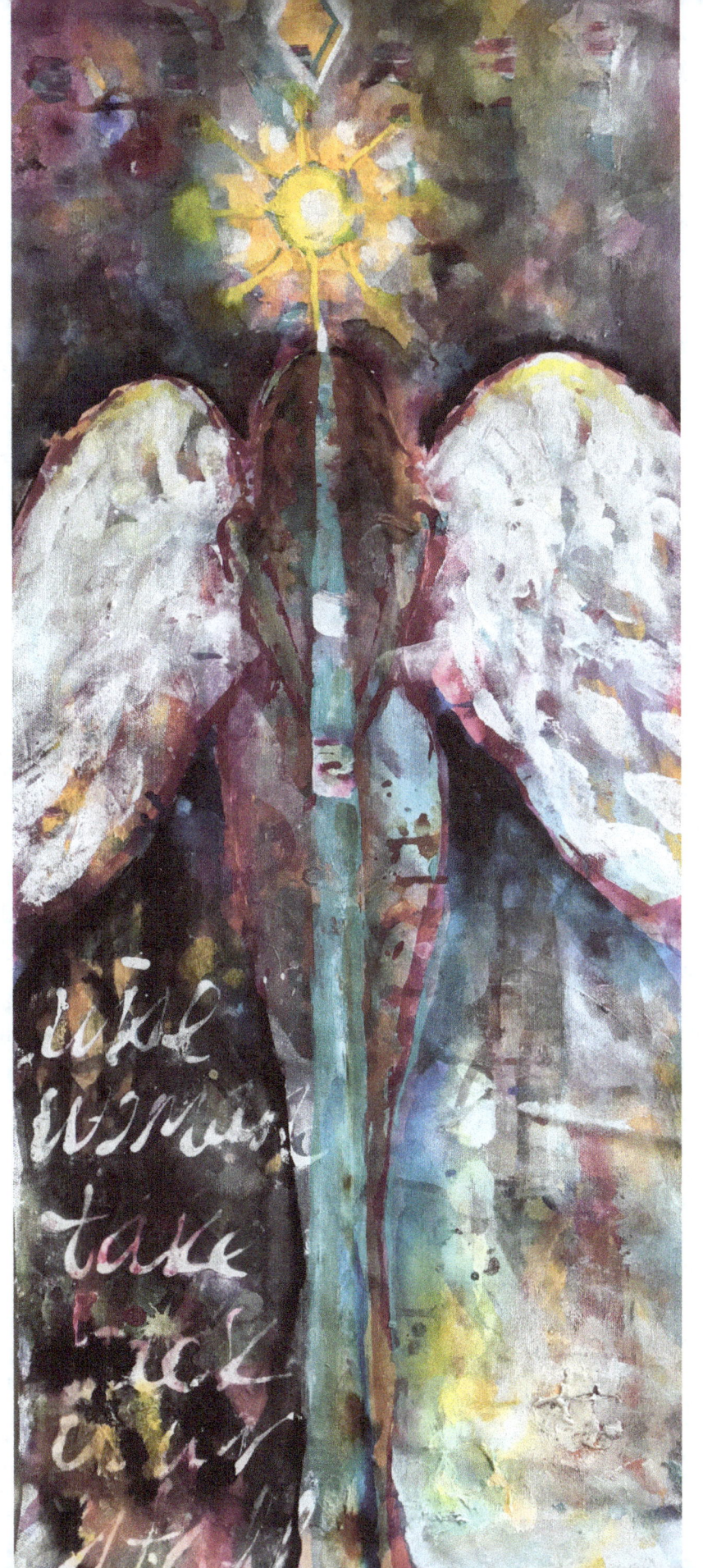

# About the Author

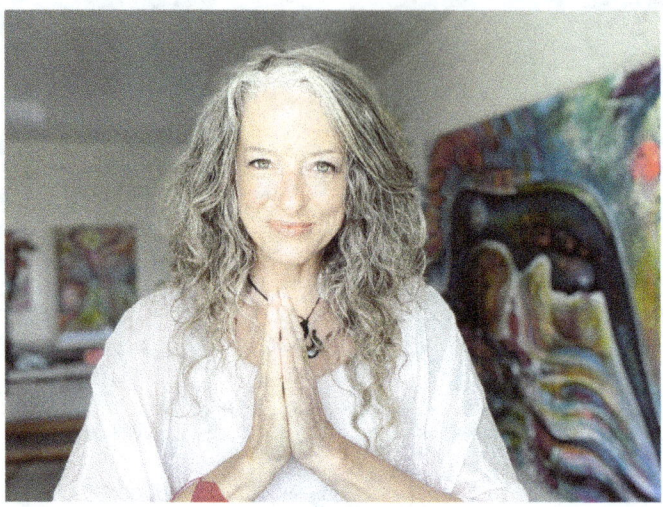

Whitney Freya grew up dreaming of becoming an artist. In 1995, while reading *Zen and the Art of Making a Living,* she came across a profound statement: "Unless you adopt an artist mentality, you won't be able to create the life of your dreams." These words sparked a flame within her, igniting a passion that has guided her career ever since.

Just four years out of college and selling books door-to-door, all she knew was that she craved a life filled with dreams. To her, the "real world" felt more like a blank canvas than anything she had ever learned in school. This sparked her curiosity: "Where do you even go to develop an artist mentality?"

Fifteen months later, in 1996, she opened The Creative Fitness Center in Nashville, TN, despite not having painted on a canvas since she was nine years old. Fueled by her desire to help herself and others create their lives as works of art, she witnessed transformation after transformation. Together with her new community, she let go of the product-focused narrative around creativity and embraced a deeply personal journey of self-discovery at the canvas.

In 2009, she launched her online program in New York City, carrying a canvas through the streets with the words CREATE CHANGE boldly displayed. She invited passersby to make their mark, handed out postcards with tips on spotting complementary colors outside the MoMA, and held book signings across the city to showcase her first book, *The Artist Within: A Guide to Becoming Creatively Fit.* In 2017, she published *Rise Above,* and in 2021, she released *30 Days to Unstoppable: Be the Dream Made Visible* along with its Companion Journal.

Today, Whitney connects with her vibrant online community and collaborates with her Creative Frequency Coaches from around the globe. She also travels to share her unique approach, which seamlessly blends the spiritual and creative aspects of our journeys. Discover more about her "practical magic" at **WhitneyFreya.com.**

www.ingramcontent.com/pod-product-compliance
Lightning Source LLC
Chambersburg PA
CBHW080408290526
45791CB00008BA/2198